Encounter

Experiencing the DIVINE PRESENCE

(Second Edition)

Edward Kleinguetl

outskirts press

Encounter
Experiencing the Divine Presence: Second Edition

v3.0

Outskirts Press, Inc.
http://www.outskirtspress.com

ISBN: 978-1-9772-5681-2

PRINTED IN THE UNITED STATES OF AMERICA

I invite all Christians, everywhere, at this very moment,
to a renewed personal encounter with Jesus.

—Pope Francis

True theology is always born out of the life of the
Church that prays, confesses, and serves.

—Patriarch Daniel of Romania

Genuine living theology is not intellectual or academic knowledge,
but a burning of the heart that draws nigh to the Person of Christ.

—Archimandrite Zacharias of Essex

The devout Christian of the future will either be a 'mystic,' one who
has 'experienced' something, or he will cease to be anything at all

—Karl Rahner, SJ

God is not a rational argument, for the Father
is in the heart of every [person].

—Robert Cardinal Sarah

IMPRIMATUR

+ Daniel Cardinal DiNardo, DD
Archbishop of Galveston-Houston
February 24, 2022

For Fr. Miron Kerul-Kmec, Jr.
and the younger generation of priests
filled with apostolic and missionary zeal,
tasked with combating secularization
and passing on the Deposit of Faith,
helping people to recognize and
achieve their divinely created purpose:
sharing in the Life of the Holy Trinity for eternity.

Table of Contents

INTRODUCTION TO THE SECOND EDITION

Does Faith Matter?

"Whoever loves me will keep my word, and my Father will love him, and we will come to him and make our dwelling with him." (John 14:23)

"If you are a theologian you truly pray. If you truly pray you are a theologian."[1] (Evagrios the Solitary)

"The devout Christian of the future will either be a 'mystic,' one who has 'experienced' something, or he will cease to be anything at all."[2] (Karl Rahner, SJ)

Does faith in God matter? This is the primordial question that must take center stage in a culture that has grown hostile toward the idea of a human-divine relationship.

We released the first edition of *Encounter: Experiencing the Divine Presence* in 2018. Since then, much has rapidly changed within our society and the Church. The cooling of faith we discussed then has evolved into a full-blown spiritual pandemic. With COVID-19, an even greater threat to humanity was exposed and, in many respects, we have focused on the wrong pandemic. A soul separated from God has a 100 percent mortality rate. St. Gregory Palamas, in a homily, described our current situation well:

1 Evagrius Ponticus, *The Praktikos & Chapters on Prayer*, trans. John Eudes Bamberger, OCSO (Kalamazoo, MI: Cistercian Publications, 1972), 65. See also Evagrios the Solitary, "On Prayer." Taken from *The Philokalia: The Complete Text*, vol. I, trans. G.E.H. Palmer, P. Sherrard, and K. Ware (London: Faber & Faber, 1979), 62.

2 Karl Rahner, "Christian Living Formerly and Today," in *Theological Investigations*, vol. 7 (New York, NY: Seabury Press, 1972), 15.

> Behold the days are coming when there will be a famine. Not a famine of bread, nor a thirst for water, but of hearing the word of the Lord. Famine means being deprived of and desiring necessary food. But there is something worse and more wretched than this famine: when someone is deprived of the necessary means of salvation and does not perceive his misfortune, *having no desire to be saved.*[3]

In a secularized world where people increasingly dismiss God, rely on human initiative, and try to create a paradise on earth as an alternative to a divinely intended purpose in the life to come, we are increasingly confronted with the question: Does faith in God really matter? Many today behave as if religion is something from a previous generation and no longer relevant for the progressive, modern person who sees God as a constraint to human existence. One bishop warned, "There is a total denial of Christianity and a dangerous tendency to replace it."[4] There is an increasing lack of desire to work for eternal salvation.

Accelerating De-Christianization

In two generations,[5] we have observed an accelerated de-Christianization in the United States, which describes itself in its Pledge of Allegiance as "one nation under God," mirroring what has happened in much of Western Europe. This is evidenced as people

3 Cf. *Saint Gregory Palamas: The Homilies*, ed. and trans. Christopher Veniamin (Dalton, PA: Mount Thabor Publishing, 2016), 15. Homily Three, no. 1. Reference is to Amos 8:11. Emphasis added by the author.

4 Archbishop Ioachim of Roman and Bacău. See Aurelian Iftimiu, "Archbishop Ioachim on Episcopal Ministry in the 3rd Millennium: Christianity is Just Beginning!" *Basilica News Agency*, online, February 21, 2022.

5 See Bishop Robert Barron with John L. Allen, Jr., *To Light a Fire on the Earth: Proclaiming the Gospel in a Secular Age* (New York, NY: Image Books, 2017), 90. Bishop Barron writes, "The dumbed-down Catholicism that I received has served us very, very poorly. I'd go so far as to say it's been a pastoral disaster. We've lost two generations because of it."

leave the Church in epidemic proportions. For every million children who are baptized and receive First Holy Communion, only 750,000 are confirmed (in the Western Church), and only 110,000 remain active in their faith by young adulthood. This is even more pronounced than in previous generations when people ceased regularly attending church. In ever greater proportion, individuals are deliberately severing their relationship with the Church, even denying they are "Catholic" when questioned about religious affiliation. These are the "Nones" that Bishop Robert Barron often references and is the fastest category in terms of religious affiliation.

Patriarch Daniel of Romania noted that Christians become increasingly secularized "when they no longer practice their faith, when they stop praying, when a free communion with God is no longer the center of their lives or felt to be a necessity."[6] This is the crux of the spiritual pandemic we face today, from which arises apatheism.

Prophetic voices such as Archbishop Fulton Sheen warned of such trends in the late 1940s.[7] Even before the health restrictions for dealing with COVID-19 forced the closure of churches, many dioceses were closing parishes because of poor attendance and a priest shortage. For example, the Diocese of Pittsburgh was collapsing its 188 parishes into 48,[8] a 74 percent reduction. It remains to be seen whether this will further accelerate post-COVID and whether those who were lukewarm in faith or simply going through the motions will return now that churches have reopened.[9]

Another alarm bell arising from a 2019 Pew Research Center survey is that over two-thirds of Catholics (69 percent) do not believe in the Real Presence of Christ in the Eucharist. Rather, they believe

---

6 Patriarch Daniel of Romania, *Confessing the Truth in Love: Orthodox Perceptions of Life, Mission and Unity*, 2nd ed. (Bucharest, RO: Basilica, 2008),

7 Cf. Joseph Pronechen, "Archbishop Sheen's Warning of a Crisis in Christendom," *National Catholic Register*, online, July 29, 2018.

8 Peter Smith, "Catholic Panel Recommends Parish Mergers," *Pittsburgh Post-Gazette*, September 16, 2017.

9 Cf. Casey Cole, OFM, "Saving a Dying, Shrinking Church," *Breaking in the Habit*, YouTube, April 15, 2020.

that the bread and wine used in Communion "are *symbols* of the body and blood of Jesus Christ."[10] Since Eucharist is the most intimate means of encounter with Christ, this represents significant erosion of a fundamental pillar of the living Church.[11] It drastically weakens the relational dimension of faith, making it increasingly superficial.

The challenge is even more significant than we may appreciate. Fr. Stephen Koeth noted that in his classes at a secular university where he teaches, there are students who are no longer exposed to basic tenants of faith, do not know parables such as the Good Samaritan, and are ignorant of Christianity in Western Culture. Accordingly, he describes the immensity of the challenge today: "We are no longer merely trying to revivify practice among people who are Catholics and who have just drifted from practice and need to be brought back to Sunday Mass. We are literally having to evangelize."[12] In many cases, that effort mirrors the early missionaries who spanned the globe to deliver the Christian message to remote corners. Today, however, these "remote corners" are much closer to home.

Evidence of the spiritual pandemic is undeniable, and the reasons for this accelerated decline in the Church are both external and internal.

External Factors: Enlightenment Influences

Externally, society as a whole and indeed many individuals have pushed God away. On a present-day list of priorities, God often is no longer first, and he may not even make the top ten. We increasingly see battle lines drawn for and against the teachings and traditions of the Church, with a growing societal aversion to organized religion

---

10 Gregory A. Smith, "Just One-Third of U.S. Catholics Agree with Their Church that Eucharist is Body, Blood of Christ," Pew Research Center, online, August 5, 2019. Survey was conducted February 4-19, 2022, among adult Catholics.

11 See Ştefana Totorcea, "Prayer and Communion are Fundamental Pillars of the Living Church: Bishop Ioan Casian," *Basilica News Agency*, online, April 21, 2022. Bishop Ioan Casian is the Romanian Orthodox Bishop of Canada.

12 Stephen Dinan, "Losing Our Religion: America Becoming 'Pagan' as Christianity Cedes to Culture," *Washington Times* online, December 30, 2019.

providing a moral compass. We are constantly bombarded with such slogans as "looking out for number one," a clear acknowledgment that our neighbor is no longer a priority, either. We find ourselves growing increasingly indifferent to the needs of others.

So, how did we get to this state of affairs? The shift in attitude began during the Enlightenment, a philosophical movement originating in France during the 18th century. It embraced a principle that humanity was inherently good and divine guidance was unnecessary. This thinking has evolved into today's "culture of individualism," wherein we place ourselves as the top priority. We may no longer recognize selfish behavior because it has become part of who we are. Further, as a society, we consider ourselves highly progressive, continuously pushing the boundaries of moral behaviors under the guise of freedom, inclusivity, and political correctness. As a result, we find ourselves pushing God further and further away: *Thanks, God, but no thanks. We have a better plan*.

St. Paisios the Athonite succinctly summarized the impact of the Enlightenment:

> Western secular society has been dominated by rationalism, a byproduct of the Enlightenment. If one looks today at Western spirituality within the lens of the Eastern Christian spiritual traditions, one sees the spiritual twilight of the West, losing sight of Christ and slipping into darkness.[13]
>
> And where does it all begin? First, we neglect our spiritual work; then we become convinced that we are really spiritual, and in the end, we come up with all sorts of nonsense.[14]

13 See St. Paisios the Athonite, "With Pain and Love for Contemporary Man," *Spiritual Counsels*, vol. 1, trans. Cornelia A. Tsakiridou and Maria Spanou, ed. Fr. Peter Chamberas and Eleftheria Kaimakliotis (Souroti, Thessaloniki, Greece: Holy Hesychasterion Evangelist John the Theologian, 2019), 235.

14 Ibid.

ter?

ur spiritual work is a good segue for examining the ding to decline.

ernal Factors: Complacency

Internally, because we live in a country built on a principle of religious freedom, we Christians became complacent with our great gift of faith. Prior generations carefully handed down this treasure, yet in the absence of persecution, we have lost appreciation for it. Thus, as Christian values are attacked today, we find ourselves sluggish to react. We no longer seem willing to take a stand, too concerned with political correctness or being labeled unwelcoming or even "non-Christian." Robert Cardinal Sarah would call this the "silent apostasy;"[15] we are renouncing our faith simply by not saying anything when our beliefs and values are threatened, bowing in many cases to societal intimidation.

Further, we do not always hand on to our children what we received from our parents and grandparents. Faith is no longer discussed at the kitchen table; religious formation has moved from the home to catechists or teachers with a huge divergence in quality or motivation; the basic principle of praying as a family is steadily eroding with the overwhelming busyness and noise of our lives. The reality is that as a society, our priorities are shifting away from faith and the Church. It is small wonder when people, especially the young, ask us, "Is faith in God relevant in my life today?"

Fr. Gabriel Bunge said the crisis of faith we are experiencing today, particularly in North America and Western Europe, is not because organized religion has lost meaning, as some would argue. The crisis exists because many have lost or have not been exposed to one of the most fundamental components of our faith: the ability to encounter

15 See Fr. Gerald E. Murray, "Cardinal Sarah and Our Silent Apostasy," *The Catholic Thing*, January 16, 2016.

Jesus through prayer. Simply put, we as a Church and a society do not know how to pray.[16]

Finally, one major reason for disaffiliation from the Church is our young people's "disillusionment and frustration that their questions about faith were never answered or that they never had the opportunity to ask them in the first place."[17] Other reasons for disaffiliation included lack of companionship on the spiritual journey and struggles with difficult issues such as abortion, marriage, and contraception. There has been limited or declining spiritual formation in successive generations—"a pastoral disaster," said Bishop Robert Barron.[18]

Re-cultivating the Spiritual Life

"We are at an inflection point,"[19] wrote Dr. Scott Hahn and Brandon McGinley in their book, *It is Right and Just*. They observed:

> Despite all the bad news both within the Church and on its peripheries, this is one of the best evangelization opportunities in centuries. So many people are looking for answers to the emptiness they feel as the old concepts and institutions that provided identity and structure fade away and as the new idolatries prove unsatisfying. It is always the right time to assert

16 See Gabriel Bunge, OSB, *Earthen Vessels: The Practice of Personal Prayer According to the Patristic Tradition* (San Francisco, CA: Ignatius Press, 2002), 9. This monk describes the "evaporation of faith" and how, despite the best efforts, Christianity seems to be growing cold. His premise is that we have lost touch with the importance of a personal prayer life which was always an essential part of the mystical tradition of the Early Church.

17 Catholic News Service, "Young Adults Want to be Heard by the Church, Study Finds," *Texas Catholic Herald*, January 23, 2018, 2. Reference is made to the survey contained in Robert J. McCarty and John M. Vitek, *Going, Going, Gone: The Dynamics of Disaffiliation in Young Catholics* (Winona, MN: St. Mary's Press, 2017). This survey was conducted from 2015-2017.

18 See Barron, *To Light a Fire on the Earth*, 90.

19 Scott Hahn and Brandon McGinley, *It is Right and Just: Why the Future of Civilization Depends on True Religion* (Steubenville, OH: Emmaus Road Publishing, 2020), 134.

> Christ, but there are times when the culture is more open than others. Despite all the apparent dangers, this is one of those times.[20]

Cardinal Sarah said, "I would say that, for a Christian, faith is man's total and absolute confidence in a God whom he has *encountered personally*."[21] It is about the encounter and a return to the relational aspect of faith that is important for spiritual renewal today. That is what animates faith and makes it relevant. Accordingly, now is the time to reconnect with our faith and our spiritual roots. The world needs the truths of authentic Christian living, the Art of Spiritual Life. To address whether faith is in fact relevant, we must address the relational aspects of faith—to come to know and love Jesus Christ in a real and personal way. This deepens our understanding of the Sacred Scriptures as living texts and begins to connect with God's divinely intended purpose. "We cannot benefit from the Gospels until we fall in love with Christ."[22] While catechesis has been declining, the relational element—the mystical tradition—has been, in our opinion, to a great extent been ignored.

Restoring the Unity Between Spirituality and Theology

"True theology is always born out of the life of the Church that prays, confesses, and serves,"[23] wrote Patriarch Daniel (Ciobotea) of Romania. Becoming Patriarch in 2007 of the second-largest Orthodox Church in the world, he was tasked with rebuilding a Church that had been subjected to a brutal Communist regime until 1989. A major focus of the patriarchate was fostering the renewal of

20 Ibid.

21 Robert Cardinal Sarah, in conversation with Nicolas Diat, *The Day is Now Far Spent*, trans. Michael J. Miller (San Francisco, CA: Ignatius Press, 2019), 24. Emphasis added by author.

22 Iftimiu, "Archbishop Ioachim on Episcopal Ministry in the 3rd Millennium."

23 Patriarch Daniel (Ciobotea), "The Unity between Theology and Spirituality," in *Patriarch Daniel: Rebuilding Orthodoxy in Romania*, ed. Chad Hatfield (Yonkers, NY: St. Vladimir's Seminary Press, 2021), 20.

the interior life and inward spiritual growth of the faithful. Today, the Church in Romania is again flourishing; parishes are filled during Sunday liturgy, especially with young families, and many people make regular visits to monasteries to seek guidance from spiritual elders—visible evidence of the fruits of this effort. Patriarch Daniel stressed, "The more we feel [Jesus's] personal loving presence, the more we hearken to his word and meet him in the fulfillment of his commandments."[24]

For faith to be relevant and take root in the heart of the believer, we cannot lose focus on the relational element. We want to make sure "the art of arts and science of sciences" is not simply science. To provide context, during the Scholastic Period in the Western Church, the study of theology shifted from monasteries to universities, at which point theology and spirituality began to go their separate ways.[25] Theology became highly intellectualized. Patriarch Daniel wrote:

> It is worth mentioning that contemporary Western theology has sought too much to make faith credible through all sorts of rational arguments, while faith is a reality that permeates our whole being and, therefore, does not confine itself to a mere intellectual convincing.[26]

In contrast, in the Patristic theology of the Early Church, a strong union between theology and spirituality remained. Many of the Early Fathers were monks, committed Christian ascetics, who "did not regard the life of prayer—conscious striving for union with God in Christ in his Spirit—as irrelevant to the practice of theology."[27] The Eastern Church, which remained entrenched in Patristic teaching, held to the axiom, "If you are theologian you truly pray. If you truly prayer

24 Ibid., 16.

25 Cf. Aidan Nichols, *The Shape of Catholic Theology* (Collegeville, MN: The Liturgical Press, 1991), 205.

26 Patriarch Daniel, "The Unity between Theology and Spirituality," 21.

27 Nichols, *The Shape of Catholic Theology*, 205.

you are a theologian." Theology in this context places significant emphasis on the relational component.

Accordingly, the focus of this work is to examine our faith through a lens of spirituality, rounding out a person's understanding of Christianity that has been more grounded in doctrinal knowledge. The Second Vatican Council advocated a shift from Scholastic theology back to Patristic teaching (*ressourcement*). We, too, must make this shift, rediscovering the Holy Fathers who strived through ascetical practices to live the commandments of Jesus and now provide us the necessary insights into building a relationship with him.

To stress the importance of spirituality, we leverage the concept of dialectic tension, wherein two elements—often contradictions—are in play to create unity. As an example of this concept, let us consider a fundamental doctrine of Christian faith: Jesus as both true God and true man, fully human and fully divine. The following is an illustration of the concept:

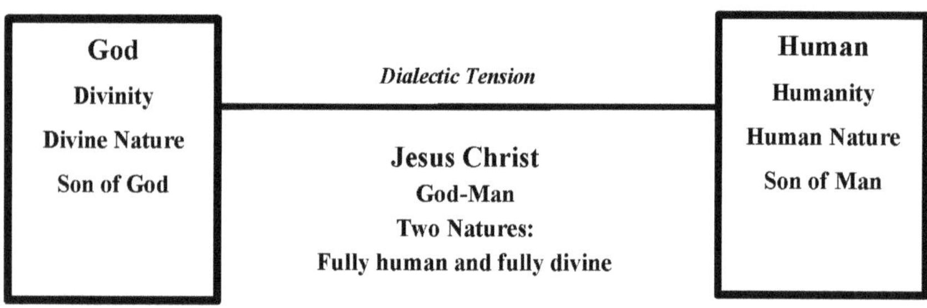

To understand who Jesus is, one must hold two elements in tension: divinity and humanity. Neither can be overemphasized at the expense of the other. At the Council of Chalcedon in 451, Jesus was defined as, "Truly God and truly man ... two natures without confusion, without change, without division, without separation." The great heresies of the Church arose when this dialectic tension was disturbed. For example, if the humanity of Jesus is overemphasized at the expense of divinity, a heretical distortion such as Arianism can arise. Conversely, overemphasis on the divinity of Jesus at the expense of his humanity leads to heresy such as Nestorianism. Thus, the concepts of divinity and humanity must remain in balance to understand who Jesus truly is. This is an example of dialectic tension.

This same concept applies to the relationship between spirituality and theology. They should not be separated, nor one emphasized at the expense of the other. Consider what Patriarch Daniel wrote about true theology being born of a Church that prays, confesses and serves.

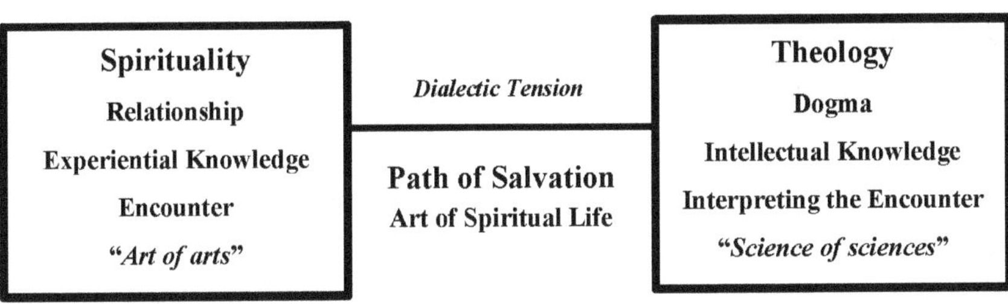

An intellectualized faith, one that overemphasizes theology while ignoring the spiritual dimension, does not have the necessary depth created through a genuine encounter with Christ, thus risking superficiality and easily dismissal as irrelevant. Secularization has competing philosophical arguments, that, for example, a person can live a good life without being rooted in the Divine. Thus, personal encounter is the critical differentiating factor between authentic Christian life and the spirituality of the age; it is essential to a living faith, life-giving and animating versus historical and incomplete. Patriarch Daniel observed, "'Social' theology separated from the spiritual experience of the Church risks becoming a fashionable ideology rather than permanent and consistent."[28] The Church

28 Patriarch Daniel, "The Unity between Theology and Spirituality," 21.

facilitates our encounters with Jesus and serves as a repository of our spiritual traditions. As Elder Porphyrios of Kavsokalyvia wrote, "Outside the Church there is no salvation, there is no life."[29] There needs to be unity between theology and spirituality.

A problem also exists if one makes the opposite separation. Many people describe themselves as "spiritual," but reject the notion of an institutionalized Church. Most do not reject belief in God, per se, but they believe spirituality and a transcendent purpose are something to be pursued individually. In contrast, Sr. Sandra M. Schneiders, a foremost authority on spirituality, would argue the spiritual traditions of the Church are precisely what we need to understand our spiritual-life experiences.[30] We receive our life-giving spiritual tradition *through* the institutionalized Church, the Christian tradition centered on Jesus Christ.[31] Divorcing the spiritual life from the Church, Schneiders says, "is a classic case of curing a headache by decapitation."[32] Spiritual traditions are handed to us by the Church, and we need them to understand, guide, and support our encounters with Jesus, our source of life. The Church provides guidance from the collective wisdom of the Holy Fathers who have undertaken the same spiritual journey before us. We have access to their writings, which offer guideposts to our experiences. They have walked the same path and have left markers for us to follow.[33] Thus, we can never separate our growth in the spiritual life from the Church, or spiritual encounter from theology, because such a separation would leave us incomplete. Christianity is not an intellectual exercise; it is a mystery of life in a divine embrace.

---

29 Elder Porphyrios, *Wound by Love: The Life and Wisdom of Elder Porphyrios*, ed. Sisters of the Holy Convent of Chrysopigi, trans. John Raffan (Limni, Evia, Greece: Denise Harvey, 2013), 87.

30 Cf. Sandra M. Schneiders, "Religion vs. Spirituality: A Contemporary Conundrum," *Spiritus: A Journal of Christian Spirituality* 3(2) (2003), 169.

31 Ibid., 171.

32 Ibid.

33 See Richard J. Fowler, *Celebration of Discipline: The Path to Spiritual Growth* (New York, NY: Harper One, 1998), 72.

A Catalyst for Spiritual Renewal

Does faith matter? The short answer: God is relevant to us today, and we need to allow him to make his way from the periphery back to the center of our lives. God is meant to be experienced. He is active and present in his Creation and wants to have a relationship with us. Faith is meant to be felt in the heart—a fire of Christian zeal, not simply intellectual concepts we retain in our minds. Pope Francis reminds us in *Evangelii Gaudium*, "The Joy of the Gospel fills the hearts and lives of all who encounter Jesus."[34] It is about experiencing the living God, not just reading about him in a book.

As human beings, we all want to be happy. Yet, what provides true and lasting happiness? What fills the deepest longing within us? Are we happier without God? Does he have a purpose for us? To answer these questions, we have developed this series of discussion topics. We want to present the evidence to allow people to decide where God belongs in their lives. Jesus tells us, "If you remain in my word, you will truly be my disciples, and you will know the truth, and the truth will set you free."[35] Simply put, we want to present that truth without being distorted or watered down by falsehoods or empty messages prevalent in secular society.

Each topic is intended to be a bite-sized, manageable piece. We invite those who are curious or have questions about faith to join in the discussion; engage the faith, learn more about it, and then, based on the facts and, more importantly, the stirrings within their hearts, decide where God belongs. Each topic is linked to Sacred Scripture, and we examine our faith through our encounters with God as he has been revealed to us by his Son, Jesus Christ. As we dig deeper to understand the truth and recognize the presence of God in ordinary moments, we learn why faith has meaning in our daily lives.

---

34 Pope Francis, *Evangelii Gaudium*, Apostolic Exhortation (Rome: Libreria Editrice Vaticana, Nov. 24, 2013), no. 1.

35 John 8:31-32. All biblical quotes contained herein are from the NABRE, 2011, unless otherwise specified.

We developed these topics to answer the questions of young people hungry to know more about their faith. We want them to know that their questions are being heard. However, the topics are equally relevant for a broader audience: those who question or have walked away from the Church; those who consider themselves "Catholic-ish", somewhat aligned to the teachings of the Church but not completely; those thinking about leaving; the spiritually hungry; and those who feel they are not getting answers to their questions about faith. By understanding the *why*, people can own their faith and belief system, rather than memorizing a textbook or what is handed down by others.[36] We want to introduce people to a God who is personal, not a theoretical concept or rational argument. By his teachings and example, Jesus models his relationship with God for us. He is the way to the Father,[37] the true light that pierces the darkness of hopelessness, disillusionment, and despair that has settled in our midst.

This book does not advocate new programs or approaches; they are not needed. We are returning to basics within our Deposit of Faith, a spiritual renewal in the Patristic tradition. We are reclaiming the unity between theology and spirituality, holding both in proper balance. It is intended for people who want clarity on their faith: authentic, not diluted, and without additives, artificial flavors, or whitewashed or sugarcoated for acceptability within secular culture. Simply the basics.

Intrigued? Want to know more? Then, let us begin the journey.

---

36 See James W. Fowler, *Becoming Adult, Becoming Christian: Adult Development and Christian Faith* (San Francisco, CA: Jossey-Bass Publishers, 2000). For those familiar with James W. Fowler's Faith Formation Theory, this is the transition from Stage 3 (Synthetic Conventional Faith) to Stage 4 (Individuative-Reflective Faith). This means one's faith is no longer dependent upon the teaching of others, but rather through critical and reflective thinking, one internalizes faith for his- or herself. In short, the person now owns the faith as his or her own.

37 See John 14:6.

Part 1

Our Desire for Encounter

The Spirituality of Encounter

"Lord, what is man that you care for him, mortal man, that you keep him in mind; man who is merely a breath, whose life fades like a passing shadow."
(Psalm 144:3-4, NAB)

"Were not our hearts burning within us?"
(Luke 24:32)

"Your most intense effort should be how you will encounter Christ, how you will be united to him, and how you will keep him in your heart." [38]
(Elder Porphyrios of Kavsokalyvia)

"Christianity ... is much more than an exterior acceptance of doctrines and rules. No one can be a true Christian at second hand; there must be a personal encounter, in which each knows, sees, tastes, and touches for himself." [39]
(Metropolitan Kallistos Ware)

Opening Gospel Passage

Luke 24:13-35 (Appearance on the Road to Emmaus).

Beginning with the Conclusion

Let us begin with a conclusion: Our purpose in life is to live in union with God. This is why we were created and why we exist—to be with the God who created the universe, the God who is "ineffable, inconceivable, invisible, incomprehensible, ever-existing, yet ever

38 Elder Porphyrios, 137.

39 Kallistos Ware, "Introduction," *St. John Climacus: The Ladder of Divine Ascent*, trans. Colm Luibheid and Norman Russell (New York, NY: Paulist Press, 1982), 7.

the same,"[40] a God beyond all our imagining. He desires a personal, intimate relationship with each of us. Our deepest longing can be fulfilled only by establishing such a relationship with him.[41] This is the God who Jesus has revealed to us, a God who cares so much for us that the very hairs on our head have been counted.[42] God's greatest desire is to draw near to us; our journey through this life is to make us accustomed to experiencing his presence. Such a relationship with God should be normal for all, not just a select few. God wants to live with us in this life, not just in heaven.

That is the conclusion. By the end of these discussions, we will have made our case, and it will be up to each individual to determine if we have proven this conclusion. We each need to consider the relevance of faith in our lives. Who is God to me, and where should he be in my life? This will allow us to answer the overarching question and theme of this book: "Does faith matter?"

Encounter

Pope Francis wrote, "The Joy of the Gospel fills the hearts and lives of all who encounter Jesus."[43] It is all about the encounter. We develop a personal relationship through encounter because our God is meant to be experienced in a personal, tangible way. We cannot know God intellectually; rather, we must experience God. To experience God, we must be attuned to the divine presence.

---

40 From the Anaphora (consecration prayer) of the Divine of Liturgy of St. John Chrysostom. *The Divine Liturgies of Our Holy Father John Chrysostom* (Pittsburgh: Byzantine Seminary Press, 2006), 72. See also Robert F. Taft, "The Authenticity of the Chrysostom Anaphora Revisited. Determining the Authorship of the Liturgical Texts by Computer," *Orientalia Christiana Periodica* 56(1) (1990): 28–29. Taft explains that Chrysostom (d. 407) used the Anaphora of the Twelve Apostles of Syrian (Antiochian) origin when he came to Constantinople and added phrases. This particular phrase was a genuine addition to the Anaphora by Chrysostom himself.

41 See Eph. 1:5–6. The God and Father of our Lord Jesus Christ "destined us for adoption to himself through Jesus Christ, in accord with the favor of his will, for the praise of the glory of his grace that he granted us in the beloved."

42 See Matt. 10:30.

43 Pope Francis, *Evangelii Gaudium*, no. 1.

Consider the encounter from our opening Gospel reading about the two disciples on the road to Emmaus. The encounter was not primarily intellectual. The disciples did not recognize Jesus as he interpreted the scriptures for them. They recognized him in the breaking of the bread, illustrating that encounters are meant to be primarily experiential. Further, this Gospel passage shows that the encounter should be deeply felt ("Were not our hearts burning within us?").

Consider the Eucharist. Intellectual learning tells us the bread and wine are transformed, becoming the body and blood of Christ—the Doctrine of Transubstantiation that most who partake likely remember from catechism class. However, what is the sensation we have when we receive him? Have we properly prepared ourselves to receive him? It is about the encounter, a genuine experience of God.

God is present in the ordinary and mundane, not just mountaintop experiences, which tend to be extraordinary events, few and far between. However, we need to be increasingly spiritually aware to recognize God in all things, especially in everyday life circumstances. St. Theophan the Recluse wrote:

> There is a moment, and a very noticeable moment, which is sharply marked out in the course of our life, when a person begins to live in a Christian way. Christian life is zeal and the strength to remain in communion with God by means of an active fulfillment of his holy will, according to our faith in our Lord Jesus Christ, and with the help of the grace of God, to the glory of his most holy name.[44]

Through this series of discussions, we will outline the case that God wants an intimate relationship with each person. This relationship begins through encounters with the divine presence, leading us to our destiny: union with God—or to remain in communion with

44 St. Theophan the Recluse, *The Path to Salvation: A Concise Outline of Christian Ascesis*, trans. Seraphim Rose (Stafford, AZ: St. Paisius Monastery), 23.

God, as St. Theophan said. We could call this a spiritual theology of encounter, or simply a spirituality of encounter. Pope Francis mentions "encounter" 34 times in *Evangelii Gaudium.*[45] We will examine our Catholic faith through this lens, because we cannot be fulfilled nor achieve our created purpose without entering into a relationship with God. It is hoped that this approach will prove why our faith is relevant in today's secularized world.

We will first examine how every person was created with a desire for encounter. Next, we will consider the Divine we encounter. Who is this God who wants a personal relationship with us? Next, we will consider the means of encounter. How do we experience this divine presence? After this, we will consider where these encounters take place. Finally, we will examine what happens because of these encounters and how they affect the journey toward our divinely intended destiny. The end goal is not the encounter itself—it is who we become because of our encounters with the divine presence. This transformation, this "becoming" on the journey from encounter to destiny is called *theosis,* a Greek term meaning "divinization" or "deification" of the human person. "Essentially, *theosis* is the core of the good news of the Gospel, namely that we are called to share in the very life of God."[46] Through our encounters with the divine presence, we are transformed, gradually becoming more like God in anticipation of our destiny. This spiritual transformation is an incremental process occurring over a lifetime and continuing into the next life until the resurrection of the dead.[47]

---

45 See William T. Ditewig, "A Spiritual Theology of Encounter," *Deacon Digest* 33(6) (2016), 9. Pope Francis uses the term *encounter* 34 times in *Evangelii Gaudium,* and unlike previous popes, he "takes the term a bit further to speak of our encounter with each other, especially with those who suffer at the margins." His lens of encounter is such that "through our encounter with God, we are led to encounter with others, and through our encounter with others, we are led again to a renewed encounter."

46 Anthony M. Coniaris, *A Beginner's Introduction to the Philokalia* (Minneapolis: Light & Life Publishing Company, 2016), 18.

47 See Nicholas Cabasilas, *The Life in Christ,* trans. Carmino J. DeCatanzaro (Crestwood, NY: St. Vladimir's Seminary Press, 1974), 43. "The life in Christ originates in this life and arises from it. It is perfected, however, in the life to come, when we shall have reached that last day."

By cultivating our personal relationship with God, we discover something amazing. God is not silent or passive in our lives, as some would like us to believe. Rather, God reaches out to us to enter into a relationship with him. The spiritual transformation, or *theosis,* is our personal submission to him alone, allowing him to take possession of us. It is how we surrender our self-will to the divine-will, to de-throne our egos and rely upon him alone. As St. Teresa of Ávila advised, "Whoever does not follow the invitation of God to enter into a personal and intimate relationship will not come to know the meaning of life or bring it to its fulfillment."[48] In essence, we become accustomed to living with God, in God, and through God in this life in preparation for an even more perfect life in eternity.

All of us must decide where God should be positioned in our lives. Will he be at the center or the periphery? Will he even have a place at all? Our objective through this series of topics is to prove the case by providing evidence that for us to achieve our human purpose, union with God, he needs to be at the center. This is the value proposition of the Gospel, the message of Jesus when he said, "I came so that they might have life and have it more abundantly."[49] As Pope Francis writes, "Those who accept his offer of salvation are set free from sin, sorrow, inner emptiness and loneliness."[50] This is the desire of every human heart, the great search for meaning and fulfillment. However, many still seek meaning and fulfillment in ways other than those presented in the Gospel.

Opposing Secular Messages

Winter is an appropriate metaphor for the situation of faith in our modern world.[51] Above, we have laid out the value proposition of the Gospel. However, we also need to lay out the challenges to

48 St. Teresa of Ávila, *The Interior Castle*, trans. Kieran Kavanaugh, OCD and Otilio Rodriguez, OCD (Mahwah, NJ, Paulist Press, 1979), 12-13.

49 John 10:10.

50 Pope Francis, *Evangelii Gaudium.* no. 1.

51 See Elizabeth A. Johnson, *Quest for the Living God: Mapping Frontiers in the Theology of God* (New York, NY: The Continuum International Publishing Group, 2007), 28.

faith that are prevalent in today's society. To foster the ability for true discernment, it is important to consider all sides of the case. Each person needs to carefully evaluate the evidence to make an informed decision about the importance of faith in their lives.

The Age of Enlightenment, which emerged in France and dominated the world of ideas in Europe during the 18th century, fostered a belief in the inherent goodness of humanity and confidence that human beings had the capacity for greatness within themselves—extolling reason over faith. This belief was subsequently challenged by the horrors of two world wars, which demonstrated the destructive and depraved depths to which human beings were also capable of falling. However, the philosophical principles of the Enlightenment are still seeded in our society, many standing in direct opposition to the Christian faith. These include:

- Atheism – outright rejection of a belief in God.
- Agnosticism – another rejection defaulting to the view that matters of God are unknown or unknowable. God may exist but is not relevant.
- Relativism – subscribing to the point that there is no absolute truth such as that expressed by Christianity.
- Secularism – humanistic values that allow a life of ethical integrity without faith. In other words, faith is not necessary for one to live a good life.
- Religious pluralism – belief that there is more than one path to holy and ethical living.
- Apatheism – espoused by those who do not actively question or reject God, as much as they do not see a reason to bother with religion.[52]

52 See Dinan, "Losing Our Religion." Per Dinan, Apathetics do not attend services, do not ascribe to a creed, and often have limited familiarity with faith. They account for a larger share of the American population than agnostics and atheists combined, and are a rapidly growing group, their numbers growing by millions each year.

These popular perspectives often leave people confused, causing them to seek meaning in many different places, often turning away from the Church. The problem is that such perspectives as relativism and subjectivism lead to spiritual drifting, subject to the whims of passing fads that have no spiritual roots.[53] British writer G.K. Chesterton is credited with saying, "When people cease to believe in God, they do not believe in nothing; they will believe in anything."[54] We lose our perspective on God, striving to mold God into our desired image of who we believe he should be, rather than recognizing humanity as being created in God's image. This diffuses our faith and erodes our foundation. Yet there is a correlation that occurs: the greater the spiritual void, the greater the frustration in finding something apart from God that will provide lasting satisfaction. Because of this, many despair or even lose hope. Cardinal Sarah wrote, "Without the nourishment of prayer, every Christian is in danger. Without the Son of God, [human beings] are lost and humanity has no more future."[55]

Archbishop Charles Chaput of Philadelphia describes contemporary American society as a "culture of individualism," self over others, where the person is the center instead of God and emphasis is placed on one's own abilities, personal success, and instant material happiness.[56] Individualism is more than simple selfishness; rather, it is innate to our culture. As it has evolved, the importance of God is gradually diminished. Accordingly, these behaviors today (e.g., "looking out for

53 See Robert Cardinal Sarah, *God or Nothing: A Conversation on Faith*, trans. Michael J. Miller (San Francisco, CA: Ignatius Press, 2015), 120.

54 Alex McFarland, *The 10 Most Common Objections to Christianity* (Ventura, CA: Regal Books, 2007), 148.

55 Sarah, *God or Nothing*, 120, 158.

56 Cf. Robert Cardinal Sarah, "You follow me," *Magnificat*, 19(4) (2017), 54. Taken from *God or Nothing*.

number one") are considered normal.[57] Many do not even realize or appreciate how our culture influences views in matters of faith such as love of God and love of neighbor. Pope Francis described this as a "seedbed for collective selfishness." He writes in *Laudato Si'*:

> When people become self-centered and self-enclosed, their greed increases. The emptier a person's heart is, the more he or she needs things to buy, own, and consume. It becomes almost impossible to accept the limits imposed by reality. In this horizon, a genuine sense of the common good also disappears. As these attitudes become more widespread, social norms are respected only to the extent that they do not clash with personal needs.[58]

We have become enslaved to a mentality of comfort.[59] A well-respected Greek monk, Elder Amphilochios of Patmos, summarizes this well: "When your heart does not have Christ, it will contain either money, property, or people instead." Let us candidly ask ourselves, "What fills our heart today?"

If removed from the center of our lives, God becomes distant and less relevant, and the importance of Christian values are continually

---

57 See Charles J. Chaput, OFM Cap., *Strangers in a Strange Land: Practicing the Catholic Faith in a Post-Christian World* (New York, NY: Henry Holt, 2017). This is an excellent book that describes the impact of this shifting culture in the United States, which began with The Age of Enlightenment or Age of Reason. It fostered a belief in the inherent goodness of humanity and confidence that human beings had the capacity for greatness within themselves, dismissing the role of God. Over time, this spawned several other movements or philosophical schools of thought including Humanism, Rationalism, and Individualism. Humanism: an outlook or system of thought attaching prime importance to human rather than divine or supernatural matters. Rationalism: a belief or theory that opinions and actions should be based on reason and knowledge rather than on religious belief or emotional response. Individualism: (1) the habit or principle of being independent and self-reliant and (2) a social theory favoring freedom of action for individuals over collective or state control. All of these schools of thought, which have influenced our culture today, illustrate a movement away from God and even communal responsibilities with an increased focus on self. Accordingly, we have developed a culture of individualism.

58 Pope Francis, *Laudato Si'* (Rome: Libreria Editrice Vaticana, May 2015), no. 204.

59 Cf. Iftimiu, "Archbishop Ioachim on Episcopal Ministry in the 3rd Millennium."

reduced. As written in the Second Letter of John, "Anyone who is so 'progressive' as not to remain in the teaching of Christ does not have God; whoever remains in the teaching has the Father and the Son."[60]

This is a realistic perspective on the attitudes and beliefs that permeate our secular society. Many voices try to drown out the message of the Gospel. It is no wonder people are confused. Hopelessness seems normal. C. S. Lewis wrote, "All that we call human history... [is] the long, terrible story of man trying to find something other than God which will make him happy."[61]

We see the experience of winter occurring today in terms of faith. Many no longer see the point of faith, believing God to be absent, or the relevance of faith, not seeing God providing purpose and meaning to daily life. "Churches are emptying, but clinics prescribing anti-depressants are full."[62] Souls are dying!

Because faith underpins hope, the crisis that has gripped our Church today is largely a loss of hope.[63] "In such a season, belief must get back to basics. To survive, people of faith need to return to the center, to the innermost core that alone can nourish and warm the heart in winter."[64] In this situation, there is only one big issue: if "something other than God" fails to fulfill the human spirit or provide us the lasting happiness we seek, then perhaps it is time to take a renewed look at what God has to offer. What fills our hearts? How can we experience the joy of the Gospel? How do we discover fulfillment of our deepest longing?

---

60 2 John 9.

61 C. S. Lewis, *Mere Christianity* (New York, NY: Macmillan, 1952), 53.

62 Cf. St. Paisios the Athonite, "Spiritual Struggle," *Spiritual Counsels*, vol. 3, trans. Fr. Peter Chamberas, ed. Anna Famellos and Andronikos Masters (Souroti, Thessaloniki, Greece: Holy Hesychasterion Evangelist John the Theologian, 2014), 301. "Without good Spiritual Fathers, the churches empty, while the psychiatric wards, prisons, and hospitals become busier than ever. People need to realize that their life is troubled because they have distanced themselves from God; they need to realize they must repent and humbly confess their sins."

63 Hieromonk Maximos Davies, "Lenten Mission 2018: Hope," delivered at St. Sophia Ukrainian Greek Catholic Church, The Colony, Texas, February 24, 2018.

64 Ibid., 29.

Keeping the Lights On

German Theologian Wolfhart Pannenberg observed, "Religions die when their lights go out, when their teachings no longer illuminate life as it is lived by their adherents. Where people experience God as still having something to say, the lights stay on."[65] Since there is sufficient emphasis in society on finding "something other than God" to make us happy, this series of discussions will make the case that only God can be the source of true happiness, that he is the fulfillment of all human longing. We believe when the evidence is independently and objectively examined, individuals will discover the Catholic Church, enriched by its Eastern Christian patrimony, has something relevant to say about human purpose standing in stark contrast to empty secular messages and distortions. We retain a living faith that is ever ancient, ever new, providing us with the means to experience the Risen Jesus in a tangible way so that we fulfill our true human purpose, which is union with God.

Perspectives to Be Leveraged

During our discussions, we will consider various perspectives. At the outset, we would like to introduce the two most significant sources, modern-era theologians, and explain the reasons why they are included. The first is Karl Rahner, SJ, a German Jesuit priest, philosopher, and theologian, considered one of the most influential Catholic theologians of the 20th century. He was part of the *Nouvelle Théologie* movement, a school of thought that emerged within the Catholic Church leading into the Second Vatican Council (Vatican II). The movement was primarily composed of French and German theologians who increasingly stood in opposition to Neo-Scholasticism, encouraging a return to the sources (*ressourcement*), namely Sacred Scripture and Patristic teaching. Their perspectives significantly influenced the Council. Rahner developed his

65 Cited by Elizabeth A. Johnson, 22.

theological framework by considering Early Greek Fathers such as St Gregory of Nyssa. His perspectives on, for example, anthropology and Christology are complementary to Eastern theological teachings and supportive of the doctrine of *theosis*. What is particularly refreshing about Rahner's approach is the belief that we can learn about God through our human experiences more so than divinely revealed truths or philosophical frameworks. Reflective of this, he wrote, "The devout Christian of the future will either be a 'mystic,' one who has 'experienced' something, or he will cease to be anything at all."[66]

The second source is Fr. Dumitru Stăniloae, a Romanian Orthodox priest, theologian, and professor, considered one of the most influential Eastern Orthodox theologians of the 20th century. In developing his theological framework, he considered the teachings of Vatican II and Catholic Theologians such as Rahner. To provide context as to why Eastern Christian perspectives are being included, we need to consider the view of Pope St. John Paul II, who believed the Church needed to learn to breathe again from both lungs, one Eastern and one Western.[67] Recent popes have described the need to rediscover the treasures of the Eastern Catholic Churches to create a true synthesis reflective of the Universal Catholic Church. These Eastern Christian perspectives provide a further richness to our Catholic faith. Many do not realize that the Catholic Church consists of 24 Churches in communion with the Pope of Rome, the Roman or Latin Church, and 23 Eastern Catholic Churches, demonstrating the true universality of the Church. Many of these Eastern Catholic Churches have Eastern Orthodox counterparts, which is why we have chosen to include a well-recognized and respected Eastern Orthodox theologian in our discussions.

There is a distinct difference between Eastern and Western

66 Rahner, "Christian Living Formerly and Today," 15.

67 See Pope St. John Paul II, *Ut Unum Sint* (Rome: Libreria Editrice Vaticana, 1995), no. 54. This Pope often spoke of the need for the Church to achieve its deepest meaning by breathing from both its lungs, one Eastern and one Western.

theological approaches, but they share common themes to consider as we reflect on our spiritual journey. In particular, many parallels exist between Rahner and Stăniloae, especially in Christology and humanity's desire for something greater, such as transcendence. Further, Eastern Orthodox theology remained more deeply rooted in Patristic teachings and the mystical tradition. Theologians such as Stăniloae often quote the axiom, "If you are a theologian you truly pray. If you truly pray you are a theologian." Accordingly, this theological approach is highly predicated on an experiential encounter with the divine presence. Archimandrite Zacharias Zacharou of Essex summarizes this perspective well: "Genuine living theology is not intellectual or academic knowledge, but a burning of the heart that draws nigh to the mystery of the Person of Jesus Christ."[68]

These discussions will also introduce other Church historical figures, from ancient times to modern. In the Supplemental Information, we have provided a section entitled Pivotal Players, which provides a brief biographical sketch of key people referenced herein.

Summary

We began our discussion by noting that God, who is beyond human comprehension and understanding, wants a personal, intimate relationship with us. This relationship is developed through encounters with the divine presence. Our God is not distant, but meant to be experienced in a tangible way, which means we must be attuned to his presence. Our relationship with God, supported by our encounters with him, is important to achieve our human purpose: union with God.

Systematically, by exploring these topics, we will make the case for why God should remain at the center of our lives and not pushed to the periphery.

---

68 Archimandrite Zacharias Zacharou, *Thirst for Life Eternal* (Essex, England: Stavropegic Monastery of St. John the Baptist, 2022), 219.

Reflection Questions

After each discussion, we will include reflection questions for individual consideration. Below are the questions for Topic No. 1:

1. God, who is beyond human comprehension, desires a personal, intimate relationship with me. What is my reaction to this?
2. On a scale of zero to ten, how would I rate the importance of faith in my life today? Zero would mean faith is not a part of my life. Ten would mean God is at the center, and my faith is the essential element of my life. Be honest; this answer will not be shared.
3. Where is God in my life today? Is he at the center of my life and in all my actions? Is he somewhere on the periphery? Is he even in my life? Again, please be honest; this answer will not be shared.
4. Do I consider myself hopeful? What do I hope in? What is the foundation for my hope?
5. What fills my heart? Is it Christ or something else?

Key Vocabulary from this Discussion

Many young people have expressed a desire to know their faith and not have it watered down. Accordingly, we have provided a Glossary of Selected Terms.

Icon of the Appearance of Our Lord on the Road to Emmaus

Anthropology

"God created mankind in his image."
(Gen. 1:27)

"Only in God does man have a unique and eternal value." [69]
(Patriarch Daniel of Romania)

Opening Scripture Reading

Gen. 1:26-31 (Creation of humanity in the divine image).

Beginning with the Beginning

Anthropology refers to our human origins. Many ask these fundamental questions: Who are we as human beings? Why were we created? What is our purpose? Sacred Scripture tells us that humanity was created in the image of God, an image impressed within every person and giving each fundamental dignity. It is the reason all human life is considered sanctified. The Early Greek Fathers said that we are patterned after the Image Absolute, Jesus Christ himself.[70]

For this discussion, let us also briefly differentiate between image and likeness:

> Image: The sum total of our possibilities.[71] It is imprinted upon us and can never be taken away.

---

69 Patriarch Daniel, *Confessing the Truth in Love*, 166.

70 See Col. 1:15. "He [Christ] is the image of the invisible God, the firstborn of all creation."

71 Cf. Anthony M. Coniaris, *Tools for Theosis: Becoming God-like in Christ* (Minneapolis: Light & Life Publishing Company, 2014), 8.

> Likeness: This is the image's fulfillment,[72] our ability to become who God wants us to be by achieving our possibilities, meaning to live in union with him—nothing less.

The human person, created in the image of God, has the capacity for God (*capex Dei*), meaning we can experience him and have a relationship with him. Even if we ignore God, we can experience this capacity through our feelings of human longing. God created this void so that he alone could fill it, allowing us to become what we were created to be by entering into communion with him. Through such communion, we find ourselves by experiencing authentic fulfillment.[73] Our hearts were made for God.

Human beings are given free choice. We can freely choose to fulfill our possibilities, to be open to God who communicates himself to us. We can become who he created us to be, or we can reject our openness to God. The desire for fulfillment or deeper purpose (transcendence) is inherent to human nature. We can seek fulfillment in the finite or the infinite, within created things or within the Creator, within absurdity and nothingness or within an Absolute Being (God) who offers us a deeper purpose. Each of us must make this choice.

God invites everyone to share his divine life through his Incarnate Son,[74] "the offer of salvation,"[75] and we can respond freely to this offer of God through Jesus. It is about the offer and our response. Accepting the offer means preparing ourselves through personal effort, submission to the will of God, and collaborating with divine assistance given us. This is a transformative journey called *theosis*.

---

72 Ibid.

73 Cf. John Cardinal O'Connor, "The One We Have Looked For," *Magnificat* 23(10) December (2021), 204.

74 See Mark F. Fischer, *The Foundations of Karl Rahner* (New York, NY: Crossroad Publishing Company, 2016), 8. "Theology presupposes anthropology. Anthropology understands the human being as one created with the ability to hear God's Word."

75 See Pope Francis, *Evangelii Gaudium*. no. 1. "Those who accept his [Jesus's] offer of salvation are set free from sin, sorrow, inner emptiness and loneliness."

God's offer is irrefutable, and his grace always available. However, we cannot become who we were created to be without divine assistance. We strive, surrendering self-will to the divine will, living in a right-ordered relationship with God. We provide the effort, and God provides the assistance (*synergeia*).

We previously mentioned that a critical element of our spiritual journey is our ability to encounter the Divine; it is about our human experiences. So, let us begin with our simplest experience with God: human longing. Every person feels a deep-seated longing within. We want to find meaning and purpose in life. We want to love and be loved. We seek happiness and joy. We find ourselves striving for something to fill that longing. Most of us know that feeling, sometimes all too well; it is a yearning of becoming something more. One author writes, "We seek for something or someone else to [quench] our inner thirst, to fill the void God created as a sacred place for himself, a void large enough that only he can fill."[76] This human longing indicates to us that there is something more. Let us consider this longing from a few perspectives.

Patristic Perspective

The Patristic Period is considered the Early Church after the time of the apostles, approximately100 to 800 CE. One of the Early Greek Fathers, St. Gregory of Nyssa, described inner longing as "the experience of our dissatisfaction." He taught that we could have all the food, honors, personal recognition, power, praise, sexual intimacy, or other pleasures that we seek, yet somehow still find ourselves empty. The feeling of fulfillment is only temporary. We remain dissatisfied and will continue to seek ways to fill this emptiness. Therefore, St. Gregory concluded that we either are the most pitiable of creatures seeking something that does not exist (absurdity of life), or there is

76 Joseph Langford, MC, *Mother Teresa's Secret Fire: The Encounter that Changed Her Life and How It Can Transform Your Own* (Huntington, IN: Our Sunday Visitor Publishing Division, 2008), 191.

something that transcends time and space that can satisfy our deepest longing. That something, St. Gregory concludes, is God. Only God can fill the "God-sized" holes in our lives.

As we continue to explore this series of topics, we will observe clear similarities between this teaching of St. Gregory of Nyssa and those of Rahner and Stăniloae.

Modern Day: The Theology of Rahner and Stăniloae

What made Rahner's theology unique and particularly refreshing was that instead of focusing on God through philosophical or theological discussions, he focused on human experience. Rahner believed that theology is anthropology and anthropology is theology. What does this mean? Based on what it means to be human, this provides us with some understanding of God. Everything we say about God is something about ourselves because we cannot know God as he is (his "essence")—he is beyond human comprehension or understanding. Even though God is the ultimate mystery, he is constantly seeking us, and we can experience him through our encounters with the world and especially other people.[77] For example, when we receive genuine acts of love from our neighbors, we experience something about God.[78] God is personal and the foundation of all; he offers himself to us, and his love is unconditional. Should we close off our openness to God, we do not just deny God; we also deny ourselves. We deny part of our own humanity because we were created in the image of God to live in relationship with him. For Rahner, theological doctrine cannot be detached from human experience. Consider our

---

77 See Karl Rahner, *Theological Investigations*, vol. 4 (Baltimore, MD: Helicon Press, 1966), 110. Cited in Karen Kilby, *Karl Rahner: A Brief Introduction* (New York, NY: Crossroad Publishing Company, 2007), 7. "Man always lives by the holy mystery, even when he is not conscious of it."

78 See Karl Rahner, *Foundations of Christian Faith: An Introduction to the Idea of Christianity*, trans. William V. Dych (New York, NY: Crossroads Publishing Company, 1990), 54. "The concept of 'God' is not a grasp of God by which a person masters the mystery, but it is letting oneself be grasped by the mystery which is present and yet ever distant."

opening discussion regarding dialectic tension between spirituality and theology: We learn about our faith and achieve an understanding of God through our lived experiences.

Stăniloae's theological framework is based on a similar principle. "Theology, properly understood, is not an abstract system, not a philosophical theory, but the expression of personal experience, of a living encounter with the living God."[79] He continues, "A theology which feeds on the prayer and spiritual life of the Church is a theology which expresses and deepens the Church's thinking, her spiritual life, and her work of sanctification and serving."[80] Stăniloae also quotes the axiom "If you are a theologian, you will pray truly. And if you pray truly, you are a theologian."[81] For Early Fathers such as St. Maximos the Confessor, *theologia* is envisioned as a relationship with God that transcends all knowledge and is considered in the Christian East as the highest form of contemplation.[82] In this sense, theology is not an intellectual activity but one of relational experience.

Consider this perspective carefully. Stăniloae is saying that a theologian has experienced God through prayer versus someone who has simply studied doctrine and written books. The emphasis is placed on experience, not intellectual insight, which is why we focus our discussions on encounter, which is often the road less traveled in catechesis.

Because the human person is created in the divine image, we have the pattern of the Divine infused within us. Thus, we can have a relationship with God (*capex Dei*); we have a natural openness to God, to realize that something infinite exists because human desire is always striving for something greater. Rahner's favorite image for such

79 Kallistos Ware, Foreword to Dumitru Stăniloae, "Revelation and Knowledge of the Triune God," *The Experience of God: Orthodox Dogmatic Theology*, vol. 1, trans. Ioan Ionita and Robert Barringer (Brookline, MA: Holy Cross Orthodox Press, 1998), xiv.

80 Ibid., 87.

81 Ibid., 86. From the writings of Evagrios the Solitary (Evagrios Ponticus).

82 Elena Vishnevskaya, "Divinization and Spiritual Progress in Maximus the Confessor," in *Theosis: Deification in Christian Doctrine*, ed. Stephen Finlan and Vladimir Kharlamov (Eugene, OR: Pickwick Publications, 2006), 142.

desire is that of a horizon.[83] Human beings know finite objects against the backdrop of an infinite horizon, the limited or finite against the unlimited. We are drawn toward something beyond us, something we can reach for but never quite grasp; we strive to move beyond the finite but can never reach the horizon. "Whenever we experience our limits, imagining what lies beyond them, we begin to transcend them."[84] Theologian Karen Kilby uses the analogy of Sir Edmund Hillary's ascent of Mount Everest. The goal is the summit, and the explorer's eyes were set on this goal. It is in the context of the infinite goal that finite acts, the individual steps, can take place.[85] Human beings have a fundamental drive to move forward toward something, to reach for that which lies beyond. Rahner says our experience of the horizon, an analogy for infinite possibility, allows us to experience the idea of "Infinite Being," or God. As humans, limited by our nature, we begin to understand the concept of limitlessness, no limits or boundaries, because we can experience that there is always something beyond us. We may recognize this as God, or we may suppress this idea. However, our experience of the infinite horizon demonstrates that we are grounded in a holy mystery, and because we are filled with desire for something beyond us, we have an openness to truth.

The concept of horizon is also present in Stăniloae's theological framework. He describes the "super-essential attributes of God," the first of which is infinity. As created, a person experiences what he calls "finitude" (what Rahner calls "limitedness") and continuously aspires to transcend this finitude. This longing for infinity sustains our movement toward the horizon, for something greater that is beyond us. As Stăniloae concludes, affirming the teachings of the Early Church Fathers, "Creation has been destined to reach direct participation in God's infinity through grace."[86] This direct participation is another way of describing our destiny: union with God. The reference

83 Fischer, 37.
84 Ibid., 14.
85 See Kilby, 4.
86 Stăniloae, "Revelation and Knowledge of the Triune God," 141–42. Discusses the "divine super-essence of infinity" and "finitude longing for infinity."

"through grace" also reminds us that divine assistance—human-divine collaboration, or *synergeia*—is required for us to achieve our destiny.

Relationship with God (God Communicating Himself to Us)

We have an initial experience of God through our human longing for something greater, something that is beyond us. We push forward but never quite reach it. We look at our finite existence against a horizon of infinite possibility. Thus, by having a concept of infinity, we can begin to understand that an Infinite Being, or God, exists. In other words, if we have a sense of infinity, something beyond our grasp, it is impossible to be an atheist.

Another key aspect of Rahner's theology is that God communicates himself to us. He taught that God's self-communication is not to be understood "in the sense that God would say something *about* himself in some revelation or other."[87] It is not about sending a message, but rather it is about forming a relationship.[88] This self-communication is grounded in holy mystery, deeply rooted within the human who is both a spiritual and personal being by nature.[89] We are spiritual in that we have the divine image within us. It is also important to understand that in God's self-communication to humanity, the Giver is himself the gift.[90] This is a profound concept: the gift is Jesus Christ, and the Giver (God) is himself the gift (Jesus) because both are of

87 Karl Rahner, *Foundations of Christian Faith: An Introduction to the Idea of Christianity*, trans. William V. Dych (New York, NY: Crossroad Publishing Company, 1990) 116.

88 See Fischer, 39. See Rahner, *Foundations of Christian Faith*, 117–118. "God's self-communication means, therefore, that what is communicated is really God in his own being, and in this way, it is a communication for the sake of knowing and possessing God in immediate vision and love."

89 See Rahner. *Foundations of Christian Faith*, 116. "A self-communication of God as personal and absolute mystery to man as a being of transcendence signifies at the outset a communication to man as a spiritual and personal being."

90 Ibid, 120. "It is decisive for an understanding of God's self-communication to man to grasp that the giver in his own being is the gift, that in and through his own being the giver gives himself to creatures as their own fulfillment."

the same essence. God literally gives himself to us in human form. Because of this gift and because we are made in the divine image, the divine presence can dwell within us. As St. Paul writes, "I live, no longer I, but Christ lives in me."[91]

"When God gives himself to us, we are changed. God's gift of self becomes a part of our very being. We become what God gives."[92] In other words, if the end goal for humanity is union with God, through *theosis*, God's gift of self (Jesus Christ) is the agent who creates the transformative change. Thus, we can become more "God-like" in our journey of transformation in preparation for our destiny.

We can become more God-like by practicing the divine attributes such as love, mercy, and compassion, as modeled for us by Jesus. The incremental transformation of *theosis* is about perfecting these attributes—albeit we will never be perfect, but we constantly strive—to be worthy of living in union with God.

Another term for human longing is desire. The natural state of the human person, as created by God, desires God. As stated by Abba Isaiah of Scetis:

> Desire is the natural state of intellect because without desire for God there is no love ... but the enemy twisted this into shameful desire, a desire for every impurity.
>
> Ambition, also, is the natural state of the intellect for without ambition there is no progress toward God, as it is written in the epistle, *be ambitious of the higher gifts* [1 Cor. 12:31]. However, our godly ambition has been turned into an ambition that is contrary to nature, so we are jealous, envious, and deceitful toward each other.[93]

---

91 Gal. 2:20.

92 Fischer, 40–41. See also Stăniloae, "Revelation and Knowledge of the Triune God," 12. "Through all things, God gives himself to man, and man to God."

93 Abba Isaiah of Scetis, *Ascetic Discourses*, trans. John Chryssavgis and Pachomios Penkett (Kalamazoo, MI: Cistercian Publications, 2002), 43-4.

Desire is not the problem. Rather, it is the distortion of this desire because of our fallen human nature that seeks finite things as a substitute for God, who alone can fill infinite longing. Said another way, only God can fill "what is not God."[94] We cannot change human anthropology, that the human person is a being made in the image of God and, through how we were created, can find true fulfillment only in him.

"Our culture often prescribes instant gratification as a cure for our deep desire for happiness."[95] Yet, something finite is only a temporary fix. Consider St. Gregory of Nyssa's "experience of our dissatisfaction." This spiritual hunger, this longing, helps us to begin to understand human purpose, that we were created for an infinite God. One of the deepest desires of the human heart is to be loved. Where does this desire come from? That desire was placed within us by God so that he alone could fill it.

Also supporting Rahner's concept that the "Giver himself is the gift,"[96] Stăniloae wrote, "Human beings are saved…through the free acceptance of communion with Christ, and in Christ with the entire Holy Trinity."[97] In other words, while we grow our relationship with Christ, God is never separable. So, spiritual writers interchangeably use such terms as "indwelling divine presence" and "indwelling Trinity."

By nature, human beings are oriented toward the infinite and desire to reach for something beyond themselves. As spiritual beings (created in the divine image), they have a "longing for truth, for

---

94 See Rahner, *Foundations of Christian Faith*. 226. "God himself has spoken his Word as our flesh (Incarnation) into the emptiness of what is not God." As previously discussed, God himself creates the emptiness so that he himself can fill it.

95 Matthew Kelly, *Perfectly Yourself*, 3rd ed. (North Palm Beach, FL: Beacon Publishing, 2017), 119.

96 See Rahner, *Foundations of Christian Faith*, 120.

97 Dumitru Stăniloae, "The Person of Jesus Christ as God and Savior," in *The Experience of God: Orthodox Dogmatic Theology*, vol. 3, ed./trans. Ioan Ionita (Brookline, MA: Holy Cross Orthodox Press, 2011), 86.

love, for fellowship, for God,"[98] Rahner said. Further, a person faces loneliness, fear, or imminent death—all basic human experiences, reinforcing this desire for a relationship with God. Thus, no complex theories are required. Through our human experiences alone, we begin to have a simple or even primitive awareness of God.[99] In time, we become increasingly aware of the presence of God in our lives through other means. However, by reflecting on this deep-seated longing that is part of our human nature, we begin to learn something about God. Even when we seek to fill this longing by finite means and experience dissatisfaction, we are given a hint that there must be something more.

For both Rahner and Stăniloae, it is not complicated. The human person is created to experience God, for an openness to God, who communicates himself to us, and whom we encounter in our everyday life and through our mundane activities. In turn, through our free will, we can choose to enter a relationship with him. God's gift of self is intended to foster a relationship, which is the cause of our transformation. It divinizes and prepares us for the ultimate fulfillment of our destiny: union with God in the life to come. We can recognize God's presence through our inherent search for truth, to recognize the possibilities for our human existence and satisfaction of our inner longing, or we can suppress this idea. We can seek true meaning in finite or created things or recognize the absurdity of trying to find something other than God that will fulfill infinite longing. To get off the treadmill of constant, fruitless searching, we must make a faith decision: our desire for something more is not grounded in nothingness, but in our ability to enter into a relationship with an Infinite Being, God.

98 Karl Rahner. *The Practice of Faith: A Handbook of Contemporary Spirituality*, ed. Karl Lehmann and Albert Raffelt (New York, NY: Crossroad Publishing, 1986), 63.

99 Ibid. Experiencing God: "Be still for once. Don't try to think of so many complex and varied things. Give these deeper realities of the spirit a chance now to rise to the surface: silence, fear, the ineffable longing for truth, for love, for fellowship, for God. Face loneliness, fear, imminent death! Allow such ultimate, basic human experiences to come first. Don't go talking about them, making up theories about them, but simply endure these basic experiences. Then in fact something like a primitive awareness of God can emerge."

The Link to *Theosis*

Theosis is the slow, incremental transformation we undergo, taking us from where we are today to our divinely prepared destiny. We achieve this by overcoming our passions, our sinful desires, and inclinations, and living lives of virtue, striving to mirror the attributes of God, such as love, mercy, and compassion. We strive in life to be more like God by following the example he gave us, his Son Jesus Christ, and strengthened by the Holy Spirit. To undergo this transformation, "we must desire, struggle, and prepare ourselves so that we are worthy, capable, and receptive enough to accept and guard this great gift from God."[100] St. Gregory Palamas wrote, "We unite ourselves to God, in so far as this is possible, by participating in the godlike virtues and entering into communion with him through prayer and praise."[101] Stăniloae would add that growth in the virtues, our spiritual strength, is based on a person's detachment from material things; a person should not be dominated by things in a selfish way.[102] Again, we see this constant emphasis on moving away from finite things to fill infinity longing.

In considering the horizon analogy in Rahner's theological framework, the self-communicating God fills a person's emptiness through uncreated grace, "the love of God has been poured into our hearts through the Holy Spirit that has been given to us."[103] Each human person has the capacity for God (*capex Dei*) and the choice of being open to the gift given by the God who communicates himself to us. In Rahner's terms, *theosis* is like the forward movement to grasp

---

100 Archimandrite George, *Theosis: The True Purpose of Human Life* (Mount Athos: Holy Monastery of St. Gregorios, 2006), 47.

101 St. Gregory Palamas, "Three Texts on Prayer and Purity of Heart," in *The Philokalia: The Complete Text*, vol. 4, comp. by St. Nikodemos (Nicodemus) of the Holy Mountain and St. Makarios of Corinth, trans. G. E. H. Palmer, Philip Sherrard, and Kallistos Ware (London: Faber and Faber, 1995), 343.

102 See Dumitru Stăniloae, "The World: Creation and Deification," *The Experience of God: Orthodox Dogmatic Theology*, vol. 2, ed./trans. Ioan Ionita and Robert Barringer (Brookline, MA: Holy Cross Orthodox Press, 2000), 39. "The human person grows in various forms of spiritual strength (the virtues) by means of a particular relationship of detached superiority to things and by the fact that he does not let himself be dominated by things in a selfish manner."

103 Rom. 5:5.

that which lies ahead. We do this by striving to follow the example of Jesus. As Stăniloae wrote, "It is toward this horizon that every human being tends and, in a certain way, partakes of through his relationship with the Incarnate *Logos* (Jesus Christ)."[104] Thus, per Stăniloae, we choose freely to enter more deeply into a relationship with God. Rahner would say our free choice is not rejecting God but being open to his self-communication and grace. Both theologians would agree that movement toward God cannot be achieved by human effort alone; divine assistance is required.

First Truth of Faith

Fr. Walter Ciszek, SJ spent 23 years imprisoned within the Soviet Union and wrote an autobiographical spiritual reflection about his experiences. In his epilogue, he states:

> Man was created to praise, reverence, and serve God in this world and to be happy with him forever in the next. That is the fact of the matter; you believe it or you don't—and this is the end of it. Philosophers may argue about it, and they have; some have managed to convince themselves and others of its truth, while others have not. But it is the first truth of the faith, and those who have faith accept it; those who do not, do not.[105]

Some simply reject this truth. However, for those willing to consider the possibility, there are indicators of this truth such as Rahner's infinite horizon or St. Gregory of Nyssa's experience of our dissatisfaction. Human longing causes us to seek something that is beyond what we know.

---

104 Stăniloae, "The Person of Jesus Christ as God and Savior," 36.

105 Fr. Walter J. Ciszek, SJ with Fr. Daniel Flaherty, SJ, *He Leadeth Me* (San Francisco, CA: Ignatius Press, 1995), 200.

Summary

The human person is created in the divine image and, thus, can enter into a relationship with God. And though God in his essence is beyond human comprehension, we can know something about him by understanding our experiences: theology is anthropology, and anthropology is theology. Using the analogy of the horizon, we have a sense of human striving to reach beyond ourselves because human nature contains a deep-seated desire for "something more." This striving allows us to recognize that we are finite yet find ourselves longing and reaching for the infinite (something we can never quite reach). This sense of infinity provides a basic sense of Infinite Being and, as such, our inability to find fulfillment in finite things. From this, we have an initial understanding of God and that only an infinite God can fill our infinite longing.

Because we can have a relationship with God (*capex Dei*), he gives himself to us through his Son, Jesus Christ; the Giver is himself the gift. The acceptance of this gift, the willingness to submit self-will to the divine will, living the life Jesus modeled for us, allows us to begin to live in a right relationship with God.

Through acceptance of the gift, we can begin to be transformed, to move toward the infinite horizon, by becoming more God-like, practicing the virtues or attributes of God such as love, mercy, and compassion. This transformation, *theosis*, is how we prepare ourselves for our true destiny: union with God. We need to be more God-like if we wish to be in union with him. As Fr. Walter Ciszek asks, "Why must we always look for more sophisticated, more meaningful, more relevant answers, when [God] has set the truth before us in so stark and simple a fashion?"[106]

106 Ibid.

Reflection Questions

1. When I think about God, do I think of him in terms of religious doctrines and concepts that I learned over time? Or do I think of him based on my own experiences? Please provide details.

2. What have my experiences with God been like? How do I personally *know* that God exists?

3. When I hear that I am made in the divine image, what does this mean to me?

4. We have said that the human person is "spiritual." What makes a human spiritual?

OUR DESIRE FOR ENCOUNTER

Real Personhood

"The concern of the flesh is death, but the concern of the spirit is life and peace."
(Rom. 8:6)

"Spirituality is the norm of human life." [107]
(St. Theophan the Recluse)

Opening Scripture Reading

Rom. 8:1-13 (The Flesh and the Spirit).

Reset to the Original Settings

On an iPhone, one can "Reset to Original Settings." It is worth considering the original settings of the human person made in the image and likeness of God. If such a spiritual person as originally created stood up, would we even recognize him or her? Or is our perception of a good and God-fearing life distorted, influenced by our secular society?

In our discussion on Anthropology, we stated that humanity was created in the image and likeness of God, the likeness being the image's fulfillment. We lost this likeness because of Adam and Eve's sin, tempted to be like God[108] instead of dependent on him as intended through Creation. Thus, our original settings—communion with God, to praise, revere, and serve him—have been distorted. For example, desire is not bad, as Abba Isaiah of Scetis said, for it is the natural

107 St. Theophan the Recluse, *The Spiritual Life: And How to be Attuned to It*, trans. Alexandra Dockham (Safford, AZ: The Holy Monastery of St. Paisius, 2017), 59.

108 See Gen. 3:5.

state of the intellect, and without a desire for God, there is no love. However, the Devil has distorted this desire causing human beings to seek fulfillment in things other than God.[109] We chase after the world, jumping on a veritable treadmill of dissatisfaction— seeking, finding, casting away, seeking again—always coming up empty. We seek carnal pleasures, intellectual pursuits, fame and recognition, or material things. St. Augustine of Hippo, in his younger days, is a perfect example of giving into passionate desires and the intellectual pursuit of wisdom.[110] In a 5G world, we are always stressed, in a hurry, and seeking immediate results. We are imprisoned by worries and concerns. We get tired and become disillusioned.[111] Our fallen human nature is enslaved, and the Devil is having a field day.[112] Simply put, we fall short of our created purpose.

The human person was created to be spiritual. This is the norm as opposed to what secular society would describe as "normal." St. Theophan the Recluse wrote that the human person has three characteristics—spiritual, intellectual, and carnal—and the spiritual person is the *real* person, or as other spiritual writers would say, the *natural* person—our true nature. As St. Theophan wrote to a young woman under his spiritual guidance:

> When the spiritual reigns supreme in someone, then although this is his exclusive character and attitude, he does not err. This is because, in the first place,

---

109 Recall the C.S. Lewis quote: "All that we call human history…[is] the long, terrible story of man trying to find something other than God which will make him happy."

110 St. Augustine of Hippo, *Confessions*, trans. Henry Chadwick (New York, NY: Oxford University Press, 2008), 201. "Late have I loved you, beauty so old and so new: late have I loved you. And see, you were within and I was in the external world and sought you there, and in my unlovely state I plunged into those lovely, created things which you made. You were with me, and I was not with you. The lovely things kept me far from you …" At the beginning of his *Confessions*, he states, "Our heart is restless until it rests in you." *Confessions*, 3.

111 Cf. Archimandrite Aimilianos of Simonopetra, *The Church at Prayer* (Alhambra, CA: Sebastian Press, 2012), 44.

112 See Bishop Joseph E. Strickland, *Light and Leaven: The Challenge of the Laity in the Twenty-First Century* (El Cajon, CA: Catholic Answers Press, 2020), 149. "Yes, Satan and his angels are real, and they are having a field day with so many things going on today."

> spirituality is the norm of the human life, and so as a result, being spiritual, he is a real person. Secondly, no matter how spiritual someone is, he cannot help but give the intellectual and carnal their rightful place; he maintains just a little of them, in subordination to the spirit. Let intellectuality not be too broad within him (in scientific knowledge, arts, and other subjects), and let carnality be firmly restrained—then he is a real, whole person. But the man of intellect (the expert, the connoisseur, the shrewd man)—and even more so the carnal man—is not a real person, no matter how appealing he seems outwardly. He is foolish. Hence the simple man who fears God is superior to the man who is diverse and elegant, but who does not have among his goals and yearnings the pleasing of God. You may judge in the same way about works of literature and art. Works in which everything is carnal are completely bad; those in which intellectuality is supreme also do not answer their purpose, although they are higher than the carnal. This judgment concerns those works that have no spiritual elements; those that are directly hostile toward all that is spiritual, that is, toward God and all divine things, are direct suggestions of the enemy and should not be tolerated.[113]

Compare St. Theophan's advice to the young woman to what is valued in secular society today: intellectual knowledge, beauty, wealth, comfort and ease, convenience. Due to our fallen human nature, we have distorted desires and often pursue that which leaves us interiorly bankrupt. We have not grown rich in what matters to God.[114] If we truly desire to achieve our divinely created purpose, we must pursue that which will prepare us for this destiny. Through

113 St. Theophan, *The Spiritual Life*, 59-60.
114 Cf. Luke 12:21. Parable of the Rich Fool.

genuine struggle, we must flee temptation, human wretchedness, and self-pity; we must learn self-control and restraint. In short, we prepare ourselves to be a vessel capable of containing the grace of God.[115]

Fully Living

St. Irenaeus of Lyons said, "The glory of God is man fully alive."[116] His statement denotes that God's greatest creation is humanity: made in his image, capable of entering into a relationship with him. Second, "fully alive" references the spiritual or natural man as originally created, in communion with and dependent upon God, not the carnal man that rejected God through the fall of Adam. The person in communion with God is living; the person separated from God is dead—spiritually dead in this life and permanently separated from God in the life to come. Thus, an individual's life as envisaged by the Creator is a manifestation of his goodness. We strive for this goodness, regaining the likeness of God, by living as God intended and as modeled by his Son, Jesus Christ.

In his final instructions to his Apostles, Jesus said: "Peace I leave with you; my peace I give to you. Not as the world gives do I give it to you. Do not let your hearts be troubled or afraid."[117] The peace offered by Jesus is not the absence of war or hostility. Rather, it is interior peace that even when we find ourselves in a whirlpool of turbulent thoughts, desires, or emotions. It is the peace we can experience even in the midst of temptations or persecution, illness, suffering, or the loss of a loved one, or when confronted with difficulties and seemingly impossible situations. When our crosses seem overwhelming, when we feel ready to collapse under the load we bear, we are offered an interior peace through complete dependence on God. Surrendering our stubbornness of heart and self-will to the divine will, we will survive the storm, which prepares us to live in communion with God for eternity. We seek first

115 Cf. Archimandrite Aimilianos of Simonopetra, 44.

116 St. Irenaeus of Lyons, *Against Heresies*, Book 4, Chapter 34, Section 7.

117 John 14:27.

the kingdom of God[118] and allow the peace of Christ to dwell in our hearts,[119] replacing doubts and fear. No sensual pleasure, recognition, or material wealth could ever compare to this.

Secular society seems to be moving in the opposite direction, the modern man becoming too progressive to need God, and the focus is toward self-love. St. Theodoros the Great Ascetic wrote, "For this terrible enemy, self-love, is the foremost of evil dispositions, and is like some tyrant with the help of which the three principal passions … overwhelm the intellect."[120] He, similar to many Holy Fathers, defined these principal passions as love of sensual pleasure, love of riches, and love of praise.[121] These passions manifest themselves in behaviors and even meet with a certain level of societal approval ("Looking out for number one;" "Just do it!"). Yet, are people today happier as a progressive society detached from God? On the contrary, we observe listlessness, emptiness, despair, disillusionment, pessimism, and a constant fruitless search for that which will satisfy.

In the desert, Jesus endured three temptations, each relating to one of the principal passions. The entire purpose of the Incarnation was to replace fallen human nature with a renewed human nature, a reset of sorts to the original settings, the spiritual or natural person undistorted by the influences of the secular world. St. Theophan wrote, "The passions are not natural to us, but alien, and the emotions of the heart are agitated and disturbed by these very passions."[122] Our objective in the spiritual life is to overcome the passions and grow in a relationship with God. He further wrote:

> From this you see that according to the natural purpose, man must live in the spirit, subordinate everything to

118 Cf. Matt. 6:33.

119 See. Col. 3:15. "And let the peace of Christ control your hearts …"

120 St. Theodoros the Great Ascetic, "A Century of Spiritual Texts," in *The Philokalia: The Complete Text*, vol. 2, trans. G.E.H. Palmer, P. Sherrard, and K. Ware (London: Faber & Faber, 1981), 27.

121 Ibid., 16.

122 St. Theophan, *The Spiritual Life*, 58.

> the spirit, be penetrated by the spirit in all that is of the soul, and even more so in all that is physical—and beyond these, in the outward things, too, that is, family and social life. This is the norm![123]

We are challenged to regain the norm of humanity, the spiritual state, to become, as St. Theophan described it, a "real person," to become as God intended us to be. We strive to overcome carnal desires and attempts to intellectualize faith as if it were an academic science. Rather, we want to regain our reverential awe of God, returning to a right-ordered relationship with our Creator, lest we lose the destiny intended for humanity.

Concluding Thoughts

Let us consider a reflection of St. Elizabeth of the Trinity, OCD, who wrote:

> To attain the ideal life of the soul, I believe we must live on the supernatural (spiritual) level. We must become aware that God dwells within us and do everything with him. Then we are never commonplace, even when performing ordinary tasks, for we do not live in these things, we go beyond them! A supernatural soul never deals with secondary causes but with God alone. Oh, how its life is simplified, how it resembles the life of the blessed, how it is freed from self and from all things! Everything for it is reduced to unity, to that *one thing necessary*, of which the Master spoke to Mary Magdalene. Then the soul is truly great, truly free, for it has enclosed its will in God's.[124]

---

123 Ibid., 59-60.

124 St. Elizabeth of the Trinity, *I Have Found God: Complete Works*, vol. 1, trans. Sr. Aletheia Kane, OCD (Washington, DC: ICS Publications, 1984), 127.

Factoring in the innate human desire for transcendency, the constant seeking for something more, St. Elizabeth tells us that the soul dwelling on the spiritual level rises above commonplace, even in ordinary tasks. In other words, mundane activities in life can bring us the fulfillment we desire—if our soul dwells in God and God in our soul. There is no reason to seek the extraordinary or the undiscovered continent. As Jesus told us, "The kingdom of God is within you."[125] We can get off the veritable treadmill of dissatisfaction, stop exhausting ourselves, and look inward. To become our truest form of self, this is the realization we must come to.

Let us consider one takeaway thought from the Prophet Isaiah: "Why spend your wages for what does not satisfy?"[126] Or, restated, why spend one's time, effort, and money on that which will only leave one empty? Internally bankrupt? Or, as C.S. Lewis stated, why pursue "something other than God" when history has shown us what that outcome will be?

Reflection Questions

1. St. Theophan the Recluse states that the "real person" is spiritual, with carnal and intellectual characteristics subordinate to this. Do I agree with this?

2. Are my priorities in life aligned with what the secular world values, or am I striving to be rich in what matters to God? Explain.

125 Luke 17:21.
126 Isa. 55:2.

Part 2

The Divine Presence We Encounter

Introduction

In Part 1, we considered a person's desire for encounter and capacity for a relationship with the Divine based on how human beings were created. In this section, we will consider the Divine. From a theological standpoint, God is a Trinity: a communion of three distinct persons (*hypostases*) who share one essence (*ousia*). We will use the term *nature* interchangeably with *essence*. To put these three divine persons into perspective, let us leverage an analogy from Catholic Theologian Elizabeth A. Johnson:[127]

> **Father:** "God beyond us." A mystery beyond all telling.[128] "Ineffable, inconceivable, invisible, incomprehensible, ever-existing, yet ever the same."[129]
>
> **Son:** "God with us (Emmanuel)." The promised Messiah and Word of God (*Logos*).
>
> **Holy Spirit:** "God within us." The outpouring of God's love, a God of absolute love.

While we will discuss the Mystery of the Trinity specifically in a separate topic, we wanted to provide the above as an introduction to each of the divine Persons.

---

127 From Elizabeth A. Johnson, *Quest for the Living God*. Cited by Heidi Russell, "Karl Rahner: Christology and Trinity," lecture notes, Christian Doctrine and its History, Loyola University Chicago (Spring 2016), 18.

128 Ibid., 17.

129 From the anaphora (consecration prayer) of the Divine Liturgy of St, John Chrysostom.

God: Creator and Father

"God replied to Moses: I am who I am."
(Exod. 3:14)

"Creation without the Creator fades into nothingness."[130]
(Gaudium et Spes)

Opening Scripture Reading

Exod. 3:1-15 (God reveals himself to Moses in the burning bush).

While Unknowable, God Can Be Experienced

God is "ineffable, inconceivable, invisible, incomprehensible, ever-existing, yet ever the same."[131] He is the Creator who holds the universe in balance; he is the ground for all beings. God is infinite, he is mystery, and beyond any human comprehension. We cannot know God; we only can know something about God.[132] Yet despite his awesomeness, God desires a personal, intimate relationship with each of us.

God is also a loving Father who created humanity, his most prized creation and infused with his own image, unlike any other part of creation. We are patterned after the Image Absolute, which is Jesus Christ. God created humanity to share his overflowing love. As St. Irenaeus of Lyons wrote, "God is man's glory. Man is the vessel which

130 Second Vatican Council, *Gaudium et Spes* (Pastoral Constitution on the Church in the Modern World), December 7, 1965, no. 36.

131 From the Anaphora (consecration prayer) of the Divine of Liturgy of St. John Chrysostom.

132 St. Gregory of Nyssa says, "the highest degree of knowledge of God is to understand that one cannot understand him." Any philosophy that attempts to explain God or assumes that God can be understood or examined loses its validity. To define God would be constrain him within limits, whereas God is limitless.

receives God's action of his wisdom and power."[133] Throughout the Old Testament, we read how God has watched over and cared for his prized creation and especially for his chosen people, Israel, despite their weaknesses and failings. The life he wants for each of us is to live in union with him and he invites us to this life through his incarnate Son.

Despite humanity's limitations, God cares for us and desires that we share in his divine nature.[134] The offer of salvation is always there. While God is the horizon for which we strive yet always remains beyond us, he is not distant. Rather, he is ever-present, revealing himself to us, desiring to be in a relationship with each of us. Each human person is created with the capacity to experience God (*capex Dei*), to enter into a relationship with him, collaborate with him (*synergeia*), and be transformed (*theosis*). Every person has the same potential to be like Mother Teresa of Calcutta because we all have the same divine image infused within us. The difference becomes the degree to which one responds to God's communication and collaborates with his divine presence.

Rahner said, "God's self-communication is a further miracle of his free love which is the most self-evident thing of all."[135] His offer of salvation is gratuitous, reflective of God's overflowing love for us, even before any rejection on our part.[136] He knocks at the door of our hearts,[137] and he "will not rest until he has moved us from the gutter to the Palace."[138] Jesus's mission through the Incarnation was the restoration of the image of God, tainted by sin, and the divinization of humanity—allowing us to realize the possibilities of a divinely created purpose.[139]

133 St. Irenaeus of Lyons, *Against Heresies*, in *The Liturgy of the Hours*, vol. 1 (New York, NY: Catholic Book Publishing Co., 1975), 337.

134 See 2 Pet. 1:3–4.

135 Rahner, *Foundations of Christian Faith*, 123.

136 Heidi Russell. "Karl Rahner: Sin, Grace, Salvation, and Revelation," lecture notes, Christian Doctrine and Its History, Loyola University Chicago (Spring 2016), 9.

137 See Rev. 3:20. See also John 15:23.

138 Coniaris, *Tools for Theosis*, 80.

139 See Archbishop Joseph M. Raya, *The Face of God: Essays on Byzantine Spirituality* (Woodland Park, NJ: God With Us Publications, 2012), 179.

Stăniloae picks up on Rahner's theme that God provides humanity with a future full of hope, even though humanity is exposed to an unforeseeable future. Referencing Rahner, he includes the following in his theological framework:

> The human being's advance into the future is a constant struggle to diminish his inner alienations as well as the distance between what he is and what he really wants to be and should be. We have to be content, therefore, with the satisfaction (individually or collectively) of an eternally distant goal, always unevenly followed and which keeps moving further, or this absolute goal is an unattainable one which, once attained, does not suppress the finite by making it disappear in the absoluteness of God.[140]

This passage contains a critical point captured by Rahner and Eastern Christian theologians. Despite our destiny to live in union with God, our human nature does not "disappear in the absoluteness of God." In other words, a person, who has been transformed or divinized, remains human by nature and does not take on the divine nature of God. Early Church Fathers St. Irenaeus of Lyons and St. Athanasius of Alexandria are both paraphrased as describing the purpose of the Incarnation as follows: "The Son of God became man, so that man might become God." A better way to describe the goal of *theosis* would be to say the person comes God-like, preparing one for union with God. However, union with God is a "union of

140 Karl Rahner, "Grundlinien einer systematischen Christologie," in *Christologie systematisch und exegetisch* (Freiburg, Germany: Herder, 1972), 62–3. Cited in Stăniloae, "The Person of Jesus Christ as God and Savior," 8.

distinct natures."[141] In other words, when in union with God, people do not become God; they remain human beings. However, they are divinized in preparation to live in this eternal relationship.

The model for a union of two distinct natures is Jesus Christ, who is both fully human and fully divine, without mixture or confusion of the two natures. Accordingly, the example of the human person living in union with God as a "union of two distinct natures" is the incarnate Jesus.

As for the offer of salvation, we can be open to it or not. Rahner would argue that our ability to accept is "enabled by God's love, by God's gift of self which grounds our freedom"[142] to make the choice. This self-communicating God is meant to be experienced,[143] and Rahner taught that our experience of God happens in this world, in time and space, in the banality of life.[144] "Every man! He has to...dig it out from under the rubbish of everyday experience."[145]

Knowledge about God, per Rahner, can be gained by understanding our human experience. For example, we understand an Infinite Being by experiencing our own limitations and striving to move beyond ourselves (transcendence). We understand what God is like, for example, when we experience an act of love from our neighbor. St. Gregory of Nyssa, who developed significant groundwork for the doctrine of *theosis*, provided a similar perspective when he wrote:

> When you hear that the Divine Majesty is exalted

141 Stăniloae, "The Person of Jesus Christ as God and Savior," 72. Union does not mean a mixing of the human and divine nature where one loses its distinct identity. The same is true in the Incarnation of Christ, where Christ has two distinct natures without mixture or confusion. See also Stăniloae, "The World: Creation and Deification," 92–3. "We have observed already that the greatest possible union with God, toward whom we ascend through virtue, cannot mean submersion within the ocean of an impersonal infinity. That would no longer signify a human being deified through grace while distinct from God by nature, but rather a single and undifferentiated divinity."

142 Heidi Russell, "Karl Rahner: Sin, Grace, Salvation, Revelation," 16.

143 See Elizabeth A. Johnson, 44.

144 See Karl Rahner, *The Practice of Faith*, 83.

145 Ibid.

> about the heavens, that its glory is inexpressible, its beauty ineffable, and its Nature inaccessible, do not despair of ever beholding what you desire. It is indeed within your reach; you have within yourselves the standard by which to apprehend the Divine.[146]

St. Gregory is saying that we cannot comprehend the Divine Majesty of God (we cannot know God), but we have the standard within ourselves to know something about God. This standard is the divine image.[147] St. Gregory adds that a purified soul, one that has been transformed through *theosis*, exhibits attributes of the Divine (love, mercy, and compassion). Thus, because we possess this divine image patterned after Jesus and because we have the example of Jesus's earthly life, we can have some understanding about God and divine perfection. St. Gregory uses the analogy of looking at the sun through a mirror, in this case, the mirror is the purified soul.[148] Like Rahner, St. Gregory implies our experiences result in our knowledge of God. Further, purification of the soul (divinization) implies accepting God's offer of salvation. This sets the foundation for the journey of *theosis*. Our spiritual transformation is cultivated by our relationship with God, surrendering ourselves to him, and allowing him to take possession of us. This prepares us for union with God. However, it should be emphasized again that this transformation is an incremental process that requires persistence, patience, effort, and assistance from the Divine (*synergeia*).

---

146 St. Gregory of Nyssa, "On the Beatitudes," in *Ancient Christian Writers: The Works of the Fathers in Translation*, vol. 18, ed. Johannes Quasten and Joseph C. Plumpe, trans. Hilda C. Graef (New York, NY: Paulist Press, 1954), 148.

147 Ibid., 85. "Beatitude, in my opinion, is a possession of all things held to be good, from which nothing is absent that a good desire may want." Goodness is one of the essential perfections of God; God lacks for nothing. Since the soul is created in the image of God, the attributes of God are present within each human person—copies of the Original Divine Pattern, or in Nyssa's terms, the Divine archetype). This sets the stage for humanity's possible future destiny through divinization.

148 See Norman Russell, *Fellow Workers with God: Orthodox Thinking on Theosis* (Crestwood, NY: St. Vladimir's Seminary Press, 2009), 117. See also Vladimir Lossky, *In the Image and Likeness of God*, ed. John H. Erickson and Thomas E. Bird (Crestwood, NY: St. Vladimir's Seminary Press, 1974), 36.

Stăniloae, like most Orthodox theologians, would take this a step further: we directly experience the mystical presence of God (apophatic or ineffable knowledge), an experience of God that is beyond our ability to define in words.[149] This direct experience is through contemplative prayer that is reflective of the Eastern Christian mystical tradition, and since Patristic times, there has been an emphasis on prayer as a direct experience of God. Stăniloae quotes the axiom, "If you are a theologian, you will pray truly. And if you pray truly, you are a theologian."[150] He explains, "Through apophatic knowledge the human subject not only knows that God is infinite, omnipotent, or loving, but also experiences this."[151]

God is Personal and Relational

First and above all, God is personal. He is a communion of three loving persons: the Most Holy Trinity. Second, because God wants a personal, intimate relationship with us, and we can enter a relationship with him, this negates some of the ideas secular society has proposed about God. Archbishop Charles J. Chaput, OFM Cap., addresses this succinctly:

> God is not an idea, or an ideology, or an equation, or magic, or a force, or an intelligent gas cloud, or a hypothesis. God is as real and as personal as you and me—only much more so, because God is the source of personhood and author of reality. We can love a person and, being personal, God can love us back. We can't love a gas cloud, and ideas don't have relationships.[152]

149 See Stăniloae, "Revelation and Knowledge of the Triune God," 95.

150 Ibid., 86.

151 Ibid., 95.

152 Archbishop Charles J. Chaput, OFM Cap., *Living the Catholic Faith: Rediscovering the Basics* (Cincinnati, OH: St. Anthony Messenger Press, 2001), 17.

Cardinal Sarah wrote, "We encounter God only in the eternal silence in which he abides."[153] Mystics can be in union with God through intense contemplative prayer. Mother Teresa is an example of this gift granted by God based on an individual's efforts.

Openness to God

The capacity for our relationship with God is a given, based on how humanity was created. Openness to God, who communicates himself to us, is a matter of free choice. Increasingly, we observe secular society trying to distance itself from God. "Today the West lives as if God did not exist,"[154] Cardinal Sarah wrote, adding:

> This estrangement from God is not caused by reasoning but by a wish to be detached from him. The atheistic orientation of life is almost always a decision by the will. Man no longer wishes to reflect on his relationship with God because he himself intends to become God.[155]

On the surface, this statement may seem extreme. However, we continuously see attempts to replace God through human initiative, a desire to be self-reliant, and build a paradise on earth without God.[156] However, this is a delusion since this life is preparation for true Paradise in the world to come. Archimandrite Sophrony of Essex wrote: "When we turn away from the path indicated by Christ—that is, from the deification of man by the power of the Holy Spirit—the whole point

153 Robert Cardinal Sarah, in conversation with Nicolas Diat, *The Power of Silence: Against the Dictatorship of Noise*, trans. Michael J. Miller (San Francisco, CA: Ignatius Press, 2017), 21.

154 Sarah, *God or Nothing*, 167.

155 Ibid., 168.

156 As an example, the World Economic Forum has discussed "The Great Reset" initiative, which includes a desire to create a new world order. At its core, this is another attempt for humanity to build a paradise on earth, excluding God and ignoring his plan for his creation. This is not unlike the European Enlightenment that emphasized reason over faith.

of man's coming into the world disappears."[157] In other words, without God, our purpose in life no longer exists—because we were created to live in union with him. Those without God often feel deep inner emptiness and frustration; they cannot find peace in this world. When we consider how we were created, why would this surprise us? Life without God is like expecting a fish to live outside of water. Our Savior made clear the path to eternal life and the immortality of the Gospel.

How do we cultivate openness to God? We begin with reverential awe, also called Fear of God, which is critical to a right-ordered relationship with our Creator. St. Theodoros the Great Ascetic makes it clear that it is not based on fear of punishment;[158] it is our fear of being separated from God for eternity. Jesus assured his disciples, "I will not leave you orphans."[159] Therefore, Fear of God means we do not fear punishment but flee the sinfulness that prevents us from being in a relationship with God and accepting his plan for our salvation. This is foundational. As St. Isaac the Syrian wrote, "The Fear of God is the beginning of virtue, and it is said to be the offspring of faith."[160]

The difference between fear of punishment and fear of separation is explained by St. Peter of Damaskos: "He who is afraid of God's punishment has a slave-like fear of God ..."[161] He describes such fear as impure because it comes from our sinfulness,[162] whereas pure

157 Archimandrite Sophrony Sakharov, *His Life is Mine*, trans. Rosemary Edmonds (Crestwood, NY: St. Vladimir's Seminary Press, 1977), 70.

158 See St. Theodoros the Great Ascetic, "A Century of Spiritual Texts," 36. "By fear he means not the initial fear of punishment, but the perfect and perfecting fear, which we ought to have out of love for him who has given the commandments. For if we refrain from sin merely out of fear of punishment, it is quite clear that, unless punishment had awaited us, we should have done things deserving punishment. But if we abstain from evil actions not through threat of punishment, but because we hate such actions, then it is from love of the Master that we practice the virtues, fearful lest we should fall away from him."

159 John 14:18.

160 *The Ascetical Homilies of Saint Isaac the Syrian*, rev. 2nd ed. (Brookline, MA: Holy Transfiguration Monastery, 2011), 113. Homily One.

161 St. Peter of Damaskos, "Twenty-Fours Discourses," *The Philokalia: The Complete Text*, vol. 3, comp. St. Nikodimos of the Holy Mountain and St. Makarios of Corinth, trans. G.E.H. Palmer, P. Sherrard, and K. Ware (London: Faber & Faber, 1984), 217.

162 Ibid.

fear arises from an awareness of God's love for us and our increasing love for him, desiring not to lose the grace he has bestowed on us.[163] Thus, a fear of punishment effectively impairs our free will, inhibiting our ability to choose God over everything else. Sin is enslavement, and Jesus reminds us that we are not slaves.[164] Quite the contrary, if we are led by the Spirit of God, we are children of God.[165] St. John the Evangelist validates this at the beginning of his gospel, telling us that by accepting Jesus, we have been given the power to become children of God.[166]

We return to a right-ordered relationship with the Divine through our openness to God. St. Paul of the Cross described it as our nothingness and the "All" of God (*Niente – Tutto*). He tells us:

> It is necessary to make the will of God the ruling principle of life, to place hope and trust solely in God, who is the highest Good, who is 'All.' Furthermore, it is necessary to admit and to recognize the human person's own creatureliness because his littleness and nothingness are manifest 'before God.' Finally, it is necessary to let this 'nothing' be filled by God's 'All.'[167]

---

163 Ibid., 272-3. "Through the power of God and through the wisdom granted him, [a person] becomes aware of his own weakness and ignorance. As a result of this he begins to give thanks with a humble soul and he trembles with fear lest he should relapse into disobedience. Because of this pure fear—fear which is not due to the fact that he has sinned—and because of the thankfulness, patient endurance, and humility which have been bestowed on him as a result of his knowledge (granted by God), he begins to have hope that by God's grace he will obtain mercy. In the light of his experience of the blessings he has received, he watches and fears lest he should be found unworthy of such gifts from God. Hence, he receives greater humility and more intense prayer from the heart; and the more these increase, together with thankfulness, the greater the knowledge he receives. Thus, he advances from knowledge to fear, and fear to thankfulness, and so he attains the knowledge that transcends all these. As a consequence, he comes truly to love his Benefactor and longs to serve him with joy, indebted as he is to God for the knowledge bestowed on him."

164 Cf. John 15:15.

165 Cf. Rom. 8:17.

166 John 1:12.

167 Martin Bialas, *The Mysticism of the Passion in St. Paul of the Cross* (San Francisco, CA: Ignatius Press, 1990), 203-4.

St. Paul of the Cross also describes separation from God, saying, "Whoever has sinned is worse than nothingness, because sin is a horrible nothing, worse than nothing."[168] Through his great love for his creation, God draws the sinner out of an abyss more dismal and deep than his nothingness, that is, out of the abyss of sin.[169] And we are drawn by our participation in the suffering of Jesus Christ, dying to self—submission to the divine will.

Summary

God is the Creator of all. Humanity is his most prized creation, which he created to share his abundant love. Because of this, he invites us to live in a relationship with him. It is beyond human capabilities to know God, but we can know something about God and enter into a relationship with him. Because of this invitation and the offer of salvation, our ultimate destiny is to live in union with God. We prepare for our destiny through *theosis*, the process of transformation, whereby we strive to become more God-like. This means being open to the offer of salvation through a right-ordered relationship with our Creator.

Mystics who are active in contemplative prayer can have some experiences of God, a sense of union of with him in this life. We call this apophatic knowledge of God, an experience beyond our ability to define it in words. Some mystics have used the analogy of a mountaintop shrouded in clouds. Occasionally, one acquires brief glimpses of the summit. However, it is beyond our abilities to comprehend it fully.

168 Ibid., 166.
169 Ibid., 167.

Reflection Questions

1. Who is God to me?
2. What do I know about God? What are my observations? How have I come to this understanding of him?
3. In the Beatitudes, there is this statement: "Blessed are the clean of heart, for they shall see God."[170] Based on our discussion that God is beyond human comprehension, what do you believe this means? How is "seeing God" possible?

170 Matt. 5:8.

THE DIVINE PRESENCE WE ENCOUNTER

Jesus: Image of the Invisible God
A: The Incarnation

"In the beginning was the Word, and the Word was with God, and the Word was God."
(John 1:1)

"For the Son of God became man so that we might become God." [171]
(St. Athanasius of Alexandria)

Opening Gospel Reading

John 1:1-18 (Prologue: Description of the Word of God).

Encountering Jesus: An Introduction

Pope Francis wrote, "The Joy of the Gospel fills the hearts and lives of all who encounter Jesus." It is all about this authentic experience. The next sentence in *Evangelii Gaudium* states, "Those who accept his offer of salvation are set free from sin, sorrow, inner emptiness and loneliness."[172] Accordingly, if we encounter Jesus by accepting this offer, it is important to understand who Jesus is and how he fits into our created purpose of living in union with God.

---

171 Cf. St. Athanasius of Alexandra, *On the Incarnation*, no. 54. Public domain text from CCEL.org, printed by Cliff Lee (2017), 93. "[T]he Word of God himself ..., indeed, assumed humanity that we might become God." The underlying Greek word used in this statement, *theopoie*, literally means "to make divine," comparable to 2 Pet. 1:4: "sharers in the divine nature."

172 Pope Francis, *Evangelii Gaudium*, no. 1.

The Image of the Invisible God

In our opening Gospel passage, we read, "No one has ever seen God. The only Son, God, who is at the Father's side, has revealed him."[173] This statement is important to our understanding of the Divine whom we encounter. "Apart from Jesus, we know nothing of God."[174] In the Letter to the Colossians, Jesus is described as "the image of the invisible God, the first born of creation."[175] Jesus is the Image Absolute in whose image humanity was created. A significant cornerstone of Rahner's theological framework is that humanity is *related* to God because each person is infused with the divine image, and the purpose for which we are created is to live in union with him. God reveals himself to us, and the ultimate revelation is manifested in the incarnate Son of God.

Further to Rahner's thinking, we can learn more about God through human experiences than we can from divinely revealed truths or philosophical proofs.[176] When we view our experiences, we begin to understand something about God. Thus, Rahner examines the "conditions of possibility."[177] What are we as humans capable of doing or experiencing? We are infused with the divine image, so we can aspire to live a noble life and imitate the divine attributes. Through many saints—modern examples such as Mother Teresa of Calcutta, Dorothy Day, Maximilian Kolbe, Pier Giorgio Frassati—we can observe that our human nature has tremendous capacity for good inspired by a great love for God.

Based on this, we can learn much about what it means to be a real person from the Incarnate Jesus, "the image of the invisible God," who was both human and divine. For example, what is God like? We can look to Jesus and his teachings to determine some of

173 John 1:18.

174 Sr. Ruth Burrows, OCD, *To Believe in Jesus* (Mahwah, NJ: Paulist Press, 2010), 15.

175 Col. 1:15.

176 See Heidi Russell, "Karl Rahner: Philosophical Foundations," lecture notes, Christian Doctrine and Its History (Loyola University Chicago, Spring 2016). See also Kilby, 56.

177 Ibid.

God's attributes: goodness, love, mercy, compassion, longsuffering, patience, purity, and having pure love for neighbor.[178] Thus, to become who God wants us to be and to fulfill our destiny, we too must follow the example of Jesus and observe his commandments, further cultivating these divine attributes.

So, let us delve further into the God-Man, Jesus Christ.

Incarnation: God's Plan for Union

The Incarnation is part of God's plan for the union between God and humanity. We have discussed humanity's capacity for God (*capex Dei*), how God gives himself to us as gift ("Giver as gift"), and how this will lead us to our ultimate destiny. Based on this perspective, we will consider the Incarnation.

At the Council of Chalcedon in 451, the Fourth Ecumenical Council, Jesus Christ was declared both fully human and fully divine: "Truly God and truly man...two natures without confusion, without change, without division, without separation."[179] What does this mean for us?

For Rahner, "Christ is integrated into a broader vision of God's single, overarching movement toward the world in grace."[180] Jesus is not God and human, but rather God *as* human, the fulfillment of the human person. Jesus is not human plus divine; rather, he is "divinized humanity." Rahner also wrote:

> We see that Christology is at once the beginning and end of anthropology, and that for all eternity such an anthropology is really theology. For God 'himself'

178 Cf. A Monk of Mount Athos, *The Watchful Mind: Teachings on the Prayer of the Heart*, trans. George Dokos (Yonkers, NY: St. Vladimir's Seminary Press, 2014), 160. The divine attributes or what God wants us to become can be seen through Jesus's life in the Gospels.

179 Cited in Kilby, 17.

180 Ibid., 16.

> has become 'man.' The less we merely think of this humanity as something added on to God, and the more we understand it as God's presence in the world ... the more intelligible does the abiding mystery of our faith become.[181]

Consider carefully what Rahner is saying. Christology is at once the beginning of anthropology, which references how humanity is made in the divine image, the Image Absolute being Christ. Christology as the end of anthropology is Christ as "divinized humanity," which is the fulfillment of creation and the purpose for which humanity was created. Said another way, Jesus, in whose image we were created, is our model for what we are to become. From the time the Holy Spirit descended on the Apostles at Pentecost, consider how the Holy Fathers and Mothers have subsequently strived to follow their teaching and live the commandments of Jesus. They struggled with overcoming passions and temptations, cultivating virtue, and preparing themselves for the life to come. These struggles, these incremental efforts, are how we become divinized, conversion and incremental transformation by practicing the God-like virtues.

Stăniloae agrees. "The humanity of human beings was not yet completed before the Incarnation of the Son of God."[182] This theological position is supported by St. Paul, who wrote, "When everything is subjected to him, the Son will also be subjected to the one who subjected everything to him (God the Father), so that God may be all in all."[183] In other words, God has filled the emptiness of all that is not God. Remember the concept of two distinct natures; humanity is not God. However, God fills and completes us by allowing us to become sharers in his divine nature.[184] He fills us with himself, provided we freely submit our will to his.

---

181 Karl Rahner, *Theological Investigations*, vol. 1 (Baltimore, MD: Helicon Press, 1963), 185.

182 Stăniloae, "The Person of Jesus Christ as God and Savior," 36.

183 1 Cor. 15:28.

184 See 2 Pet. 1:4.

The Eastern Christian perspective is similar, "Only through God incarnate can man become fully human;"[185] in other words, become what they were created to be: divinized humanity. St. Irenaeus of Lyons stated, "the glory of God is the human person fully alive"—fully alive being the divinized person.

The Incarnation is the fulfillment of creation. Rahner wrote:

> We are entirely justified in understanding Creation and Incarnation not as two separate and juxtaposed acts by God 'outwards' which have their origins in two separate initiatives of God. Rather in the world as it actually is, we can understand Creation and Incarnation as two moments and two phases of the one process of God's self-giving and self-expression.[186]

The Incarnation[187] is the fulfillment of what the human person is to become, the climax of history in God's plan of salvation. Jesus as Savior is at once both the offer of salvation by the God, who give himself to his creation (the gift), and the perfect acceptance of that gift.[188] Not only is the Incarnation a historical event, but it is also both irrevocable and irreversible because God himself has acted in the world.[189] Christ accomplished his redeeming work during his time on earth, yet it still plays out in history. As Stăniloae wrote, "God undertakes an action whereby he lays an immovable foundation for the communion between himself and us, uniting our nature with his nature within one of the divine persons."[190] Archbishop Joseph Raya wrote:

---

185 Ware, Foreword to "Revelation and Knowledge of the Triune God," xii.

186 Rahner. *Foundations of Christian Faith*, 197.

187 For Rahner, the Incarnation is not just the moment of conception, but the entire life, ministry, words, and deeds of Jesus, culminating in his death.

188 Rahner, *Foundations of Christian Faith*, 195.

189 Ibid. "The absolute savior, that is, the irreversibility of the history of freedom as the self-communication of God which succeeds, is, first of all, a historical moment in God's salvific activity in the world, and indeed in such a way that he is part of the history of the cosmos itself. He cannot simply be God himself as acting in the world, but must be part of the cosmos, a moment within its history, and indeed at its climax."

190 Stăniloae, "Revelation and Knowledge of the Triune God," 69. Note continued emphasis on the Trinity.

> Without this Incarnation, in which the Son of God, God himself, became the Son of man and specifically Son of a human mother, Mary, Christianity has neither meaning nor relevance.[191]

What are the implications for us in terms of the Incarnation? "The Incarnation of God is...the unique, *supreme,* case of the total actualization of human reality."[192] In a particular human being, "God and the world become one, without ceasing to be that what each are."[193] In Rahner's view, from the beginning God created "what is other than himself in order to give himself to it."[194] St. Paul similarly described this when he wrote, "the love of God has been poured out into our hearts through the Holy Spirit that has been given to us."[195] In the case of humanity, the perfect example of accepting this gift is through the Incarnation of Jesus, who lived in absolute obedience to God by surrendering his self-will to the divine will. "The Incarnation makes accessible the Trinity and our participation in the divine nature, which is our end objective in *theosis*. Because God became a human being, the gulf between divinity and humanity collapsed."[196] Stăniloae would add:

> To reach this goal [of union] or to fulfill this meaning toward which our being tends, we not only ascend

191 Raya, *The Face of God*, 23.

192 Rahner, *Theological Investigations*, vol. 4, 110. Cited in Kilby, 20. Human striving for self-actualization is also part of Maslow's Hierarchy of Needs.

193 Kilby, 28. See also Stăniloae, "Revelation and Knowledge of the Triune God," 80–1. "According to Christian faith man remains defined as man even within the highest degree of union with God and even as he participates in God's infinity. To express the matter more exactly, in union with God the believer is strengthened to the greatest possible extent precisely in our own character (nature) as creature distinct from God." Thus, even in union with God, a human person is not given the essence of God.

194 Ibid.

195 Rom. 5:5.

196 Fischer, 72. See also Rahner, *Foundations of Christian Faith*, 213. "We are trying to reflect upon the mystery which is called in theological language the mystery of 'God becoming man.' Here lies the center of the reality from out of which we Christians live, and which we believe. It is only here that the mystery of the divine Trinity is accessible to us, and only here the mystery of our participation in the divine nature is promised to us in a definitive and historically tangible way."

> to communion with [the] supreme Person, but that Personal reality also descends to be with us. For love demands that each of those who love one another moves toward the other. Through all things, God gives himself to man, and man to God.[197]

Stăniloae sees the Incarnate Christ as the bridge[198] between God and humanity:

> As God, [Jesus] becomes transparent and visible in his humanity; as man he punctuates the maximum approach in his position as God in relation to us and as obedient Son in relation to the Father. One and same Person is asking of us a maximum responsibility as God and is manifesting a maximum responsibility toward the Father for our sake. He gives us commandments while he prays together with us. He demands obedience from us while he asks us to receive his love and to follow his example of humility, meekness, and service. In both cases he is the perfect man because at the same time he is also God.[199]

In summation, the Incarnation is the ultimate act of God's solidarity with humanity, and specifically the poor and those on the margins. Reflecting back to the concept of the Giver as gift, Pope St. Leo the Great writes, "the divine nature and the nature of a servant were to be united in one person so that that Creator of time might be born in time, and he through whom all things were made be brought forth in their midst."[200] He also describes the incarnate Christ as "true

197 Stăniloae, "Revelation and Knowledge of the Triune God," 12.

198 Stăniloae, "The Person of Jesus Christ as God and Savior," 83. "He is the bridge between the Father, with whom he is of one essence according to divinity, and us, with whom he is of one essence according to humanity."

199 Ibid., 24.

200 St. Leo the Great, Letter 31, in *The Liturgy of the Hours*, vol. 1 (New York, NY: Catholic Book Publishing Co., 1975), 321.

and perfect man,"[201] aligned with Rahner's description of "divinized humanity" and our previous description of real personhood.

The divinization of the human person to live in union with God was made possible through the Incarnation, Christ being divinized humanity. Jesus is the perfect example of accepting God's gift of God, modeling the right-ordered relationship of surrender of self-will to the divine will. Thus, if we, who have been made in the image of God with a capacity for God, follow the example of the one who perfectly accepted the gift of the self-communication of God, we too can fulfill the purpose for which we were created. Jesus is our way[202] because he is also our goal.[203]

We also want to consider the perfect acceptance of the gift. As St. Paul writes, "He emptied himself and took the form of a slave."[204] This self-emptying, or *kenosis*, is important when considering how Jesus accepted the gift. He modeled this self-emptying in a very dramatic way when he washed the feet of his disciples at the Last Supper,[205] taking on the role of a slave and telling his disciples he has given them a model to follow.[206] We become more God-like by our submission to the will of God and allowing him to take possession of us. This prepares us for our destiny.

Following the example of Jesus means striving to live a life of self-denial. This daily movement toward the horizon of infinite possibility, toward God, who seeks a relationship with us, is the essence of *theosis*. It is the same ascetic struggles of the Holy Fathers who went before us and strengthen us by their spiritual counsels. The key is that we must freely choose self-denial, placing the divine will over our own. This challenge is increasingly difficult given the culture of individualism

201 Ibid., 320.

202 See John 14:6. "Jesus said to him, 'I am the way and the truth and the life. No one comes to the Father except through me.'"

203 Stăniloae, "The Person of Jesus Christ as God and Savior," 20.

204 Phil. 2:7.

205 See John 13:1–17.

206 Cf. John 13:15.

that has emerged in secular society, where we often find ourselves in the center instead of God. Thus, the example of Jesus shows us how to live in a right-ordered relationship with God by placing him at the center of all that we do, seeking first the kingdom.[207]

Summary

Through the Incarnation, God reveals himself through his Son, Jesus Christ, the "image of the invisible God." Jesus is both fully human and fully divine, with no confusion or mixture between these two natures. Jesus is both the gift and the Giver because he in his divinity and the Father are of one essence. We referred to Jesus as "divinized humanity," which is the end goal for humanity through *theosis*. Accordingly, Jesus models the perfect acceptance of the gift through self-surrender. This occurs through self-emptying, or *kenosis*, whereby Jesus came to us without claiming equality to God; his humility was illustrated, for example, when he washed the feet of his disciples.[208] It is also illustrated in the Garden of Gethsemane when he surrenders his will to the Father: "Not my will but yours be done."[209] Thus, Jesus models the perfect acceptance of the gift and becomes our "way" to the Father.[210] Following this example and living by the commandments of Jesus is how we prepare ourselves for our destiny.

In Topic No. 2, we first introduced Rahner's concept of "Giver as gift." These three simple words provide a profound reflection on the significance of the Incarnate Christ to us. Below is a summary for further reflection.

207 See Matt. 6:33.

208 See John 13:1-17.

209 Luke 22:42.

210 See John 14:4-6. Jesus tells his disciples, "Where I am going you know the way." Thomas objects that they do not know where he is going, so how can they know the way. Jesus replies, "I am the way and the truth and the life." Consider the implications: Jesus is the way because he demonstrates how to enter into relationship with God through self-surrender. He is the truth, that the goal of humanity is "divinized humanity." He is the example of the "life," the purpose of humanity to live union with the Triune God.

"The Giver is himself the gift." **Jesus is:**	
God	Jesus is consubstantial with the Father (same essence): • "In the beginning was the Word, and the word was with God, and the Word was God" (John 1:1). • "The Father and I are one" (John 10:30). • "Image of the invisible God" (Col. 1:15). • "In these last days, (God) spoke to us through a Son" (Heb. 1:2).
Gift	Jesus is God's gift to humanity: • "For God so loved the world that he gave his only Son, so that everyone who believes in him might not perish but might have eternal life" (John 3:16). • "I came so that they might have life and have it more abundantly" (John 10:10).
Our Model	Jesus is our example of how to accept God's gift: • "Not my will but yours be done" (Luke 22:42). • "I am the way and the truth and the life" (John 14:6). • "If anyone wishes to come after me, he must deny himself and take up his cross daily and follow me" (Luke 9:23).
Our Goal	Jesus is "divinized humanity": • "We will…make our dwelling with him" (John 14:23) • "Remain in me, as I remain in you" (John 15:4). • "I am the vine, you are the branches. Whoever remains in me and I in him will bear much fruit, because without me you can do nothing" (John 15:5). • "Whoever acknowledges that Jesus is the Son of God, God remains in him and he in God" (1 John 4:15). • "You may come to share in the divine nature" (2 Pet. 1:4).

The Incarnation is also relevant because it is a historical event whereby the God who is beyond time and space entered into his creation. This act makes his offer of salvation both irrevocable and irreversible. He cannot take it back.

Finally, Creation and the Incarnation are not separate, distinct actions but part of a single process that brings humanity to its fulfillment. God joined himself to humanity through Jesus; thus, the divide between God and humanity collapses. Jesus becomes the bridge in our relationship with God.

Reflection Questions

1. Who is Jesus to me? How do I think of him? Do I focus on the human side of Jesus, or do I focus on the divine?
2. When I reflect on the Incarnation, what are its implications?
3. What are my thoughts about God's offer of salvation? How relevant is this to me today? Please be honest. Answers will not be shared.

THE DIVINE PRESENCE WE ENCOUNTER

Jesus: Image of the Invisible God B: The Mission and Life of Jesus

"The Spirit of the Lord is upon me..."
(Luke 4:18)

"Living faith moves people, regenerates them and changes them, whereas words alone remain fruitless. The best form of mission is through our good example, our love and our meekness." [211]
(Elder Porphyrios of Kavsokalyvia)

Opening Gospel Reading

Luke 4:16-21 (Jesus begins his ministry in Nazareth).

Introductory Comments

The Letter to the Hebrew states:

> In times past, God spoke in partial and various ways to our ancestors through the prophets; in these last days, he spoke to us through a son, whom he made heir of all things and through whom he created the universe.[212]

Through Jesus, who is described in the opening of the Gospel of John as the "Word of God" or *Logos*, God speaks to us directly versus using intermediaries. This fulfills the prophecy contained in Isaiah

211 Elder Porphyrios, 187.
212 Heb. 1:1-2.

about the virgin who shall bear a child who will be named Emmanuel ("God with us").[213] The Incarnation is the ultimate sign of God's desire to be with his Creation.

Examining the Mission of Jesus

Jesus said, "I am the way and the truth and the life."[214] To achieve our created purpose, we must accept the offer of salvation. Jesus described the terms and conditions of this acceptance: "If anyone wishes to come after me, he must deny himself and take up his cross daily and follow me."[215] In the Gospel of Luke, this is described as a daily action, which in terms of *theosis*, requires daily choices to follow Jesus as intentional disciples. Recall Jesus's examples: obedience, self-denial, humility. It also is worth noting the criteria Jesus set for judging worthiness to enter the kingdom of heaven. "Amen, I say to you, whatever you did for one of these least brothers of mine, you did for me."[216]

In our opening Gospel passage, Jesus begins his public ministry by reading a proclamation from the Prophet Isaiah.[217] Consider Jesus's stated purpose for this mission, comparing it to the situation of his time and that of the present day.

Luke 4:18–19, 21	**Situation at the Time of Jesus**	**Situation Present Day**[218]
"The Spirit of the Lord is upon me, because he has anointed me."		

213 Isa. 7:14.
214 John 14:6.
215 Luke 9:23.
216 Matt. 25:40.
217 See Luke 4:16–30.
218 Pope Francis, *Misericordiae Vultus*, Papal Bull (Rome: Libreria Editrice Vaticana, 2015), no. 16.

Luke 4:18–19, 21	Situation at the Time of Jesus	Situation Present Day[218]
"To bring glad tidings to the poor…"	The "overwhelming majority of the population in Palestine"[219] The lowest class of Jews were uneducated and illiterate. Many of the *marginales*, the social and religious outcasts, were the wretched of the earth: the sick, blind, lame, poor, diseased, deranged and mentally ill, captives and prisoners, the hungry. Some were day laborers.	"To bring a word and gesture of consolation to the poor…"
"He has sent me to proclaim liberty to captives and…"	Those living "outside the Law." This included "sinners," such as prostitutes and tax-collectors, also those condemned by the religious authorities (scribes and Pharisees).	"To proclaim liberty to those bound by new forms of slavery in modern society…"
"Recovery of sight to the blind…"	Those who could not see the truth that the love of God extends to all	"To restore sight to those who can see no more because they are caught up in themselves…"

219 Albert Nolan, *Jesus Before Christianity* (Maryknoll, NY: Orbis Books, 2013), 33.

Luke 4:18–19, 21	Situation at the Time of Jesus	Situation Present Day[218]
"To let the oppressed go free…"	Overwhelmingly, members of this group depended on others for material assistance, and on Jewish leaders for their sense of righteousness or holiness before God.[220]	"To restore dignity to all those from whom it has been robbed."
"And proclaim a year acceptable to the Lord."		
"Today this scripture passage is fulfilled in your hearing."	Jesus essentially came to give hope to the vulnerable, marginalized, and outcast, and despite what the religious authorities might teach, God loved them. They were not encumbered by a burden of debt to God for sin. In his life and ministry, Jesus identified with the poor and outcasts (solidarity), restoring their dignity.	"The preaching of Jesus is made visible once more in the response of faith that Christians are called to offer by their witness."

The mission of Jesus was to restore basic human dignity to people stripped of it. He ministered to the poor and marginalized, those who had been alienated or forced to the fringe of society. He identified with the poor, the sinners, and the sick[221]—seeking out the lost sheep

220 Steve Krupa, SJ, "The World of Jesus: Parties and Sects within Judaism," lecture notes, Foundations of Christian Spirituality, Loyola University Chicago (Fall 2014), 4.

221 See Nolan, *Jesus Before Christianity*, 27.

of Israel.[222] Thus, if we wish to exhibit the God-like virtues—to be like God in terms of love, mercy, and compassion—we are called to be intentional disciples, following the example of Jesus. Today, we encounter Jesus in our daily mundane lives, especially when we experience the broken Body of Christ.[223] We do not have to look far to see the poor, the marginalized, and those who live on the fringe. Pope Francis said to reporters after his election, "Oh, how I wish for a Church that is poor and for the poor!"[224]

If we are open to the offer of salvation, allowing God's uncreated grace to flow into us, we must share that grace—the love of God—with those around us. We need to be loving, merciful, and compassionate, especially to those in greatest need. As Rahner wrote, "An absolute love that gives itself radically and unconditionally to another person affirms Christ implicitly in faith and love."[225] We essentially love Jesus by loving others. "By doing so, we realize the possibility of becoming one with God"[226] —reminiscent of our destiny.

The Teachings of Jesus

Through Jesus, God shows his solidarity with those on the fringes of society. Knowing that the mission of Jesus was to the poor and marginalized, let us consider his birth. He humbly entered the world. "He emptied himself, taking the form of slave."[227] He was born amid the livestock, his crib was a feed trough, and he was wrapped in swaddling clothes, rags and scraps of cloth. He was born in a manger because

222 Consider Luke 10:10. At the conversion of Zacchaeus, Jesus says, "For the Son of Man has come to seek and to save what was lost."

223 See Rom 12:5. "So we, though many, are one body in Christ and individually parts of one another."

224 Edward Pentin, "Pope: 'How I Wish for a Church That is Poor and for the Poor!" *National Catholic Register Online*, March 16, 2013. Also cited in Sarah, *God or Nothing*, 142.

225 Rahner, *Foundations of Christian Faith*, 296. See also Stăniloae, *The Person of Jesus Christ as God and Savior*, 7–8. He includes this quote from Rahner and concurs with this assessment.

226 Fischer, 106.

227 Phil 2:7.

there was no room in the inn.[228] This is analogous to what the homeless experience today. Jesus came into this world humble and vulnerable.

"In the society in which Jesus lived, money was the second most important value. The dominant value was *prestige*,"[229] The perception was that the *Messiah* would certainly be someone of prestige. Yet Jesus said, "Whoever wishes to be great among you [prestige] shall be your servant [humility]; whoever wishes to be first among you shall be your slave."[230] He taught, "Amen, I say to you, whoever does not accept the kingdom of God like a child [vulnerable] will not enter it."[231] When he entered Jerusalem, Jesus was not seated upon a magnificent horse, but on a donkey—a beast of service. At the Last Supper, Jesus washed the feet of his disciples,[232] an act of service (*diakonia*) and an ultimate act of humility performed by a slave. Then he told his disciples, "I have given you a model to follow, so that as I have done for you, you should also do."[233]

Wealth was considered by the religious authorities as a reward from God for virtuous living (rich = virtuous; poor = sinner). Yet Jesus taught, "Blessed are the poor in spirit, for theirs is the kingdom of heaven."[234] He advised the crowds, "Do not store up for yourselves treasures on earth...But store up treasures in heaven."[235] When the rich young man went away sad, Jesus noted, "Amen, I say to you, it will be hard for one who is rich to enter the kingdom of heaven."[236] In the Parable of the Rich Fool, he warned of the dangers of wealth and focusing on oneself.[237] Jesus turned the social conventions of his time upside down.

228 See Luke 2:7.
229 Ibid., 67.
230 Matt. 20:26.
231 Mark 10:15. The most vulnerable of society, the *anawim*, were the widow the orphan, and the resident alien. They had no voice.
232 See John 13:1-15.
233 John 13:15.
234 Matt. 5:3.
235 Matt. 6:19-20.
236 Matt. 19:23.
237 Luke 12:13-21.

At the Presentation of Jesus in the temple, Simeon made this prediction to his mother Mary: "Behold this child is destined for the fall and rise of many in Israel, and to be a sign that will be contradicted."[238] Throughout the Gospel accounts, we begin to see how this played out. The religious authorities—scribes, Pharisees, Sadducees), those considered righteous at the time—rejected the teaching of Jesus and the kingdom of heaven (the fall). Those who were outcasts and sinners had their friendship with God restored (the rise). The Gospel of Luke portrays tax collectors and sinners drawing near to Jesus to listen to the word of God, in contrast to the Pharisees who generally criticized and rejected his teachings, fiercely clinging to the status quo.[239] However, as Jesus said at the repentance of Zacchaeus, "The Son of Man has come to seek and to save what was lost."[240] This was the ultimate liberation, freeing those bearing heavy burdens placed upon them by the scribes and Pharisees. They no longer relied on these authorities for their well-being.[241]

Jesus changed the teachings of his time on riches, honor, and pride. These were the three temptations Jesus experienced in the desert. He recommended that his followers embrace spiritual poverty and endure insults and contempt, from which would come genuine humility.[242] This was radical, and we can imagine the crowds murmuring, just as they did after the Bread of Life Discourse in John's Gospel, "This teaching is hard; who can accept it?"[243] Are we any more able to accept this teaching today? Yet, this is the example Jesus gave us, our model for living in a right-ordered relationship with the Father.

---

238 Luke 2:34.

239 Ex. Luke 15:1-2.

240 Luke 19:10.

241 See Matt. 23:3-4: "For they preach and do not practice. They tie up heavy burdens [hard to carry] and lay them on people's shoulders, but will not lift a finger to move them."

242 See William A. Barry, SJ, *Finding God in All Things* (Notre Dame, IN: Ave Maria Press, 1991), 102-3.

243 John 6:60.

Obedient unto Death

In the Crucifixion, we see Jesus's obedience unto death. First, consider his obedience to the will of God, and submission to the divine will, which is best demonstrated in the agony in the garden of Gethsemane. In the Sacred Scriptures, Jesus experiences fear and uncertainty. Yet, he consented to what God asked of him: "Still, not my will but yours be done."[244] This complete surrender to God was the model for acceptance of God's gift. Yet why crucifixion and death?

Dr. Heidi Russell observes that Christ does not atone for our sins through crucifixion by paying a debt to an angry God, a position taken by certain evangelical theologians. Rather, our sins crucify Christ, but out of God's great love for humanity, he forgives us and draws us into the divine embrace of the Trinity. Every time we fail to recognize God in our midst, we crucify Jesus again.[245] This includes failing to recognize Jesus in his most distressing disguises.[246]

Within Rahner's theological framework, the Incarnation is not an afterthought to Creation or the consequence of humanity's fallen nature.[247] Christ is not simply a remedy for our sins because, as Rahner states, sin "cannot be allowed to be the driving motor of the story of God's involvement in the world."[248]

As Catholic Christians, we are accustomed to seeing crucifixes in our churches. Consider this salvific act in light of a self-communicating God who chose to become part of human history. God embraces our sinfulness, willingly surrendering himself to human judgment. In the Gospel of John, Jesus responds to Pilate's questions by saying, "For

244 Luke 22:42.

245 Heidi Russell, "Karl Rahner: Christology and Trinity," lecture notes. Excursus discussed during class lecture. In addition, per Russell, Rahner sees the crucifixion as a symbol of God's love, not his anger.

246 Term used by both Saint Teresa of Calcutta and Dorothy Day in describing the poorest of the poor.

247 See Kilby, 28. See also Stăniloae, "The Person of Jesus Christ as God and Savior," 9. Describing the fulfillment of the human person in Christ, he wrote: "He was created for Christ, or rather that the human person's divine image is perfected in Christ."

248 Ibid., 29.

this I was born and for this I came into the world, to testify to the truth."[249] As Pope St. John Paul II wrote, "But then: 'What is truth?' and here ended the judicial proceeding in which man accused God (Jesus) before the tribunal of his own human history, and in which the sentence handed down did not conform to the truth."[250] Pilate finds no guilt in Jesus,[251] and because of this, tells the Jews to crucify Jesus themselves,[252] and washes his hands of the whole affair.[253] Pope St. John Paul II wrote, "Therefore, the condemnation of God by man is not based on truth, but on arrogance."[254]

Our arrogance crucified Jesus. "The cross is our false judgment of God—a judgment not based on truth, but our ego, our arrogance and underhanded conspiracy, our attempts to protect the status quo, to maintain our power and control."[255] Consider how the people in authority reacted to the love of God as manifested in Jesus. For example, Jesus healed a crippled woman on the Sabbath,[256] and the synagogue official tries to condemn this act of mercy: "There are six days when work should be done. Come on those days to be cured."[257] Confronted with the love of God, we try to dismiss or eliminate it. Yet how does God react to us? Our sin "is not overcome by wrath; it is overcome by love. God brings resurrection out of our crucifixion. In that response is the forgiveness of our sins—that God looks at us for who we truly are. He sees the truth."[258] We, in turn, failed to recognize the truth of God's love in our midst. "God sees all that we have done and failed to do, and he loves us *unconditionally*."[259] As Dr. Russell writes:

---

249 John 18:38.
250 Pope St. John Paul II, *Crossing the Threshold of Hope* (New York, NY: Alfred A. Knopf, 1995), 65.
251 See John 18:39.
252 See John 19:7.
253 See Matt. 27:24.
254 Pope St. John Paul II, *Crossing the Threshold of Hope*, 65.
255 Heidi Russell, *The Source of All Love* (Maryknoll, NY: Orbis Books, 2016), 162.
256 See Luke 13:10–17.
257 Luke 13:14.
258 Heidi Russell, *The Source of All Love*, 163.
259 Ibid.

> God enters into solidarity with us, into union with us, and draws us into the divine embrace of the Trinity. God's reaction to human sinfulness is not anger and wrath. God's response is the gift of self, and that self is unconditional love and forgiveness.[260]

The crucifixion of Christ is our false judgment, wherein we rejected the truth and punished him by death, to which God responds with his overflowing love and forgiveness as manifested in the Resurrection. This is the truth of the depth of God's love for his creation and establishes the bedrock for our salvation. As we look at our society today, has much changed? We continue to reject the truth and the path to salvation.

The Resurrection

God's response to our rejection is the Resurrection. The empty tomb itself does not produce faith. This is particularly true in the Gospel of Mark with its original ending.[261] While all the Gospel accounts point to an empty tomb as physical evidence of the Resurrection, it is not so much about the empty tomb, but the encounter of the disciples with the Risen Lord that provides the tangible evidence. These encounters transform the disciples and the surrounding community. It affirms Jesus's message about life in God and the victory of the cross as the victory over meaninglessness. Faith in the Resurrection is affirmed at Pentecost with the outpouring of the Holy Spirit upon the Church, forming believers into the body of Christ. It is the Holy Spirit who

260 Ibid.

261 The original Gospel of Mark ends at Mark 16:8. The women discover the empty tomb and encounter the angel. As written, "Then they went out and fled from the tomb, seized with trembling and bewilderment. They said nothing to anyone, for they were afraid." Most scripture scholars accept the Gospel of Mark as having been written "in the late 60s or just after '70." See Raymond E. Brown, *An Introduction to the New Testament* (New York, NY: Doubleday, 1997), 164. The longer ending appended to the Gospel of Mark, sometimes called the Marcan appendix, was added in the 2nd century CE. See also John R. Donahue and Daniel J. Harrington, *The Gospel of Mark* (Collegeville, MN: Liturgical Press, 2002), 463.

makes Christ's "yes" (the positive response to our God who reveals himself to us) our "yes."[262] This helps us consider the Trinity in this light: God beyond us (Father), God with us (Emmanuel/Christ), and God within us (outpouring of God's love through the Holy Spirit—see Rom. 5:5).[263]

The Ascension

It is worth noting that from an Eastern Christian perspective, the Ascension of Jesus also has great significance because it is Jesus's transition; he completes his work on earth and lays the foundation for the work of the Holy Spirit through the Church. He unites earth and heaven, restoring the totality of the universe.[264] Thus, the salvific work can be continued. What was visible transitions and, thus, the Redeemer's visible presence has passed into the sacraments,[265] per Pope St. Leo the Great. The Ascension of Jesus brings his body into a state of spiritualization.[266]

By implication, the resurrected body of Jesus was partially spiritualized, which is the reason the disciples do not recognize him. It also explains how he enters a locked room to meet the disciples. Full spiritualization at the Ascension would also equate to Jesus being taken from the sight of his Apostles.[267] Stăniloae mentions, "Christ's

262 See Heidi Russell, *The Source of All Love*, 163. "Jesus says yes for us when we ourselves cannot or will not."

263 See Elizabeth A. Johnson, 204. She writes that the first believers in Jesus "experienced the saving God in a threefold way as beyond them, with them, and within them." This understanding underpins Paul's divine blessing, "The grace of the Lord Jesus Christ, the love of God, and the fellowship of the Holy Spirit be with all of you" (2 Cor. 13:13).

264 Raya, *The Face of God*, 70.

265 Pope St. Leo the Great "Sermon No. 2, On the Ascension." In *The Liturgy of the Hours*, vol. 2 (New York, NY: Catholic Book Publishing Company, 1976), 937.

266 See Dumitru Stăniloae, "The Church: Communion in the Holy Spirit," ed./trans. Ioan Ionita (Brookline, MA: Holy Cross Orthodox Press, 2012), 2. The full pneumatization of Christ allows the divine life to shine forth from his body into those who believe. Thus, his presence remains in the Church. Pneumatization and spiritualization are used interchangeably as are transparent and radiant.

267 See Acts 1:9. "As they were looking on, he was lifted up, and a cloud took him from their sight."

body became radiant…because the light of God's infinite power and love shines forth from Christ."[268] Peter, James, and John experienced a foretaste of this radiance during the Transfiguration of Jesus on Mount Tabor. Virtually every book about *theosis* has an icon of the Transfiguration on the cover. It is through this event that the glory of God is revealed and validates that Jesus is, in fact, the way: "This is my beloved Son, with whom I am well pleased; listen to him."[269] Patriarch Daniel of Romania elaborates further, saying, "The moment of the Transfiguration on Tabor confirms the mystery of the true human image: a man shining from within, from the presence of God in him."[270]

Stăniloae states, "The Ascension of Christ's body into heaven is also our own ascension, the ascension from our passions to be in unity with him; it is the ascension begun for us through the Lord's Ascension, to be continued until its perfection."[271] St. John Chrysostom described Christ's Ascension as the long-awaited return of humanity into heaven.[272]

> Today, the angels have obtained what they were always waiting for; today the archangels have received what they ardently desired. They have seen our nature upon its royal throne, shining with immortal glory and beauty.[273]

In other words, Christ's work has raised our fallen image and placed it on the path for divinization, to seek union with God. Humanity can once again take its rightful and intended place in heaven. However, each of us must still make the free-will decision to accept the offer of salvation, of continuing our work of seeking personal perfection to take our rightful place.

---

268 Stăniloae, "The Church: Communion in the Holy Spirit," 4.

269 Matt. 17:5(b).

270 Patriarch Daniel, *Confessing the Truth in Love*, 55.

271 Stăniloae, "The Person of Jesus Christ as God and Savior," 154.

272 St, John Chrysostom, quoted in Jean Daniélou, SJ, "The Joy of Angels," *Magnificat* 18(7) September (2016), 407. Taken from *The Angels and Their Missions*, trans. David Hermann (Baltimore, MD: The Newman Press, 1957).

273 Ibid.

Accepting the Offer of Salvation ... or Not

For Rahner, the self-communication of God includes two components. There is the *offer* ("Giver as gift") and there is our free-will response to accept or reject this self-communication.[274] Stăniloae reminds us, "By creating human beings, God has committed himself to leading them to deification [divinization]."[275]

For Rahner, sin occurs when we close ourselves to the self-communicating God and refuse to respond to his gift. Stăniloae wrote, "Sin is the closing of the human vis-à-vis God (as infinite source of power), the will to not take him into account, to forget about him. Sin is also closing vis-à-vis one's neighbors."[276]

Acceptance of the offer implies a turning away from sin, a complete surrender to God, and, for Rahner and Stăniloae, ultimate freedom as opposed to enslavement to sin and material things. "Those who accept the offer of salvation are set free from sin, sorrow, inner emptiness and loneliness."[277] God desires the salvation of all,[278] but not all will accept it. Yet, God's self-communication through the Incarnation is both irrevocable and irreversible. Accordingly, the

274 See Rahner. *Foundations of Christian Faith*, 118. "At this point it is already clear from our general anthropology that God's self-communication to man as a free being who exists with the possibility of an absolute 'yes' or 'no' to God can be present or can be understood in two different modalities: in the modality of the antecedent situation of an offer and a call to man's freedom on the one hand, and on the other hand in the once again two-fold modality of the response to this offer of God's self-communication as a permanent existential of man, that is, in the modality of acceptance or in the modality of a rejection of God's self-communication by man's freedom."

275 Stăniloae, "The World: Creation and Deification," 44.

276 Stăniloae, "The Person of Jesus Christ as God and Savior," 70. Stăniloae goes on to say that sin cannot exist in Jesus because "Christ's humanity is completely open to the Father and to the Holy Spirit and participates in perfect communion of the Son with the Father and Spirit." In addition, because of God's love *par excellence* toward his creatures, Jesus cannot be closed to love of neighbor (71).

277 Pope Francis, *Evangelii Gaudium*, no. 1.

278 See Raya, *The Face of God*, 68. "Such an act of love on the part of God is for the entire world, and not the private possession of some elect. God is uniting to himself—deifying and redeeming— the whole world, all of humanity, all the people of the earth, their cultures, their achievements, their creations of beauty. This cosmic dimension of the Incarnation is an essential part of the redeeming mission of Christianity. It should always be present in our announcement of the Good News and in our celebrations."

possibility of conversion always remains. By accepting the offer of salvation, we are placed on the path of transcendence as intended by God and on the journey of transformation, which allows us to fulfill our destiny: union with God in the life to come.

Summary

Jesus is the Word (*Logos*) who reveals the Father to us. In the context of Giver as gift, Jesus is not only the gift of the God who communicates himself to us, but he also models the perfect acceptance of the gift. Jesus further demonstrates God's solidarity with the poor and the marginalized by entering human history through humble circumstances reflective of his teachings. He overturned the social conventions of his time, placing no value on prestige, wealth, and honor. Rather, he focused on humility, spiritual poverty, service, self-emptying, and self-surrender to the will of God.

Through the Incarnation, God demonstrates his great love and his desire to be with his Creation. He responds with overflowing love even when we condemn him and, through our arrogance, attempt to maintain the status quo. His response to the Crucifixion is the Resurrection.

Our faith in the Resurrection is affirmed by the encounter with the Risen Jesus, not the empty tomb. The Ascension of Jesus is our ascension, elevating our human nature from our passions and sinfulness. Through the Ascension, humanity (through the human nature of Jesus) again takes its rightful place in heaven and provides the opportunity for humans to ascend to their rightful place.

Reflection Questions

1. What are my reactions to the life and mission of Jesus? What parts of his message do I find the most compelling? What parts do I find most difficult? How different are Jesus's teachings from the messages I hear in society today?

2. We discussed God's overflowing love for us, reflected through the life of Jesus. How do I react to this constant response of love (e.g., God's response to the Crucifixion was the Resurrection, his response to rejection is love)?

3. Do I find myself trying to hold on to the status quo? What are my greatest struggles with change?

The Holy Spirit: Key to the Divine Indwelling

"But when he comes, the Spirit of truth, he will guide you to all truth." (John 16:13)

"What counts in God's eyes is true faith in him and in his only Son. It is for this that the grace of the Holy Spirit is given us; the Lord seeks hearts overflowing with love for him and their neighbor, and this is the throne where he would sit and reveal himself in the fullness of his glory." [279] ***(St. Seraphim of Sarov)***

Opening Gospel Reading

John 16:5-15 (Jesus foretells the coming of the Advocate).

The Mission of the Holy Spirit

At Pentecost, a new reality entered the world. The descent of the Holy Spirit allows Christ's work of salvation to continue through the Church, even though Jesus has ascended and sits at the right hand of the Father. There are two missions of the Father, the Word (*Logos*) and the Spirit (*Pneuma*). These Divine Persons of the Trinity were sent into the world and the work of *both* is required for us to attain our destiny, union with God.[280] Rahner describes the human person as a finite spirit whom God fulfills with his gift of self ("Giver as gift"). Thus, "God

279 Valentine Zander, *St. Seraphim of Sarov*, trans. Sr. Gabriel Anne SSC (Crestwood, NY: St. Vladimir's Seminary Press, 1975), 93.

280 See Vladimir Lossky, *The Mystical Theology of the Eastern Church* (Crestwood, NY: St. Vladimir's Seminary Press, 1998), 156.

is accomplishing the union of finite spirit (the human person) and the Holy Spirit as humanity's fulfillment."[281] The Incarnation completes the creation of humanity, and the Holy Spirit guides humanity to fulfill its destiny. This double arrangement "of the Word and the Paraclete [Advocate] has as its goal the union of created beings with God,"[282] wrote Eastern Orthodox Theologian Vladimir Lossky.

Scriptural Foundation

We read about the descent of the Holy Spirit in the Acts of the Apostles.[283] We know that *something* happened. There were physical signs such as "a noise like a strong driving wind, and it filled the entire house."[284] There were "tongues as of fire, which parted and came to rest on each of them."[285] A clear transformation occurred with disciples, previously scared and timid, cowering behind locked doors for fear of the Jews.[286] With the Pentecost event, their fear evaporated, and they boldly began to proclaim the Gospel message. They could not tell people fast enough about Jesus. Something transformational happened. Today, we as a Church are proof that something happened because the transmission of faith that began at Pentecost. Jesus ascended into heaven, and with the arrival of the Holy Spirit, the Church was established

Before Jesus's crucifixion, he spoke to his disciples about sending another Advocate,[287] that he would not leave them orphaned and that he would come to them.[288] He said that it is better he goes, because otherwise, the Advocate would not come,[289] i.e., the two-fold mission could not be completed. Jesus explains that the Spirit of truth will

281 Fischer, xxiii.
282 Lossky, *In the Image and Likeness of God*, 109–10.
283 See Acts 2:1–13.
284 Acts 2:2.
285 Acts 2:3.
286 See John 20:19.
287 Cf. John 14:6.
288 John 14:18.
289 Cf. John 16:7.

guide them to all truth: "He will not speak on his own, but he will speak what he hears."[290] Jesus also tells them that the Spirit will glorify him "because he will take from what is mine and declare it to you."[291] This is the scriptural foundation for the remainder of our discussion.

The Ongoing Work of Salvation

Post-Ascension, the work of building up the Church began with the descent of the Holy Spirit at Pentecost; this is how Jesus remains active in the Church today. He told his disciples, "Whoever loves me will keep my word, and my Father will love him, and we will come to him and make our dwelling with him."[292] In other words, Christ remains present in the hearts of all believers, and the Church is built up through cooperation with these believers. Yet if Jesus has ascended to the Father, how does he remain active in the Church and in our hearts?

Previously we mentioned that through his Ascension, Jesus was fully spiritualized. He continues to save us, because he continues to dwell in us through the Holy Spirit, the indwelling divine presence. "In this way the power for our salvation and deification [divinization] shines forth within us from Christ's spiritualized body."[293] It is the Holy Spirit who allows the deified body of Christ to shine forth from the hearts of those with faith, drawing them into union with God. Archbishop Joseph Raya explained it as follows: "Because the Holy Spirit animates the Body of Christ, it is he who is the life of the Church and who unites her to the Lord."[294] Thus, we see the unification of the two missions of the Father and how the Church is a means to encounter the Divine.

---

290 John 16:13.

291 John 16:14.

292 John 14:23.

293 Stăniloae, "The Church: Communion in the Holy Spirit," 2.

294 Archbishop Joseph M. Raya, "Where His Body Is, There We Gather," *Magnificat,* 23(9) (2021), 160. Taken from *The Face of God*.

Sometimes people see the Ascension and Pentecost as transition events, in which Jesus ascends to the Father and the Holy Spirit descends to take over the work of building up the Church. This implies that the Church is solely the work of the Holy Spirit. Yet this is not correct. Instead, "the Holy Spirit must be considered as the Spirit of Christ; therefore, he should never be seen as separated from Christ in any way."[295]

The Incarnate Jesus (God as man) is our model of the divinized person to which humanity aspires. Stăniloae wrote:

> Through the Incarnation, Crucifixion, Resurrection and Ascension, Christ lays the foundation of the Church in his body, and through these events, the Church exists in its potential form. However, the Son of God became man not for himself but so that he could extend salvation from his body, as divine life within us. This divine life, extended from his body into those who believe, is the Church. This life shines forth from his body, which was raised up to the full state of pneumatization [spiritualization] through his Ascension and sitting at the right hand of the Father, within the deepest intimacy of the infinite life and love that God directs toward human beings."[296] .

It is the innate desire for transcendence instilled in each person by which the finite strives for the infinite. By ascending in his human nature to the Father, Jesus is filled bodily with the Holy Spirit (fully spiritualized). As such, the Father and Christ as God can be the fullness of the Spirit shining forth from the perfectly spiritualized body of Christ. While his body can no longer visibly appear, Jesus can permeate the hearts of those who believe in him—just like when

295 Stăniloae, "The Church: Communion in the Holy Spirit," 2.
296 Ibid.

passing through the locked doors of the room after the Resurrection. Thus, Christ dwells in our hearts, the indwelling of Christ's deified body in human beings through the Holy Spirit.[297] It also fulfills what Jesus said to his disciples regarding the Holy Spirit: "He will take from what is mine and declare it to you." Accordingly, the Risen Lord is with us until the end of the age,[298] his spirit in the heart of believers, and the Holy Spirit continuing to guide us to "all truth." Further, as St. Paul writes, "If the Spirit of the one who raised Jesus from the dead dwells in you, the one who raised Christ from the dead will give life to your mortal bodies also, through his Spirit that dwells in you."[299] Thus, we can see the connection between the Father's two missions and how they unfold in the Church.

We mentioned earlier that divinization involves the union of two distinct natures. It is through the Holy Spirit that God and humanity can be in union yet remain distinct from one another.[300] In fact, certain Holy Fathers, such as St. Seraphim of Sarov, consider *theosis* to be the acquisition of the Holy Spirit. As written in the Letter to the Ephesians, God "has destined us for adoption to himself through Christ Jesus, in accord to the favor of his will."[301] We are adopted children because we do not become consubstantial with God the Father as Christ. Despite entering into union with God, our nature remains distinct. In other words, we become partakers of the divine nature, but do not become the divine nature. So, what Christ possesses by nature, we share in by participation or adoption. To this end, we cannot achieve our status as adopted children without the Holy Spirit. St. Paul wrote, "The love of God has been poured into our hearts through the Holy Spirit that has been given to us."[302] If we consider Jesus as the "love

297 Ibid., 4.
298 See Matt. 28:20.
299 Rom. 8:11.
300 See Raya, *The Face of God*, 50. "St. Athanasius of Alexandria says, 'Without the Holy Spirit we are strangers and far from God.'"
301 Eph. 1:5.
302 Rom. 5:5.

of God," the gift reflecting the depth of God's love for humanity,[303] we can understand how the spirit of Christ can dwell in the hearts of believers through the Holy Spirit. Thus, we are given the power to develop ourselves into the model of the divinized person represented by the Incarnate Christ. This allows us to fulfill our deepest longing—seeking infinite fulfillment versus seeking fulfillment in finite things—and achieve our destiny.

Through his Ascension, Jesus raised our nature to the possibility of union with God and, at Pentecost, the Holy Spirit descended, reconciling the Father with our human nature.[304] As Lossky wrote, Pentecost confers the presence of the Holy Spirit and the first fruits of sanctification upon human persons. "It signifies the end and final goal and, at the same time, marks the commencement of the spiritual life."[305] This provides the possibility for humanity to be divinized; however, continuing in the spiritual life requires ongoing human collaboration with the divine presence (*synergeia*).

The initial descent of the Holy Spirit gathered together the followers of Jesus into communion with one another, the tongues of flame came to rest on each, and brought the Church into existence.[306] From this point forward, the Church is maintained in Christ through the Holy Spirit. Lossky differentiates between the coming of the Holy Spirit at Pentecost, the unifying bond, and the personal coming of the Holy Spirit to individuals, which Stăniloae describes as occurring when "being asked for through prayers and the avoidance of sin."[307] Again, he reminds us that *theosis* continues through human effort—avoiding sin, practicing the virtues—in collaboration with divine assistance that allows us to persevere in our struggles. Trying to live

303 See Elizabeth A. Johnson, 40. "Rahner placed his interpretation of the Incarnation within the framework of God as love."

304 See Stăniloae, "The Church: Communion in the Holy Spirit," 4.

305 Lossky, *The Mystical Theology of the Eastern Church*, 170.

306 See Lossky, *The Mystical Theology of the Eastern Church*, 167. "The first communication of the Holy Spirit was made to the whole Church, to the Church as a body. Here the Spirit is bestowed upon all in common as a bond of unity."

307 Stăniloae, "The Church: Communion in the Holy Spirit," 8.

God-like virtues prepares one to become a recipient of deifying grace of the Holy Spirit through which union with God is possible. Pentecost provides the first fruits, with the final fruits attained when human beings fulfill their destiny. The spiritual life, *theosis,* involves lifelong effort and only reaches fulfillment at the resurrection of the dead in the life to come.

We should also mention the gifts of the Holy Spirit. "In the theology of the Eastern Church, the Person of the Holy Spirit is distinguished from the gifts he bestows on men."[308] This is based on the words of Jesus, mentioned above under the scriptural foundation: the Spirit will glorify Jesus, "because he will take from what is mine and declare it to you."[309] That which is taken from the Father and Son, which is common to them, is the divinity that the Holy Spirit bestows on those in the Church, making them "partakers of the divine nature."[310]

The gifts are "often described by the names of the seven spirits, which are found in a passage from Isaiah."[311] These are "a spirit of wisdom and understanding, a spirit of counsel and of strength, a spirit of knowledge and fear of the Lord."[312] However, in Orthodox theology, there is typically no distinction between these gifts and God's deifying grace[313]—these gifts and deifying grace are terms used synonymously. In an upcoming topic, we will further discuss the concepts of "becoming partakers of the divine nature," the "operations" of God—also called uncreated energies, and grace, all of which are interrelated.

Finally, the Holy Spirit increases the intensity of Christ's presence in the Church and the hearts of believers. It is the Holy Spirit who allows the deified body of Christ to shine forth from the hearts of those with faith. Stăniloae wrote:

308 Lossky, *The Mystical Theology of the Eastern Church*, 162.
309 John 16:14.
310 See Lossky, *The Mystical Theology of the Eastern Church*, 162.
311 Ibid.
312 Isa. 11:2.
313 See Lossky, *The Mystical Theology of the Eastern Church*, 162.

> The Spirit remains forever in this shining forth. The expression 'the Holy Spirit remains in the Church' is not contrary to this permanent shining forth. The expression is correct only in the sense that the Lord himself, who as a man is on the divine throne together with the Father, is at the same time within the hearts of those who believe and within the communion among them, namely in the Church; thus, by shining forth from Christ, the Holy Spirit shines forth from the Church, in which Christ dwells. Given that Christ is both on the divine throne and comes continuously from the throne to those who receive or have the faith and who develop it through *good works*—coming more intensely to those who advance in their faith—the Spirit also comes from beyond the Church, or beyond the intimacy of the believers. That is why on one hand the Church has the Spirit constantly, and on the other hand (the Church) asks for him constantly. She asks for him because she has him, for the Spirit gives her the strength to ask for him through prayer, so that he may continue to come more and more.[314]

The intensity of the indwelling divine presence increases as individuals continue the ascetical struggles to overcome the passions and temptations, and cultivate the virtues. It is the Holy Spirit that prepares the kingdom of God within us.[315] In coming to dwell in us, "he makes of our being the throne of the Holy Trinity, for the Father and the Son are inseparable from the deity of the Spirit. Through the coming of the Holy Spirit, the Trinity dwells within us and [divinizes]

314 Ibid., 7–8. See also Rom. 8:26–27. "In the same way, the Spirit comes to the aid of our weakness, for we do not know how to pray as we ought, but the Spirit itself intercedes with inexpressible groanings. And the one who searches hearts knows what is the intention of the Spirit, because it intercedes for the holy ones according to God's will."

315 See Luke 17:21.

us; confers upon us the uncreated energies,"[316] and prepares us for union with God.

Within the Church, we have both the Risen Lord and Holy Spirit whom we can encounter; we experience both the Resurrection and Pentecost through the Holy Mysteries of Initiation: Baptism is our personal participation in the Resurrection; Chrismation (Confirmation) involves us in Pentecost. Through these Holy Mysteries, the Spirit "recreates our nature by purifying it and uniting it to the body of Christ,"[317] and we receive the uncreated and deifying grace conferred by the Holy Spirit.

After the Holy Mysteries of Initiation, the spiritual life continues. Good works, as described by Stăniloae above, are the cultivation of the virtues, which St. Gregory Palamas says helps us regain the likeness of God. Good works move us closer to God, preparing us for our destiny. They also intensify the experience of the Risen Jesus within the hearts of the faithful. Thus, in this manner, the work of divinization and sanctification continue within the Church.

Receiving and Retaining the Divine Indwelling

Baptism is the commencement of the spiritual life, our regeneration and purification of the soul to its original state. However, the spiritual life continues through *synergeia*. "'Synergy' consists of divine initiative and human response."[318] This is similar to Rahner's concept of the gift offered by the self-communicating God ("Giver as gift") and humanity's free-will response to be open to the gift. In response to our human efforts, God provides us with deifying grace to strengthen us. St. Silouan the Athonite said:

316 Lossky, *The Mystical Theology of the Eastern Church*, 171.

317 Ibid., 170.

318 John Breck, "Prayer of the Heart: Sacrament of the Presence of God," *Saint Vladimir's Theological Quarterly* 29(1) (1995): 37. See also Vishnevskaya, "Divinization and Spiritual Progress in Maximus the Confessor," 134. "The essential conditions for fulfilling the divinizing process are the divine initiative and willing human cooperation."

> The Lord does not manifest himself to the proud soul. All the books in the world will not help the proud soul to know the Lord, for her pride will not make way for the grace of the Holy Spirit, and God is known only through the Holy Spirit.[319]

Pride is an impediment to grace and the Holy Spirit; thus, in our good works we endeavor to cultivate a spirit of humility. Further, St. Silouan reemphasizes that our destiny cannot be achieved solely through human effort. Through the Holy Spirit, we gain knowledge of spiritual mysteries, what the Holy Fathers often call "knowledge from above," and this is our way to Christian perfection. Cardinal Sarah said, "God is not a rational argument, for the Father is in the heart of every [person]."[320] God is relational, his presence in the heart of those who are open to the offer of salvation. "The abiding in us of the Father and the Son, inseparable from them the Holy Spirit, will give us true knowledge of God."[321] As Jesus said, "Whoever loves me will keep my word, and my Father will love him, and we will come to him and make our dwelling with him."[322] St. Silouan adds:

> Unless the Lord grant him knowledge in the Holy Spirit, man cannot know how greatly he loves us, for there is no earthly science that can teach the human mind of the love the Lord has for men.[323]

Accordingly, divinization involves true communion with the Holy Spirit in the depth of the human heart. It is not simply intellectual knowledge; rather, it is the experience of divine love. It is God's initiative and our response to that initiative. St. Paisius Velichkovsky wrote:

---

319 Archimandrite Sophrony Sakharov, *St Silouan the Athonite*, trans. Rosemary Edwards (Crestwood, NY: St. Vladimir's Seminary Press, 1991), 306-7.

320 Sarah, *God or Nothing*, 114.

321 Archimandrite Sophrony, *His Life is Mine*, 30.

322 John 14:23.

323 Archimandrite Sophrony, *St Silouan the Athonite*, 304.

> First, one must clean the royal house from every impurity and adorn it with every beauty, then the king may enter into it .... For the Holy Spirit does not dwell in a man until he has been cleansed from the passions of the soul and body .... First of all, one must banish within himself self-love in all forms of desiring objects of the world .... Humility never fails, it lies beneath everything.[324]

Baptism begins the spiritual life, which must be sustained through ongoing effort and openness to the Holy Spirit; deifying grace is bestowed upon us as gift commensurate with our efforts. St. Theophan the Recluse summarizes this well, writing:

> We, the baptized, have received a talent, which is the grace of the Holy Spirit. This talent ... acts within us on its own at first, until we have grown up. As we approach maturity, grace, although it is ready to act, does not act. It waits until we freely and willingly incline to it, when we ourselves desire its full action within us and begin to seek it. As soon as we begin seeking, grace immediately resumes its work within us, rousing us, directing us, and strengthening us.[325]

Grace resuming its work is the shining forth that Stăniloae referenced, whereby the Holy Spirit allows the deified body of Christ to shine forth from the Church and in the heart of all believers. It is the two-fold mission of the Father in drawing us back into union with him and strengthening us to carry out his will.

---

324 St. Paisius Velichkovsky, "Field Flowers," in *Little Russian Philokalia*, vol. 4 (Platina, CA: St. Herman of Alaska Brotherhood, 1994), 82.

325 St. Theophan, *The Spiritual Life*, 120.

Summary

The Father has two missions associated with the salvation of humanity: the Word (*Logos*) and the Spirit (*Pneuma*). Both are required. Jesus promises to send us "another advocate," not allowing his disciples to be orphaned and leading them to all truth. At Pentecost, the disciples' transformation is evident: they go from fearful and timid to boldly proclaiming the Gospel. It is through the Holy Spirit that the Risen Christ can dwell in the hearts of believers and remain present in the Church, even though he is no longer visible and seated at the right hand of the Father. "The Holy Spirit shines forth in the Church in which Christ dwells." Through the Holy Spirit, humanity is drawn into union with God—the human and divine natures are united yet remain distinct.

The Holy Spirit is key to the indwelling divine presence, and we must be open to the gift of God's deifying grace given through the Holy Spirit. Through our spiritual lives, this requires human-divine collaboration (*synergeia*), divine initiative and human response to this initiative.

Reflection Questions

1. What is my personal perception of the Holy Spirit?
2. How does the Holy Spirit allow the Risen Christ to be present in the hearts of believers?
3. How does the miracle of Pentecost continue today?

Supplemental Discussion:

The *Filioque*: Controversy over the Procession of the Holy Spirit

Filioque is Latin for *and the Son*, which was added to the Nicaean Creed in the West in the 6th century. The Creed recited before then came from the work of the First and Second Ecumenical Councils, Nicaea I (325) and Constantinople I (381), which produced the Nicaean-Constantinopolitan Creed (NCC). In the second council, the procession of the Holy Spirit was stated as being "from the Father." This is the original NCC used by both Eastern and Western Churches. The *Filioque* had been accepted by the Roman Church in 1014—arguably to avoid confrontation with the Frankish kings and key supporters of the Roman Church.[326] All the Churches of the East rejected it.

Perhaps the most significant issue with the *Filioque* is its unilateral insertion into the NCC by the West. It overrode the creed adopted by the Ecumenical Councils, which many saw as an unacceptable and noncanonical action. The second major issue is concern about theological confusion this phrase could create. Some believe it overrides the two missions of the Father (Word and Spirit) and implies a "double procession" of the Holy Spirit (*processio*, proceeds from the Father *and the Son*). The Eastern Orthodox Churches, Oriental Orthodox Churches, and Assyrian Church of the East reject this position. Some also believe this could imply subordinationism[327] or even Sabellianism.[328] Supporters of the Orthodox position cite John 15:26, which states, "When the Advocate comes whom I will send you from the Father, the Spirit of truth *that proceeds from the Father*, he will testify to me." The Eastern belief is that the Spirit is *sent* by the Son but *proceeds* from the Father as the sole origin or cause of the Spirit. This, in essence, is the controversy.

Modern day Eastern Orthodox theologians labeled as "rigorists," including Stăniloae, Lossky, and John Romanides, argue against

326 See "Filioque," *Wikipedia*.

327 The Doctrine of the Trinity is that the three Persons are equal. Various heretical forms of subordinationism had existed in the Church, such as the Son is subordinate to the Father, and the Spirit is subordinate to the Son. This position rejects the equality of personhood in the Trinity.

328 Sabellianism was a heresy rejecting the doctrine of the Trinity. It was named for the priest Sabellius of the 3rd century who said there was only one God who had different modes (or faces) when he acted as Father, as Son, and as Spirit. This is also referred to as Modalism, also a heresy.

the double procession and consider this position heretical. Some more liberal theologians, such as Metropolitan Kallistos Ware, do not believe this is an insurmountable theological argument.[329] For example, St. Maximos the Confessor in the 7th century suggested that the Holy Spirit proceeds from the Father *through* the Son, wording that eliminates concerns about the double procession. Other suggested wording is the Spirit *reposes* or *dwells* in the Son; St. John of Damaskos described the Spirit as "taking origin from the Father and reposes in the Word."[330] This is one of the sources of current theological dialogue between the Roman Catholic and Eastern Orthodox Churches. It should be noted that the *Filioque* has been removed from the NCC in Eastern Catholic Churches.

329 See "Filioque," *Wikipedia*.

330 St. John of Damaskos, *Dialogue Contra Manichaes*, 5. Cited in Patriarch Daniel of Romania, *Confessing the Truth in Love*, 97.

THE DIVINE PRESENCE WE ENCOUNTER

The Holy Trinity: A Model for Relationship

"Go, therefore, and make disciples of all nations, baptizing them in the name of the Father, and of the Son, and of the Holy Spirit..."
(Matthew 28:19)

"The Trinity is the foundation upon which the Christian religion stands and from which all its theology and spiritual life proceed." [331]
(Archbishop Joseph M. Raya)

"Salvation ... is not an abstract notion but union with God the Holy Trinity in the Person of our Lord Jesus Christ." [332]
(Metropolitan Hierotheos Vlachos of Nafpaktos)

Opening Gospel Reading

Matt. 3:13-17 (The Baptism of Jesus).

Introduction

"The mystery of the Holy Trinity is the very heart of any authentic Christian theology and spirituality,"[333] wrote Patriarch Daniel of Romania. From a theological standpoint, God is a Trinity, a communion of three distinct persons (*hypostases*) who share one essence (*ousia*). The term *nature* is also used herein interchangeably with essence. Our focus in this discussion is the relationship between

331 Raya, *The Face of God*, 23.

332 Metropolitan Hierotheos of Nafpaktos, *A Night in the Desert of the Holy Mountain: Discussion with a Hermit on the Jesus Prayer*, 3rd ed., trans. Effie Mavromichali (Levadia, Greece: Birth of the Theotokos Monastery, 2009), 50.

333 Patriarch Daniel, *Confessing the Truth in Love*, 86.

the three divine persons. Previously, we considered the three using the description of theologian Elizabeth Johnson:

> **Father:** "God beyond us." A mystery beyond all telling.[334] "Ineffable, inconceivable, invisible, incomprehensible, ever-existing, yet ever the same."[335]
>
> **Son:** "God with us (Emmanuel)." The promised Messiah and Word of God (*Logos*).
>
> **Holy Spirit:** "God within us." The outpouring of God's love, a God of absolute love.

An alternative way to consider this relationship is that of the Father with two missions, the Word and the Spirit. Both are sent into the world and essential to the work of assisting humanity in achieving its divinely created purpose.

The Early Church Fathers believed that the Mystery of the Trinity was revealed at the Baptism of Jesus, referred to in the Eastern Churches as the Theophany. The Troparion[336] for the Feast of the Theophany is the following:

> At your baptism in the Jordan, O Lord, worship of the Trinity was revealed.
>
> For the Father's voice bore witness to you, calling you his beloved Son,
>
> and the Spirit in the form of a dove confirmed the truth of these words.

334 Elizabeth A. Johnson, 17.

335 From the anaphora (consecration prayer) of the divine Liturgy of Saint John Chrysostom.

336 See Bogdan G. Bucur, "Exegesis of Biblical Theophanies in Byzantine Hymnology: Rewritten Bible?" *Theological Studies* 68(1) (Mar. 2007), 94. The Early Eastern Church typically communicated key theological concepts through hymnology, namely the troparion and kontakion, which developed between the fourth and early fifth centuries. These succinct, one-stanza hymns are packed with theology, bursting with meaning, and were a means of catechizing the faithful, many of whom were illiterate.

> O Christ God, you appeared and enlightened the world. Glory to you![337]

In Eastern Christian theology and even in liturgical prayer, there is greater emphasis on the Trinity than in the Western Church. In Rahner's theological framework, God, who is love, creates that which is not God with an emptiness that only his love can fill. On the other hand, Stăniloae begins with the Trinity: "If God is love, then he cannot be merely one person loving himself alone, for self-love is not true love. As the God of love, he is shared, mutual love, a community of persons loving one another."[338] He wrote about the communion in the Godhead, saying, "This implies perfect love. For love seeks complete unity and reciprocal affirmation of the persons who love one another."[339] The force of this love, God's overflowing love, manifests itself in creation. Thus, the created world and in particular, humanity made in the divine image are drawn into communion with this Trinity. Sometimes union with God is referred to as sharing in the life of the Holy Trinity.

Stăniloae addresses some key points in the doctrine: unity through perfect love and a self-giving relationship. This is a perfect union and, as Lossky states, the Trinity represents a theology of union.[340] The divine persons have one nature (substance), a single will, a single power, and a single operation.[341] Jesus describes his unity with the Father, "The Father and I are one."[342] In Last Supper Discourses in the Gospel John, Jesus also states several times, "I am in the Father and the Father is in me."[343] He also mentions that the Father will send another advocate, referencing the Holy Spirit as part of this relationship.[344]

---

337 Troparion for the Theophany. *The Divine Liturgies*, 313.
338 Ware, foreword to "Revelation and Knowledge of the Triune God," xx.
339 Stăniloae, "Revelation and Knowledge of the Triune God," 68.
340 See Lossky, *The Mystical Theology of the Eastern Church*, 67.
341 Ibid., 53.
342 John 10:30.
343 See John 14:10, 14:11, and 14:20.
344 See John 14:16.

The only difference among the three divine persons are the properties of unbegotten (Father), filiation[345] (Sonship, "begotten, not made" per the Nicaean Creed—"consubstantial with the Father"), and procession (Holy Spirit).[346] Unbegotten means God existed before time and space without beginning or end. As for the Son, we describe him in the Nicaean Creed as "begotten, not made," which means he was not created by God; rather, he is in essence God. This was in response to Arianism, one of the early heresies that taught that Jesus was a creature (created) and not divine. This heresy was rejected at the First Nicaean Council (325). As for the Holy Spirit, this also comes from the Nicaean Creed: "I believe in the Holy Spirit, the Lord, the giver of life, who proceeds from the Father..." This refers to procession. In the Gospel of John, Jesus said the Father will *send* another advocate. Thus, the divine persons are identical except for these three specific properties. Filiation and procession are comparable to the two missions of the Unbegotten Father.

There is complete equality among the divine persons of the Trinity. Father, Son, and Holy Spirit are not three "modes" of the one God (the heresy of Modalism). The Son is not subordinate to the Father, nor the Holy Spirit subordinate to the Son (the heresy of Sabellianism or subordinationism).

The Trinity is inseparable. If we say the Holy Spirit dwells in our hearts, we also have the Father and Son. Similarly, when Paul writes that it is Christ dwelling in him,[347] he also has the Father and the Holy Spirit. In a previous discussion, we noted that it is the Holy Spirit that allows the Risen Christ to dwell in the hearts of believers and to remain active in the Church. That is why this idea of the indwelling divine presence is also considered the indwelling Trinity.

This union of the divine persons in Trinity provides some

345 Filiation is defined as "the fact of being a child of a certain parent." It is derived from the Latin, *filius*, meaning "son."

346 See Lossky, *The Mystical Theology of the Eastern Church*, 54.

347 See Gal. 2:20.

perspectives on humanity's destiny of union with God. The unity of the Trinity has a single will, power, and operation. *Theosis* involves self-surrender of our human will to the divine will a unified will. This unity of will and way of acting reflects perfection, the objective of divinized humanity, to act perfectly in accord with God's will—a single will, as in the Trinity. While perfection is not possible, we strive for this as part of the spiritual life. (Recall Rahner's analogy of striving for the infinite horizon.) However, this ideal of alignment of wills, human and divine, and living the God-like virtues, is like the principles of unity within the Trinity. Jesus also refers to this unity between human and divine when he says to his disciples, "On that day you will realize that I am in the Father and you are in me and I in you."[348] In another analogy of union, Jesus says, "I am the vine; you are the branches."[349]

In his Letter to the Philippians, St. Paul writes, "Have among yourselves the same attitude that is also yours in Christ Jesus"[350]—or, said another way, "You must have the same attitude that Jesus had."[351] Consider the term "attitude." It comes from the Greek word *phroneō*, which can be translated to "be of the same mind." This returns us to the idea of a union of wills, human and divine, to be single-minded. Accordingly, we again see this idea of union being illustrated by Jesus's dwelling within us. *Theosis* involves this ongoing effort to deny oneself, to surrender like Jesus to the Father's will—a single will, which is one of the attributes of union within the Trinity itself. Accordingly, we can reflect upon this model of the Holy Trinity in terms of our own human destiny and its implications for our daily lives.

The primary difference between the unity within the Trinity and humanity's union with God is this: the three divine persons share a common nature, whereas union with God refers to the union of two

348 John 14:20.
349 John 15:5.
350 Phil. 2:5.
351 Phil. 2:5. New Living Translation.

distinct natures (human and divine). We become *sharers* in the divine nature;[352] we do not become divine in nature. We participate in the life of the Trinity, possessing by grace what the Trinity is by nature. We do not become members of the Trinity. "He [God] destined us for adoption to himself through Jesus Christ, in accord with the favor of his will."[353] In other words, we become children of God through adoption (participation), whereas Jesus is a Son by nature (filiation, begotten of the Father). We align our human will with God, but it is not the same will. We remain human, and God remains divine. However, we share or participate through alignment of will.

Patriarch Daniel of Romania wrote:

> Orthodoxy offers a very special synthetic theological-spiritual vision, integrating life and the whole of reality created by God. Through the theology and testimony of its spirituality, Orthodoxy helps Western Christianity rediscover the mystery of the Holy Trinity as the source of life and meaning of the Church and of Christian existence in general.[354]

Summary

A central mystery of the Christian faith is that God exists as a Trinity, a communion of three divine persons who are equal, sharing one nature (essence), one will, one power, and one operation. As Stăniloae explained, if God is love, self-love is not true love. Accordingly, God is a community of persons united in self-giving love. Not only does the Trinity give us a model for having a relationship with one another, the Trinity is a model for our human destiny, union

352 See 2 Pet. 1:4.
353 Eph. 1:5.
354 Patriarch Daniel, "Spiritual Life and Theology in Contemporary Orthodoxy: A Short Presentation," in *Patriarch Daniel: Rebuilding Orthodoxy in Romania*, ed. Chad Hatfield (Yonkers, NY: St. Vladimir's Seminary Press, 2021), 33.

with God, which involves self-surrender to God and the alignment of our human will with that of God. Recall Jesus's self-surrender in the Garden of Gethsemane: "Not my will but yours be done."[355] Through this union, we participate in the life of the Trinity; however, we do not become part of the Trinity. We also have described this union between humanity and God as that of two distinct natures, whereby each nature remains the same.

Reflection Questions

1. How have I thought of the Trinity in the past? Has my thinking changed based on this discussion? If yes, what has changed?
2. How is the Mystery of the Trinity relevant to me? What are the implications in terms of *theosis*?

355 Luke 22:42.

THE DIVINE PRESENCE WE ENCOUNTER

The Operations of God

"He has bestowed on us the precious and very great promises, so that through them you may come to share in the divine nature..."
(2 Pet. 1:4)

"We should fight ... until we come to perceive unceasingly the energy of the Holy Spirit within us and rise with the Lord's help above [the] passions."[356]
(St. Diadochos of Photiki)

Opening Scripture Reading

2 Pet. 1:1-11 (The Power of God's Promise; Sharing in the Divine Nature).

Introduction

Let us review some key points. First, we began with our conclusion: that our God is ineffable and inconceivable, completely beyond our human comprehension; "the God who made the universe and holds it in existence"[357] desires to have a personal, intimate relationship with us. While we cannot comprehend God in his essence, we can experience God in the ordinariness of life. God is active in creation, not just a passive participant or disinterested spectator. Further, per Rahner's theological approach, it is through these experiences that we can learn something about God.

---

356 St. Diadochos of Photike, "On Spiritual Knowledge and Discrimination," in *The Philokalia: The Complete Text*, vol. 1, comp. St. Nikodimos of the Holy Mountain and St. Makarios of Corinth, trans. G.E.H. Palmer, P. Sherrard, and K. Ware (London: Faber & Faber, 1979), 294-5.

357 Clarence Enzler, *Everyone's Way of the Cross* (Notre Dame, IN: Ave Maria Press, 1986), Station No. 3.

We also described human destiny as union with God, a union of two distinct natures. God remains God in his essence, and we retain our human nature. In other words, God invites us to participate in the life of the Trinity, but we do not become part of the Trinity. We also noted that we could not achieve this destiny without divine assistance (*synergeia*). Our union with God is brought about through deifying grace of the Holy Spirit. Living the God-like virtues in the spiritual life prepares one to become a recipient of such grace (*theosis*).

Finally, as we see our human limitations, our inner longing for something more, we develop a sense of God as Infinite Being. Remember St. Gregory of Nyssa's description of the experience of our dissatisfaction. We also discussed our striving for the infinite horizon and the concept of *theosis*, the incremental transformation through our striving to draw closer to God by practicing the God-like virtues to achieve our ultimate destiny. These key concepts provide the groundwork for this next topic, which will describe how we can genuinely experience God, who is always active in his creation.

When we experience God through his operations, we will consider two different perspectives. The first is the Eastern Christian concept of God's operations as uncreated energies, also referred to as deifying grace; the other is a Western Christian concept of uncreated grace, as defined by Rahner. In each case, these theologians attempt to explain how human beings, who cannot know God in his essence, can genuinely experience God and have a relationship with him. For both, God's interaction with his creation is through his operations.

Scriptural Context of *Theosis*

Before delving into these two approaches, let us first consider the common scriptural foundation for this concept of union with God. One of the primary scriptural references related to *theosis* is 2 Peter

1:4: God has bestowed on us the "precious and very great promises, so that through them [we] may come to *share* in the divine nature" (NABRE 2011). Other translations say, "*sharers* in the divine nature" (AMP, AMPC), "*partakers* of the divine nature" (NASB, ESV, and KJV 1900), or "*participants* of the divine nature" (NRSV). In all these translations, the meaning is similar. We are *sharers, partakers,* or *participants* in the divine nature,[358] but we do not *become* the divine nature. This scriptural reference is foundational in understanding the concept of a union between two distinct natures because the ultimate promise of Christianity is access to God,[359] union with God, to become God-like, but not becoming God.

Eastern Christian Perspective: The Operations of God as Uncreated Energies

St. Gregory Palamas is the primary figure associated with the Eastern Christian theological concept of uncreated energies. Palamas, first and foremost, was a monk and mystic for more than 20 years on Mount Athos and only later in life named Archbishop of Thessaloniki. His primary emphasis was "upon *theosis* as the true goal of all human endeavor."[360] Palamas and, in general, Eastern Orthodox theology gravitate to the idea that divine transcendence is a property of God. The God of Sacred Scripture "is a 'hidden God' who only reveals himself when he so desires and on conditions which he himself fixes."[361] There is a belief that God willingly does all the work regarding humanity's ability to achieve divinization, as long as the human person freely consents through the perseverance necessary to align self-will with the divine will. This reinforces that divinization can only be achieved through collaboration (*synergeia*).

358 The Greek word for "divine" is *theios* (Strong's G2304), which means *of God.*

359 See Doru Costache, "Experiencing the Divine Life: Levels of Participation in St. Gregory Palamas' *On the Divine and Deifying Participation,*" *Phronema* 26(1) (2011), 9.

360 Gerry Russo, "Rahner and Palamas: A Unity of Grace," *St. Vladimir's Theological Quarterly* 32(2) (1988), 160.

361 Ibid.

1. The Operations of God in his Creation

How can we know something about God? We can experience God through his activity, his "operations." We experience God as he reveals himself through grace, light, wisdom, goodness, love, and life, just to name a few ways.[362] Stăniloae explained it this way:

> God in his entirety makes himself known known to us and, frequently enough, causes us to *experience* him through each operation and, through them, the same God in his entirety makes himself known to us as bearer of a number of general attributes. God is good. But how many nuances does this goodness of his not have as we see it shown to us in innumerable operations that correspond to the needs we have at each moment and the needs of all? Through his attributes, God makes something of his being evident to us, but this something is made specific within one vast and uninterrupted symphony of continually new acts that guide creation and each element of it separately toward the final goal of union with him.[363]

Thus, God's essence is beyond our reach, but he comes to us through a range of experiences that are intended to draw us closer to him. Stăniloae described these operations of God, above, as "new acts that guide creation" for "the needs we have at each moment." In other words, if we are open to God, he gives us what we need when we need it. Through our experiences of God's operations, we begin to gain an understanding of the attributes of God: love, mercy, compassion, wisdom, omnipotence, omniscience, beauty,

362 See Stăniloae, "Revelation and Knowledge of the Triune God," 126.
363 Ibid., 128.

etc. Through these operations or energies, God manifests himself to his creation in unlimited ways.

Here is an example illustrating this point. One of the divine attributes of God is love. A person facing a desperate situation prays faithfully to God for guidance through seemingly endless darkness. At some point, an unexpected door opens, revealing a path forward, a light in the darkness. The person finds immense joy and relief in finding an answer to the desperate situation through prayer, and the uncertainty in his or her life can now be overcome. This is an experience of God's love (the divine attribute) through his operations or a new act (revealing an answer to the person in need). So, in this case, the person does not *know* God in his essence. God remains a mystery, but the person has *experienced* the love of God, a divine attribute, through a specific action of revelation. Thus, the person can know *something* about God, having experienced his love toward his creation through an act of revelation. This is a genuine experience of God, and the experience is through his operations, to which God has made himself known.

What does love look like? The reality is that we cannot see love; however, we can infer something about the attribute of love through our life experiences and, as such, know something about love. For example, we can experience a genuine act of love by a neighbor; however, we can never plumb the true depths of love. It is the same with God. We can learn something about him through our experiences in life, and these experiences draw us toward God, who reveals himself to us in our faithfulness and needs. However, God is limitless.

We could also say that we *participate* in this operation. In the case of the person seeking an answer, she directly experienced relief, a reward for perseverance and struggle. Consider, too, that God can reveal himself in different ways. Through prayer, an idea may be given, involving a solution not previously considered. Alternatively, we may suddenly hear something in a homily that resonates with us, unlocking a missing piece. Perhaps God sends someone to us at the right time with the advice we need. The point is that there are endless possibilities of how God can choose to reveal himself to us. We simply need to be constantly open to him and his presence.

2. Differentiating Essence and Uncreated Energies

Theologians historically faced the challenge of explaining how the union of two distinct natures takes place. St. Gregory Palamas developed a theological framework to explain this union, creating a distinction between the essence of God that is beyond us and the operations of God that we can experience, the latter of which he called "uncreated energies." Essentially, he develops the same conclusions: We cannot know God in his essence; however, we can know something about God through his energies (operations). Palamas indicated the only true knowledge of God comes through direct revelation and personal experience.[364] Consider the case of the person facing a desperate situation. God revealed an answer and the person experienced relief.

These energies are operations of God coming from his attributes (e.g., God's love), they are considered part of God, thus "uncreated," not something created such as a human being. The argument is that if the energies we experience are created, we do not have the ability to truly experience a genuine encounter with God or be in a relationship with him. "The bridge between humanity and God collapses together

364 See Costache, 13.

with the possibility of [having] a direct experience of God in the present life."[365] Therefore, Palamas argues that these energies of God must be uncreated. He further explains that our union with God occurs through our *participation* in these uncreated energies. Consider the scriptural reference above regarding human destiny to become "sharers," "partakers" or "participants" in the divine nature.

As humanity, we have a desire for transcendence, the finite being drawn to infinity, which describes our desire for God (knowingly or unknowingly). Our true, divinely created purpose is union with God, and we continually strive toward achieving this through divinization. Palamas wrote:

> We unite ourselves to God, in so far as this is possible, by participating in the godlike virtues and by entering into communion with Him through prayer and praise. Because the virtues are similitudes of God, to *participate* in them puts us in a fit state to receive the Divine.[366]

Think of it this way: if humanity strives to fulfill its destiny by pursuing God-like virtues with humility as the foundation, then we will continue to experience the energies of God as he reveals himself to us, suggesting an ongoing relationship, and leading us on the path to divinization.

3. Essence and Energies: An Analogy

Archimandrite George Kapsanis, the former abbot of Grigoriou Monastery on Mount Athos, differentiates between essence and energies through an analogy of electricity. There are three ways to consider this situation. First, if we could unite directly with God, we would lose our distinct nature.

365 Ibid.
366 St. Gregory Palamas, "Three Texts on Prayer and Purity of Heart," 343.

Archimandrite George writes, "If we were able to unite with the essence of God, we would become gods by essence. Then everything would become a god."[367] Thus, God would be diffused to an indistinct power dispersed throughout the world—in men, animals, and objects.[368] This is what Hinduism espouses. Thus, there must be some distinction between divine and human nature. "If we grasp a bare electric wire, we will die."[369]

Second, if the energies were created, we would no longer be able to enter a relationship with or participate in the divine life. In this case, only God would have his essence, and we could not participate in this essence. God would remain a self-sufficient God, closed within himself, and unable to communicate with his creation.[370] If the energies of God were not of the divine essence, we could not be deified nor united with God, because nothing created can deify.

Thus, we have the third possibility, which is the Eastern Christian theological position that God communicates himself through his energies, and the distance between God and humanity is effectively bridged.[371] As Archimandrite George noted, our touching of a live wire (the essence) causes death. However, he adds, "if we connect a lamp to the same wire, we are illuminated. We see, enjoy, and are assisted by, the energy of the electric current, but we are unable to grasp its essence."[372] This concept is similar to Rahner's perspectives on uncreated grace.

367 Ibid.
368 Cf. Ibid., 39–40.
369 Archimandrite George, *Theosis*, 39.
370 Cf. Ibid., 40.
371 Cf. Ibid., 41.
372 Ibid., 39.

4. The Uncreated Energies: Light and Grace

One other thought: the two most common references to uncreated energies are grace, as in deifying grace, and light.[373] Grace could encompass various experiences of God, such as the person facing a desperate situation. We described her experience of God's love, mercy, and compassion during her time of need. All these operations or energies could be broadly categorized as God's grace and, as such, uncreated grace (part of who God is). Rahner has a similar perspective about experiencing God, who comes to us in our everyday human experience.

There is also the idea that mystics who achieve a certain level of pure prayer can experience union with God in this life. This concept is not unique to Eastern Orthodox spirituality. Western Christian mystics such as St. Teresa of Ávila and St. John of the Cross said that in the deepest levels of prayer, there is a direct experience of God. In St. Gregory Palamas's theological framework, he described light as an uncreated energy because many mystics experienced a sense of brightness, light, or radiance. St. Gregory was a monk and mystic who spent more than twenty years in the monasteries of Mount Athos,[374] which is the epicenter of Eastern Orthodox spirituality, especially regarding the hesychast tradition (Jesus Prayer),[375] faithfully practiced and preserved by monks for centuries. Practitioners of hesychast prayer report experiences of light, which creates a sense of the divine presence during prayer. Mystics also mention "the development of a very

373 See St. George Greek Orthodox Cathedral, "God's Uncreated Energies," http://www.stgeorgegreenville.org/OrthodoxLife/Chapter2/Chap2-5.html.

374 John Meyendorff, "Doctrine of Grace in St. Gregory Palamas." *St. Vladimir's Seminary Quarterly* 2(2) (Winter 1954), 20.

375 From *hesychia*, which in Greek means stillness, watchfulness, and interior silence of the heart. Beginning with the Early Desert Fathers, this referred to a unique form of contemplative prayer known as the hesychast tradition of prayer, which is also sometimes referred to as Prayer of the Heart or, more commonly, the Jesus Prayer.

intense feeling" during the process of the soul's ascent to God.[376] According to the hesychast tradition, a holy person who is completely purified (through prayer, ascetical practices, etc.) attains union with the Divine and experiences a vision of divine radiance.[377] This radiance is believed to be the same light manifested to Jesus's disciples on Mount Tabor at the Transfiguration. Accordingly, this radiance is sometimes referred to as "Tabor Light."[378] In *The Triads*, his defense of the hesychast tradition, Palamas wrote:

> But it is not yet union, unless the Paraclete (Holy Spirit) illumines from on high the man who attains in prayer the stage which is superior to the highest natural possibilities, and who is awaiting the promise of the Father, and by his revelation ravishes him to the contemplation of light.[379]

The notion of the Holy Spirit enlightening the person from on high reminds us that deifying grace of the Holy Spirit enables a union with God. "Superior to the highest natural possibilities" refers to transcendence, which is that which every person innately desires.

This experience of light described by Palamas and other hesychasts prompted Barlaam of Calabria to denounce it as a heresy.[380] From this controversy came the rejection of the concept of uncreated energies by the Christian West. The

376 Ivan V. Popov, "The Idea of Deification in the Early Eastern Church," in *Theosis: Deification in Christian Doctrine*, vol. 2, ed. Vladimir Kharlamov (Eugene, OR: Pickwick Publications, 2011), 75.

377 Union with the Divine is not unique to the hesychast prayer tradition. Well-known examples of Western saints with similar experiences include the Spanish mystics St. Teresa of Ávila and St. John of the Cross. What is unique to the hesychast tradition is the experience of light and the belief this is the same light as experienced by Christ on Mount Tabor at the Transfiguration.

378 See "Tabor Light," *Wikipedia*.

379 St. Gregory Palamas, *The Triads*, trans. Nicholas Gendle (Mahwah, NJ: Paulist Press, 1983), 65.

380 See "Hesychast Controversy," *Wikipedia*.

Orthodox position is that "Divine uncreated light has the purpose of uniting creation with God."[381] Proponents would point to the Gospel of John, for example, as the Gospel of Light (Jesus is referred to as "the light of the human race; the light that shines in the darkness, and the darkness has not overcome it"[382]) and the Letters of John ("God is light, and in him there is no darkness at all"[383]). They also point to the light encountered by St. Paul on the road to Damascus.[384]

Palamas took the position that if there was no experience of the Divine (actual divine energies, as opposed to something created), then a person could not transcend nature and could not be born from above.[385] Consider, too, Jesus's statement to Nicodemus: "Amen, amen, I say to you no one can enter the kingdom of God without being born of water and the spirit." He adds, "You must be born from above."[386] In other words, a true experience of the Divine is required for a person to transcend his or her nature. Rahner would concur; it is about the experience.

Palamas describes three levels of participation or spiritual perceptions relative to communion with God, through which one can progress through spiritual practices and perfection. He refers to these as learning (sensorial experience), understanding (reasoning, intellectual), and enlightenment

381 St. George Greek Orthodox Cathedral, "God's Uncreated Energies." Reference made to a quote by St. Maximos the Confessor.

382 John 1:3–5.

383 1 John 1:5.

384 See Acts 9:3–4.

385 See Costache, 14. He quotes from Palamas' *On the Divine and Deifying Participation*: "If the deifying gift of the Spirit bestowed upon the saints [holy people] is created, like some natural feature or resemblance even though deified the saints could not transcend nature and would not be born of God." Like most Orthodox writers, Costache refers to *saints*, which means those pursuing holiness in this life.

386 See John 3:1–21. The conversation between Jesus and Nicodemus.

(noetic,[387] spiritual[388]), the latter being the ultimate height of contemplation. This last stage is the one "that transcends natural capacity of the mind."[389] Consider the human desire for transcendency and, through our creation, we have capacity to achieve it. It should be noted that these three levels of participation are not dissimilar to those described by Western Christian mystics: purgative, illuminative, and unitive. Palamas taught that only the latter of these levels was a true, direct experience of God and, as such, one of uncreated light, an "immediate and deifying experience."[390] Given Palamas's Athonite experience, he states that the spiritual elders make deliberate efforts at ascetical practices, trying to master their nature to attain a measure of detachment or personal freedom—surrendering more and more to the presence of God. Participation in the deifying experience, experiencing the energies, is how Palamas said the union between human and divine occurs. For the dedicated monastic mystics, this union can occur in this life, albeit through temporary experiences. However, for most, the spiritual life is a gradual transformation caused by increasingly saying yes to God, drawing closer to him. This transformation, *theosis*, is never completed until the next life at the resurrection of the dead.

Finally, in terms of Palamite thinking, there is delineation between participation in the uncreated energies, such as those experienced by the Holy Fathers through hesychast prayer ("immediate and deifying participation"), and providential or mediated participation in the "effect" of God's uncreated

387 *Noetic* is the adjective form of *nous*. The *nous* is the rational part of the soul (some say the mind). In the hesychast prayer tradition, the objective is to place the *nous* into the heart in order to achieve stillness and be free of distractions. It is to feel the presence of the divine, not to rationalize or think about. This can only be achieved with great practice and discipline. We will discuss prayer as a means of encounter in a later topic.

388 See Costache, 14–5.

389 Ibid., 12.

390 Ibid., 16.

energies.[391] This providential participation, the experience of uncreated grace, would be analogous to our theoretical person who faced a desperate situation and experienced the energies or operations of God. This person's experience was less direct (sensorial) compared to that of the mystic engaged in the highest form of contemplation. Still, the experiences of God through his operations continue to draw us into a deeper relationship with him. In the example of Rahner's infinite horizon, we experience our limitedness in striving for the limitlessness. Palamas taught, "All are in God yet not all are equally receptive to God's presence. The Spirit shines wholly and continually to all creation yet the receptive capabilities vary from one being to another."[392]

While not all Orthodox theologians accept the uncreated light as Tabor Light, most believe in an experience of light and the presence of the Divine. The monks clearly have some type of mystical experience through their prolonged practice of the Jesus Prayer. It is not whether God's presence can be felt; rather, it is whether this is *uncreated* light or *uncreated* energy, as Palamas would argue.

Pope St. John Paul II, in addressing the hesychast controversy, prefaced his comments, "We must not forget what unites us is greater than what divides us."[393]

> The hesychast controversy marked another distinctive moment in Eastern theology. In the East, hesychasm means a method of prayer characterized by a deep tranquility of spirit, which is engaged in constant contemplation of God by invoking the name of Jesus. There was

391 Ibid., 16.

392 Ibid., 17.

393 Pope St. John Paul II, "Eastern Theology has Enriched the Whole Church," Angelus address, August 11, 1996 (Rome: L'Osservatore Romano, 1996), no. 1.

> no lack of tension with the Catholic viewpoint on certain aspects of this practice. However, we should acknowledge the good intentions which guided the defense of this spiritual method, that is, to emphasize the concrete possibility that man is given to unite himself with the Triune God in the intimacy of his heart, in that deep union of grace which Eastern theology likes to describe with the particularly powerful term of "*theosis*." 'divinization'[394]

While not trying to resolve the controversy associated with uncreated energies, in particular the concept of uncreated light, the Pope acknowledges the spirit of tranquility associated with practice and the ability of a person to experience intimacy with God—both important to the process of divinization. There is a grace associated with the prayer, and there is clearly an experience of the divine presence.

Historically, the concept of uncreated energies has been a major obstacle between East and West. The Roman Catholic Church initially rejected the concept. However, in recent years, there has been a more positive view of Palamite thinking, a better understanding of his concept of essence and energies, and it is no longer considered an insurmountable theological division between Roman Catholicism and Eastern Orthodoxy.[395]

5. Concluding Thoughts on Palamas's Perspectives

Our primary takeaway should be that we can experience

394 Ibid., no. 2.

395 See Jeffrey D. Finch, "Neo-Palamism: Divinizing Grace, and the Breach between East and West," in *Partakers of the Divine Nature: The History and Development of Deification in the Christian Traditions*, ed. Michael J. Christensen and Jeffery A. Wittung (Grand Rapids, MI: Baker Publishing Group, 2008), 243–45. French argues that Palamas's thinking is compatible with Roman Catholic teaching and just another way of approaching an ineffable mystery.

the operations or uncreated energies of God in our daily lives as he chooses to reveal himself. Essentially, if we are faithful in the spiritual life—overcoming the passions and cultivating the God-like virtues—God will give us what we need when we need it based on our perseverance.

Western Christian Perspective: The Operations of God as Uncreated Grace

We have noted that Rahner emphasized God's self-communication and the human capacity to experience God (*capex Dei*). This self-communication was not a word about God, but the gift of God's very self ("Giver as gift").[396] Rahner wrote, "The term 'self-communication' is really intended to signify that God in his own most proper reality makes himself the innermost constitutive element of man."[397] The first distinctive feature of Rahner's understanding of grace is that it is, most fundamentally, God's self-communication."[398] Because God gives himself to people and dwells within them, they are gradually transformed.[399] Thus, if the Giver is gift and the gift is grace, it would be uncreated because the gift is God's very self. With the divine indwelling, we gradually can overcome bad habits and particular sins—the passions—to practice the virtues, and to progress through our spiritual lives to our divinely designated destiny. Similar to the Eastern Christian perspective, Rahner believes this involves gradual transformation.

God's self-communication can be understood through our finite life experiences when considered against a horizon of infinite possibility. He is calling us to something greater than ourselves. "A second distinctive feature of Rahner's understanding of grace has to do with where Rahner *locates* grace, with where he understands

396 Heidi Russell, "Karl Rahner: Sin, Grace, Salvation, and Revelation," 7.
397 Rahner, *Foundations of Christian Faith*, 116.
398 Kilby, 21.
399 Ibid., 22.

grace to be offered and perhaps received."[400] He believes grace is experienced in our "transcendental experience," or our striving to move past our limitedness toward the horizon of infinite possibility. It is in this striving that we experience God's grace.[401] Grace can move us into a closer relationship with God. Rahner uses the term "unthematic" to describe the experiences of God amid daily human experience. He wrote:

> The transcendental experience of God in the Holy Spirit is, however, given only unthematically in everyday human experience, where it is overlaid and hidden by concern with actual realities with which we are taken up in our social world and environment. This transcendental experience of God in the Holy Spirit in everyday life remains anonymous, unreflective, and unthematic.[402]

The notion of the Holy Spirit in our lives as being "unthematic" directly parallels the Eastern Christian perspective. First, consider what Jesus tells Nicodemus: "The wind blows where it wills, and you can hear the sound it makes, but you do not know where it comes from or where it goes; so it is with everyone who is born of the Spirit."[403] This implies the Spirit operates in an unstructured way. Second, consider Stăniloae's perspective of how we experience God through his operations in "new acts that guide creation" for "the needs we have at each moment." In other words, there is no simple list of God's operations or energies. We experience these energies as grace and, from these experiences, we can infer the divine attributes of God (love, mercy, compassion, etc.). We experience these operations in our particular need. These operations are unstructured or, using Rahner's term, unthematic. We cannot try to rationalize these encounters with words; rather, we simply need to

400 Ibid., 23.
401 Ibid.
402 Rahner, *The Practice of Faith*, 80.
403 John 3:8.

experience them. Through these experiences, we begin to understand something about God: his love, mercy, compassion, forgiveness.

Using the earlier analogy, the person facing a desperate situation experiences his or her limitedness (finitude) in attempting to resolve the situation. Yet, as Rahner taught, human beings have a capacity and openness to the self-communicating God. It is in this striving that we can experience grace; it is offered, and we can be open to it or reject it. Accepting this grace, the offer of God's very self, we can modify our transcendence, which has "the effect of altering our relationship to our horizon, to the 'mystery' [God] which surrounds us."[404] In other words, we are drawn into a closer relationship with God.

God gives himself in grace, yet he remains a mystery because we can never surpass God on the horizon of infinite possibility. Accordingly, as Palamite teaches, we can never really know God, but we can learn something about him through our life experiences; we can experience God's grace, his gift of himself. In other words, without ceasing to be God, ungraspable and incomprehensible to the human mind, God somehow draws near and offers himself to us.[405] As Rahner wrote:

> A man as spirit in love for truth reaches—so to speak—the frontier of the absolute (i.e., God as horizon), about which he has no longer anything to say, which sustains and is not sustained: the absolute which is there even though we cannot reach out and touch it, which—if we talk about it—as again concealed behind our talk as its ground.[406]

In other words, it remains about the experience because in talking about it, the reality of what happens is concealed in mystery (God is mystery), and words cannot properly express our experiences of the

404 Kilby24–5.
405 Ibid., 25.
406 Rahner, *The Practice of Faith*, 63–64.

Divine. Another way to consider this is that it is about the experience itself, and not the intellectualizing of it.

A third distinctive feature of Rahner's concept of grace is its universality. It is not limited to selected individuals but always offered to everyone. God is always drawing near, always offering himself to humanity. "Grace...always surrounds man, even the sinner and unbeliever, as the inescapable setting of his existence."[407] Palamas would agree: "The Spirit shines wholly and continually to all creation."[408]

To summarize Rahner's view of uncreated grace: (1) It is the gift of God's self; (2) it is offered, and we experience it in our striving for transcendence, pushing beyond our limitations; and (3) it is universally available to all, including sinners and nonbelievers. This offer of grace requires a response, and humanity is free to choose. We can reject or accept God's offer of self, "but to protect the gratuity of grace, one must acknowledge that *acceptance* of God's grace is always undergirded and empowered by that same grace."[409] In other words, God's offer can only "be accepted in and through the grace of God."[410] We cannot save ourselves. Salvation is only through God's gracious gift of self, which, reemphasizing what was said above, "is a permanent offer to every human being."[411] Uncreated grace is linked to the Incarnation [God's gift of self, "Giver as gift"], to the indwelling of the Holy Spirit in the individual's soul, and to the Church through membership.[412]

To understand Rahner, it is important to reemphasize his belief that uncreated grace is meant to be experienced. Theologian Mark Fischer authored a book paraphrasing Rahner's major work, *Foundations*. When summarizing Rahner's concept of grace, Fischer raises this

---

407 See Rahner, *Theological Investigations*, vol. 4, 56. Cited in Kilby, 25.

408 Costache, 17.

409 Heidi Russell, "Efficacious and Sufficient Grace: God's One Offer of Self-Communication as Accepted or Rejected," *Philosophy & Theology* 22(1–2) (2010), 353.

410 Ibid., 361. Consider that we as human beings are striving toward God, who is infinite, while we ourselves are finite. We need divine assistance to proceed (*synergeia*).

411 Ibid., 362. It is permanent because the Incarnation is irrevocable.

412 Thomas Louis Knoebel, "Grace in the Theology of Karl Rahner: A Systematic Presentation" (PhD diss., Fordham University, 1980).

question: What is the difference between grace and the other basic structures of transcendence (mystery, freedom of choice, openness, created versus Creator, etc.)?[413] The answer is that grace remains free and cannot be predicted or manipulated. While grace is hidden, it is not beyond our possibility to experience it.[414]

1. An Illustrative Example

A distinctive feature of uncreated grace is that it is freely offered. We experience this grace when we face our finiteness and strive for transcendence, which is our effort to move beyond these limitations. There is a profound meaning to this statement, which is best illustrated through an example.

A prominent man in Los Angeles had a son who was well educated and had a promising future. Unfortunately, he was murdered by a gang member, who was about the same age as the victim and who had committed the crime as part of his gang initiation rite. Without question, it was a senseless murder, and the young gang member received a very long prison sentence. The father of the victim struggled with the senselessness of the crime and had a hostile view of the gang member. Consider this in light of our discussion above. We know that God's mercy and forgiveness is infinite. Any sin can be forgiven with genuine repentance. However, the father's personal limitations initially kept him from forgiving. Consider what Rahner is telling us: We experience grace when we transcend our limits.

A year after the trial, the father of the gang member reached out to the father of the victim. The father of the victim was initially reluctant, but eventually agreed. When they met, the victim's father found his anger diminishing as he began

413 See Fischer, 44.
414 Ibid.

to realize the father of the gang member had also lost a son, first to poverty, then to the gang, and now to a lengthy prison term. He found they had much in common. At the end of the meeting, the father of the victim accepted the condolences of the father of the gang member. Now consider the element of grace. The father of the victim, limited by human frailty, initially was unable to forgive. Later, his heart was moved to compassion. He experienced grace as he moved beyond his previous limitation—transcendence—and he began to understand more about the compassionate heart of Jesus, compassion being a divine attribute, knowledge of which is inferred by the experience of grace.

Consider, too, Stăniloae's perspective of "new acts that guide creation" for "the needs we have at each moment." In this case, God revealed himself to the father of the victim through the father of the gang member. Remember, God is active in his creation and can reveal himself in many ways.

After the initial meeting, the two fathers met several more times to share their mutual pain of loss. Afterward, the father of the victim felt an urge to visit the young gang member in prison, which he did, and *forgave* him! He could not bring his son back, but he could empathize with the other father who had also "lost" a son. Again, consider Rahner's concept of experiencing grace through the experience of our limitedness—in this case, inability to forgive—and when striving to move beyond the limitation, forgiving the gang member. This is another example of transcendence, the gradual progress in moving beyond our limitedness.

Over time, the two fathers began to speak together to audiences of parents about the problems of gangs, violence, and remaining engaged with their children. Both had pain to share, and it had an impact on people who heard the message. Further, the young gang member repented, embraced Christianity, and asked the father of the victim to forgive him. At the first parole hearing, the father of victim spoke on behalf of the gang member, who received a reduced sentence. Again, consider the transcendence that occurred in the victim's father, from the initial limitation of being unable to forgive, to embracing the gang member and advocating for him. God granted this father the grace of conversion and change of heart. That grace also influenced the gang member and his father as well as many people to whom the two fathers spoke.

This example illustrates how uncreated grace can gradually transform an individual striving for transcendence, moving past human limitations. Through this conversion of heart, one begins to understand the infinite compassion and forgiveness of God, inferred from the experience, and one continues to strive for the horizon of infinite possibility. In turn, this provides a perspective on the spiritual life and the gradual, incremental process of divinization. Finally, we can appreciate how God chooses to reveal himself, unique to every circumstance. For the victim's father, it began through the visit by the father of the gang member and through his humility and desire to offer comfort. This is an example of God's operations, of his active participation in his creation. The key is for s to be attuned to the presence of God and open to the offer of salvation.

Summary

We have previously described God as beyond human comprehension. However, despite this, our God desires to enter into a relationship with us and draw us closer to him and our divinely intended purpose: union with him. We cannot become God, but this union involves participating in the divine nature through the deifying grace of the Holy Spirit. We experience God's divine nature through his operations, active presence, and participation in his creation. We considered two complementary perspectives on God's operations, one from the Christian East, uncreated energies, and one from the Christian West, uncreated grace. Both gave us an appreciation for how God operates, and through these operations, we can infer something about God, such as his divine attributes: love, mercy, compassion, forgiveness. If we are faithful in the spiritual life, God will give us what we need when we need it, depending on our perseverance. We can begin to understand God's infiniteness—as an example, God's infinite willingness and desire to forgive—in light of our human frailties and limitations. A parallel in the Gospel is the Parable of the Prodigal Son.[415] The Father is capable of forgiving the prodigal son of an egregious and unforgivable sin (infinite mercy), whereas the older son, who was not harmed per se, could not forgive (limitedness).

The following schematic provides a summary:

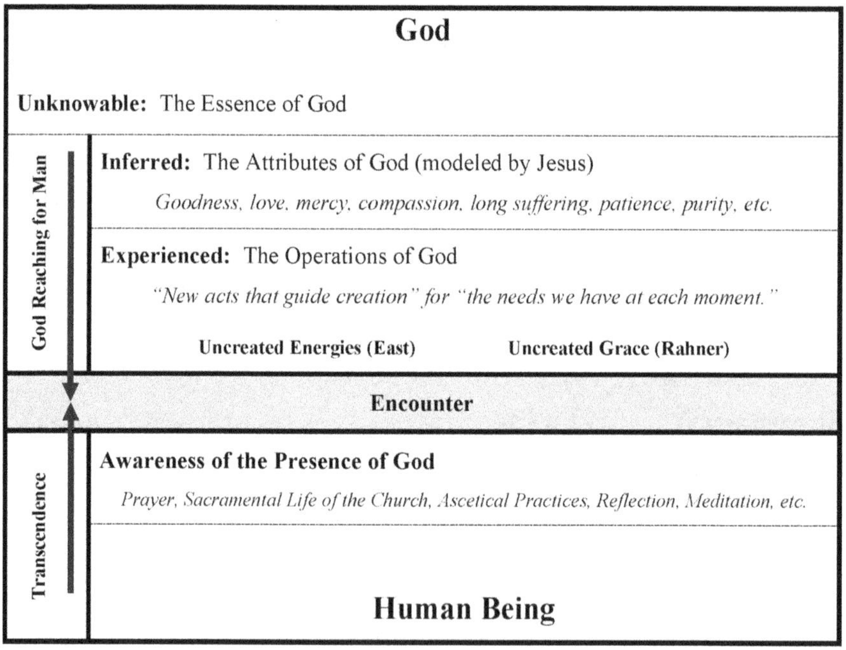

God

Unknowable: The Essence of God

God Reaching for Man

Inferred: The Attributes of God (modeled by Jesus)

Goodness, love, mercy, compassion, long suffering, patience, purity, etc.

Experienced: The Operations of God

"New acts that guide creation" for "the needs we have at each moment."

Uncreated Energies (East) **Uncreated Grace (Rahner)**

Encounter

Transcendence

Awareness of the Presence of God

Prayer, Sacramental Life of the Church, Ascetical Practices, Reflection, Meditation, etc.

Human Being

415 See Luke 15:11-32.

Rahner makes a profound statement for us to reflect upon: "The devout Christian of the future will either be a 'mystic,' one who has 'experienced' something, or he will cease to be anything at all." Stăniloae supported with a famous axiom, "If you are a theologian, you will pray truly. And if you pray truly, you are a theologian." What both are saying to us is that it is about our experiences of God, the encounter, whereby we come to understand something about God. It is not about intellectualizing or understanding doctrines. In fact, Rahner used the term "unthematic" for such experiences, meaning unstructured and beyond pat explanations. Thus, both theologians and Palamas tell of our need to be attuned to the presence of the Divine in his creation and to recognize his activities and operations when we experience them.

Reflection Questions

1. How have I personally experienced the presence of God in my life? Recall a specific experience and write it down. Remember the specifics. How did God reveal himself to me?

2. We have described grace as the divine assistance we receive to move beyond our human limitations, generally when we strive to be more God-like and live the virtues. When have I found myself moved beyond my limitations (overcoming an inability to forgive, overcoming stereotypes or personal prejudices, suddenly moved with compassion for a stranger)? Describe the experience in detail. Did I recognize God revealing himself to me through this particular experience? When I look back, do I view that experience differently today? If yes, why? Be detailed.

Part 3

Means of Encounter

Introduction

In Part 1, we discussed our desire for encounter. Our God, who is beyond human comprehension, desires a personal, intimate relationship with each of us. Because of our desire for greater purpose and meaning in life, which is part of our human nature, we are seeking something infinite. The reality is that only God can fill our infinite longing. This longing gives us a simple experience of God, a sense of Infinite Being. Further, we are created in the divine image and, because of this, have the capacity to experience God and our divinely created purpose, union with him. To pursue this destiny, we must strive for a spiritual transformation.

In Part 2, we discussed the Divine we encounter: God the Creator, Jesus as the image of the invisible God, and the Holy Spirit. We considered this Trinity a model for our relationship and created purpose, union with God. Our union is enabled by our ability to share or participate in the divine nature. We also discussed one means of experiencing God, through his operations, by which God remains active in his creation. Through our experience of these actions, being attuned to the presence of God, we begin to understand something about God and ourselves because we are created in his image.

In our last topic, we concluded with a statement by Rahner: "The devout Christian of the future will either be a 'mystic,' one who has 'experienced' something, or he will cease to be anything at all." It is about experiencing God; it is about the encounter. However, to experience God, we must be attuned to his presence. In this next series of topics, we will examine means of encounter to help us become more spiritually attuned.

Prayer
A: General Overview

"Lord, teach us to pray..."
(Luke 11:1)

"The true beginning of prayer is warmth of the heart, which scorches passions, fills the heart with the joy and delight of unshakable love, and strengthens it with sure conviction."[416]
(St. Gregory of Sinai)

Opening Gospel Reading

Luke 11:1-13 (Jesus's teachings on Prayer).

The Significance of Prayer

Patriarch Daniel of Romania wrote:

> The first and ultimate source of love, of true joy and true peace, is *prayer*. Nothing in this world can replace prayer. Therefore, prayer as communion with God is the life of the Christian soul.[417]

Metropolitan Archbishop Antony Bloom adds, "Prayer is the search for God, encounter with God, and going beyond this encounter in

416 St. Gregory of Sinai, "Instruction to Hesychasts," in *Writings from the Philokalia in Prayer of the Heart*, trans. E. Kadloubovsky and G.E.H. Palmer (London: Faber and Faber, 1992), 90.

417 Patriarch Daniel, *Confessing the Truth in Love*, 106.

communion."[418] The Holy Spirit allows the Risen Jesus to dwell in the hearts of believers. St. Teresa of Ávila believed the gate of entry to the heart is prayer.[419] Through prayer, our encounters with God through the Church and in the Holy Mysteries become more personal, more intimate, when we enter into an even deeper relationship with him. Prayer and the sacramental life of the Church were always meant to go together because one without the other leads to an incomplete spirituality. However, it seems as if we have forgotten to teach people how to pray, which reduces the richness of the encounter with Jesus in the Sacraments and the Liturgy.

Stăniloae wrote, "In general it is a good thing to pray in all circumstances, because in itself prayer is a means of making the soul sensitive to the presence of God."[420] God is ever-present within his creation, and through prayer, we become more attuned to him, especially in everyday life. We do not need to be mystics in the classical sense, such as the monks on Mount Athos or St. Teresa of Ávila. We can still experience the Holy Spirit's movements through greater personal awareness. Solitude is less a place than a state of being. Consistent prayer draws us more deeply into the endless mystery that is God.

The Eastern Church has a rich mystical prayer tradition focused on *hesychia*, which refers to inner stillness of the heart. Such prayer is called noetic, hesychast, Prayer of the Heart, and most commonly, the Jesus Prayer. Some monks simply refer to it as "the prayer." All refer to the same practice: the repetitive invocation of the name of Jesus to create stillness in one's heart. Prayer is person-to-person contact with God, so the soul must be open, calm, and serene to meet him and experience his presence.[421] The importance of such prayer cannot be overstated as part of the spiritual life by which we fulfill our destiny.

---

418 Metropolitan Anthony Bloom and Georges LeFebvre, *Courage to Pray* (Crestwood, NY: St. Vladimir's Seminary Press, 1973), 5.

419 St. Teresa of Ávila, 38.

420 Stăniloae, "Revelation and Knowledge of the Triune God," 119.

421 See Raya, *The Face of God*, 212-3.

Winter is an appropriate metaphor for what the Church is experiencing today, a cooling of faith that has turned into a virtual ice age. People increasingly seek answers away from the Church, no longer convinced of the need for God or salvation. Yet this crisis of faith is not because structured religion has lost meaning, as some argue. The crisis exists because many have lost or have not been exposed to one of the most fundamental components of spiritual life: the ability to encounter Jesus through prayer. Simply put, we as a Church and a society do not know how to pray.[422] In the Early Church, personal prayer was an essential part of the mystical tradition, something still strongly emphasized in the Christian East. Some in the Christian West, such as Basil Pennington, OCSO noted that pure, contemplative prayer was the norm in the Church until the Scholastic era.[423] Thus, he and others would concur that we have lost something of our tradition, and to recover it, we can look to the Christian East.

While there have been various calls throughout the years for a deeper encounter with Jesus, in late 2019, an increased urgency for prayer as a means for renewal in the Church emerged. This was a theme stressed in books released by notable Catholic authors Matthew Kelly and Cardinal Sarah.[424] "It is time for us to become a spiritual people again,"[425] Kelly wrote, adding:

> Nothing will change a person's life like really learning how to pray. It's one of life's most powerful lessons. And yet, astonishingly, we don't teach people how to talk to God. We don't teach them to pray with their hearts in a deeply personal way. It is one of the areas

---

422 See Gabriel Bunge, OSB, *Earthen Vessels*, 9.

423 See Cyprian Consiglio, *Prayer in the Cave of the Heart: The Universal Call to Contemplation* (Collegeville, MN: The Liturgical Press, 2010), 56.

424 Matthew Kelly released *Rediscover the Saints* in August 2019, and the English translation of Robert Cardinal Sarah's book, *The Day is Now Far Spent*, was released in September 2019.

425 Matthew Kelly, *Rediscover the Saints* (Assam, India: Blue Sparrow Books, 2019), 31.

> of singular importance where we have fallen short as a Church.[426]

Cardinal Sarah wrote, "The chief preoccupation of all disciples of Jesus must be their sanctification. The first place in their lives must be given to prayer, to silent contemplation, and to the Eucharist."[427] Especially as the Church emerges from the COVID-19 crisis, as parishes reopen and the true extent of the spiritual pandemic is realized, it is time to reconnect to our spiritual roots. Elder Thaddeus of Vitovnica wrote, "The only cure for man's illness is a return to a life centered on Christ the God-man, the only one who can fulfill all of mankind's needs."[428] Archbishop Charles Chaput wrote, "Without passion in our hearts for the living person of Jesus Christ, our faith is empty. *With* it, all things are possible."[429]

A tree in winter needs to return to its roots, and so must we as a Church.

It is worth noting the different types of prayer, such as the Divine Liturgy, the Mass, the Daily Hours (Horologion), the rosary, and devotions such as the Chaplet of Divine Mercy. Our discussion, though, is specifically about contemplative prayer that fulfills the teaching of the Psalmist: "Be still and know that I am God!"[430] We come before the Lord in reverence, stripping away concerns, distractions, or thoughts.[431]

---

426 Ibid.

427 Sarah, *The Day is Now Far Spent*, 30.

428 Cf. *Our Thoughts Determine Our Lives: The Life and Teachings of Elder Thaddeus of Vitovnica*, comp. St Herman of Alaska Brotherhood, trans. Ana Smiljanic (Platina, CA: St. Herman of Alaska Brotherhood, 2017), 9.

429 Archbishop Charles J. Chaput, *Things Worth Dying For: Thoughts on a Life Worth Living* (New York, NY: Henry Holt, 2021), 238.

430 Psalm 46:10.

431 See Kallistos Ware, *The Philokalia: Master Reference Guide*, comp. Basileios S. Stapkis, ed. Gerald Eustace Howell Palmer and Philip Sherrard (Minneapolis: Light & Life Publishing Company, 2004), x. These distractions in the Eastern Christian tradition are called *logismoi*, which "are essentially a train of thoughts that befog and pollute the mind so that bit by bit it drifts away from reality into a world of fantasy and delusion. In the writings of the Desert Fathers, *logismoi* are thoughts caused by demons. They are important because all battles are won or lost first in the internal dialogue of the mind.".

As sung in the Cherubic Hymn of the Divine Liturgy, "Let us now set aside all earthly cares that we may receive the king of all." In the silence of our hearts, we are alone with God and can develop a personal, intimate relationship with him. Archbishop Joseph Raya noted:

> Masters of spirituality such as Maximos the Confessor and John Climacus insist that the activity of the soul in prayer is essentially concentrating on a divine person and a self-surrender to him in order to be united and identified with him.[432]

Recalling the axiom that a theologian is one who truly prays, we should note that prayer is theology carried through to its ultimate realization.[433]

Scriptural Foundation

Let us ground our discussion in the words of Sacred Scripture. We have mentioned that Jesus is our "way" to the Father. "Prayer is a constant motif in Luke-Acts, and the critical moments of Jesus's ministry are punctuated by prayer."[434] In the Gospel of Luke, eight specific instances of Jesus praying are mentioned, including four in which he withdraws into solitude. These occur each time before he teaches or heals. Thus, Jesus models the importance of prayer.

In the Gospel of Matthew, Jesus gives his disciples specific instructions:[435] "When you pray, go to your inner room, close the door, and pray to your Father in secret. And your Father who sees in secret will repay you."[436] Early Christians interpreted this "inner room" as the human heart, which is the core of the Jesus Prayer tradition. The

---

432 Raya, *The Face of God*, 212.

433 Ibid.

434 Luke Timothy Johnson, *The Gospel of Luke*, ed. Daniel J. Harrington. In the "Sacra Pagina" series, vol. 3 (Collegeville, MN: Liturgical Press, 1991), 69.

435 See Matt. 6:5–8. Teaching about prayer.

436 Matt. 6:7.

Desert Fathers, who emulated Jesus's withdrawal into the desert, knew that Christianity was a divinizing process that took place gradually within the human heart, an interior intersection where man and the Triune God meet.[437] Jesus also tells his disciples not to multiply words like the pagans: "Do not be like them. Your Father knows what you need before you ask."[438] The Jesus Prayer has a single petition: "Have mercy on me."[439] If God already knows our temporal needs ("give us this day our daily bread"), we pray and trust him to do so. Thus, all we truly need is to surrender to his will and invoke his mercy.

St. Paul says in his letter to the Thessalonians, "Pray without ceasing. In all circumstances, give thanks, for this is the will of God for you in Christ Jesus. Do not quench the Holy Spirit."[440] In the hesychast prayer tradition, those monks who are practitioners of the highest form of contemplation strive to maintain the prayer in their hearts day and night. Further, we experience the operations of God in his creation through the actions of the Holy Spirit. Thus, St. Paul's admonition to not quench the Holy Spirit, not to restrict or impede his actions in our lives, is apropos.

Rahner's Perspectives on Prayer

Rahner emphasizes that we come to know something about God through our human experiences. First and foremost, in his discussion on prayer, he reminds us that humanity does not "evaporate" into the essence of God. Rather, God in sober reality created an "other"—that which is not God—who, "despite being radically dependent on God, can freely stand before him and *relate* to him."[441] Rahner further emphasizes that we must develop practices of meditation and prayer,

437 See George Maloney, SJ. *Prayer of the Heart: The Contemplative Tradition of the Christian East* (Notre Dame, IN: Ave Maria Press, 2008), 19 and 43.

438 Matt. 6:8.

439 The most common form of the Jesus Prayer is: "Lord Jesus Christ, Son of God, have mercy on me, a sinner." The shorter version favored by many Greek monks is similar: "Lord Jesus Christ, have mercy on me."

440 1 Thess. 5:17–19.

441 See Rahner, *The Practice of Faith*, 85.

solitude, and endurance to develop an awareness of God. Otherwise, all we have are conceptual-thematic expressions of God that are false,[442] an intellectualized faith instead of experiential.

For Rahner, there are no words that can describe God. We cannot reduce God to talk and concepts; we can never fully understand God. Rather, through our encounters with the Divine, we obtain a "primitive experience of God," meaning that we can only have a sense of God in his mystery. This primitive experience is "unthematic"[443] and buried in our daily routines. As we cultivate our practices of prayer and meditation, we get a sense of how primitive and deeply rooted is our relationship with God.[444] Therefore, Rahner encourages us "to awaken in ourselves this primitive experience of God," this experience of God as the ineffable and incomprehensible.[445] We can experience the operations of God and recognize them if we are properly attuned, learning to recognize God in all things. St. John Chrysostom said, "If you accustom yourselves to pray fervently, you will not need instruction from your fellow servants because God himself, with no intermediary, enlightens your mind."[446] Thus, contemplative prayer is crucial in cultivating our awareness of the presence of God and entering more deeply into a relationship with him.

Significance of Hesychast Prayer

Hesychast prayer tradition began with the Desert Fathers, who withdrew to the Egyptian desert beginning in the 3rd century. It is

442 Ibid., 63.

443 In Rahner's view, concrete concepts and talk about God would be considered thematic. But God in his mystery cannot be confined to concepts and boundaries; thus, our experience of God is considered unthematic. As an example, Jesus describes the Holy Spirit to Nicodemus: "The wind blows where it wills, and you can hear the sound it makes, but you do not know where it comes from or where it goes; so it is with everyone who is born of the Spirit" (John 3:8). This is an example of Rahner's concept of the unthematic.

444 Ibid., 64.

445 Ibid.

446 Stăniloae, "Revelation and Knowledge of the Triune God," 119.

the oldest form of contemplative prayer in the Church, having been faithfully practiced and preserved by the Christian East. St. Gregory Palamas identified three levels of participation or spiritual perceptions associated with prayer, of which noetic prayer was the highest. He also explained that those who achieved this level of prayer can have a direct, immediate experience of union with God in this life, which he described in terms of experiencing uncreated light. Palamas wrote:

> When a hesychast concentrates his attention on his own interior—of his soul as well as his body, he does not seek for any particular 'psychological state,' but he seeks Christ Himself who lives in him, the Kingdom which is 'within us' and appears to us in a manner more real than that in which the Apostles had contemplated it on Tabor.[447]

Why is this experience even "more real" than what the Apostles experienced on Mount Tabor? Because they were still on the outside, looking in. Now, with the presence of Christ's spirit dwelling in the hearts of the faithful, and through the Holy Spirit, we can experience Christ's actions.[448]

Hesychia refers to interior stillness. The hesychast Prayer of the Heart "is the highest form of prayer in which the *nous*, the rational part of the soul or mind, is kept in the heart by the grace of the Holy Spirit, and prays there without distraction."[449] The *nous* can be described as the rational part of the soul or the mind. Inner stillness is achieved when the *nous* is freed from its enslavement to reason, the passions, and the surrounding world. Thus, when freed from distractions,[450] one

447 Meyendorff, "Doctrine of Grace in St. Gregory Palamas," 21.

448 Ibid., 20–1.

449 Elder Ephraim, *My Elder Joseph the Hesychast* (Florence, AZ: Saint Anthony's Greek Orthodox Monastery, 2013), 692.

450 When we discuss the Wisdom of the Desert Fathers, we will discuss practices such as the cultivation of the virtue of humility and detachment from material things, which assists this process. Further, the Holy Mysteries such as the Mystery of Repentance of the Holy Eucharist also cultivate the soul for this type of prayer.

is left to pray with the heart[451]—to feel and experience the prayer rather than to simply think about or recite it. This deep tranquility of spirit is achieved through the constant contemplation of God by invoking the name of Jesus. Prayer of the Heart is contrasted to other types of prayer, such as liturgical prayer, which leverages the mind's rational faculties.

The Holy Fathers explain that this level of contemplative prayer requires considerable time and discipline to achieve. One hermit described the practitioner as an "athlete of prayer"[452] and said, "The athlete must accept that he must struggle for many years."[453] Elder Joseph the Hesychast of Mount Athos advised his disciples:

> Man's *chief* aim should be to *find* God. In finding God, he finds true happiness. The interior prayer we have been discussing (Jesus Prayer) leads man to him. We can never thank God sufficiently for revealing himself to us. We can never even thank him enough for the other goods he bestows upon us. God need not have created man: he had a host of angels. Yet he created man and countless marvelous things for him.[454]

Let us consider this advice. First, Elder Joseph represents an Athonite monk like St. Gregory Palamas. Similar to Rahner, Elder Joseph implies that God created humanity to have someone who can relate to him. He also advised, "True Orthodox theology is experience; it is the knowledge of God which is given to the person whose heart and *nous* [mind] have been purified and illuminated."[455] Consider this in light of Stăniloae's perspective that a theologian must be a person of prayer with actual experience rather than just doctrinal knowledge. Further, Rahner says that we must have this primitive experience of God through practices such as meditation and prayer, or we have

451 See Met. Hierotheos, 208.
452 Ibid., 114.
453 Ibid., 151.
454 Elder Ephraim, 475.
455 Ibid., 483.

only an intellectual perspective: concepts and a false sense of piety. Therefore, it is inescapable that an experience of the Divine must be grounded in prayer.

Cultivation of this prayer is not just about practicing the mechanics of the prayer itself. Hesychasts undergo personal purification of soul and body to be freed from distractions. These spiritual disciplines include the practice of the virtues beginning with humility, ascetical practices such as fasting and self-denial (*áskēsis*), detachment from disordered passions such as material possessions (*apatheia*), mourning of our sinfulness (compunction or *penthos*), sober vigilance (*nepsis*), and forgiveness of others (*aphesei*), to name a few. In addition to these spiritual disciplines, the Holy Mysteries, particularly the Mystery of Repentance and Mystery of Holy Eucharist, help a person delve more deeply into prayer; at the same time, contemplative prayer makes the reception of the Holy Mysteries a much more personal encounter.

Becoming an athlete of prayer, as the hermit described, requires years of practice and self-surrender; it is the ultimate response to the self-communicating God. However, no one achieves these heights of contemplation without divine assistance. St. Paul wrote, "The Spirit too comes to the aid of our weakness; for we do not know how to pray as we ought, but the Spirit itself intercedes with inexpressible groanings."[456] This is why some Holy Fathers consider divinization (*theosis*) as the acquisition of the Holy Spirit; it is through the Holy Spirit that the Holy Trinity dwells within the hearts of the faithful. "The love of God has been poured into our hearts through the Holy Spirit that has been given to us."[457]

Not every person is called to a life of contemplation or monastic life, but the Jesus Prayer can be used by anyone. Through prayer, we become more attuned to God's operations in our daily lives. Prayer also increases our desire for God, to reach for the infinite horizon, to enter into a personal relationship with him.

---

456 Rom. 8:26.
457 Rom. 5:5.

Summary

Contemplative prayer reflects our ability to encounter the divine presence and is one way to develop a personal, intimate relationship with God, who is forever reaching out to us. Contemplative prayer was a part of the Church for many years, lost outside of the monasteries in the Western Church when theological training shifted to the universities, but faithfully practiced and preserved in the Eastern Church. It provides a foundation for other means of encounter, such as the Holy Mysteries. We must reclaim this lost contemplative prayer practice to live the spiritual life properly.

Prayer requires constancy and consistency, accompanied by other spiritual disciplines such as ascetical practices and living a life of virtue. As with any skill, this requires patience, perseverance, time, and effort. Further, our prayer must be in harmony with our lives. We cannot live reckless or careless lives and expect to achieve a fruitful prayer relationship with God.

The Jesus Prayer is the most ancient form of contemplative prayer today.

Reflection Questions

1. Do I have a daily Rule of Prayer? What prayers or practices do I perform daily? How faithful am I to the practice?
2. Have I experienced contemplative prayer? What was my experience? Do I regularly practice contemplative prayer? Why or why not?
3. Would I like to cultivate a personal relationship with Jesus? If so, am I willing to work at it like any other relationship?

Prayer
B: The Jesus Prayer

"But when you pray, go to your inner room, close the door, and pray to your Father in secret. And your Father who sees in secret will repay you."
(Matt. 6:6)

"Learn to love prayer. In order not to live in darkness, turn on the switch of prayer so that divine light may flood your soul. Christ will appear in the depths of your being. There, in the deepest and most inward part, is the Kingdom of God. The Kingdom of God is within you." [458]
(Elder Porphyrios of Kavsokalyvia)

Opening Gospel Reading

Matt. 6:5-8 (Jesus's teaching on prayer).

The Case for the Jesus Prayer

In our previous discussion, we considered the importance of contemplation for entering into a deeper relationship with God. There are numerous contemplative prayer traditions and movements in the Church. Historically, we have taught the Jesus Prayer in our retreats and during parish missions for four specific reasons:

1. ***It is the oldest*** of the contemplative prayer traditions, beginning with the Desert Fathers.

2. ***It is the most used*** form of contemplative prayer,

458 Elder Porphyrios, 113.

especially within the Eastern Christian Churches and the patrimony of the Universal Catholic Church.

3. ***It requires humility***, and is the only tradition that approaches God humbly, acknowledging we are sinners. Consider the Parable of the Pharisee and the Publican.[459]

4. ***It evokes simplicity*** by asking for the one thing we need from God: mercy. He knows what we need before we ask.[460] So, we trust God to provide and, therefore, seek his mercy.

The Jesus Prayer returns us to our spiritual roots: authentic, not diluted, without additives, preservatives, or artificial flavors. Such prayer is foundational to the Art of Spiritual Life, a deeply personal relationship with God.

An Ancient Prayer Focusing on Interior Stillness

We need silence more than we realize. With the busyness of our lives, it is hard to slow down and take time for Jesus. Yet, whether we realize it or not, we need Jesus more than we need food, water, light, or life itself. It is in silence that we encounter the Divine. Cardinal Sarah writes, "We encounter God only in the eternal silence in which he abides."[461]

Jesus himself reinforces the importance of prayer and often withdrew to spend time with his Father. Before beginning his ministry, he spent 40 days in the desert to pray. Before Jesus taught, preached, or healed, he often went off to a secluded place to pray. Luke tells us

459 See Luke 18:9-14.
460 See Matt. 6:8.
461 Sarah, *The Power of Silence*, 21.

that the reason Jesus went to Mount Tabor, where he was transfigured, was to pray.[462] Also in Luke, Jesus tells his disciples the Parable of the Persistent Widow[463] and the passage begins with this statement: "And he told them a parable about the necessity to pray always without becoming weary."[464] Jesus prayed, and he encouraged his disciples to pray.

Prayer can be described as the workings of the Holy Spirit within us. Our desire is to get in touch with these workings of the Spirit; our intention is direct contact with the Divine. This requires us to listen for the Spirit working in the stillness and silence of our hearts. Yet, when we take time to sit in silence to be with the Lord, one is bombarded by thoughts, making it harder to hear the voice of Jesus. We need stillness, and the Jesus Prayer is a powerful tool to help us achieve this objective. It is like listening at the feet of Jesus as Mary did, which Jesus described as the "better part," compared to Martha, who was overwhelmed with the chores of hospitality.[465]

Placing Jesus at the Center of Our Lives

The Jesus Prayer places him at the center of our lives. The following is an overview of its most common form:

462 Luke 9:28.
463 See Luke 18:1-8.
464 Luke 18:1.
465 See Luke 10:38-42

Breathing[466]	Prayer[467]	Observation
Inhale	*Lord, Jesus Christ*[468]	***A profession of faith:*** Acknowledging Jesus as Lord, the center of our lives and as the Son of God.
Exhale	*Son of God*	
Inhale	*Have mercy on me*	***A desire for repentance and reconciliation:*** Acknowledging who we are ("a sinner") and our request of Jesus ("have mercy on me"). In addition, the prayer is grounded in humility—the foundation for attaining all the other virtues. Humility is part of the movement away from self, surrendering self-will to the Divine will.
Exhale	*A sinner*	

This prayer acknowledges a complete surrender to God, allowing Jesus to lead us in the spiritual life to the Father. The Jesus Prayer is the only contemplative prayer tradition that approaches God with such a profound sense of humility, which is key to the process of divinization. In today's world, there seems to be a loss of respect for God. This prayer focuses on the right-ordered relationship between Creator and creature, acknowledging the vast difference between

466 Some Spiritual Fathers would advise their disciples that the prayer is said on a single breath: (Inhale) "Lord Jesus Christ, Son of God"; (exhale) "have mercy on me, a sinner." Either way is acceptable, as long as the prayer itself becomes as natural as breathing. To some, this two-breath approach more readily adapts to a natural breathing pattern. Ultimately, it is up to the practitioner to decide what is better.

467 In the writings of the Holy Fathers, one may encounter variants of the Jesus Prayer. Some Greek Fathers use a shorter version: "Lord Jesus Christ, have mercy on me." Others may exclude the phrase "a sinner," originally added in the Russian/Slavic tradition in the 18th century. Each still contains the two key components of the prayer: the invocation of the name of Jesus and the request for what we most need: mercy. Herein we use the most common form and that which we were taught by our Spiritual Fathers.

468 Acts 4:12: "There is no salvation through anyone else, nor is there any other *name* under heaven given to the human race by which we are to be saved."

them and asking for the one thing most needed by us: Mercy. We need not ask for anything else because Jesus tells us: "Your Father knows what you need before you ask Him."[469] Thus, all we need is God's mercy.

It is important to note that the Jesus Prayer is performed without mental forms or focusing on images, such as an icon. It does not involve imagination or any form of thoughts, such as Ignatian spiritual practices. Rather, it is solely intended as a means to experience the presence of God. The breathing is meant to be natural, such that the prayer takes root in the heart, even when the practitioner is unaware of it ("pray without ceasing").

Practicing the Jesus Prayer[470]

The following are some practical thoughts on saying the Jesus Prayer:

1. **Posture** – Position your body comfortably, spine erect, using a chair or cushions. Athonite elders recommend a low stool, closer to the ground as a posture of humility. Bow your head to come humbly before the Creator. Recall the Publican (tax collector) who "would not even raise his eyes to heaven."[471]

2. **Be Grounded** – Be aware of your physical senses. Close your eyes and gradually become aware of the physical senses of your body. Feel them as they flow through you.

3. **Open Your Awareness to God's Presence** – Feel the presence of God all around. Feel that presence within. Breathe in the Divine with every breath. Breathe God out and let yourself rest in his presence. Begin slow, steady breathing with

469 Matt. 6:8.
470 See Ken Kaisch, *Finding God: A Handbook of Christian Meditation* (New York, NY: Paulist Press, 1994), 199-200.
471 Luke 18:13.

deep, natural breaths—not prolonged, but natural. Release outside thoughts and distractions.

4. **Move Thoughts from the Head to the Heart** – With every breath, allow your sphere of energy to slowly sink from the head to the heart. This may be very difficult at first; slowly allow the energy within to become heavier and heavier, sinking to the heart one inch at a time. Center yourself in your heart. This is why the Jesus Prayer is also referred to as "Prayer of the Heart."

   St. Ignatius Brianchaninov wrote: "The attentiveness of the mind during prayer attracts the heart in sympathy. When attentiveness becomes natural to prayer, then the mind can descend into the heart for most profound prayerful worship."[472]

5. **Begin the Words of the Prayer** – When a rhythm of breathing has been established, synchronize your breathing with the reverent repetition of the prayer. Slowly say the words from the heart: "*Lord, Jesus Christ, Son of God, have mercy on me, a sinner*." Let your heart repeat these words slowly, over and over again, feeling God's presence within. St. John Climacus writes: "The beginning of prayer is the expulsion of distractions from the very start by a single thought."[473] In this case, that single thought is the Jesus Prayer.

6. **Be Attentive** – When your attention wanders, be patient. Thoughts and distractions are likely to emerge in one's consciousness during the Jesus Prayer (we can experience interior chaos, a constant bombardment of thoughts).

472 St. Ignatius Brianchaninov, *The Refuge: Anchoring the Soul in God*, trans. Nicholas Kotar (Jordanville, NY: Holy Trinity Publications, 2019), 219.

473 St. John Climacus, *The Ladder of Divine Ascent*, trans. Colm Luibheid and Norman Russell (New York, NY: Paulist Press, 1982), 276. Step 28: On Prayer. The Greek term used for thought, *monologistōs*, can also mean "by a repeated short prayer."

Slowly refocus on the prayer, releasing the thoughts. "The goal is not to suppress the thoughts during prayer, but only to ignore them, to let them be and to let them go—and to *prefer* Jesus, to choose him anew whenever we wander."[474]

Fr. Thomas Keating, OCSO provided one of the best analogies for unwanted thoughts. He described human consciousness as a river and our thoughts as boats going down the river.[475] Suddenly in prayer, we realize that we are on one of these boats. Keating wrote: "If you find yourself on a boat, just get off. There should be no self-recriminations, no sighs, no annoyance that you had a thought. Any such reflection is another thought, another boat."[476]

We should not judge ourselves for having a thought. Just gently let it go and return to the prayer. Remember the intention: to enter into prayer, to cultivate the relationship with God. God is more interested in our intention than whether we do the prayer perfectly, which we cannot. Gently we bring ourselves back to attentiveness (head in the heart, rhythmically breathing, and the slow repetition of the prayer: *Lord, Jesus Christ, Son of God, have mercy on me, a sinner*).

Consider the Four "R's" related to interior stillness:

- Do not **<u>Resist</u>** the thought. We are human beings; rational thought is part of who we are. It was a gift from our Creator.
- Do not **<u>Retain</u>** the thought. Once you realize your mind has wandered, gently release the thought. If you find yourself on a boat, simply get off.

---

474 Langford, 196.
475 See Thomas Keating, *Intimacy with God* (New York, NY: The Crossroad Publishing Company, 2002), 61-3.
476 Ibid., 63.

- Gently **Return** to the prayer. Reestablish the rhythm and pattern.
- Do not **Regret** the thought. The purpose of the prayer is intention—to build a relationship with the unseen God, who knows this intention. Regret is another thought, another boat going down the river. Regret is also a demon who can bring despair and discouragement, preventing us from continuing our prayer or simply giving up.

The repetition of the prayer is not a monotonous attempt to gain God's attention,[477] trying to wear God down, but an attempt to gather oneself in recollection by clearing the mind of everything except Jesus. The goal is to make this prayer so connected with one's breathing that it becomes, as the experienced Spiritual Fathers say, truly rooted in our hearts and continues as unconscious or self-activating prayer.

Regarding distractions (*logismoi*), the "enemy" who despises prayer will do *anything* to disrupt our efforts. Assaults come from the left ("vain thoughts and sinful imaginings"[478]) and from the right ("edifying memories" or "beautiful thoughts"[479]). All such thoughts are meant to disrupt us from our prayer. Keep in mind what is important to God. He is pleased when we persevere in our prayer; we stay the course, no matter how intense the distractions become.

Finally, here is the reality. Our practice is not "never let your attention in prayer be stolen." It will most definitely be stolen, perhaps every three seconds or every 30 seconds.

477 Cf. Matt. 6:7.

478 Aleksei Pentkovsky, "Introduction," in *The Pilgrim's Tale,* trans. by T. Allan Smith (Mahwah, NJ: Paulist Press, 1999), 108.

479 Ibid.

Our practice is to cultivate the habit of returning to the prayer, returning to the present, which cultivates stillness.[480]

7. **Conclude the Jesus Prayer** – When ready, let the feeling return to your hands, feet, and face. Take a deep breath and slowly open your eyes. This prayer was intended for monastics to perform in their cells. Accordingly, each person chooses when to conclude praying. The prayer is not about completing a specified number of repetitions. It is most important is to spend quality time in silence with Jesus.

8. **Use a Prayer Rope** – Eastern Catholic and Orthodox monastics often use a prayer rope to count the number of recitations of the Jesus Prayer. It also helps one remain focused on the prayer. Tradition has it that St. Pachomius (292-348), an Egyptian and early Desert Father, invented the prayer rope as an aid for illiterate monks to accomplish a consistent number of prayers and prostrations in their cells. Prayer ropes come in varying lengths; however, ropes with 100 beads (usually with a knotted cross on the end) and 33 beads are the most common.

The Jesus Prayer is meant to be personal, done in private to reflect the instructions of Jesus in Matt. 6:6: "Enter the inner room, close the door, and pray to your Father in secret." St. Isaac the Syrian tells us we cannot taste honey by reading a book.[481] God is not meant to be intellectualized; he is meant to be experienced. Similarly, we can continue to discuss the history and merits of the Jesus Prayer; however, it is more vital to experience the prayer, taste its sweetness, and be sustained by its fruits. Take time to pause, to be still, and to enter into the Jesus Prayer.

---

480 Martin Laird, *Into the Silent Land: A Guide to the Christian Practice of Contemplation* (Oxford University Press, 2006), 43.

481 See *The Ascetical Homilies of Saint Isaac the Syrian*, 153. Homily Four. "Therefore, O man, pay attention to what you read here. Indeed, can these things be known from [*writings of*] ink? Or can the taste of honey pass over the palate by reading books? For if you do not strive, you will not find, and if you do not knock at the door with vehemence and keep constant vigil before it, you will not be heard."

Summary

A personal relationship with God revolves around encounter. The Jesus Prayer is a means for cultivating such a personal, intimate relationship. It also enriches other means of encounter such as through the liturgy and the sacramental life of the Church. Encountering Jesus provides us with the openness to receive the graces he wishes to give us, which assist us in our spiritual life. We listen at the feet of Jesus.

Reflection Questions

1. What have my experiences with the Jesus Prayer been like? Provide details.
2. Do I think the Jesus Prayer is something that I should add to my personal Rule of Prayer?

Additional Resources

The following are resources that have been developed in support of this topic.

Edward Kleinguetl. *The Fruit of Silence: The Jesus Prayer as a Foundation to the Art of Spiritual Life*. Parker, CO: Outskirts Press, 2020.

______. *The Fruit of Prayer: Spiritual Counsels of the Holy Fathers*. Parker, CO: Outskirts Press, 2021.

2022 Proclaimed a Solemn Year of Prayer

Patriarch Daniel and the Holy Synod of the Romanian Orthodox Church have proclaimed 2022 as a Solemn Year of Prayer and a commemorative year of three hesychast saints: St. Symeon the New Theologian, St. Gregory Palamas, and St. Paisius of Neamţ (Velichkovsky), three key figures we regularly reference in our works. The commemoration notes the 1,000th anniversary of the repose of

St. Symeon and the 300th anniversary of the birth of St. Paisius; all three saints reflect periods of spiritual revival in the Church. In his remarks immediately after the proclamation, Patriarch Daniel noted:

> Without prayer there is no Church and no Christian life. When we lose the joy and peace of mind, it is a sure sign that we are not praying properly and as much as we should. The Orthodox Christian must pray as much as possible because prayer brings much holy love into the heart; it unites us with God the Merciful; it helps us to see in every man a brother and in every beauty of creation a gift from God. Prayer helps us to face the hardships of life and to taste the light and joy of the Resurrection and eternal life in this world.
>
> Nothing can replace prayer, and no activity is more precious than prayer, for it gives us inspiration and strength to speak the kind word and to do good.
>
> In the context of the restrictions caused by the global pandemic situation of the last two years, it has become even more necessary to emphasize the practice of prayer in the life of the Church and of the faithful. Prayer is a source of joy and spiritual strength, a source of peace and love for God and for our neighbors. It is, as the holy ascetics said, 'the spiritual breath of the soul.'
>
> All the good deeds of the Christian and all the pure thoughts are the fruits of their prayers and of those who pray for them: priests, parents, godly friends, and good people.[482]

This focus on prayer, *hesychia*, and renewal of interior life is an appropriate response in combatting today's spiritual pandemic.

---

482 Aurelian Iftimiu, "Patriarch Daniel Proclaims 2022 Solemn Year of Prayer, Commemorative Year of Hesychast Saints," *Basilica News Agency*, online (Jan. 1, 2022).

Icon of the 2022 Patron Saints of Romania

(Courtesy of Basilica News Agency)

MEANS OF ENCOUNTER

Divine Revelation
A. Sacred Scripture

"All scripture is inspired by God and is useful for teaching, for refutation, for correction, and for training in righteousness..." (2 Tim. 3:16)

Read the Holy Scriptures, dear friend, read the Scriptures and be immersed in them; receive their sweetness, nourishment, and delight, which is not empty and transient. [T]he soul cannot show forth any spiritual fruit unless it is first enlightened by Holy Scriptures.'[483] ***(St. Nikodemos the Hagiorite)***

Introduction to This Two-Part Topic

Revelation is "the act of revealing or disclosing." From a theological standpoint, revelation is God's disclosure of himself and his will to his Creation, or an instance of such disclosure and communication, something disclosed, or something that contains such disclosure as the Bible. The Catholic Church recognizes two sources of revelation as the foundation for its theological teachings, Sacred Scripture and Sacred Tradition, both of which make up the Sacred Deposit of Faith (*Depositum Fidei*). While all Christians acknowledge the importance of Sacred Scripture, the same cannot be said of Tradition. Accordingly, we will explore Tradition as a theological source. This source is foundational to our discussion on other means of encounter: the Holy Mysteries, Liturgy, and the Church. However, it is important to understand what we mean when we say Sacred Scripture is a source

483 St. Nicodemos of the Holy Mountain, *A Handbook of Spiritual Counsel*, trans. Fr. Peter A. Chamberas (New York, NY: Paulist Press, 1989), 188.

for our theological belief because Sacred Tradition is grounded upon this source.

Opening Scripture Reading

2 Tim. 3:10-17 (Being grounded in Scripture).

The Importance of Sacred Scripture

Every religious tradition has its sacred texts: Judaism has the Torah; Islam has the Qur'an; Christianity has the Bible, both the Old Testament or Hebrew Scriptures shared with Judaism, and the New Testament or Christian Scriptures, the latter universally accepted by all major Christian traditions. Through the Scriptures, we learn much about our faith, how God created us and how he has cared for his people. It also shows people's fidelity or breaking covenant with God and the consequences of their actions. In the Gospels, we learn from the teachings of Jesus—the gift of the Giver— through his recorded actions and specific teachings. In the rest of the New Testament, we learn what happened in the Church after the Ascension of Jesus and Pentecost, how the teachings of Jesus were applied and interpreted, and receive guidance for living a life of authentic discipleship. Thus, the Scriptures are a means for an encounter through meditation and reflection, and a means of interpreting our encounters through the commandments of Jesus and teachings of his first disciples.

As Christians, we anchor our theological beliefs on these sacred texts. However, there are implications when we refer to Scripture as "the foundation of our beliefs." We will explore these implications.

The Authority of Scripture

We believe that Sacred Scripture's authority is based on three principles:

1. Inspiration - Scripture as the inspired word of God.
2. Inerrancy - Scripture as being inerrant or without error.
3. Canonicity – Assumes books or writings were inspired and the determination of which were accepted into the official "Canon," including how this determination was made. By Canon, we simply recognize specific books or writings as being divine and inspired.

Inspiration

We believe that Sacred Scripture is the inspired word of God. The issue with inspiration is at the heart of the Bible's authority for theology. The Bible is considered divine and an authority in theological studies. However, we face challenges when evaluating what is meant by "inspired."

1. How do the stories in Genesis 1 and 2 reconcile with scientific discoveries that point to the "Big Bang" theory[484] and evolution?
2. Is the Book of Jonah a story about a whale swallowing people, or is it about how God demonstrates his mercy?
3. Historical facts about the Babylonian Captivity within the Book of Daniel are in error.

Keep these thoughts in mind as we examine how Sacred Scripture is the divinely inspired word of God.

Let us begin with Judaism. The Israelite religion gradually

484 The "Big Bang" theory was developed by Fr. George Lemaître, a Belgian-born astronomer and physicist who received his doctorate from MIT, and was a devout Roman Catholic priest. He believed his theory, widely accepted in the scientific community, was proof that the birth of the universe was the work of God, the Prime Mover. Pope Pius XII publicly favored this theory, writing in conclusion, "Therefore, there is a Creator. Therefore, God exists!"

became a scriptural religion based on sacred texts. There are references to Josiah's religious reforms and the adoption of the Book of Deuteronomy as a charter of national reform in 622 BCE. Ezra decided to use the Pentateuch (the Torah) to reconstruct Jewish national life after the Babylonian Exile. Only over time did the Jewish people become known as "People of the Book," as they have remained until today. Before this, Judaism had based its religious authority in other things: Oral tradition, customary laws, teaching of the priesthood at the Temple or in shrines, and messages of the prophets.

Christianity took a similar approach. It was easier to conserve a book or series of writings than an entire institutional fabric and way of life, the latter being considered Sacred Tradition.

The Jewish understanding of scriptural inspiration was simple: God dictated, and the authors listened. Some Christians also found this notion helpful. Two passages in the New Testament are often referenced when considering how the Scriptures are inspired. The first is from our opening reading:

> All scripture is inspired by God and is useful for teaching, for refutation, for correction, and for training in righteousness ...[485]

The Greek word for "inspired by God," *theopneustos*, means "breathed out by God." In other words, produced by the breath or spirit of God. This implies no constructive role for human authors. The second passage is:

> Know this first of all, that there is no prophecy of scripture that is a matter of personal interpretation, for no prophecy ever came through human will; but

485 2 Tim. 3:16.

> rather human beings moved by the Holy Spirit spoke under the influence of God.[486]

The Greek word for "moved," *pheromenoi*, is a nautical metaphor that could be translated as "propelled." Scriptural writers are like sailing ships borne forward by the wind. In this case, a human factor is acknowledged but viewed as entirely dependent on God. Over time, various historical theories about biblical inspiration were developed: literary analysis, form criticism, comparative literature from other cultures, and biblical archeology. Questions emerged, such as which authors were inspired and what part of the writing was related to the material or the environment where it was developed. Without going into the details of each method of analysis, the result was a theory that the inspiration of individuals is based on the collective effort of those involved. All sorts of people acted as instruments of inspiration to various degrees.

Accordingly, let us consider these issues when we view Scripture in terms of divine inspiration:

1. The literal sense—what an author intended; this would be real and also accessible to historical investigation.
2. We should regard an individual book of the Bible as an accumulation of literal senses, of which the principal sense would be that of the book in final form, which is the sense of the final editor.
3. The revealed meaning of a book must be sought beyond its literal sense, such as in the interrelationship of biblical books taken as a whole.
4. Revealed meaning found in the Canon must be made within the Tradition of the Church and not without it.

486 2 Pet. 1:20-21

Inerrancy

Inerrancy implies Scripture is without error. However, to what extent is this true? For example, biblical archeology has determined the walls of Jericho fell almost 1,000 years before the arrival of the Hebrews. What about the three challenges we raised at the beginning: The Genesis accounts of creation in light of scientific knowledge, errors in historical facts about the Babylonian Captivity in the Book of Daniel, and the account of Jonah and the whale being literal or a revelation of God's mercy.

Accordingly, what does "inerrancy" mean relative to Sacred Scripture? Two factors should be considered: the literary form or genre used by the author and the message regarding human salvation.

1. Literary Form – Pope Leo XIII made the point that the sacred writers make accommodations to their audience. Accordingly, one should be aware of the literary form of the book. There has always been an awareness of literary form within the Church. For example, in the 13th century, the Latin text of the Bible was rearranged into three sections: historical, didactic, and prophetic literature. Today, this process is much more refined, given an understanding of the context in which the book was written, the culture, and the general literary background. By understanding the literary genre, one can determine the kind of truth to be found in a given biblical book. We look through the medium of the literary form of a work for the original intention of its author, and having found this intention, we decide how to apply the Church's faith that Scripture is God's truth in each particular case.

   The Bible is free from error in the sense that the meaning intended by its writers is error-free. Investigation of literary form will help one to judge the intended meaning, while the doctrinal affirmation of inerrancy informs us that this meaning will not be overthrown by growth in scientific or historical understanding.

2. Economy of Salvation – The intention of the biblical author, located by reference to the literary form, must be judged in terms of its relevance to human salvation. "The Scriptures teach us how to go to heaven, not how the heavens go."[487] If the Bible is the record of revelation, then it must be ordered to the same goal as revelation itself, humanity's salvation, and evaluated in this light. Inspiration has the effect of rendering Scripture inerrant under one formal perspective only, that of relevance to human salvation.

   Another way to consider this is that the Scriptures, like the *Logos* (The Word of God, Jesus), are simultaneously human and divine.

Now let us apply these thoughts to the original three challenges raised at the beginning. First, consider how the stories in Genesis 1 and Genesis 2 align with the findings of science. The biblical truth is not whether the world was created in seven days, but that God was the Creator and Prime Mover, a belief that the originator of the Big Bang theory, Fr. George Lemaître, believed he proved and Pope Pius XII concurred. This is a divine truth that will not be overturned by growth in scientific or historical understanding. A second divine truth is that human beings were endowed with the divine image. How this occurred in light of evolution is less important than the truth. Accordingly, Genesis is not intended to be a scientific journal, but a revelation of specific truths. Again, Scriptures are intended to teach us how to go to heaven, not how the heavens go.

For the second question—whether the Book of Jonah is a story about whales swallowing people or to convey the message that God's salvation is intended for all (confirmed by Jesus)—we look at the

487 Nichols, 137. Quote attributed to Galileo.

literary form. This book is meant to be a symbolic message of hope. Jesus stated:

> At the judgment, the men of Nineveh will arise with this generation and condemn it, because they repented at the preaching of Jonah; and there is something greater than Jonah here.[488]

Thus, it is less relevant whether the story of Jonah is literal, but that a sign led to repentance, whereas the scribes and Pharisees had missed it. Similarly, the Book of Daniel contains historical inaccuracies. Again, it is likely this book was an allegorical message to the people of Israel to persevere under Greek persecution leveraging the story of the Babylonian Captivity. Thus, in these cases, we look to both the literary form and the message (intent) associated with human salvation to ascertain the divine truths.

Canonicity

First, let us define the term "Canon." Simply put, it is the list of books that Christianity considers sacred (inspired). Canonicity considers which books should be included within the collection of Sacred Scripture that we refer to as the Bible. We need to initially consider some factors. First, the Bible itself is a collection of works, the word "Bible" coming from the Greek *biblios* meaning book. The Bible is best thought of as a library. The books contained therein are diverse texts and, for example, the Old Testament (Hebrew Scriptures) has four mini-canons or collections. The Catholic Church did not formalize its final Canon until the Council of Trent in 1546, although the books therein had been accepted since the Patristic Period (ending ~800).

Canonicity can be considered in two parts: the Old Testament or Hebrew Scriptures and New Testament or Christian Scriptures. While

488 Matt. 12:41. See also Luke 11:32.

there is agreement by most Christians on the Canon for the New Testament; such is not the case for the Old Testament.

1. Old Testament (Hebrew Scriptures)

In Judaism, the Hebrew Scriptures are divided into three sections: the *Torah* (the Law), *Nebi'im* (the Prophets), and *Ketubim* (the Writings). The *Torah* includes the Pentateuch (Genesis, Exodus, Leviticus, Numbers, and Deuteronomy). The *Nebi'im* is further divided between the "Former Prophets"— Joshua, Judges, Samuel, and Kings, referred to as the Historical Books—and the "Latter Prophets," — Isaiah, Jeremiah, Ezekiel, and the 12 named prophets. The *Ketubim* contains the remainder, including the Wisdom Literature. Accordingly, there are four mini-collections within the Hebrew Scriptures and there were four stages in the formation of the Canon. They are:

Mini-Collection	Description	Timing/Commentary
Pentateuch	Five books of the *Torah* (or Law).	*Before 400 BCE* Ezra used this as the basis for reconstructing Jewish society after the Babylonian Exile.[489]
History Books	Former Prophets in the Hebrew Canon.	*Some writing before the Exile; completed after* A history of God's will and judgments.

489 Babylonian Exile was 598 – 538 BCE. The Babylonians conquered Judah and forced the Jewish people into Exile. After the Persian Empire defeated the Babylonians, Cyrus allowed the Jews to return.

Mini-Collection	Description	Timing/Commentary
Prophets	Latter Prophets in the Hebrew Canon.	*Before 190 BCE* Warnings to the Jewish people prior to the Babylonian Exile.
Writings	Other works written by the ancestors.	During the biblical period, no one was sure what was included. Some consider Wisdom literature similar to other literature of neighboring countries. It was clear that at the time of Jesus, the Hebrew Canon had not been closed.

The reason Catholics and Protestants have different canons for the Old Testament reflects the history of the Jewish people. The largest Jewish community outside Palestine was in Alexandria. Jewish scholars translated the Hebrew Scriptures into Greek, the common language of the Middle Eastern world. This translation is known as the Septuagint (or LXX). The Jewish scholars in Alexandria favored the inclusion of more works in the Writings than Jewish scholars in Palestine. The primary differences are the seven books, referred to as the Apocrypha by Protestants and Deuterocanonical by Catholics.[490] Because Gentile Christians spoke Greek, it was natural for them to use Greek translations of the Hebrew Scriptures.

490 These seven deuterocanonical books are Tobit, Judith, Wisdom, Sirach (Ecclesiasticus), Baruch, 1 and 2 Maccabees. There are additions to other books not accepted by the Protestants in the Old Testament canon including additions to Esther, Jeremiah (as included in the Septuagint), additions to Daniel including the Prayer of Azariah, the Song of the Three Holy Children, and the last chapter which is the story of Susannah.

In contrast, the Palestinian Jews began to standardize their scriptures, preferring a shorter canon that excluded the Deuterocanonical Books. Accordingly, the primary differences in the Hebrew Scriptures comes down to the perspectives of the Jewish scholars in Palestine versus those in Alexandria. Some traditions believe the Jewish Council of Jamnia in 94 CE was where the Canon of Hebrew Scriptures was finalized, excluding the Deuterocanonical Books. However, the authority of this council is still debated. More likely, the differences in the Canon of Hebrew Scriptures were evolutionary. At the time of Jesus, the Canon was not yet final. However, Protestant Reformers accepted the Canon approved by the Council of Jamnia.

One argument raised by the Protestant Reformers against the inclusion of the seven Deuterocanonical Books was that no Hebrew translation could be found. However, with the discovery of the Dead Sea Scrolls in the Wadi Qumran in 1947, fragments containing Hebrew texts were found for six of the books, but not the Book of Judith. Accordingly, most Protestant Bibles today contain the seven books, albeit in a separate section entitled Apocrypha. The Eastern Orthodox accept these seven books in their Canon, along with other writings not accepted by Catholics or Protestants.[491]

2. New Testament (Christian Scriptures)

While Catholics, Eastern Orthodox, and Protestants agree on the Canon of the New Testament, it is worth noting why books were included or excluded from the Canon and the timing by which the New Testament came into

491 Additional writings accepted by the Eastern Orthodox in the Old Testament Canon include 1 and 3 Esdras, 2 and 4 Esdras (the latter in an appendix in the Slavonic bible), Prayer of Manasseh, 3 Maccabees, 4 Maccabees (in an appendix in the Greek bible), Psalm 151, and the Odes.

being. This timing also helps set the stage to understand the importance placed on Tradition.

Before 50 CE, there was little effort to put the Gospels into writing. In fact, scripture scholars generally consider the Gospels to have evolved in three stages:

- Stage 1 – the actual sayings of Jesus.
- Stage 2 – the oral tradition about Jesus after the Ascension.
- Stage 3 – the written tradition that emerged as the four Gospels.

Four distinct causes explain why the faith was placed into writing:

1. Geographical dispersion – The Church began to gain converts living far away from the mother Church in Jerusalem, including the inclusion of Gentile converts without first requiring them to become Jews.
2. Passage of time since Christ's ministry – as the years mounted after Jesus's ministry, the oral tradition could not be sustained. Eventually, the Twelve Apostles would die, as would those who had known them. Accordingly, the finer or more circumstantial points of the oral tradition would be lost.
3. The threat of heresy – Individuals might choose an interpretation of Jesus's ministry and sayings that did not coincide with the rest of the Church. For example, the Johannine letters were written to combat Gnosticism, a heresy that emerged implying only certain people had the "secret knowledge" required for salvation.

4. Encouragement for those facing persecution – Throughout the Roman Empire, various communities faced persecution. So certain writings were to encourage the perseverance of believers, such as 1 Peter, Revelation, etc.

Many writings existed during this early period. Three criteria were used to determine which books to include in the Canon:

1. Apostolic Connection – Usually, the writings were associated with a specific Apostle. Doubts about apostolic association arose with the Letter to the Hebrews and the Book of Revelation. Further, scripture scholars no longer believe all the letters attributed to Paul were actually written by him. Today, apostolic authority is considered more broadly. If an apostle was said to "stand behind" a writing in such a way that the essential drift of his teaching is preserved within it, then this is regarded as adequate grounds for maintaining its apostolicity and inclusion into the Canon.

2. Orthodoxy – Conformity to the emerging rule of faith of the Church. For example, in about 190 CE, a bishop in Antioch stopped people from using the so-called Gospel of Peter on the grounds its author did not consider the human body of Jesus as real.

3. Writing valued by the Church – This meant that the writing was respected for its apostolic origin.

Similar to the Hebrew Canon, the Christian Canon came together as different collections.

Mini-Collection	Description	Timing/Commentary
Pauline Corpus	Letters of St. Paul and those attributed to him.	*~ 90 CE* The Acts of the Apostles was written near 90 CE, and people began to realize the huge importance of Paul. So, they gathered his letters and those attributed to him in a single collection.
Four Gospels	Matthew, Mark, Luke, and John	*~ 200 CE* Gospels written between 46 and 200 CE by different authors to different communities under varying circumstances. Collection brought together about 200 CE, likely because certain groups and sects used other gospels, now referred to as "apocryphal gospels."
Remainder of the New Testament	Everything else. Note that the Acts of the Apostles was always considered a second part or sequel to the Gospel of Luke.	*~ 400 CE* A bit unclear as to what was to be included, similar to the Writings in the Old Testament. Based on Patristic discussions, the present 27-book canon was widely accepted by the Greek and Latin Churches by the end of the 4th century.

Again, it is important to note that before the Council of Trent, there was no universally agreed-upon canon for the New Testament within the Catholic Church. However, the Pauline collection and the Gospels remained constant through the discussions of what should or should not be included. The canon as it exists today was generally accepted by the end of the 4th century.

3. Importance of a Single Canon

For Christians, there is only one Canon, and it includes the Old and New Testaments. The reason is that the Creator and Savior, creation and redemption, the natural and supernatural belong together in one unbreakable union. The one *Logos*, finally revealed in Jesus Christ, is, as Justin Martyr insisted, at work in both. Further, the Holy Fathers whose writings are part of Sacred Tradition, are deeply engrained with the teachings of Sacred Scripture, their foundation for teaching. This is clear in collections such as the *Philokalia* and many other writings in this Patristic vein.

Summary

Most major religions have texts that they consider Sacred Scripture. For Christians, Scripture is a major source of revelation and a theological source for our beliefs. Three assumptions are associated with the sacred texts: they are inspired, free from error or inerrant, and accepted by Christians as the inspired texts worthy of inclusion in the canon. The Canon of Sacred Scriptures for Christians, also known as the Bible, includes both the Old Testament (Hebrew Scriptures) and New Testament (Christian Scriptures) as a single canon.

Scripture is also a means for an encounter through meditation and reflection, such as through *Lectio Divina,* and it is a means of interpreting our encounters with the Divine in light of the commandments of Jesus and through the teachings of his disciples. Through Scripture, we learn of God's plan for our salvation and, specifically, through the Gospels, we come to know Jesus Christ, the way to the Father. Thus, we come to know the person to whom we pray.[492] Jesus wants us to know him in truth and that he is the one on whom we can rely. Heed the words of St. Nikodemos: "Read the Holy Scriptures, dear friend, read the Scriptures and be immersed in them; receive their sweetness, nourishment, and delight, which is not empty and transient." [493]

Catholics, Eastern Orthodox, and Protestants agree on the 27-book canon for the New Testament. Protestants do not accept seven books as part of the canon associated with the Old Testament for distinct reasons, but while not considered inspired, generally include them within the standard Protestant Bible in a separate section entitled the Apocrypha. The reason for this difference goes back to disagreement between Jewish scholars outside Palestine and those inside Palestine.

While the Canon of the Bible for the Catholic Church was not officially approved until the Council of Trent in 1546, today's 27-book New Testament canon was accepted by all Christians by the end of the 4th century.

Reflection Questions

1. What are my own thoughts about Sacred Scripture? What does the Bible mean to me?

2. Do I use the Bible (Scriptures) to reflect on my faith? What parts do I prefer the most? Why?

3. What role does the reading of Scripture play in my daily Rule of Prayer?

---

492 Sr. Ruth Burrows, OCD, *Essence of Prayer* (Mahwah, NJ: Paulist Press, 2006), 176-77.
493 Ibid., 188.

MEANS OF ENCOUNTER

Divine Revelation
B. Sacred Tradition

"For I received from the Lord what I also hand on to you..."
(1 Cor. 11:23)

"You must draw instruction and guidance from the teaching of the Holy Fathers and check yourself against the Word of God expressed in Sacred Scripture." [494]
(The Pilgrim's Tale)

"The words of Holy Scripture and the words of the Saints, inspired by the Holy Spirit, help us continually rekindle the sensation of God within our heart." [495]
(Archimandrite Zacharias of Essex)

Opening Gospel Reading

John 21:24-25 (Conclusion of the Gospel of John).

Introduction

Sacred Tradition is a major source of revelation within the Catholic and Eastern Orthodox Churches. It is not accepted to the same extent, if at all, by Protestants, who gravitate more toward Sacred Scripture alone (*sola scriptura*) as the source of revelation. Accordingly, this topic is a prerequisite to upcoming discussions. The reality, which we also heard in our Gospel reading for this topic, is that not everything

494 *The Pilgrim's Tale*, 208-9.

495 Archimandrite Zacharias (Zacharou) of Essex, "Introduction" in *Sermons on the Spiritual Life: Saint Philaret of Moscow* (Riverside, CA: Patristic Nectar Publications, 2020), x.

was written down. Information circulated from the Apostolic Age (to ~100 CE) was passed on in the Patristic Period (to ~800 CE) and handed down to us as oral tradition and practices that are significant to our faith. Sacred Tradition is anchored by Sacred Scripture; the two are not separable in terms of the foundation, though this is a proper order. The writings of the Holy Fathers also provide us perspective on how to follow Jesus's commandments. In Catholic and Eastern Orthodox teaching, Sacred Tradition is considered a living reality and, along with Sacred Scripture, forms a single Sacred Deposit of Faith.[496]

When Tradition is capitalized in this context, it refers to Sacred Tradition. The word tradition comes from the Latin, *trader,* which means "to hand on." Sacred Tradition is the Scripture as it is lived out in the Church. Specifically, it is the Word of God that the prophets and Apostles received through the inspiration of the Holy Spirit. This message was then "handed on" to the Christian world by the Church through the guidance of the Holy Spirit.[497]

In this time of spiritual pandemic, we have been advocating a return to our roots, the Early Church teachings of the Holy Fathers. Accordingly, this topic provides important insights into the early development of our Christian faith and the wellspring from which the Holy Fathers continue to draw.

---

496 See Patriarch Daniel, *Confessing the Truth in Love*, 233. As a point of clarification, the Orthodox perspective is that there is only one source of Divine Revelation, the Person of Christ, to whom both Sacred Scripture and Sacred Tradition bear witness. Thus, the Revelation of Christ through these two forms constitutes the "Apostolic Tradition." "The form of Scripture is fixed once for all, but the form of Tradition is renewed from generation to generation in order to remain faithful to the original Revelation of Christ and to make it relevant to every generation. "

497 Divine Revelation was fulfilled, completed, and perfected in Christ, the fullness and mediator, author and interpreter, purpose and center of public revelation. St. Thomas Aquinas and others taught that all public revelation ended with the death of the last apostle, St. John the Evangelist (~100 CE). However, the teachings of the Apostles including the commandments of Jesus have continued to be handed on through the generations under the guidance of the Holy Spirit operating within the Church.

The Nature of Tradition

Christian Tradition consists of the way of life and worship that is the Church. As stated by the Church Fathers at the Council of Trent, "These truths and rules are contained in the written books and unwritten traditions which have come down to us." They conclude, therefore, "All traditions concerning faith and morals...come from the mouth of Christ or are inspired by the Holy Spirit and have been preserved in continuous succession in the Catholic Church." In simplest terms, the beliefs of the Early Church were not only contained in Scripture, but also handed down through the rites, rituals, and prayers to comprise what is considered Sacred Tradition.

The notion of Tradition within Scripture begins with the Gospels. Christian revelation in terms of the teachings of Jesus were spoken until the Gospels were put into writing. Similarly, in Judaism, much of the oral tradition in the time of Jesus eventually found its way into a significant 2nd-century sourcebook, the Talmud. Accordingly, there not just with a culture of manuscripts, but also a culture of manuscripts and memory. In the Gospel of John, Jesus says: "The Advocate, the holy Spirit that the Father will send in my name—he will teach you everything and remind you of all that I told you."[498] In Paul's letters, he speaks of what has been "received" or "transmitted," or handed down. Accordingly, these are Scriptural examples of Tradition in action.

Tradition is seen as the life and consciousness of the Church, of which Scripture forms an essential part. This Tradition also includes the rites and liturgies that have been handed down since the time of the Apostles, reflective of their interpretations. The writings and teachings of the Holy Fathers also provide guidance for following the teachings of Sacred Scripture to achieve eternal life. Accordingly, the Catholic view of Tradition is actually the revelation of its transmission. Traditions have always been part and parcel to the Scriptures from

498 John 14:26.

Judaic times through Christian times. The unwritten traditions are manifestations of how the essential meaning underpinning the Scriptures was passed on to subsequent generations, and how the faith and teachings were lived out after the Ascension.

Church Fathers, Councils, and Creeds

The Patristic Period is often considered the most significant in terms of Tradition. During this period, the First Seven Ecumenical Councils of the undivided Church were held, defining significant doctrines, including: the nature of Christ as fully human and fully divine, the Trinity as three Divine Persons sharing one essence, and Mary as the *Theotokos* (God-bearer). This period came closest to that of the Apostles, through whom the truths of faith were originally handed down. The Apostles received Divine Revelation once and for all, revelation believed to have ended with the death of the last Apostle, and this revelation has been handed down through the teachings and life of the Church. The Patristic Period also was when the Creed, worship in the form of liturgy, and the Church and its structure were developed.

Nouvelle Théologie and its *ressourcement* was a movement leading up to Vatican II advocating a return to the sources. This movement considered the teachings of the Early Church Fathers from the Patristic Period when the fundamental doctrines of faith were developed through the First Seven Ecumenical Councils. This was a highly formative period when the Christian religion was condensed into the basic format that is recognizable today. The Creed was formulated, the most significant being the Nicaea-Constantinople Creed (NCC), and the liturgical traditions in the East and West were developed. Also, an ordered communion of local Churches evolved under bishops and centered on the local Church of the city of Rome, coupled with the development of a sacramental system presided over by the threefold ministry of bishops, presbyters, and deacons. Thus, much of what we consider part of the Church today was developed during the Patristic Period.

1. Theology of the Early Church Fathers:

The Patristic Period was a time of significant theological development, which was very diverse—from the backward Latin-speaking Church to the sophisticated Greek-speaking Church, to the Syriac and non-Greek-speaking Churches. Three characteristics distinguish this period.

a. Focus on Fundamentals

Theology focused on the principal Christian dogmas of God, Christ, the Holy Spirit, and the Church. This is in contrast to the later Scholastic Period, where theology focused on numerous secondary or peripheral questions. Note that *ressourcement* was a reaction against Scholasticism and Neo-Scholasticism, which had become the predominant theology of the Catholic Church up to the time of Vatican II and was heavily based on doctrine. *Ressourcement* placed the focus back on the teachings of the Patristic Church, and one could say the Church was returning to its roots. In contrast, the Eastern Orthodox had maintained its Patristic roots,[499] so with *ressourcement,* it was not surprising to see commonalities between Rahner's and Stăniloae's theological frameworks. As for the Protestants, the Reformation was, in its own way, a reaction against Scholasticism, but in many cases, it jettisoned the Tradition in favor of Sacred Scripture alone.

Patristic theology can be described as follows:

- Theocentric—presenting God as the primary reality.

499 The Eastern Churches did not have the equivalent of a Scholastic movement that significantly swayed the focus from experience to doctrine. In essence, these Churches remained more closely aligned to their Patristic roots.

- Christocentric—Creation stems from God and returns to God, shepherded by the Spirit of Christ.
- Ecclesiocentric—Christ gives the Spirit as head or source of the Church. From the Greek *ekklēsia,* meaning "church."
- Mysteriocentric—the Church's life is fully realized through the celebration of the Holy Mysteries (Sacraments).

b. Pastoral Fruitfulness

Most of the Early Church Fathers during the Patristic Period were pastors, often bishops, who wrote to answer the needs of the Church. Such writings included sermons, replies to inquiries, exhortations, manuals of instruction, and refutations of heresies. While time-bound, these writings lay out the intrinsic finality or purpose of theology itself: Not just laying out Christian truths for their own sake but aiming to communicate the results of exploring faith to build up God's people in wisdom and understanding. Many of these writings remain classics.

2. The Creed

The formulation of the creed is a summary of Divine Revelation. While not specifically stated in Scripture, the Creed summarizes the beliefs of the Church. The most notable creed is the Nicaea-Constantinople Creed (NCC), which was developed during the Patristic Period and reflected the fundamental beliefs of the Early Church Fathers, including Christological and Trinitarian beliefs. After the First Seven Ecumenical Councils, the NCC, used by most mainline Christian denominations, has not been altered, with the notable exception being the insertion of *Filioque* by the Western Church.

The Liturgy

The liturgy is one aspect of Tradition handed down to us by the Patristic Church. The maxim *lex orandi, lex credendi* means "the law of prayer is the law of believing." Therefore, one of the best guides to what the Church believes is what the Church says when it prays, referring specifically to the Church's official public prayer. The highest form of this is the liturgy, the Eucharist, and other liturgical rites, which are the central acts of our faith. The liturgical traditions handed down from the early Church have theological significance, as they reflect the beliefs as understood by the Early Church Fathers. Pope Pius XII's papal encyclical letter *Mediator Dei*, stated, "The Church prolongs the priestly mission of Jesus Christ mainly by means of the sacred liturgy"[500] The intercessory activity of Christ before the Father is said to be continued in the liturgy of the Church.

Christian Art

The Christian faith also began to be expressed in visual images that emerged as part of the Tradition. The dominant Christian art form in the Early Church was the icon, which was more than a painting or a picture. Icons are images that reflect an underlying reality and often convey key theological concepts. One challenge often voiced by various Protestants is whether the depiction of Christ in Christian art—icons, paintings, statues, and such— violates the First Commandment's prohibition of making images. However, the Sacred Tradition would refute this. The true image of God was made by God himself in the Incarnation. In Christ, the invisible God is made visible[501] and this gives a rationale for depicting Christ and, by extension, Christian art.[502] In his treatises, *On the Divine Images*, St.

500 Pope Pius XII, *Mediator Dei,* Papal Encyclical (Rome: Libreria Editrice Vaticana, Nov. 20, 1947), no. 3.

501 See Col 1:15.

502 See Nichols, *The Shape of Catholic Theology*, 188-9. "With the incarnation, God makes himself visible in the life of Jesus, which is human life in every sense and therefore a life capable of depiction in artistic terms."

John of Damaskos defended Christian art against those who saw it as fundamentally blasphemous:

> Now that God has been seen in the flesh and has associated with humankind, I depict what I have seen of God. I do not venerate matter, I venerate the fashioner of matter, who became matter for my sake and accepted to dwell in matter and through matter worked through my salvation, and I will not cease reverencing matter, through which my salvation was [effected].[503]

He adds:

> I venerate the image of Christ, as God incarnate; of the mistress of all, the Mother of God, as the mother of the Son of God; of the saints, as friends of God, who struggled against sin to the point of blood, have both imitated Christ by shedding their blood for him who shed his blood for them, and lived a life following his footsteps.[504]

Throughout the ages, great significance is placed on the veneration of icons in the Eastern Churches, especially in the personal piety of the faithful who often have icon corners in their homes. The iconostasis in the church provides significant symbolism to the liturgy that unites heaven and earth in praise of God in a foretaste of eternal life.

Periods of Church History

The Apostolic Period lasted until ~100 CE, considered when the last apostle died. The Patristic Period (~100-800) was known for its

503 St. John of Damascus, *Three Treatises on the Divine Images*, trans. Andrew Louth, 1st ed. (Crestwood, NY: St. Vladimir's Seminary Press, 2003), 29.

504 Ibid., 34-5.

pastoral fruitfulness. Many of the Early Church Fathers explored the meaning and practice of faith. This also was when the First Seven Ecumenical Councils of the undivided Church defined critical doctrines. When referring to the Early Church, herein, this includes the Apostolic and Patristic Periods.

The Scholastic Period (800-1700) reflected a theological movement wherein critical thought was dominated by academics, first in cathedral schools, and by the 12th century, by faculties of theology in the medieval universities of Europe.[505] The development of theology shifted from monasteries to academic institutions in Europe and became increasingly academic. It was a time when dogma was defined and defended in an increasingly diverse context. Much of this theological approach was grounded in Aristotelian philosophy. One of the best-known theologians of this period was St. Thomas Aquinas, a philosopher, theologian, and Dominican priest. His epic work was the *Summa Theologiae*, a guide for theologians and seminarians. Neo-Scholasticism was a revival and development of medieval scholasticism in Roman Catholic theology and philosophy that began around 1840. This was the dominant theological method taught to seminarians until Vatican II.

Nouvelle Théologie advocated[506] a return to the sources, primarily Sacred Scripture and the teachings of the Patristic Church. The movement began in the mid-20th century as a reaction against Neo-Scholasticism and strongly influenced the teachings of the Church that came from Vatican II. Patristics and Scripture study were reintroduced or expanded in seminary curriculums, while

505 See Nichols, 291. Some Church Historians would characterize the period from 800 to 1100 as Early Scholasticism, the zenith as 1200-1300, and period of decline being 1660-1760. The restoration of dogmatic theology began approximately 1840 in a movement known as Neo-Scholasticism.

506 Sometimes the term *Nouvelle Théologie* ("New Theology") is used to describe this school of thought in Catholic theology, primarily supported by French and German theologians, which stood as a counterpoint to the dominance of Neo-Scholasticism and was an effort to fundamentally reform Catholic theology. This school of thought significantly influenced the reforms of Vatican II.

scholastic theology and philosophy were phased out. The Church was returning to its roots.

Also, the Patristic Period is particularly interesting because of its strong union between theology and spirituality. Many of the Early Church Fathers were monks, committed Christian ascetics, who "did not regard the life of prayer—conscious striving for union with God in Christ in his Spirit—as irrelevant to the practice of theology."[507] In other words, theology and spirituality had not yet gone their separate ways.[508] After this point, we see a separation, at least in the Western Church as it enters the Scholastic Period.

The Christian East, on the other hand, retained a greater connection with Patristic theology. There was no equivalent to the Scholastic movement, nor a substantial disruption such as the Protestant Reformation. The Holy Fathers in the East have followed a common golden thread, which has not changed since the Desert Fathers, the earliest Holy Fathers, to the present day. For example, a pivotal point in the evolution of this thread was the publication of the *Philokalia* in the 18th century, written to return to the golden age of hesychast masters, those who strove through ascetical practices to follow the commandments of Jesus. The focus was always on deepening their relationship with Jesus in anticipation of gaining union with God in eternity. Holy Fathers, such as St. Isaac the Syrian and St. John Climacus, were frequently quoted by the Philokalic Fathers and were clear influences on many; Post-Philokalic Fathers, who embraced the writings of the *Philokalia*, continued this tradition. Holy Fathers have changed, the times and circumstances have changed, but that golden thread has remained.

The *Philokalia* was at the forefront of a significant spiritual renewal, including the Russian Spiritual Renaissance of the 19th century. Much of Europe was succumbing to the secularizing influences of

507 Nichols, 205.
508 Cf. Ibid.

the Enlightenment—not dissimilar to today. Accordingly, three monks on Mount Athos and their followers launched a counter-response to the disturbing trend they were observing, advocating a return to the Holy Fathers and the Tradition—a return to basics.[509] The tradition of these Holy Fathers is alive today, as evidenced by Elder Ephraim of Arizona, a monk who died in December 2019 and was a disciple of Elder Joseph the Hesychast.

Patriarch Daniel of Romania also stressed the importance of returning to the Holy Fathers to rebuild people's interior lives after decades of Communist repression:

> The Patristic and Philokalic renewal is reflected in the translation of the work of the Church's Holy Fathers and great confessors as well in studies or commentaries on these works, undertaken in order to highlight better their timeliness and their depth of thought and the Christian experience throughout the centuries—during very different historical circumstances—of great theologians and spiritual men: martyrs, shepherds, teachers, ascetics, servants, parents, and children, witnesses and saints of the Church of Christ. In other words, Patristic renewal is not just a simple cultural phenomenon; not only does it correspond to the need for information, but it also imposes itself as a necessity for the Church's own life, as a sensitization and rejuvenation of her consciousness expressed together with the Tradition as living memory of the Holy Spirit.[510]

He recognized that the Sacred Tradition of the Church provides

---

509 St. Paisius Velichkovsky produced the Slavonic collection of the *Philokalia*, which significantly influenced mysticism in Romania and Russia. St. Nikodemos the Hagiorite and St. Makarios of Corinth produced the Greek collection. There is an 80-percent overlap between the two.

510 Patriarch Daniel, "Spiritual Life and Theology in Contemporary Orthodoxy," 25.

a foundation from which to rebuild, that renewal efforts are required both in theology and spirituality, which he described as "something which goes with the character of a living church."[511] Similarly, in a world gripped with unbelief, we, too, can return to the Holy Fathers for their guidance and witness. We can restore the equilibrium in the dialectic tension between spirituality and theology, not forgetting the intense mystical tradition that is part of our Deposit of Faith.

The Influence of the Golden Thread: *Ressourcement*

This golden thread is evident in the writings of Stăniloae, who places great emphasis on experience, especially experiences of prayer as the foundation of theology. So, when we consider *ressourcement* as a return to the sources leading up to Vatican II, it is clear how such theologians as Rahner gravitated to the teachings of the Early Church Fathers, particularly those of the Christian East. From this, we also appreciate what Pope St. John Paul II meant when he said the Church needed to learn to breathe again from both lungs, one Eastern and one Western. The Christian East preserved much of Patristic theology and the mystical tradition. These are the spiritual treasures that underpin our encounters with the Divine. They support our efforts to examine our faith and beliefs from the perspective of the spirituality of encounter.

Eastern Catholic Bishops at Vatican II, while small in number,[512] had a considerable influence on the resultant teachings. Patriarch Maximos IV (Sayegh) of the Melkite Greek Catholic Church was considered one of the ten most dominant personalities of the

---

511 Ibid., 24.

512 There was 130 Eastern Catholic Bishops at Vatican II, out of an approximate total of 2,600 bishops. See Dar Al-Kalima, "The Melkite Church at the Council: Discourses and Memoranda of Patriarch Maximos IV and of the Hierarchs of His Church at the Second Vatican Ecumenical Council," trans. Bishop Nicholas Samra (Manuscript submitted for publication; originally published as *L'Eglise Grecque Melkite au Concile*, 1967), 232. Note that the Melkite Greek Catholic Church delegation consisted of one patriarch and 16 bishops.

Council.[513] Thus, this convergence in theological thinking between East and West since the Council is not surprising. It is evidenced by comparing the theological framework of Rahner and Stăniloae, West and East, where theology and spirituality are realigned.

Looking Ahead to the Upcoming Discussions

Now that we have addressed the two sources of Divine Revelation included in our Sacred Deposit of Faith, Sacred Scripture, and Sacred Tradition, we are ready to examine the Holy Mysteries, Liturgy, and the Church as means of encounter. These three topical areas were significantly influenced by Sacred Tradition, much of it formulated during the Patristic Period. We will also discuss how we encounter the Divine through love of neighbor, reflective of Jesus's mission and teachings. This concept was significantly influenced by Sacred Scripture and how the Early Church lived out Jesus's directives to feed the hungry, cloth the naked, and do other charitable acts.

Attempts to Distort the Deposit of Faith

Today, we are faced with many distortions and attempts to "modernize" Christian teaching by being more inclusive, politically correct, less restrictive, more liberated, or more appealing to mass media. Matthew Kelly aptly wrote, "Every type of perversion and depravity has become someone's personal preference and right"[514] and many want a Christianity that will endorse such immoral behavior. Some of the challenges come from within the Church, such as the German "Synodal Path" (*Der Synodale Weg*), wherein positions have been proposed "that Divine Revelation in Scripture and tradition is not binding over time."[515] The belief is that a Church that takes cues from secular culture,

513 See *History of Vatican II*, vol. I, gen. ed. Giuseppe Alberigo, trans. Joseph A. Komonchak (Maryknoll, NY: Orbis Books, 1996), 380.

514 Matthew Kelly, *Life is Messy* (North Palm Beach, FL: Blue Sparrow, 2021), 39.

515 George Weigel, "Liquid Catholicism and the German Synodal Path," *First Things*, February 16, 2022.

a Christianity that is easier for more people to embrace, will attract more members. *Do not be deceived!* Jesus was clear: "Amen, I say to you, until heaven and earth pass away, not the smallest letter or the smallest part of a letter will pass from the law ..."[516] He did not create latitude for alternative interpretations. St. Paul warned:

> Let us be children no longer, tossed here and there, carried about by every wind of doctrine that originates in human trickery and skill in proposing error. Rather, let us profess the truth in love and grow to the full maturity of Christ the head.[517]

Jesus is not trying to fill a quota; he wants to save the courageous few willing to deny themselves, take up their crosses daily, and follow him.[518] Salvation is open to all, and God desires that all be saved. This is the Good News of the Gospel and our source of hope. However, there are conditions that Jesus set forth: we need to enter through the narrow gate; we need to make a free-will decision to accept the offer of salvation—on God's terms, not our own. We do not dictate the terms. We must repent and believe in the Gospel[519]—the Gospel as presented by Jesus and not distorted by the spirit of the age (*Zeitgeist*). Sacred Scripture and Sacred Tradition do not change. "Jesus Christ is the same yesterday, today, and forever. Do not be carried away by all kinds of strange teaching."[520]

Summary

For Catholics and Eastern Orthodox, Sacred Scripture and Sacred Tradition are both sources of Divine Revelation and the foundation for our theological beliefs. We also considered Sacred Tradition as a source of Divine Revelation. While Sacred Scripture is the primary

516 Matt. 5:18.
517 Eph. 4:14-5 (NAB).
518 Cf. Luke 9:23.
519 Cf. Mark 1:15.
520 Heb. 13:8-9.

source, Tradition was how the faith was lived, handed down from the Apostles and their followers, through the writings and teachings of the Holy Fathers throughout the ages, and subsequently lived out in the life of the Church. From this Tradition, we have received prayers, rites, rituals, the liturgies, a sacramental system presided over by the ministries of bishops, priests, and deacons, and the Church as a communion of churches. These were the fundamentals of the Church, most of which remain recognizable today.

Lex orandi, lex credendi loosely means, "the law of praying is the law of believing." This is a well-known expression in the Church. The implication is that how we pray, like the liturgy, points to our beliefs and theology. Thus, Tradition handed to us underpins the beliefs of the earliest Christians and, as such, becomes a source of revelation, pointing to what they believed.

This two-part discussion has provided the context for the remaining topics in this section, covering our means for encountering the Divine.

Reflection Questions

1. Of the Tradition (prayers, rites, rituals, liturgies, sacramental system, threefold orders of clergy, the Church), of which am I most familiar? Least familiar?

2. Which part of the Tradition is the most important to me on my personal faith journey?

3. Which part of the Tradition do I struggle with? Why?

Supplemental Discussion:

A Summary of the First Seven Ecumenical Councils

The table below summarizes the First Seven Ecumenical Councils of the Church. All occurred during the Patristic Period, where significant doctrine was defined. Most heresies regarding Jesus either over-emphasized his humanity (e.g., Arianism) or his divinity (e.g., Nestorianism).

Year	Name of Council	Primary Topic(s) Addressed
325	First Council of Nicaea	Addressed prevalent heresy: – Arianism - denied the divinity of Christ, believing Christ to be created (albeit a creature above all other creatures). Declared Christ was of the same substance as the Father (affirmed divinity of the *Logos*) and initial formulation of the Nicaean Creed expressing beliefs of the Church.
381	First Council of Constantinople	Addressed heretical views: – Arianism – Still not fully resolved within various jurisdictions of the Church. – Apollinarism – believed Christ had a human body, but only a divine mind. – Sabellianism – Anti-Trinitarian view that there is one God who operates in three modes (also called modalism); denies three persons. Defined the Holy Spirit and the Doctrine of the Trinity; adjusted the previously developed Creed, today known as the Nicaea-Constantinople Creed.

Year	Name of Council	Primary Topic(s) Addressed
431	Council of Ephesus	Addressed heretical views: – Nestorianism – tried to dilute the humanity of Jesus, over-emphasis on divinity. – Pelagianism – human effort alone can merit salvation; divine assistance is not required. Re-confirmed full divinity and full humanity of Jesus, Declared Mary as *Theotokos* ("God-bearer") vs. *Christotokos* ("Christ-bearer"). This reaffirms the divinity of Christ. Reconfirmed need for divine assistance.
451	Council of Chalcedon	Addressed heretical views: – Monophysitism – believed divine and human nature of Christ were fused into one new single nature. His human nature was "dissolved like a drop of honey in the sea." Overemphasis on the divine. Reaffirmed the two natures of Christ, that he was fully human and fully divine without mixture or confusion.
553	Second Council of Constantinople	Addressed heretical views: – Origenism Condemned Origen and his teachings; condemned *apocatastasis*, a belief that everything would be restored to its original or pre-Fall condition, denying eternal damnation.

Year	Name of Council	Primary Topic(s) Addressed
680-81	Third Council of Constantinople	Addressed heretical views: – Monothelitism – a belief that Christ had two natures, but only one, divine will. Fully human and fully divine meant that Christ had a human will. Otherwise, he could not have been an example for humanity in accepting God's will.
787	Second Council of Nicaea	Addressed controversy over Christian art: – Iconoclasm – a controversy over divine images, primarily icons. During 726-87, images were banned, and there was a deliberate destruction of religious symbols, motivated by First Commandment against graven images, and further influenced by the rise of Islam with its condemnation of idols. The Council supported the veneration of icons.

MEANS OF ENCOUNTER

Holy Mysteries (Sacraments)

"Go, therefore, and make disciples of all nations, baptizing them in the name of the Father, and of the Son, and of the Holy Spirit..."
(Matt. 28:19)

"Through the sacred Mysteries, as through windows, the Son of righteousness enters into this dark world."[521]
(Nicholas Cabasilas)

"The purpose of our life here is to restore communion with God through the Holy Eucharist."[522]
(Bishop Ioan Casian Tunaru of Canada)

Opening Gospel Reading

Matt. 28:16-20 (The Commissioning of the Disciples).

Channels of Grace

At the Ascension and strengthened by the gift of the Spirit, the Redeemer's visible presence passed into the sacraments, wrote Pope St. Leo the Great. "Our faith is nobler and stronger because sight has been replaced by a doctrine whose authority is accepted by believing hearts, enlightened from on high."[523] Each of the Holy Mysteries represents opportunities for encounters with the Divine, especially in the regular

521 Cabasilas, 50. He also adds, "For this reason, the most sacred Mysteries may fittingly be called 'gates of righteousness,' for it is God's supreme loving-kindness and goodness towards mankind, which is the divine virtue and righteousness, which has provided us with these entrances into heaven" (52-3).

522 Totorcea, "Prayer and Communion are Fundamental Pillars of the Living Church."

523 Pope St. Leo the Great, Sermon No. 2 on the Ascension." In *The Liturgy of the Hours*, vol. 2, 937-38.

participation in Holy Repentance and reception of Holy Eucharist. Through the Holy Mysteries, Jesus shows the depth of his overflowing love for us. We will consider each of these in the context of *theosis*.

The Roman Catholic and Eastern Churches accept the same seven Holy Mysteries. They are believed to have been instituted by Jesus and entrusted to his Church. They are visible rites seen as signs and effective channels of God's grace to all those who receive them through proper disposition. In the Christian East, the term Holy Mystery is used, *mystērion* being Greek for "mystery." Thus, emphasis is placed on the mystery of the ritual. The Holy Mysteries are considered vessels for mystical participation in divine grace. In general, everything which is in and of the Church is considered sacramental or mystical.

In the Roman Catholic Church, *sacrament* comes from the Latin, *sacramentum*, meaning "sign of the sacred." The Sacraments are considered to have a visible and invisible reality; visible as a reality open to the human senses, but invisible when being grasped in its God-given depths with the eyes of faith. In many ways, the term *sacrament* emphasizes the former and mystery the latter. Both East and West believe in the Holy Mysteries as a means of divine encounter and, especially in the case of Eucharist and Repentance, divine assistance, what we have also referenced as deifying grace, for achieving humanity's ultimate destiny, union with God. Nicholas Cabasilas explains, "This is the way in which we draw life into our souls—by being initiated into the Mysteries, being washed, and anointed and partaking of the holy table. When we do these things, Christ comes to us and dwells in us."[524]

The Holy Mystery of Baptism

Baptism is our personal participation in Easter, the death and resurrection of Christ. In Baptism, we are clothed with Christ and

524 Ibid., 60.

initiated into the Church. We are claimed for Christ, our fallen human nature replaced by the renewed human nature won by Christ—a dignity that can never be revoked. We are reminded of this during Bright Week, the week immediately after Easter, and other selected times in the Church calendar. In the Eastern Churches, the usual "Holy God" sung for the Thrice-Holy Hymn is replaced by "All you have been baptized into Christ have been clothed with Christ. Alleluia!"[525] In the Resurrection Matins, the Eastern Churches sing:

> It is the day of Resurrection, O People, let us be enlightened by it. The Passover is the Lord's Passover, since Christ our God, has brought us from death to life and from earth to heaven. Therefore, we sing the hymn of victory.[526]

How does Baptism assist in the journey of *theosis* when most of us were baptized as infants and have no recollection? The answer is that we need to acquire (or reacquire) the grace of our Baptism in our lives, to claim it and make it our own. St. Theophan explained:

> We, the baptized, have received a talent, which is the grace of the Holy Spirit. This talent ... acts within us on its own at first, until we have grown up. As we approach maturity, grace, although it is ready to act, does not act. It waits until we freely and willingly incline to it, when we ourselves to desire its full action within us and begin to seek it. As soon as we begin seeking, grace immediately resumes its work within us, rousing us, directing us, and strengthening us.[527]

At Baptism, we receive grace and the openness to the working of

525 Thrice-Holy Hymn used on Pascha (Easter), Bright Week, Pentecost, Nativity, Theophany, and Lazarus Saturday. Taken from *The Divine Liturgies*, 31.

526 Resurrection Matins, Resurrection Canon, Ode 1, Hirmos.

527 St. Theophan, *The Spiritual Life*, 120.

the Holy Spirit, always ready to act in us, but requiring us to pursue the Christian life. When a person decides to be subject to divine action, then God begins to act through the grace each received at Baptism. As St. Theophan described it, "There is a moment, and a very noticeable moment, which is sharply marked out in the course of our life, when a person begins to live in a Christian way."[528] Christian life begins with this zeal. However, the grace to live such a life is already bestowed upon a person through Baptism, waiting to be activated by a free-will decision. When we decide to live in a Christian way, activating our Baptismal grace, we will likely stumble and fall—human nature is weak. Baptism is one-time event, so when we fall, we need to be restored to our original state of grace. St. John Climacus wrote:

> Repentance is the renewal of baptism and is a contract with God for a fresh start in life. Repentance is critical awareness and a sure watch over oneself. Repentance is the daughter of hope and the refusal of despair. The penitent stands guilty—but undisgraced.[529]

In Baptism, we were washed clean and set free from sin, having been clothed in Christ. Repentance restores us to this state of cleanliness.

The Holy Mystery of Repentance (Confession)

The first words of Jesus in his public ministry were, "Repent, for the kingdom of heaven is at hand."[530] To become an authentic disciple of Christ, a person consciously decides to align with Jesus's teachings and commandments. The Holy Mystery of Repentance is the concrete expression, beginning, and completion of repentance. It gives us the chance to express our sins to our confessor and be

528 St. Theophan, *The Path to Salvation*, 23.
529 Climacus, 121. Step 5: On Penitence.
530 Matt. 4:17.

forgiven. Patriarch Daniel of Romania said, "Repentance becomes the resurrection of the soul from the death of sin and the rediscovery of man in communion with God."[531] Accordingly, "repentance must be a permanent state for all Christians."[532]

In Eastern Christian theology, unlike in the Roman Church, there is less delineation between mortal and venial sin. All sin is considered separation from God. The small sins can easily become habit and can cause a contraction of our hearts.[533] There is a strong belief that these smaller encroachments need to be kept in check, so poisonous weeds do not take root in our hearts. Thus, the Eastern Spiritual Fathers place greater emphasis on daily examination of conscience and seeking the Holy Mystery of Repentance more regularly. As St. John Climacus wrote: "In fact nothing gives demons and evil thoughts such power over us as to nourish them and hide them in our hearts unconfessed."[534] Further, as Pope Francis wrote: "The confessional must not be a torture chamber, but an encounter with the Lord's mercy which spurs us on to do our best."[535]

However, Repentance is not simply the Holy Mystery. Repentance, first and foremost, is a state of mind, a constant acknowledgment that we are sinners and need to mourn our sins,[536] both of which are important in our upward movement to God. Through this ongoing state of repentance, "each day the soul is

531 Deacon Iulian Dumitraşcu, "Repentance Must Be a Permanent State for All Christians, Say the Patriarch of Romania," *Basilica News Agency*, online, February 20, 2022.

532 Ibid.

533 See *Catechism of the Catholic Church ("CCC")*, no. 1865. While the Roman Church still refers to "grave sin," there is a discussion of the proliferation of sin similar to the concerns of the Eastern Churches. "Sins creates a proclivity to sin; it engenders vice by repetition of the same acts. This results in perverse inclinations, which cloud conscience and corrupt the concrete judgment of good and evil. Thus sin tends to reproduce itself and reinforce itself, but it cannot destroy the moral sense at its root."

534 Climacus, 211. Step 23: On Pride.

535 Pope Francis, *Evangelii Gaudium*, no. 44.

536 *Penthos*, also called compunction, is mourning for our sinfulness (e.g., "Spare your people, O Lord") and an important part of repentance as a state of mind. Some Greek fathers also describe the gift of tears associated with such mourning, a reflection of unworthiness and a desire for the mercy of God. This also helps to cultivate the virtue of humility.

strengthened and becomes a fertile field, providing the fruits of the Holy Spirit to harvest."[537] "If a person has not repented, if one has not changed his or her way of life, thinking, attitudes, and opinions and if that person does not stand forever tearfully before God, then it is not true repentance."[538]

In the Christian East, the practice of can be illustrated as such:

Repent > Confess > Commune > Maintain Vigilance

There is a significant linkage in the Eastern Churches between the Holy Mystery of Repentance and Holy Eucharist. St. Nikodimos the Hagiorite wrote, "For without Communion, man reverts to his previous condition, and 'the last state of that man becomes worse than the first.'"[539] The confessional practices in the Christian East since the 8th century have been adapted from the monastic *exomologesis* (confession). Its purpose is to restore the person as worthy of receiving the Holy Eucharist. This is particularly noticeable in many Orthodox Churches, where the faithful do not receive Communion as frequently as in the Catholic Church, even on Sundays. The reception of Communion is a matter of conscience, repentance, and direction by one's Spiritual Father.

We have reflected on the words of the Jesus Prayer, *Lord Jesus Christ, Son of God, have mercy on me, a sinner*. The prayer reflects the ongoing state of repentance, acknowledging our sinful nature and our desire for mercy. The Jesus Prayer "leads in the last analysis to the embracing of our souls by the Holy Spirit."[540]

---

537 Archimandrite Christoforos Stavropoulos, *Partakers of Divine Nature*, trans. Rev. Dr. Stanley Harakas (Minneapolis, MN: Light & Life Publishing Company, 1976), 53.

538 Ibid., 55.

539 St. Nikodimos the Hagiorite, *Concerning Frequent Communion of the Immaculate Mysteries of Christ*, trans. George Dokos (Thessaloniki, Greece: Uncut Mountain Press, 2006), 73. He references Matt. 12:45.

540 Ibid., 77.

The Holy Mystery of Chrismation (Confirmation)

Chrismation is our personal participation in Pentecost, the coming of the Holy Spirit upon us.[541] We receive the seal of the gift of the Holy Spirit.[542] The significance of the descent of the Holy Spirit at Pentecost is worth considering. At the Annunciation, the Holy Spirit descends upon the Virgin Mary, the *Theotokos* ("God-bearer"). At the Theophany, the Spirit descends upon Jesus as he emerges from the Jordan River for his earthly ministry. However, at Pentecost, the Holy Spirit descends upon all humanity. We see the effects of the Holy Spirit, as described in the Acts of the Apostles, transforming individuals fearfully locked behind doors to proclaim boldly the gospel message. The Troparion for Pentecost Sunday follows:

> Blessed are you, O Christ our God. You have shown the fishermen to be all-wise, sending down upon them the Holy Spirit. Through them you have the whole world in your net. O Lover of us all, glory to you![543]

At the time of Jesus, it was unthinkable to consider fishermen as all-wise. Yet something powerful clearly happened. We today are proof of this "something," gathered together as Church. Someone handed the Gospel message to us, and that transmission began with those fishermen on Pentecost.

In the Holy Mystery, the Holy Spirit comes to dwell in us, bringing to life the graces we received in Baptism.[544] Jesus assured us at the Last Supper that he would not leave us orphans[545] and would send

541 Not all Orthodox theologians agree that Chrismation is a personal participation in Pentecost. Rather, the broader view is that the *whole* rite of initiation (Baptism, Chrismation, and Eucharist) is entrance into the life of the Trinity, without taking Chrismation in isolation. In the Eastern Churches, Baptism and Chrismation are never separated.

542 See Rom. 8, 1 Cor. 6, and 2 Cor. 21–22.

543 Troparion for Pentecost Sunday, *The Divine Liturgies*, 205.

544 See Anthony M. Coniaris, *Achieving Your Potential in Christ: Theosis* (Minneapolis: Light & Life Publishing Company, 2004), 81.

545 Cf. John 14:18.

another Advocate, "the Spirit of truth."[546] Same as Baptism, we need to reclaim the graces of Chrismation through Repentance and other actions that prepare our hearts as a suitable dwelling for the Spirit, by, for example, cultivating the virtue of humility through ascetical practices.

Achieving *theosis* is predicated on collaborating with the divine presence, which means collaborating with the Spirit of God dwelling within us. The graces granted through the Spirit are many-fold: wisdom, understanding, counsel, fortitude, knowledge, piety, and fear of the Lord[547]—deifying grace that assists us in achieving our destiny. In summary, the Spirit gives us the strength and guidance to live our lives in a manner pleasing to God, drawing us closer to him, becoming more God-like and preparing us for our final destiny: union with him.

The Holy Spirit is the fulfillment of Christ's promise, teaching us what we need to know and reminding us of all that Jesus taught.[548] In other words, the Holy Spirit becomes our guide during our spiritual life and *theosis* can only be realized in the Holy Spirit,[549] drawing us to life in the Holy Trinity. Consider that in the Eucharistic celebration, bread and wine are transformed into the Body and Blood of Christ through the invocation of the Holy Spirit in the *Epiklesis*. The same Holy Spirit has the power to transform our lives from fear and doubt to faith and constancy. Cultivating a spirit of humility and ascetical practices of self-denial create fertile ground within our hearts, opening them for collaboration with the Spirit.

Certain Holy Fathers, such as St. Seraphim of Sarov, describe the aim of the spiritual life as acquisition of the Holy Spirit. This can also be defined in terms of *theosis,* becoming God-like, sharing in his divine nature because the Holy Spirit seeks to divinize us and

546 See John 14:16–17.
547 See also Isaiah 11:2.
548 See John 14:26.
549 Stavropoulos, 29.

make us temples of God's presence,[550] guiding us toward our ultimate destiny. St. Paul validated this when he wrote, "Do you not know your body is a temple of the Holy Spirit within you, whom you have from God, and that you are not your own?"[551] He also wrote:

> We even boast of our afflictions, knowing that affliction produces endurance, and endurance, proven character, and proven character, hope, and hope does not disappoint, because the love of God has been poured out into our hearts through the holy Spirit that has been given to us.[552]

Essentially, St. Paul is describing *theosis* because afflictions represent the daily crosses we must bear[553] and the terms and conditions of discipleship, accepting "the offer of salvation." There is no salvation without the cross.

Our collaboration with the Spirit, who has been poured into our hearts, gives us the strength to turn toward God daily, and assists us in the journey of *theosis*.

The Holy Mystery of Eucharist (Communion)

Bishop Ioan Casian Tunaru said, "The purpose of our life here is to restore communion with God through the Holy Eucharist"[554] and "the Eucharist represents eternal life in advance in the Church."[555] Sr. Ruth Burrows describes the criticality of Eucharist with respect to our transformation:

> Eucharist is the sacrament of Jesus's sacrifice, of his

550 Coniaris, *Achieving Your Potential in Christ*, 139.
551 1 Cor. 6:19.
552 Rom. 5:3–5.
553 See Luke 9:23.
554 Totorcea, "Prayer and Communion are Fundamental Pillars of the Living Church."
555 Ibid.

> total, loving surrender to the Father and the Father's embrace of him in Resurrection. This divine 'exchange' becomes ours, and we are taken into the triune life of love. Our offerings, representing ourselves, become the sacrifice of Jesus. The whole meaning of our Christian existence lies in allowing God to effect this transformation. In a mysterious but real way, we are to become the reality and presence of Jesus in the world .... Eucharist is a worship and love that are wholly worthy: the worship and love of the Son.[556]

Consider Eucharist in light of our discussion on anthropology. We who are made in the image of God strive to regain the likeness of God—the essence of *theosis*. Similar to the transformation of the bread and wine into the Body and Blood of Christ, we strive to be transformed, to become more Christ-like, to become divinized humanity. We begin this journey through self-surrender, like Jesus, striving to become who we were created to become.

In addition to effecting our transformation, Eucharist is a foretaste of our destiny, for we receive the divinizing presence of Christ within us.[557] Professor Mary Healy wrote:

> When we receive him in Holy Communion, we welcome him into our hearts with hospitality full of reverence and zeal .... We keep our hearts pure by being quick to repent wherever there is sin, and making quick use of the Sacrament of [Confession]. A curious thing happens as we draw closer to the Lord. Instead of becoming more otherworldly or inward-looking, we are propelled outward. *The love of Christ compels us, because we are convinced that one has*

556 Burrows, *Essence of Prayer*, 72.
557 Coniaris, *Achieving Your Potential in Christ*, 81.

> *died for all.* The closer we come to Jesus, the more we are filled with God's unconditional love, and the more we long to give it away to the lost and the broken.[558]

Healy reinforces some key points: the linkage between repentance and Eucharist, being united with Christ and vessels of God's unconditional love, and how inflamed we are with love of Christ. We wish to express this outpouring of love to our neighbor. *Theosis* involves our constant movement in the direction of God, our desire to be in union with him, and pursue the abundant life Jesus promised.[559] Consider this, too, with Sr. Ruth Burrows' thought that we, in a mysterious and real way, are to become the reality and presence of Jesus in our world. "It is not possible, however, for us to live in God without tasting God, without God living in us, without receiving God within us."[560] Eucharist is the sacrament of union, a deepening of our sense of being united with and transformed by the Lord. As Jesus said,

> Amen, amen, I say to you, unless you eat the flesh of the Son of Man and drink his blood, you do not have life within you. Whoever eats my flesh and drinks my blood has eternal life, and I will raise him on the last day.[561]

Archimandrite Christoforos Stavropoulos writes:

> It is the Eucharist which unites us, in a mystical and spiritual manner with God and which produces our divinization. The Mystery of the Body and Blood is a concrete realization of the unity of our human nature with Christ, and concurrently, of our unity with members of the Church.

558 Mary Healy, "Apostolic Intimacy, Apostolic Charity," *Magnificat,* 23(8) (2021), 401.
559 See John 10:10.
560 Stavropoulos, 56.
561 John 6:53–54.

> The Sacrament of the Holy Eucharist is closely related to Holy Baptism. The work of the renewal and *theosis* of human beings, which was performed once through Holy Baptism, is confirmed by the Eucharist, which is constantly repeated. The Eucharist feeds the believer with the Body and Blood of Christ. It strengthens us and moves us forward. It unites us closely with the Savior and leads us firmly toward *theosis*.
>
> With Holy Communion, we relive the miracle of [Christ's] divine incarnation. It is in this Holy Mystery that human beings are interpenetrated by the Divine, just as a rod of iron, thrust into a searing flame soon becomes itself a fire engulfed in flame.[562]

Eucharist is an intimate encounter with the Risen Christ. Consider the woman in the Gospel who had been afflicted by hemorrhages for 12 years and believed that if she touched the garment of Jesus, she would be healed. When she did, she was immediately cured.[563] Our encounter with Jesus in the Eucharist is similar; we touch him and he touches us, we are healed and made whole. We are strengthened by the presence of Christ to live in a Christian way.[564] St. Gregory of Nyssa wrote, "What heals us from death and corruption is the life-giving, immortal, and incorruptible body of Christ. Only he has acquired this quality."[565]

Because the Holy Eucharist can enflame and divinize us, many of the Holy Fathers have encouraged more frequent reception of Communion. These include St. Basil of Caesarea, St. Nikodemos the Hagiorite, and St. John of Kronstadt, the latter of whom encouraged even lay faithful to participate in Eucharist daily. Of course, Eucharist

562 Stavropoulos 56–57, 59.

563 See Matt. 9:20-22, Mark 5:25-34, and Luke 8:43-48.

564 Inspired by Fr. Miron Kerul-Kmec's homily, St. Nicholas Byzantine Catholic Church, Barberton, OH, November 7, 2021. See YouTube or Podbean, "The Art of Spiritual Life."

565 Totorcea, "Prayer and Communion are Fundamental Pillars of the Living Church."

should be received worthily and well, which places increased emphasis on Repentance, thus creating a cycle of upward turning to God. Reception of Eucharist reinforces our commitment in Sacramental Confession to avoid sin.

The Holy Mystery of Crowning (Matrimony)

We believe that God established marriage as a divine institution. In Genesis, God creates a companion for the man: a woman. It is written, "That is why a man leaves his father and mother and clings to his wife, and the two of them become one body."[566] Jesus reaffirms this teaching when he describes God's intention.[567] We believe that the husband-wife union is modeled after the life of the Trinity, which remains in relationship through self-giving love. Pope St. John Paul II wrote, "God in his deepest mystery is not a solitude, but a family, since He has in Himself fatherhood, sonship, and the essence of the family, which is love."[568] He associates this "love" with the third Person of the Trinity, the Holy Spirit.[569] How do the husband and wife become one? Catholic Apologist Scott Hahn would say that the becoming of one is "so real that, nine months later, they give it a name."[570] Just like the Trinity is a communion of persons, so is the family, modeled after the divine life of God himself.

In the Eastern Churches, the bride and groom are "crowned," with crowns or wreaths of flowers. The crowns have two meanings. First, they reveal that the man and woman, in their union with Christ, participate in his kingship. Second, as in the ancient Church, crowns symbolize martyrdom as the word "martyr" means "witness." The common life of the bride and groom is to bear witness to the presence of Christ in their lives and in the world. Martyrdom is

566 Gen 2:24

567 See Matt. 19:5.

568 Pope St. John Paul II, Homily, Puebla de Los Angeles, January 28, 1979 (Rome: Libreria Editrice Vaticana).

569 Scott Hahn, *First Comes Love* (New York, NY: Doubleday, 2002), 42.

570 Ibid., 46.

usually associated with death. So, the reality of God's kingdom in the life of the husband and wife will necessarily take the form of dying to oneself, to one's will, and the giving of one's life totally to the other and, through the other, to Christ.[571]

The Mystery of Holy Orders

The Holy Mystery of Orders provides the bishops, priests, and deacons with the graces to carry out their work. The Sacrament is associated with the laying of hands on the candidate for ordination. In the two Letters to Timothy,[572] he is reminded of the graces he received through laying on of hands to carry out his work. This act of ordination has continued in the Church ever since the time of the Apostles. There is also an important concept known as Apostolic Succession, which assures the uninterrupted transmission of spiritual authority from the Apostles through successive popes and bishops. Thus, each bishop can trace his lineage of ordination to the Twelve Apostles. As successors of the apostolic witnesses, the bishops canonically select and ordain individuals to serve the Body of Christ as priests and deacons. Through ordination, priests are given the authority to celebrate Baptism, Chrismation, the Holy Eucharist, Holy Matrimony; hear Confessions; and perform the Rite of Unction. Only bishops can ordain other members of the clergy. In the Eastern Churches, a deacon does not administer sacraments.

The Mystery of Holy Unction (Anointing of the Sick)

Holy Unction is a sacrament of healing. Jesus healed others by laying his hands upon them. For example, when Jairus, a synagogue official, requests Jesus to heal his daughter, he asks, "My daughter is at the point of death. Please, come lay your hands on her."[573] There is

571 "Marriage in the Eastern Orthodox Church," *Wikipedia*.
572 See 1 Tim. 4:14 and 5:22, and 2 Tim 1:6.
573 Mark 5:23.

a healing element associated with the laying of hands on a person. In terms of the Sacrament itself, the Epistle of St. James states:

> Is anyone among you sick? He should summon the presbyters of the church, and they should pray over him and anoint [him] with oil in the name of the Lord, and the prayer of faith will save the sick person, and the Lord will raise him up. If he has committed any sins, he will be forgiven.[574]

Generally, someone who is ill or having major surgery is anointed. If death is more likely, then confession and Holy Communion are also included. This final communion is called *viaticum*, or food to prepare someone for the life to come.

Summary

The Holy Mysteries or Sacraments are means for encountering Christ and receiving grace, or divine assistance, for our spiritual journey. These consist of outward signs meant to be visible to the human senses and an inward reality meant to be seen with eyes of faith. Both the Catholic and Eastern Churches recognize seven primary ritual sacraments. These are meant to initiate believers into the life of Christ and his Church, namely Baptism and Chrismation, and further sustain them on their spiritual journey. To this end, two of these are received more frequently than the others. The Holy Mystery of Repentance represents the renewal of our Baptismal promise, restoring us the original cleanliness of our Baptism. In Holy Eucharist, we receive Jesus in a very personal way, having his divinizing presence within us. We cannot achieve our destiny of living in union with God without God's presence within us. Accordingly, Eucharist brings Christ into our hearts. Also, there is a connection between Repentance and Eucharist, the former preparing us to be in a proper

574 Jas. 5:14–15.

disposition to receive him and the latter reinforcing and sustaining the spirit of repentance. The Early Church Fathers stressed the importance of proper preparation to receive Christ—repentance, fasting, and prayer—which can increase the intensity of the encounter. Romanian Bishop Ioan Casian said in his Easter pastoral address: "Prayer and communion are fundamental pillars of the living Church."[575]

Reflection Questions

1. How important are the Holy Mysteries to my spiritual journey? Are there sacraments that I dismiss because I do not consider them important? If yes, why? Be honest.

2. What are my perspectives on Confession? Do I take advantage of the opportunity to renew my Baptismal promise? Why or why not? What holds me back?

3. What are my perspectives on the Holy Eucharist? How important is the reception of Eucharist to me as part of my spiritual journey? Do I understand the connection between Confession and Communion, the importance of preparing to receive Jesus in a personal way?

575 Totorcea, "Prayer and Communion are Fundamental Pillars of the Living Church." Author's Note: Assumes proper preparation for the reception of Holy Eucharist (Communion), including the Holy Mystery of Repentance.

Liturgy

"They devoted themselves to the teaching of the apostles and to the communal life, to the breaking of the bread and to the prayers." (Acts 2:42)

"The Divine Liturgy constitutes the most profound vision of God as a mystery of love and communion ..." [576] ***(Patriarch Daniel of Romania)***

Opening Scripture Reading

Acts 2:42-47 (Communal Life of the Early Church).

A Meeting of Heaven and Earth

The Divine Liturgy is the highest form of prayer.[577] It provides a sense of beauty, heaven and earth coming together in worship and giving us a sense of the sacred. *Liturgeia* means "work of the people." It is communal prayer that is meant to engage all the senses: sight, sound, smell, touch, and taste. It was said that when St. Vladimir the Great, Grand Prince of the Kievan Rus, initially sent his emissaries to Constantinople to investigate the Christian faith, they attended a Divine Liturgy at Hagia Sophia, the great patriarchal church, and in their report to the prince, they said,

576 Patriarch Daniel, "The One Church and the Many Churches," in *Patriarch Daniel: Rebuilding Orthodoxy in Romania*, ed. Chad Hatfield (Yonkers, NY: St. Vladimir's Seminary Press, 2021), 47.

577 Aurelian Iftimiu, "The Year 2022 is an Opportunity to Reflect on the Romanian Hesychasts, Patriarch Daniel Says at Bucharest Clergy Conference," *Basilica News Agency*, online (June 8, 2022).

> We knew not whether we were in heaven or on earth. For on earth there is no such splendor or such beauty, and we are at a loss how to describe it. We know only that God dwells there among men .... For we cannot forget that beauty.[578]

This profound proclamation confirms the beauty and sacredness of the liturgy. It is a meeting with God and communion with him.[579] In addition, the Church represents our public prayer, which is a complement to our personal prayer. These two are not meant to be separated. To opt out of communal celebration and focus only on personal prayer "is self-indulgent, seeking our own satisfaction instead of the pure love of God and our neighbor."[580] "The liturgy is a moment when God, out of love, desires to be in profound union with [humanity]."[581] Patriarch Daniel of Romania summarizes this well, writing:

> The Divine Liturgy is the mystery of change, of transfiguration, and of renewal; it expresses the presence of the kingdom and anticipates its fulfillment .... The Divine Liturgy constitutes the most profound vision ... of God as a mystery of love and communion; of humanity as created in the image of God; of creation, the gift of God, called mysteriously to become a sacrament of his presence; and of his love, called to transfiguration and eternal joy in the communion of the holy and life-giving Trinity. Herein is the meeting of time and eternity, of heaven and earth, of God and humankind, of matter and the Spirit of God; here God acts, and humankind responds actively. In the Divine Liturgy dogma and hymnody, words and symbols,

578 Stephen Freeman, "The Beautiful God," *Glory to God for All Things* (Ancient Faith Ministries, May 25, 2010).

579 Patriarch Daniel, *Confessing the Truth in Love*, 199.

580 Burrows, *To Believe in Jesus*, 81.

581 Sarah, *God or Nothing*, 124.

> action and doxology, the banality of everyday life and the radical newness of the Spirit of God, the burden of this life and the joy of encountering God—everything converges to celebrate the living God who shares in our life so that we may share in his. This is why nothing can better express the mystery of the Church and her vocation than the Divine Liturgy.[582]

Worship During the Apostolic Period

Through our Sacred Tradition, liturgical worship was handed down from Apostolic times, *lex orandi, lex credendi*. The liturgy is a key expression of our faith, filled with theology and symbolism. In the Early Church, we get a sense of what worship was like in our reading of the Acts of the Apostles, which mention the teaching of the apostles, the communal life, the breaking of the bread, and the prayers. From the beginning, this worship was Eucharistic in nature, with a focus on "the breaking of the bread." Recall the encounter of the two disciples on the road to Emmaus and how they had recognized Jesus in the breaking of the bread.[583]

Not surprisingly, Early Christian worship was modeled after Jewish liturgical worship in synagogues. Beginning at the time of Ezra, we see in the Book of Nehemiah a reading from the law (*Torah*), and explanation of the law by the Levites, and prayer.[584] Jewish worship would then conclude with the sharing of a meal.

Worship During the Patristic Period

The emissaries from St. Vladimir of Kiev observed a very ornate liturgy in the patriarchal church of the capital city of the Eastern Roman

582 Patriarch Daniel, "The One Church and the Many Churches," 46-7.
583 See Luke 24:35.
584 See Neh. 8:1-8, and 9:1-37.

Empire. Compare this also to an early description of liturgical worship by St. Justin Martyr in his *First Apology*, written between 153-55.

> But we, after we have thus washed him (baptized) who has been convinced and has assented to our teaching, bring him to the place where those who are called brethren are assembled, in order that we may offer hearty prayers in common for ourselves and for the baptized [illuminated] person, and for all others in every place, that we may be counted worthy, now that we have learned the truth, by our works also to be found good citizens and keepers of the commandments, so that we may be saved with an everlasting salvation. Having ended the prayers, we salute one another with a kiss. There is then brought to the president of the brethren (presider or priest) bread and a cup of wine mixed with water; and he taking them, gives praise and glory to the Father of the universe, through the name of the Son and of the Holy Spirit, and offers thanks at considerable length for our being counted worthy to receive these things at his hands. And when he has concluded the prayers and thanksgivings, all the people present express their assent by saying "Amen." This word Amen answers in the Hebrew language to *genoito* [so be it]. And when the president has given thanks, and all the people have expressed their assent, those who are called by us deacons give to each of those present to partake of the bread and wine mixed with water over which the thanksgiving was pronounced, and to those who are absent they carry away a portion.[585]

In this account of worship in the Ancient Church, we recognize the parts of the liturgy as still celebrated today. Even the order is the

585 St. Justin Martyr, *First Apology*, Chap. 65.

same, noting that the Kiss of Peace in the Eastern Christian liturgy is exchanged *prior* to the Eucharistic Prayer, with all liturgical traditions being derived from a common source. Justin Martyr further describes the Ancient Church's belief in Eucharist:

> And this food is called among us *Eukaristia* [the Eucharist], of which no one is allowed to partake but the man who believes that the things which we teach are true (acceptance of faith), and who has been washed with the washing that is for the remission of sins, and unto regeneration (baptism), and who is so living as Christ has enjoined (living as authentic disciples). For not as common bread and common drink do we receive these; but in like manner as Jesus Christ our Savior, having been made flesh by the Word of God, had both flesh and blood for our salvation, so likewise have we been taught that the food which is blessed by the prayer of his word, and from which our blood and flesh by transmutation (transubstantiation) are nourished, is the flesh and blood of that Jesus who was made flesh. For the apostles, in the memoirs composed by them, which are called Gospels, have thus delivered unto us what was enjoined upon them; that Jesus took bread, and when He had given thanks, said, "This do ye in remembrance of Me, this is My body;" and that, after the same manner, having taken the cup and given thanks, He said, "This is My blood;" and gave it to them alone.[586]

Comparing this description of Eucharist to the teachings of Christ in the Gospels, we see how Divine Revelation in Sacred Scripture is manifested in the life of the Church. We also see how Scripture and Tradition transmit faith to believers.

586 Ibid., Chap. 66.

The earliest documentary evidence for the liturgy in Rome comes from the Order of Hippolytus (~220), which described the Eucharist as having three parts:

1. The faithful offer their gifts. From these gifts, the deacons take bread and wine and present them to the bishop.
2. The bishop pronounces over these gifts the solemn Eucharistic prayer (*Eucharisteia*) ...
3. The Eucharistic bread is then broken and distributed; in the same manner, the consecrated wine is given to everyone.[587]

Again, in this description, we see similarity between what was recorded in the Ancient Church and what occurs in the liturgy today.

Historical Development of the Liturgy

The liturgy of the Church has been handed down as part of Sacred Tradition, so we should note its historical development from the Early Church to modern times. All major liturgies consist of the same two primary parts, the Liturgy of the Word or Catechumens and the Liturgy of the Eucharist or Faithful. Justin Martyr's description of liturgy, noted above, stated that only a baptized person who holds to the true beliefs can be admitted to the Eucharistic celebration. We still see this today where, in both East and West, catechumens are dismissed before the Liturgy of the Eucharist.

1. The Eastern Church

The Liturgy of Saint James of Jerusalem is the oldest surviving liturgy developed for use in the Church. Most authorities propose a 4th-century date. This is still used on rare occasions, such as for the Feast of St. James, in the

587 Theodor Klauser, *A Short History of the Western Liturgy*, trans. John Halliburton (London: Oxford University Press, 1969), 14-5.

Antiochene Rite, Churches that trace their liturgical heritage to the Patriarchate of Antioch. The Divine Liturgy of St Basil is also attributed to the 4th century when he was Bishop of Caesarea. It is derived from the Jerusalem liturgy and is still used by the Eastern Orthodox and Eastern Catholic Churches of the Byzantine Rite, Churches that trace their liturgical heritage to Patriarchate of Constantinople. This is the most dominant group of Eastern Christians.

The third liturgy and the most commonly used by Eastern Orthodox and Eastern Catholics of the Byzantine Rite is the Divine Liturgy of St. John Chrysostom. It is also believed to be derived from the Jerusalem liturgy, which was also in use in Antioch where St. John Chrysostom spent time as a deacon and priest. The anaphora, or Eucharistic prayer, was believed to have been written by St. John when he was Archbishop of Constantinople (398-404). Thus, one can see that the liturgies of the Eastern Church were developed during the Patristic Period and are still used in Churches today.

2. The Western Church

While the Mass of the Roman Rite is the dominant liturgy of the Roman Catholic Church, its historical development and subsequent broad-scale usage are more complicated than in the Christian East. However, there are some general characteristics. First, as Latin began to replace Greek as the liturgical language, prayers were often shortened or simplified. Further, the word *Missa* (Mass) began to replace the term Divine Liturgy. This comes from the Latin *missio*, which means "being sent" or "mission."

Second, many Western Rites were associated with different geographical locations or monastic orders. Initially, the most common was the Gallican Rite, which arose in Gaul (modern-day France). It is actually not a single rite, but a family of rites within the Latin Church that were used by the majority of Western Christians for the better part of the first millennium. One of the initial Gallican rites used the Liturgy of Jerusalem-Antioch, which had been translated into Latin. Thus, there is a clear connection between the Gallican Rite and the Christian East.

While we noted the three parts of the Eucharistic celebration attributed to St. Hippolytus and part of the Church of Rome, herein called the Roman Rite, this was limited geographically. The Leonine Sacramentary,[588] traced back to the fifth or sixth centuries, is the oldest surviving book of Mass prayers, according to the Roman Rite. The Gelasian Sacramentary, traced back to the sixth or seventh centuries, is the second oldest book of Mass prayers, according to the Roman Rite. Therefore, for a long time, there were numerous rites in the Christian West.

In the 11th century, Pope Gregory VII tried to require all other Western Bishops to adhere to the liturgical practices of Rome. However, liturgical uniformity actually came from itinerant Franciscans from the 1320s onward. They adapted liturgical books in anticipation of papal visits, and suddenly the Rite of Roman Church was seen as the preferred rite.[589]

At the Council of Trent in 1545, the Roman Catholic Church adopted the Tridentine Mass. This became the dominant Western liturgy until the reforms of Vatican II when the Mass as we know it emerged as the *Novus Ordo Missae* (the New Order of Mass). On December 4, 1963, the Vatican Council issued *Sacrosanctum Concilium*, which stated:

The rite of the Mass is to be revised in such a way that

588 The Leonine Sacramentary, so named because it was originally ascribed to Pope Leo the Great, is also referred to as the Verona Sacramentary.

589 See Klauser, 94-5.

> the intrinsic nature and purpose of its several parts, as also the connection between them, may be more clearly manifested, and that devout and active participation by the faithful may be more easily achieved.[590]

The key was that the Council wanted to expand participation, something much more apparent in the Eastern liturgies, which are also celebrated in the vernacular (language of the people). Accordingly, while Latin is still considered the official liturgical language of the Roman Church, the Mass has been translated into languages such as English to encourage greater participation.

The Tridentine Mass is still occasionally celebrated and referred to as Mass in the Extraordinary Rite. While it is no longer the norm, there remain traditionalist Catholic groups that prefer the sacredness they associate with this celebration.

Liturgical Development in Context

This brief history demonstrates how liturgical worship evolved from what was described in the Acts of the Apostles to the worship described by St. Justin Martyr and St. Hippolytus. One can appreciate how Sacred Tradition has been handed down from the Apostolic to Patristic Period to our present age. In the East, the liturgies remain those that emerged in the Patristic Church. In the West, it was the Roman Rite emerged in later centuries as the dominant liturgy. However, we did describe the *ressourcement* that evolved leading into and significantly influencing Vatican II. This is true of the liturgical reforms, where several practices were adopted from the Christian East, including a focus on a participative liturgy, use of the vernacular for liturgical worship, and a preference for Communion under both species.

590 Second Vatican Council, *Sacrosanctum Concilium*, no. 4.

Liturgy as a Means of Encounter

Liturgy is meant to engage all the senses: sight, sound, smell, touch, and taste. We enter a sacred place, an activity of communal worship where, in a mystical sense, heaven and earth unite in worship.[591] The encounter with Jesus in the liturgy is twofold, both through the Word and in the Eucharist. In the Liturgy of the Word, Christ nourishes us through the words of Sacred Scripture. We hear his teachings, and the whole of Scripture tells the story of God's great love for humanity, which culminates in sending us his Son, and through whose Spirit the work through the Church continues. Stăniloae wrote, "The living dialogue of the Church with Christ is conducted principally through Scripture and tradition."[592]

With Vatican II, a greater emphasis was also placed on the homily to educate and break open the Scriptures. Particularly in the Western Church, emphasis on Sacred Scripture was significantly increased. Some argue that before the Council, significant emphasis was placed on dogmatic theology. In the Modern Church, the emphasis is placed on nourishing people with the Word, bringing the mission and teachings of Jesus into context to assist believers in the spiritual life. This also prepares the faithful to receive Eucharist, gaining an ever-clearer understanding of the person of Jesus through the Word. Thus, the Liturgy of the Word has increased in significance as a means of encounter, gaining greater insights into Jesus and the whole of salvation history.

In the Liturgy of Eucharist, Christ comes to us as the Lamb of God, who takes away the sin of the world.[593] The sin, singular, is the Fall of Adam, and Jesus came to us incarnate to restore our

---

591 In the Eastern Churches, the sense of the mystical experience of heaven and earth united in worship is heightened through the significant use of incense, liturgical movement, and the icons of Christ, the *Theotokos*, and other saints that visually represent the heavenly host. The *iconostasis* or icon screen separates the body of the church from the altar (the holy table), also increasing a sense of the sacred.

592 Stăniloae, "Revelation and Knowledge of the Triune God," 40.

593 See John 1:29. This is John the Baptist's testimony regarding Jesus: "Behold, the Lamb of God who takes away the sin of the world."

relationship with the Father. Jesus is physically present and nourishes us in the Holy Eucharist. It is important to understand that we predominantly receive Holy Communion within a liturgical setting. As stated within the documents of Vatican II, Eucharist is "the source and summit of the Christian life."[594] It is a true encounter with Jesus. We should prepare ourselves for the reception of Jesus, beginning with the Holy Mystery of Repentance before the liturgical celebration. We further prepare ourselves by learning more about Jesus and God's plan for humanity by being nourished in the Liturgy of the Word. Our awareness of God's great love for his Creation and his personal communication to us through his Son (Giver as gift) increases our desire for our destiny and provides instruction on how to achieve it. Finally, we receive Jesus in a personal, intimate way in the Eucharist; we are united with Jesus, which encourages us with a foretaste of our destiny, of being united with God, the union of two distinct natures.

As our understanding of Eucharist increases, we approach Jesus with greater reverence and respect, recognizing his presence in our midst. We desire to receive him more and spend more time with him in prayer. We are encouraged to a life of authentic Christian discipleship, the life modeled by Jesus. Living the Christian life transforms us and prepares us along the journey to humanity's ultimate purpose. We allow Jesus to show us the way because he is "the way."[595]

The Liturgy after the Liturgy[596]

What happens as a result of our encounter? In the final analysis, it is about who we become. Do we become more God-like? Consider the following:

594 Second Vatican Council, *Lumen Gentium* (Dogmatic Constitution on the Church), Nov. 21, 1964, no. 11.

595 John 14:6.

596 See Coniaris, *Tools for Theosis,* 85-86.

> There was an elderly Russian monk who was responsible for the formation of the novices within his community. One day he asked the three novices, "What is the most important part of the liturgy?" The first novice said, "Certainly it is the Word of God, hearing what Jesus has to say to us." The second said, "Surely it is the consecration when Christ becomes present in the bread and wine." The third answered, "It must be when we partake of the Holy Mysteries, where we receive Christ in the Eucharist." The elderly monk smiled, pointed to the back of the church, and wisely said, "The most important part of the liturgy is what happens when you leave those doors."[597]

There is an organic link between the "Sacrament of the altar" and "the sacrament of the neighbor."[598] *Theosis* is about who we become from these encounters. Are we truly transformed? Do we become more God-like? Do we exhibit the divine attributes of God, such as love, mercy, and compassion? Does our capacity to love others increase? This is who we are called to be. God does not need our love, mercy, and compassion—we need his! Those near us need to experience God's love, mercy, and compassion *through* us. Consider the example in the Parable of the Ungrateful Servant,[599] which tells us that we need to give what we have received.

Summary

In *Sacrosanctum Concilium*, a document from Vatican II, the liturgy can be summarized from the aspect of our spiritual journey:

---

597 Story told by Bishop Nicholas (Samra), Eparchy of Newton (Melkite Greek Catholic). Homily Friday Evening Vespers, Sacred Heart Co-Cathedral, Houston (Sept. 11, 2009).

598 Patriarch Daniel, *Confessing the Truth in Love*, 145.

599 See Matt. 18:21-35

> In the earthly liturgy we take part in a foretaste of that heavenly liturgy which is celebrated in the holy city of Jerusalem toward which we journey as pilgrims, where Christ is sitting at the right hand of God, a minister of the holy of holies and of the true tabernacle; we sing a hymn to the Lord's glory with all the warriors of the heavenly army; venerating the memory of the saints, we hope for some part and fellowship with them; we eagerly await the Savior, our Lord Jesus Christ, until he, our life, shall appear and we too will appear with him in glory.[600]

The liturgy is communal prayer in which heaven and earth are united together in worship in a mystical way. We gain a sense of the sacred and a foretaste of eternity. Jesus comes to us in every liturgy as the Word (*Logos*) and the Lamb of God, speaking and uniting himself to us.[601]

The critical word to the liturgical experience is "engaging." Believers must be drawn into the experience, which necessitates executing worship well—a reverential pace, proper liturgical flow, ease of participation, impactful message in the homily–to create the proper environment for encounter.

Developing a greater appreciation for the beauty and context of the sacred liturgy establishes the groundwork for a genuine encounter, to enter into sacred time, experience the mystical union of heaven and earth united in worship, and receive a foretaste of our human destiny.

Reflection Questions

1. What role does the liturgy play in my daily Rule of Prayer? Am I drawn to the liturgy, to listen to the Word and receive the Eucharist?

---

600 Second Vatican Council, *Sacrosanctum Concilium*, no. 8.
601 Coniaris, *Tools for Theosis*, 74.

2. Do I have a sacred experience when I participate in liturgy? What enhances or takes away from my experience?

3. How do I personally prepare for Eucharist? Do I appreciate the gift given to me in the real presence of Christ?

4. Does my participation in liturgy change who I am? Please explain.

Supplemental Discussion:

Catholic Churches by Patriarchal Church

The Catholic Church is a communion of 24 Churches: The Roman Church and 23 Eastern Catholic Churches. Most of them received their liturgical traditions from five major historical Patriarchal Churches in the Early Church. The following is a brief categorization of these Churches:

Patriarchate	**Rites and Associated Catholic Churches** (The Universal Catholic Church consists of a communion of 24 Churches)	
Rome	**Latin Rite (1)** Roman	
Constantinople	**Byzantine Rite (14)** Albanian **(D)** Belorussian **(D)** Bulgarian **(D)** Croatian and Serbian **(D)** Greek **(D)** Hungarian **(D)** Italo-Albanian **(A)**	Macedonian **(D)** Melkite **(D)** Romanian **(D)** Russian **(D)** Ruthenian **(D)** Slovak **(D)** Ukrainian **(D)**
Alexandria	**Alexandrine Rite (3)** Coptic **(C)**, Ethiopian **(C)**, Eritrean **(C)**	

Patriarchate	**Rites and Associated Catholic Churches** (The Universal Catholic Church consists of a communion of 24 Churches)
Antioch	**West Syriac (3)** Maronite **(A)**, Syriac **(C)**, Syro-Malankara **(C)**
	East Syriac (2) Chaldean **(B)**, Syro-Malabar **(B)**
Jerusalem	*None*
	Armenian Rite (1) Armenian **(C)**

Counterparts to Eastern Catholic Churches

(A) No Eastern counterpart.

(B) From the Assyrian Church of the East. Nestorian Church.

(C) From the Oriental Orthodox Churches. Rejected the Council of Chalcedon.

(D) From Eastern Orthodox Churches. Result of Great Eastern Schism in 1054.

MEANS OF ENCOUNTER

Church

"And he gave some as apostles, others as prophets, others as evangelists, others as pastors and teachers, to equip the holy ones for the work of ministry, for building up the body of Christ."
(Eph. 4:11-12)

"The Church and its role as an institution integrates the world into Christ. It is not concerned with only a part of life but all of life." [602]
(Valeriu Gafencu)

"Outside the Church, far from the Holy Trinity, we lost Paradise, everything. But outside the Church there is no salvation, there is no life." [603]
(Elder Porphyrios of Kavsokalyvia)

Opening Scripture Reading

Ephesians 4:7-16 (Building up the Body of Christ).

Church as a Means of Encounter

"The encounter with the risen Christ constitutes the Church,"[604] said Bishop Ioan Casian of Canada. In describing the work of salvation through Christ and the Holy Spirit, it is noted, "The result of this work of Christ in the believers' hearts through the Holy Spirit is the Church; in other words, Christ's work bears fruit as Church."[605] The work of

602 Monk Moise, *The Saint of the Prisons: Notes on the Life of Valeriu Gafencu*, trans. Monk Sava, Oaşa Monastery (Triada, 2019), 230.
603 Elder Porphyrios, 87.
604 Totorcea, "Prayer and Communion are Fundamental Pillars of the Living Church."
605 Stăniloae, "The Person of Jesus Christ as God and Savior," 155.

salvation cannot be separated from the Church. Accordingly, we will consider how the two missions of the Father, Christ, and the Holy Spirit, operate within the Church.

We need the Church to create the environment in which to cultivate our faith. Pope Francis often refers to the Church as a field hospital for sinners—not a museum of saints. One Spiritual Father often called the Church the "Twelve-Step Program for Repentant Sinners." Any journey is easier when we know that we are not alone. Jesus himself said, "For where two or more are gathered in my name, there am I in the midst of them."[606]

The Church mediates our encounters with Jesus. First, we have the encounter with Christ in the liturgy through the Sacred Scriptures and Eucharist. Second, the Church mediates our encounters with Christ through the Holy Mysteries. Finally, the Church is a repository of our spiritual traditions. Elder Porphyrios wrote, "Outside the Church there is no salvation, there is no life."[607]

Unfortunately, today many people in the United States and Western Europe describe themselves as "spiritual," but reject the notion of an institutionalized Church. They believe spirituality and a transcendent purpose are something to be pursued individually. Yet as Sr. Sandra M. Schneiders, a foremost authority on spirituality, would argue, the spiritual traditions of the Church are precisely what we need to understand our spiritual life experiences.[608] We receive our life-giving spiritual tradition *through* the institutionalized Church, the Christian tradition centered in Jesus Christ, which has been institutionalized in the Roman and Eastern Catholic Churches.[609] Divorcing the spiritual life from the Church, Schneiders said, "is a classic case of curing a headache by decapitation."[610] The Church hands us these spiritual

606 Matt. 18:20.
607 Elder Porphyrios, 87.
608 See Schneiders, "Religion vs. Spirituality," 169.
609 Ibid., 171.
610 Ibid.

traditions, and we need them to support our encounters with Jesus, the source of life. The Church is where we can receive guidance from the collective wisdom of the Holy Fathers who precede us. We have access to the writings of those who have also undergone the ascetic struggles in following the commandments of Jesus, which provide guideposts for our own experiences.[611] Many others have walked the same spiritual path and have left markers for us to follow.[612] Thus, we can never separate our growth in the spiritual life from the Church. We gather as a community because we would be incomplete without it.

Perspectives on Ecclesiology

The Church is a means of encounter because it provides access to the liturgy, the sacramental life, and the repository of spiritual traditions and teachings of the Holy Fathers who strove for the same destiny. But to clarify what is meant by "Church," we should consider Ecclesiology, the study of theological doctrine as applied to the nature and structure of the Church. It comes from the Greek *ekklēsia* meaning "church."

The Eastern Christian belief is that "the Church is an image of the Holy Trinity."[613] "Just as in the Trinity the persons are equal, so in the Church no one bishop can claim to wield absolute power over the rest."[614] The Orthodox perspective was always one of collegiality, a communion of equal persons. However, from a historical perspective, the Bishop of Rome was seen as *primus inter pares*, the first among equals, given the nature of the Roman Church being founded on two

611 A corollary is the relationship between spirituality and theology. Spirituality drives theology, not the other way around. Consider this analogy: Spirituality is a flowing river. Theology and the Tradition of the Church are like the embankment, helping guide us and interpret our spiritual encounters with the Divine (the author's own analogy).

612 See Richard J. Fowler, 72.

613 Lossky, *The Mystical Theology of the Eastern Church*, 176. See also Veli-Matti Kärkkäinen, *An Introduction to Ecclesiology: Ecumenical, Historical & Global Perspectives* (Downers Grove, IL: InterVarsity Press, 2002), 17–25. "The Church as an Icon of the Trinity: Eastern Orthodox Ecclesiology."

614 Kärkkäinen, 20.

apostles, St. Peter and St. Paul. Collegiality refers to the governance of the church while respecting the proper autonomy of each bishop who is in communion with all other bishops. This stems from the idea that the apostles were in communion with one another and shared equally in responsibility for the Church, Peter being the "first among equals." However, the Catholic view of Papal Primacy caused in part the Great Eastern Schism of 1054, when the Eastern Orthodox and Catholic Churches separated. Many Eastern Orthodox continue to view the Catholic Church as having separated itself from the "one holy, catholic, and apostolic Church."

In contrast to the Eastern perspective, the Catholic Church had a much more hierarchical view of Church structure, especially prior to Vatican II, and less emphasis on collegiality. The fundamental teaching was that only the Catholic Church contained the fullness of truth, with the Eastern Orthodox referred to as "schismatics" (separated in a pejorative sense from communion) and Protestants referred to as "heretics." However, in Vatican II, this perspective changed:

> This is the one Church of Christ which in the Creed is professed as one, holy, catholic and apostolic, which our Savior, after His Resurrection, commissioned Peter to shepherd, and him and the other apostles to extend and direct with authority, which he erected for all ages as "the pillar and mainstay of the truth." This Church constituted and organized in the world as a society, *subsists* in the Catholic Church, which is governed by the successor of Peter and by the bishops in communion with him, *although many elements of sanctification and of truth are found outside of its visible structure*. These elements, as gifts belonging to the Church of Christ, are forces impelling toward catholic unity.[615]

615 The Second Vatican Council, *Lumen Gentium*, no. 8. Sections highlighted by the author.

Lumen Gentium, a key document from Vatican II, recognized that elements of sanctification and truth are found outside the Catholic Church. In particular, the Catholic Church has shown great respect for the Eastern Orthodox, who preserve the same seven ritual sacraments and have a mutual understanding of the Eucharist—important to both Catholic and Eastern Orthodox ecclesiology. This is expressed, for example, in *Orientalium Ecclesiarum*, a document from Vatican II. [616] Further, the document acknowledges and shows respect for the patriarchal structure of the Eastern Churches[617] and states that the sacraments of the separated Eastern Churches are valid. Converts need only make a profession of faith, and clerics are considered to have valid orders.[618] If necessitated for pastoral reasons, separated Eastern Christians can be admitted to the sacraments of Penance, Eucharist, and Anointing of the Sick from the Catholic Church, as could Catholics from non-Catholic ministers of the separated Eastern Churches.[619] Further, the document expressed a genuine desire for movement toward unity between East and West.[620] Thus, the term "separated churches" became more prevalent after Vatican II, a reference to the break in communion between East and West, and allowing for a shared theology.

In contrast, certain Eastern Orthodox jurisdictions do not consider Catholic sacraments as valid, including the priesthood, believing that Apostolic Succession was broken when the Catholic Church separated itself from "the one holy, catholic, and apostolic Church." Their perspective is that the Eastern Orthodox held to the one, true faith and the Catholic Church not only separated itself, but also added to teachings that were over and above the Seven Ecumenical Councils, an example being the addition of the *Filioque* to the Nicaean-Constantinople Creed. Such an addition is considered heretical.

616 See Second Vatican Council, *Orientalium Ecclesiarum* (Decree on Eastern Catholic Churches), Nov. 21, 1964, no. 1.
617 Ibid., no. 7–11.
618 Ibid., no. 25.
619 Ibid., no. 26.
620 Ibid., no. 30.

Eastern Christian ecclesiology is heavily based on Patristic teachings, particularly the Early Greek Fathers of the Church, which is seen as the image of the Trinity, predicated on the communion (*koinonia*) of the Divine Persons. The Eastern position is that the Church is fundamentally one. "The division of the churches cannot be viewed or seen as anything else but sin. Just as there are no divisions in the Trinity, there also cannot be division in the one Church, which is the image of the Trinity."[621] *Koinonia* is the theological expression for approaching the inner mystery of the church, showing it has its origins in God.[622] This idea of a "communion" was developed by various Eastern theologians and "has fundamentally designated the church's fellowship with God through Christ and the Spirit, together with the common fellowship of the faithful with one another."[623]

Lossky describes the Church has having two aspects: one is the role of Christ (Christological) and the other is influenced by the Holy Spirit (Pneumatological),[624] both of which are in harmony with each other, same as the persons of the Holy Trinity. As Lossky explains, two Divine Persons were sent into the world, the Son and the Holy Spirit, but their roles are not the same. His writings suggest the Church "is at once the body of Christ and the fullness of the Holy Spirit, 'filling all in all.'" [625] Within the body, we have unity because of the incarnate Christ's human and divine natures. The fullness of the Spirit is present to each person, who is both an individual containing all the necessary attributes for a relationship with the Divine, and at the same, a collective member of the Body of Christ. The Holy Spirit rests upon the humanity of the Son, Head of the Church, and communicates to each member of this body, thereby creating, so to speak, many Christs, many of the Lord's anointed. Because the Church is the work

621 Peter Anthony Baktis, "Orthodox Ecclesiology for the New Millennium," *Pro Ecclesia* 10(3) (Summer 2001), 327.

622 See Philip Kariatlis, "Affirming Koinonia Ecclesiology: An Orthodox Perspective," *Phronema* 27(1) (2012), 51.

623 Ibid., 52.

624 See Lossky, *The Mystical Theology of the Eastern Church*, 174.

625 Ibid.

of Christ and the Holy Spirit, the doctrine of the Church has a double foundation—it is rooted upon both Christ and the Holy Spirit.[626]

The Church is the body of Christ, and Christ dwells in the hearts of believers through the Holy Spirit. We can consider these two a dialectic. There are two missions: redemption and sanctification. Orthodox theologian Dr. Philip Kariatlis stated: "Whilst Christ became incarnate and, in this way, gave the church its 'body,' it was the Spirit who breathed life into this body thereby 'animating' it—i.e., giving it a spiritual or Spirit-filled existence—and preparing it for its universal mission in the world."[627]

The theological reality is that Christ and the Spirit always work together in guiding the Church. "*Koinonia* essentially signifies the church's intimate unity with God the Father mediated through Christ and the Holy Spirit."[628]

The Role of Christ: Eucharistic or Christological Ecclesiology

The sacramental life is at the heart of Eastern Orthodox ecclesiology. As Lossky wrote, "The sacrament life— 'the life in Christ'—is thus seen to be an unceasing struggle for the acquisition of grace, which must transfigure nature; a struggle in which victories alternate with falls, without man ever being deprived of the objective conditions of salvation."[629]

Paraphrasing Lossky, Finnish Theologian Veli-Matti Kärkkäinen wrote, "In the Church and through the sacraments human nature enters into union with the divine nature. Human nature becomes consubstantial with the deified humanity, united with the person of Christ in the power of the Holy Spirit. This union is fulfilled in

626 Ibid.
627 Kariatlis, 57–58.
628 Ibid., 53.
629 Lossky, *The Mystical Theology of the Easter Church*, 180.

the sacramental life."[630] Going back to the Patristic teachings of the Fathers, "the ecclesiological rule...says wherever the Eucharist is, there is the church." [631] Or, said another way, "the church makes the Eucharist and the Eucharist makes the church."[632] One of the key implications of this is that *ekklēsia* is not just any assembly, but God's people gathered for Eucharist.[633]

While Holy Eucharist is celebrated by each local church, it is the same Eucharist shared by all churches; thus, there cannot be any compromise on the principles of collegiality and communion. Eastern Orthodox Metropolitan Bishop Kallistos Ware would remind people that we "cannot isolate the Eucharist from the context of unity."[634]

This Christological element also supports the mission of the Church, which we have described as "The Liturgy after the Liturgy." At the end of the day, it is not the encounters that matter. *Theosis* is about who we become as a result of our encounters. Do we become more God-like? Do we exhibit the divine attributes of God, such as love, mercy, and compassion? Does our capacity to love others increase?

Some Orthodox theologians, such as Stăniloae, warn that this view of church and *koinonia* is too narrow and diminishes the importance of the Holy Spirit. Remember, the concept of dialectic and the roles of both: Christ and the Holy Spirit are both necessary in sustaining the Church.

The Role of the Holy Spirit: Pneumatological Ecclesiology

Kärkkäinen wrote, "As the Spirit inspires and empowers the process of deification, the role of the Spirit comes into focus."[635]

630 Kärkkäinen, 21.
631 Ibid.
632 Ibid.
633 Ibid.
634 Referenced by Kärkkäinen, 21.
635 Ibid., 23.

Christology and pneumatology are seen as simultaneous in the context of Eastern Orthodox ecclesiology. Pentecost is not a continuation of the Incarnation but a separate action or sequel. Christ provides the solid foundation of the Church, and the Holy Spirit provides it with a dynamic character. As St. Paul noted, there are different gifts of the Holy Spirit bestowed upon members of the Church. While there is a hierarchy, from the Eastern Christian perspective, all members of the Church are considered equal[636] and can participate in the divine life and receive the gifts of the Holy Spirit.

Lossky writes about this simultaneous action of the two aspects of the Church:

> In its first aspect the Church appears as the body of Christ; in its second, as a flame having one single base but forking into many divided tongues. The two aspects are inseparable, and yet, in the first the Church exists in the (divine nature) of Christ, while in the second we can catch a glimpse of its own being, distinct from its head.[637]

Lossky explains that the Holy Spirit did not come into the world as Christ did. Rather, the Holy Spirit remains hidden.

> He hides himself, identifying himself so to speak, with the human persons upon whom he confers a second nature—deity, the deifying energies. He becomes the source of personal deification, of the uncreated treasure in each person. He brings to each person its ultimate perfection, but he does not become the person of the Church. [638]

---

636 Ibid., 22.
637 Lossky, *The Mystical Theology of the Eastern Church*, 192.
638 Ibid., 192–93.

In other words, the Church remains the body of Christ, not the body of the Holy Spirit. Yet the Holy Spirit provides the dynamic character and enables the deification of each person, bringing him to his ultimate perfection. Lossky adds, "The Holy Spirit does not contain the unity of human and divine nature as Christ does, but gives himself separately to each person."[639]

Certain Holy Fathers, such as St. Seraphim of Sarov, describe the objective of *theosis* as the acquisition of the Holy Spirit. The Spirit is the agent providing the necessary grace for divinization, perfection, and sanctification—while at the same time following the example of Jesus and keeping his commandments.

Eucharistic Ecclesiology as *Koinonia* and Emphasis on the Local Church

Greek Orthodox Theologian John Zizioulas sees the Eucharist as center of the Church: "For Orthodoxy, the church is in the Eucharist and through the Eucharist."[640] This position evolved from St. Paul's perspective that blends the notion of the local church becoming the Church through Eucharistic celebration.[641] However, many theologians see a Church based solely on the Eucharistic celebration or other sacraments as too limited and narrow. The Church modeled in Acts 2 was more than Eucharistic. The early members devoted themselves to teaching, prayer, and providing for the needs of all, in addition to the breaking of the bread.[642] *Ekklēsia,* in this context, was "being called together by God to form an assembly of chosen people." They were called to unity by an invitation from God and understood themselves to be a people gathered led by God in Jesus Christ.[643] Thus, *koinonia* is the heart of New Testament ecclesiology, but it is not solely defined by

639 Ibid.
640 Ibid., 96. Zizioulas cited by Kärkkäinen.
641 See Baktis, 322.
642 See Acts 2:42–47, discussing communal life post-Pentecost.
643 See Kariatlis, 56.

the Eucharistic celebration. Similarly, in Base Christian Communities that have emerged in the Roman Catholic Church in Latin America, "the essential constitutive elements of the church are present, namely the gospel, the Eucharist, and the presence of apostolic succession in the person of the bishop."[644] Thus, while Eucharist is an essential part of communion, it is not the sole defining feature of the Church.

Another Perspective on Church: *Sobornost*

The term *sobornost* emerged during the Russian Spiritual Renaissance of the 1800s. It was meant to emphasize the cooperation of people over individualism. Some believe it was a reaction to the focus on individualism emerging in Western European philosophical thought. One way to consider *sobornost* is to visualize the parish church in the middle of the village, established to pull together the surrounding people. While today most parishes are much larger than a small village church in a rural area, we can illustrate the same point by considering a 7,000-family parish in a community significantly impacted by Hurricane Harvey in September 2017. Numerous parishioners were affected by flooding. The Church helped organize teams to assist parishioners in need, made cleaning supplies available, coordinated shelter and housing for those displaced, hosted evening meals at the church hall, and raised funds to provide relief to those with limited or no flood insurance. The Church was at the center of the community, a modern-day example of *sobornost*.

In such cases, parishioners are pulled together to focus on the community's collective needs. This creates a sense of communion within the parish, the binding force holding the community together. This concept is a complementary and pragmatic perspective, similar to the theological views of ecclesiology whereby the Holy Spirit creates the bond within the Body of Christ.

---

644 See Kärkkäinen, 180. References *Lumen Gentium*, no. 26.

In many cases, we have lost the sense of *sobornost*, the parish church in the middle of the community. In many respects, this is similar to the Apostolic community in Jerusalem as described in the Acts of the Apostles, in which there was teaching, preaching, and care for those in need. Putting the parish church and its community at the center of our lives could be one antidote for the increasingly prevalent culture of individualism that pushes God and neighbor to the periphery.

Summary

The Church creates an environment to cultivate our faith. It facilitates our encounters with Jesus. First, we have the twofold encounter with Christ in the liturgy through the Sacred Scriptures and Eucharist. Second, the Church mediates our encounters with Christ through the Holy Mysteries. Finally, it serves as a repository of our spiritual traditions that help guide and interpret our encounters by drawing upon the collective wisdom of the Holy Fathers before us. They were on the same journey, striving for the same destiny.

Some today believe spirituality is a private affair and struggle with the concept of an institutionalized Church. Yet, if spirituality is left to individuals, they are dependent upon their own experiences, denying the importance of more than 2,000 years of Church knowledge institutionalized for our benefit. This is precisely why we need the Church.

Both Christ and the Holy Spirit became part of human history to build up the Church. Christ pulls together the Church as his body in a tangible sense; the unity of Christ with the Church is an image of the destiny of humanity living in union with God. However, the Holy Spirit is also active in the Church and, though invisible, holds the Body of Christ together and helps cultivate individuals' talents for the benefit of all. Both are required for building up the Church; the two missions of the Father are often described as redemption and sanctification.

These components, Christological and Pneumatological, are held in dialectic tension.

The models of ecclesiology we discussed all involve relationships, people in communion with one another. Eucharistic celebration is clearly one element of unity among each church as all celebrate the same Eucharist. However, if we look at the Church as described in the Acts of the Apostles, it involved more than the breaking of the bread. It included preaching, teaching, and looking out for the needs of those in the community. The concept of communion and oneness are critical, and we begin to appreciate what Jesus asked of his Father when he prayed at the Last Supper: "[T]hat they may be brought to perfection as one."[645]

Reflection Questions

1. How do I define the Church?
2. What role does the Church play in my life today? Please be specific.
3. Do I share the concerns of some about an "institutionalized" Church? Why or why not? What are my specific concerns?
4. Ideally, where should the Church be today in my life and my community? Is it there? If not, what can I specifically do to help build up the Body of Christ?
5. Do I recognize the talents I have been given can serve the Church? Do I use them to serve? Why or why not?
6. What are my thoughts about *sobornost* as presented in this discussion? Is this an image of what I would like my parish community to be? Please be specific.

645 John 17:23.

MEANS OF ENCOUNTER

Love of Neighbor

***"Lord, when did we see you hungry and feed you, or thirsty and give you drink?"* (Matt. 25:37)**

***"True theology is always born out of the life of the Church that prays, confesses, and serves."*[646] (Patriarch Daniel of Romania)**

Opening Gospel Reading

Luke 10:25-37 (Parable of the Good Samaritan) or
Matt. 25:31-46 (The Judgment of Nations).

Love of God Manifested in Love of Neighbor

To this point, we have discussed our interior relationship with the Divine as we encounter Jesus in prayer, Sacred Scripture, the writings of the Holy Fathers, liturgy, and the community of believers. While God is the ultimate mystery, Rahner explained we can experience him through our encounters with the world and especially other people. Accordingly, our focus will now shift to how we encounter the divine presence through our love of others, all of whom are also made in the divine image. Love in this context refers to the Greek *agapé*, which is the highest form of love, such as God's love for man—absolute, unconditional love—and man's love for God—striving for absoluteness but imperfect.

646 Patriarch Daniel, "The Unity between Theology and Spirituality," 20.

Scriptural Foundation

Throughout Sacred Scripture, we hear of God's concern for the *anawim,* the poor and marginalized who depend solely on the Lord for their deliverance. In the Old Testament, they often are represented as widows, orphans, and resident aliens dwelling among the Israelites—those who had no one to stand up for them. God's concern for them in the Old Testament is a message central to Jesus's teachings.

Jesus, asked by the Pharisees what the greatest commandment was,[647] replied, "You shall love the Lord, your God, with all your heart, with all your soul, and with all your mind. This is the greatest and first commandment."[648] In other words, we are to love God with our entire being. The other means of encounter—prayer, Sacred Scripture, the Sacred Tradition, the liturgy, the Holy Mysteries, and the Church—cultivate our love for God by responding to his love for us. However, Jesus went beyond the original question, saying, "The second [commandment] is *like* it: You shall love your neighbor as yourself."[649] From these words, Jesus created an indelible link between love of God and love of neighbor. St. John the Evangelist wrote, "Beloved, if God so loved us, we also must love one another."[650] The author also says, "If anyone says, 'I love God,' but hates his brother, he is a liar; for whoever does not love a brother whom he has seen cannot love God whom he has not seen."[651]

In Luke's account of the greatest commandment, the scholar who questions Jesus asks a follow-up question, "And who is my neighbor?"[652] In response Jesus tells the Parable of the Good Samaritan,[653] essentially changing the preconceived definition of

647 See Matt. 22:35–40 and Mark 12:28–34. Luke 10:25–28 is similar.
648 Matt. 22:37–38.
649 Matt. 22:39.
650 1 John 4:11.
651 1 John 4:20.
652 Luke 10:29.
653 See Luke 10:30–37.

neighbor from being a narrow legal definition—who is worthy of my love—to one of self-giving: our neighbor is anyone in need.

Jesus's definition of neighbor is relevant for us. If we follow "the way" of Jesus, we need to reflect on his stated mission to the poor, the marginalized, and excluded. Second, Jesus tells us in the Gospel of Matthew how we will be judged worthy or not of the kingdom: "Amen, I say to you, whatever you did for one of these least brothers of mine, you did for me."[654] Linking this to *theosis*, the process of our divinization involves practicing such God-like virtues as love, mercy, and compassion. The Good Samaritan parable highlights that the "neighbor" was the one who treated the person in need with mercy.[655] In the Gospel of John, Jesus tells his disciples, "I give you a new commandment: love one another. As I have loved you, so you also should love one another."[656] Then he adds, "This is how all will know you are my disciples, if you have love for another."[657] Thus, we have a definition of neighbor and the specific commandment to love others.

Solidarity with the Body of Christ is a key tenant of ecclesiology, and by extension, to Catholic Social Teaching. St. Paul wrote, "So, we though many, are one body in Christ and individually parts of one another."[658] As one body, we are responsible for each member. Jesus addresses this in his Parable of Lazarus and the Rich Man, where the rich man dines in sumptuous splendor and ignores the needs of the poor man lying at his door.[659] Accordingly, we can conclude from the teachings of Jesus the importance of love of neighbor as a means to our salvation.

---

654 Matt. 25:40.
655 See Luke 10:37.
656 John 13:34.
657 John 13:35.
658 Rom. 12:5.
659 See Luke 16:19–31.

Example of Solidarity with the Body of Christ (or "Today, Who Is My Neighbor?")

Mother Teresa of Calcutta told a story regarding how we encounter Jesus.

> I remember one of our sisters, who had just graduated from the university. She came from a well-to-do family that lived outside of India. According to our rule, the very next day after joining our society, the postulants must go to the home for the dying destitute in Calcutta. Before this sister went, I told her, 'You saw the priest during Mass—with what love, with what delicate care he touched the body of Christ. Make sure you do the same thing when you get to that home, because Jesus is there in distressing disguise.'
>
> So she went, and after three hours, she came back. That girl from the university, who had seen and understood so many things, came to my room with such a beautiful smile on her face. She said, 'For three hours I've been touching the body of Christ!' And I said, 'What did you do? What happened?'
>
> She said, 'They brought a man from the street who had fallen into a drain and had been there for some time. He was covered with maggots and dirt and wounds. And though I found it very difficult, I cleaned him, and I knew I was touching the body of Christ!'
>
> *She knew!* [660]

This example provides context for the concept of solidarity and encountering the divine presence in others. We are all members of a

660 Mother Teresa of Calcutta, *In the Heart of the World: Thoughts, Stories & Prayers* (Novato, CA: New World Library, 1997), 55–56.

single body, all created in the same divine image. Do we recognize Jesus in others, especially when he comes to us in distressing disguise?

Social Concerns in the Patristic Period

Almsgiving and care for those in need were clear themes in the Early Church. For example, in the post-Resurrectional community in Jerusalem, the Apostles instituted the first deacons to take responsibility for food distribution so they could remain focused on the word of God.[661] Many of the Early Desert Fathers, who withdrew to the Egyptian desert for solitude to focus on prayer, performed manual labor such as basket weaving. They would sell their products, retain a small amount to purchase needed provisions, and give most of their earnings to the poor. St. Basil the Great spent five years in the Egyptian desert and, when he returned, created a "city of mercy" called the Basiliade, a home for the poor and a hospital that provided hospice care. He wrote numerous homilies on social justice. For example, in one entitled "I Will Tear Down My Barns," he wrote: "Do not become a dealer in human misery. Do not attempt to turn the chastisement of God into an opportunity for profit. Do not chafe the wounds of those who have already been scourged."[662] This advice is as relevant in modern times as in the 4th century.

St. John Chrysostom was one of the most noted commentators on social concerns and the plight of the poor. While a priest in Antioch, he wrote a series of homilies on the Parable of Lazarus and the Rich Man. "He knew from experience the sufferings of the poor and the sick and was struck in contrast by the arrogance of the rich."[663] As Archbishop of Constantinople, St. John "denounced luxury and

661 See Acts 6:1–7.

662 St. Basil the Great, *On Social Justice*, trans. C. Paul Schroeder (Crestwood, NY: St. Vladimir's Seminary Press, 2009), 64.

663 St. John Chrysostom, *On Wealth and Poverty*, trans. Catharine P. Roth (Crestwood, NY: St. Vladimir's Seminary Press, 1984), 9.

license,"[664] even taking Empress Eudoxia to task. This led him twice into exile, where he died. In the troparion for his feast day, he is known for teaching us a "disdain for wealth." The following is an excerpt from one of Chrysostom's homilies.

> Do you want to honor Christ's body? Then do not scorn him in his nakedness, nor honor him here in the church with silken garments while neglecting him outside where he is cold and naked. For he who said, 'This is my body,' and made it so by his words, also said: 'You saw me hungry and did not feed me,' and 'inasmuch as you did not do it for one of these, the least of my brothers, you did not do it for me.' What we do here in the church requires a pure heart, not special garments; what we do outside requires great dedication.
>
> Let us learn, therefore, to be men of wisdom and to honor Christ as he desires. For a person being honored finds greatest pleasure in the honor he desires, not the honor we think best. Peter thought he was honoring Christ when he refused to let him wash his feet; but what Peter wanted was not truly an honor, *quite the opposite!* Give him the honor prescribed in his law by giving your riches to the poor. For God does not want golden vessels, but golden hearts.
>
> No one has ever been accused for not providing ornaments, but for those who neglect their neighbor a hell waits with an inextinguishable fire and torment in the company of the demons. Do not, therefore, adorn the church and ignore your afflicted brother, *for he is the most precious temple of all.*[665]

---

664 Ibid., 10.

665 St. John Chrysostom, "Homily No. 50, Gospel of Matthew," In *The Liturgy of the Hours*, vol. 4 (New York, NY: Catholic Book Publishing Corp., 1975), 182–183. Emphasis added by the author.

Chrysostom clearly speaks to "the Liturgy after the Liturgy." We can observe that there was concern for the poor and marginalized in the Early Church, and, sadly, one could argue that the message has not changed much between the 4th and 21st centuries. Many of the same social concerns remain. Have we, too, passed by Jesus silently crying out to us in need and failing to recognize him?

Perspectives from Rahner and Stăniloae

Rahner taught that we experience the mystery of God by experiencing other people. "Whenever we truly love another, we are in a situation of faith."[666] He also wrote:

> In this appeal what is said in Matthew 25 would have to be taken seriously and interpreted radically, and indeed from 'below' (humanity), from the concrete love of neighbor, and not merely from 'above' (divine).

In other words, it is not a one-way street: divine to human love. We are called to be like God in our love for our neighbor. Rahner goes on to say:

> If we do not turn the saying of Jesus that *he himself* is truly loved in every neighbor into an 'as if' or merely into a theory ..., then when this saying is read from out of the experience of love itself, it says that an absolute love which gives itself radically and unconditionally to another person affirms Christ implicitly in faith and love. And this is correct. For a merely finite and ever unreliable person cannot by himself justify the sense of absolute love, which is given him, a love in which

666 Fischer, 105–6.

> a person 'involves' and risks himself absolutely for the other person.[667]

Through love of neighbor, God makes a transcendental appeal, inviting us to love absolutely as God loves, despite our finite and unreliable nature. Love is not an idea, because ideas cannot be loved. Love is a reality, and true love is not individualistic and exclusive, but a concrete expression.[668] Such love responds to God's invitation to have a relationship with him by perfecting our love of neighbor, a concrete reality. "By doing so, we realize the possibility of becoming one with God."[669] This also aligns with the teaching from 1 John that we cannot love God whom we cannot see if we cannot love the neighbor whom we can see. Said another way, loving our neighbor is a way of drawing deeper into the mystery that is God.

Stăniloae expresses the relationship between God and man similarly:

> Such a relationship (between God and man) is analogous to the relationship of one human person to another, a relationship in which the liberty of both is preserved. In this relationship, man exists for the sake of another person and is at the service of the other, although through this, he himself is enriched. Each man exists for the sake of others in a way that he does not exist for the sake of material things.[670]

Rahner says, "When we love our neighbor, we are loving in the way God deserves to be loved, namely, in a concrete manner."[671] Both Rahner and Stăniloae express how in loving others—Mother

667 Rahner, *Foundations of Christian Faith*, 295–96.
668 Ibid., 296.
669 Fischer, 106.
670 Stăniloae, "Revelation and Knowledge of the Triune God," 9–10.
671 Fischer, 112.

Teresa's Gospel on Five Fingers[672]—we are called to a standard of absolute love, which, in turn, is the love we should have for God. This affirms our faith in Jesus Christ, for he said, "This is how all will know you are my disciples." The bar for this standard is set extremely high; we struggle to properly respond to God's invitation to us. Yet we have a definitive guide. Jesus is our "way," and he modeled his absolute love for humanity, emptying himself and offering his very life on the cross. This is absolute, unconditional love and illustrates our radical dependency on God: "Father, into your hands I commend my spirit."[673] Acknowledging this dependency prepares us for surrender of our will to the will of God—the alignment of wills, complete submission, and dethronement of the ego.

Modern Catholic Social Teaching

While there were teachings on social concerns in the Early Church, modern Catholic Social Teaching is uniquely Catholic. This modern period began in 1891 with Pope Leo XIII's encyclical letter, *Rerum Novarum,* which discussed labor conditions and the need for just wages. Reflections on social concerns continue today with, for example, the writings of Pope Francis including *Evangelii Gaudium* and *Laudato Si'.* Catholic Social Teaching begins with the person and message of Jesus. Same as at the time of Jesus, we as Christians cannot ignore the toil, suffering, and poverty that afflict the lives of most people in the world.[674] Jesus deliberately went to the outcast and marginalized, restoring their dignity and telling them through his actions that they mattered to God. As authentic and intentional disciples of his, we are called to do likewise.

672 See Leo Maasburg, *Mother Teresa of Calcutta: A Personal Portrait,* trans. Michael J. Miller (San Francisco, CA: Ignatius Press, 2010), 36. "Mother Teresa sometimes held up five fingers of one hand to explain this. The whole Gospel, she said, could be counted on five fingers: 'You-did-it-to-me!'" See references Matt. 25:40. In a letter dated June 1990, Mother Teresa tells her congregation "Remember the five fingers—you-did-it-to Me." See Mother Teresa, *Come Be My Light: The Private Writings of the Saint of Calcutta,* ed. Brian Kolodiejchuk, MC (New York, NY: Doubleday, 2007), 314.

673 Luke 23:46.

674 See David J. O'Brien and Thomas A. Shannon, *Catholic Social Thought: The Documentary Heritage* (Maryknoll, NY: Orbis Books, 2004), 2.

Catholic Social Teaching tries to create a balance between individual freedom and concerns for society as a whole. The United States Conference of Catholic Bishops identifies seven themes in Catholic Social Teaching;[675] three of them are relevant to our encounter with Jesus through our neighbor.

1. **Dignity of Human Life**

   Every human is made in the divine image, patterned after the Image Absolute, Jesus Christ. In Rahner's theological framework, he places importance on humanity being *related* to God. Accordingly, each person, from the unborn child to the drug addict collapsed on the sidewalk, possesses fundamental dignity because each is infused with the divine image.

   Catholic social concern has focused on anything that could de-dignify the human person, including the most vulnerable in society. This is the reason the Church has taken strong positions on abortion, euthanasia, and the death penalty. All human life is precious to God because all are made in the divine image. Issues such as racial injustice or other types of discrimination, human trafficking, and unfair labor practices also de-dignify the human person. Embryonic stem cell research and cloning are concerns because they threaten the value of human life. Thus, the issue becomes whether a practice enhances or threatens the dignity of human life.

2. **Preferential Option for the Poor and Vulnerable**

   Who are the most vulnerable in our society? A basic moral test is to examine how well these members are faring.[676] This concept originated in the Catholic Bishops' Conferences of Latin America and has also been adopted by the United States Conference of Catholic Bishops. Further, Pope St. John Paul II

675 See United States Conference of Catholic Bishops ("USCCB"), "Seven Themes of Catholic Social Teaching." http://www.usccb.org.

676 Ibid.

spoke about a "preferential option for the poor," reinforcing this concept. Deep divides between rich and poor are a concern if the poor are left behind or alienated. In his mission, Jesus, specifically reached out to the poor, the sick, and the marginalized. These were people segregated from society, told by the religious authorities that they were estranged from God, and classified as "sinners." There was a perception that poverty and illness were retribution from God. Consider the account of the man born blind.[677] The disciples asked Jesus, "Who sinned, this man or his parents, that he was born blind?"[678] Jesus responded that it was neither.

In the Old Testament, concern for the most vulnerable—widows, orphans, resident aliens, those in debt—was addressed through regular jubilees. Pope Francis took a similar initiative when announcing an extraordinary Holy Year, the Jubilee of Mercy (December 8, 2015–November 20, 2016), especially reaching out to those who felt alienated by the Church.

Jesus is also clear about the consequences of indifference to the needs of those around us. St. John Chrysostom summarizes the issue quite well in a sermon:

> And where was Lazarus lying? Not in the road, not in a street, not in an alley, not in the middle of the marketplace, but at the gate of the rich man, where he had to go in and out, so he could not say, 'I did not see him, passed and my eyes did not see him.' He lies at your entrance, the pearl in the mud, and you do not see him? [679]

The rich man had to step over Lazarus each day to enter

677 See John 9:1–41.
678 John 9:2.
679 See Chrysostom, *On Wealth and Poverty*, 106.

his house. After three or four days of seeing him, the rich man should have been moved to pity, but he was not.[680]

As intentional and authentic disciples of Jesus Christ, we are called to show concern for the poor and most vulnerable. This includes, for example, the poor and the exploitation of undocumented immigrants through unsafe conditions, unfair wages, and such. In a consumeristic and disposable society such as the United States, Pope Francis warns about consciences becoming blunted and there being no place for the poor.[681] For example, when we encounter a homeless person on the street, do we walk away or cross to the other side? Do we even notice anymore? Do we recognize Jesus in distressing disguise, silently crying out for help? Recall Mother Teresa's Gospel on Five Fingers: "You did it to me." Elder Arsenie Papacioc of Romania said, "The beggar stretches out his hand not to ask, but to give you the kingdom of heaven, and you do not notice!"[682] Do we recognize the face of Jesus in our neighbor?

3. Solidarity

We are one body in Christ and individually responsible for one another.[683] We are a single global human family and are accountable for the suffering of our brothers and sisters. As Mother Teresa described it, if the ocean was missing a single drop, the entire ocean would be impoverished by the loss of that drop. At the core of solidarity are peace and justice.[684] As intentional and authentic disciples of Jesus Christ, we cannot ignore the needs of the global human family.

As an example, moral theologian Fr. Humberto Miguel

680 Ibid., 21.
681 See Pope Francis, *Evangelii Gaudium*, no. 2.
682 Elder Arsenie Papacioc, a Romanian Orthodox monk.
683 See Rom. 12:5.
684 See USCCB, "Seven Themes of Catholic Social Teaching."

Yáñez, SJ, speaks about the situation in his native Argentina. He notes that there is not only a division between wealth and poverty, but the latter can be further divided between poverty and deep poverty.[685] Deep poverty creates a culture of poverty, which injures people, creates hopelessness and despair, weakens social bonds, increases violence, and is perpetuated when people remain in this situation. Yáñez states, "The poor themselves, many of them young people with a history of deprivation and aggression, are growing up in institutionalized violence and will return to society what they have received from it; poverty has brought crime and violence."[686] In other words, it is not just a matter of people stealing to feed their families. Rather, a history of deprivation brings about a culture of violence, which no longer simply focuses on basic necessities. This is an indictment of an entire society that tolerates long-standing experiences of deprivation. Yáñez refers to this as *cultural poverty* and notes the following challenges:

- If culture is the way humans express meaning, here it refers to the group of marginalized and excluded people who develop a new way of expressing their fundamental existence.
- Life loses its value, but the people are determined to give some meaning to an existence too absurd to accept.
- Unemployment leads to a crisis and reformation of social roles; the emergence of dysfunctional, depressed, devaluated males and female heads of households who suffer from overwork and lack of understanding in a stressful and lonely situation.

685 Humberto Miguel Yáñez, "Opting for the Poor in the Face of Growing Poverty," in *Applied Ethics in a World Church: The Padua Conference*, ed. Linda Hogan (Maryknoll, NY: Orbis Books, 2008), 14.

686 Ibid.

- In this sense, cultural poverty generates more poverty: weaker links, declining motivation, and shrinking horizons.[687]

Cultural poverty creates despair with no optimistic outlook, which denigrates into violence and other expressions, all of which reflect the de-dignification of the human. It is a self-perpetuating cycle, spiraling increasingly downward without any sense of hope. The experience of long-term deprivation produces a jaded outlook on life and is an indictment of the legitimacy of social systems within a particular country. It is an erosion of the social fabric.

For us as Catholics in the U.S., there are key lessons. As the divide between rich and poor increases, we need to be cognizant of increasing feelings of exclusion, hopelessness, and despair. Evidence of this includes recent clashes associated with racial tension, indicative of underlying resentment and similar to Yáñez's description of cultural poverty. Second, we cannot simply ignore the plight of others beyond our borders from social and economic injustice, strife, discrimination, and ideological and religious intolerance. This economic hopelessness continues to drive massive migration here from the Caribbean and Latin American countries; religious intolerance creates refugees from the Middle East. Pope Paul VI taught that if we desire peace in the world to work for justice.[688] Finally, Pope Francis tells us in *Evangelii Gaudium* that we must say 'no' to an Economy of Exclusion,[689] in which others are written off or lose their sense of dignity. In the Church, there are no "have's" and "have nots." All are made in the image of God, all are members of the one body of Christ, and all are welcome at the Eucharistic table.

687 Ibid., 15.

688 See USCCB. Reference to Pope Paul VI, "For the Celebration of the Day of World Peace," Rome, January 1, 1972.

689 Pope Francis, *Evangelii Gaudium*, no. 53.

Intentional and authentic discipleship requires empathy and compassion, just as Jesus had for the socially marginalized of his time. Do we recognize our solidarity with the human family, that we are all members of one body in Christ? How do we react to the least among us?

Encounter through Love of Neighbor

Through prayer, Sacred Scripture, Sacred Tradition, the Holy Mysteries, the liturgy, and the Church, we deepen our individual relationship with God. However, the true question is, "Who do we become through these encounters?" Are our hearts truly transformed? Do we experience the type of deep conversion, *metanoia,* like Zacchaeus when he encountered Jesus?[690] Do we love the God we cannot see by loving the neighbor we can?[691] American Catholic social activist Dorothy Day wrote:

> How can I help but think of these things every time I sit down...and look around the tables filled with the unutterable poor who are going through their long-continuing crucifixion. It is surely an exercise of faith for us to see Christ in each other. But it is through such exercise that we grow and the joy of our vocation assures us we are on the right path.
>
> The mystery of the poor is this: That they are Jesus, and what you do for them you do for him. It is the only way we have of knowing and believing in our love. The mystery of poverty is that by sharing in it, making ourselves poor in giving to others, we increase our knowledge and belief in love.[692]

---

690 See Luke 19:1–10.

691 See 1 John 4:20.

692 Dorothy Day, *Selected Writings*, ed. Robert Ellsberg (Maryknoll, NY: Orbis Books, 2005), 330. From an article written by Day, "The Mystery of the Poor," April 1964.

This topic is the essence of *theosis,* the process of divinization in which we prepare for our destiny. It is not easy. That is why it requires incremental effort, daily choices we make to see the presence of God in our midst and respond to his invitation to love—especially in the distressing disguises of the poor, the suffering, and the immigrant. This is not a theory or nice idea; it is who we are called to be as authentic disciples of Jesus. It is how we will be judged for meriting entrance into the Kingdom.

Jesus tells us, "I have come to set the earth on fire, and how I wish it were already blazing!"[693] He expresses his deepest desire for a difference in our world, for authentic Christian witnesses who stand in stark contrast to darkness, hate, and indifference. He says, "How great is my anguish until it is accomplished!"[694] How do we as Christians set the earth on fire, and how do we not let our world be overcome by darkness? When we see injustice, is it easier to look the other way, to accept status quo, or to be indifferent? Yet love (*agapé*) can truly conquer all. Consider Mother Teresa of Calcutta, who in 1985 was described by United Nations Secretary General Perez de Cuellar as *the most powerful woman in the world.*[695] Yet she was a frail, elderly, and sickly woman. Mother Teresa transcended religion, ethnicity, and nationality to show us what it means to be an intentional, authentic disciple of Jesus Christ. She proved that such discipleship could set the earth on fire. Consider the perspective of modern-day Catholic apologist Matthew Kelly: "How would the world be different if we Christians simply *behaved* as Christians? Imagine."[696] Imagine, indeed.

Summary

Love of God manifests itself in our love of neighbor. God has always had special compassion for the poor and those without a voice,

693 Luke 12:49.
694 Luke 12:50.
695 Spoken by UN Secretary General Javier Perez de Cuellar. See Maasburg, 109.
696 Matthew Kelly, *Rediscover Jesus* (North Palm Beach, FL: Beacon Publishing, 2015), 183.

the *anawim*, those dependent upon God alone. "This poor one cried out and the Lord heard, and from all his distress he saved him."[697] Jesus reinforced this message in his teaching, "Whatever you do for one of these least brothers of mine, you did for me,"[698] and in his ministry, he reached out to the poor, the sick, the disabled, and the marginalized. Jesus broadened the definition of neighbor; it was not just those who deserve help, but those who need help.

Catholic Social Teaching is uniquely Catholic and attempts to address injustice and the sacredness of human life. The principles of such social teaching are based on the life and mission of Jesus. Three of the principles are: the dignity of human life, preferential option for the poor and vulnerable, and solidarity. Jesus said all will know that we are disciples by how we love one another.[699] Can we really make a difference in our world? Consider the example of Mother Teresa of Calcutta, who despite her diminutive stature and health issues, was consider the most powerful woman in the world.

Also consider the example of St. Seraphim of Sarov. He greeted every person he met as if he were reverencing an icon; bowing, making the sign of the cross, and saying, "Christ is risen! O my joy!" He was acknowledging the divine image in each person. Just as an icon is an image of Christ, the human, too, is an image of Christ, endowed with the divine image patterned after the Image Absolute, Christ himself. Love of neighbor is a means for encountering Christ, especially in his most distressing disguises. Louise Zwick, co-founder of Casa Juan Diego in Houston, a Catholic Worker House of Hospitality, which welcomes immigrants and the poor, tells visitors and volunteers, "We greet every person who knocks on our door as if he or she were Jesus. And Jesus never asked someone first if he or she had papers or was legal."[700]

---

697 Psalm 34:7. Consider too the refrain from the song based on this psalm by John Foley, SJ, "The Lord hears the cry of the poor, blessed be the Lord."

698 Matt. 25:40.

699 See John 13:35.

700 Louise Zwick, orientation and background information provided to high school youth from St. Martha Catholic Church, Kingwood, Texas, prior to commencing a service project at Casa Juan Diego, November 22, 2014.

Reflection Questions

1. Who is my neighbor? How do I answer this question? What is the basis for determining who is included in this definition?

2. Do I regularly feel compassion for those in need? Whom do I encounter: The homeless? The undocumented worker? The drug addict or prostitute? Do I find myself recognizing Christ, even in his most distressing disguises?

3. Do I struggle with feeling compassionate toward different groups? Who are these groups? What is my struggle? Please be specific.

4. We described three tenants of Catholic Social Teaching: The dignity of the human person, the preferential option for the poor and vulnerable, and solidarity. Can I relate to any of these? If so, which ones? Why?

5. When I consider how Jesus reached out with compassion to those who were marginalized, what are my thoughts? Can I follow his example? Why or why not?

Part 4

Where We Encounter

WHERE WE ENCOUNTER

Introduction

So far, we have considered our desire and capacity for encounter, the Triune God that we encounter, and the means for such encounter. In this next series of topics, we will consider the location of this encounter. One important premise is that our God is not distant, but ever-present in his creation. Consider the words of the Prophet Isaiah:

> I am the Lord, and there is no other. I have not spoken in secret from some place in the land of darkness. I have not said to the descendants of Jacob, 'Look for me in an empty waste.'[701]

"According to biblical thought, the heart is the center of all life,"[702] physical, mental, and spiritual[703]—body, mind, and soul. "It is the organ of reason, intelligence, and therefore knowledge of God. As such, it is the most intimate point of encounter between God and the human person."[704] Our encounter is within us.

St. Augustine of Hippo lamented in his *Confessions*, "Late have I loved you, beauty so ancient and so new: late have I loved you. And see, you were *within* and I was in the external world and sought you there."[705] We are not required to look hard for God in dark or far-away places. He is always close. Rahner would say the self-communicating God is "readily available." We simply need to become more attuned

---

701 Isa. 45:18(b)–19.

702 Breck, 37.

703 Consider this in light of Jesus's response when asked about the greatest commandment. "You shall love the Lord, your God, with all your heart, with all your being, with all your strength, and with all your mind." See Luke 10:27.

704 Breck, 37.

705 St. Augustine, *Confessions*, 201. Book 10, xxvii, (38). Emphasis added by the author.

to his presence, accepting his free gift of grace. It is about finding God in all things, not just in the extraordinary, but in the ordinary—in the banality of life, as Rahner would say.

The mission of the Father allows the spirit of Christ to dwell in the hearts of the faithful through the power of the Holy Spirit. We also spoke of the Indwelling Trinity. As Theologian Mark Fischer wrote, "God first addresses the human being personally, in the person's heart."[706] Ultimately, the process of divinization is based on a true, sustained conversion of heart or *metanoia*, a conversion occurring as a result of our encounters. Robert Cardinal Sarah wrote, "[F]aith is strengthened by way of the heart, through a personal encounter with and experience of Jesus."[707]

706 Fischer, xviii.
707 Sarah, *God or Nothing*, 147.

WHERE WE ENCOUNTER

An Interior Experience

"The kingdom of God is within you."
(Luke 17:21, Orthodox Study Bible)

"The Lord seeks hearts overflowing with love for him and their neighbor, and this is the throne where he would sit and reveal himself in the fullness of his glory. For in the heart he builds his kingdom."[708]
(St. Seraphim of Sarov)

Opening Gospel Reading

Luke 17:20-21 (The Coming of the Kingdom).

Scriptural Foundation

Let us consider some scriptural references describing encounters with Jesus.

- Jesus tells his disciples, "Whoever loves me will keep my word, and my Father will love him, and we will come to him and make our dwelling with him."[709]
- The author of the Book of Revelation writes, "Behold, I stand at the door and knock. If anyone hears my voice and opens the door, [then] I will enter his house and dine with him, and he with me."[710]
- After two disciples encounter the Risen Jesus on the road to

708 Cf. Zander, 93.
709 John 14:23.
710 Rev. 3:20.

Emmaus, one asks the other, "Were not our hearts burning within us?"[711]

- In Jesus's teachings, he says, "Go to your inner room, close the door, and pray to your Father in secret."[712]

Each of these passages refers to an interior place or experience. However, the challenge we face today is that, for many, faith is no longer deeply rooted. Our practices are superficial. We may attend Mass on Sunday because it is expected or because we did with our parents, yet without true understanding. In these cases, it is easy to fall away, and some may question the value of church and faith altogether. Jesus talked about this in the Parable of the Sower and the Seed.[713]

> Some (seed) fell on rocky ground, where it had little soil. It sprang up at once because the soil was not deep, and when the sun rose, it was scorched, and it withered for lack of roots.[714]

Sadly, this is the crisis of faith we see all too often settling in around us—a faith that is no longer deeply rooted. This was exacerbated by the COVID-19 pandemic when churches were forced to close. If God is no longer at the center, we lose our foundation, our rock. We drift, and we despair. Imagine what happens then in time of crisis: "The rain fell, the floods came, and the winds blew and buffeted the house. And it collapsed and was completely ruined."[715] One person, who had been away from the Church for a long time and endured much personal suffering, said upon his return, "A tree in winter needs its roots." How true! We need to experience that which gives life.

---

711 Luke 24:32.
712 Matt. 6:6.
713 See Matt. 13:1-9.
714 Matt. 13:5-6.
715 Matt. 7:27.

The one issue Jesus had with the scribes and Pharisees was their superficial faith.

> Woe to you scribes and Pharisees, you hypocrites. You cleanse the outside of cup and dish, but inside they are full of plunder and self-indulgence. Blind Pharisee, cleanse first the inside of the cup, so that the outside may also be clean.[716]

Compare this statement to the story of Zacchaeus.[717] When Jesus planned to dine at Zacchaeus's house, those around him "began to grumble,"[718] and they had a label for this chief tax collector—a big, scarlet "S" for "sinner." Yet, Zacchaeus had a notable change of heart, offering to give half his possessions to the poor and making four-fold restitution to anyone he defrauded. This type of conversion is what the Holy Fathers referred to as *metanoia*, a deep interior conversion. Jesus said in return: "Today salvation has come to this house because this man too is a descendant of Abraham."[719] Jesus restores to Zacchaeus his dignity, saying he is worthy of forgiveness. And Jesus adds some of the most comforting words in the Gospel, "For the son of man has come to seek and save what was lost."[720] It is a reminder of why God sent us his Son as a personal invitation to return to him.

> Return to me with your *whole heart*, with fasting, weeping, and morning. Rend your *hearts*, not your garments, and return to the Lord, your God, slow to anger, abounding in steadfast love, and relenting in punishment.[721]

The message is clear: God is asking for interior conversion and not

716 Matt. 23:25-26.
717 See Luke 19:1-10.
718 Luke 19:7.
719 Luke 19:9.
720 Luke 19:10.
721 Joel 2:12-13.

superficial window dressing. It is about true change, not simply following precepts of the law. "Blessed are the clean of heart," Jesus says, "for they shall see God."[722] This speaks to our human destiny as well. To achieve union with God, we must be transformed, overcoming temptations and our passions, to bear our crosses, to be more God-like and practice the virtues, to be more loving, merciful, and compassionate. Like Jesus, we must be moved to pity, to feel genuine solidarity with those around us, especially when we encounter Jesus in his most distressing disguise. It is about the heart, not the externals. Beginning with the Early Desert Fathers, many believed that Christianity was a divinizing process that gradually took place within the human heart; the interior focus where man and the Triune God meet.[723]

Apostolic and Patristic Period Perspectives

The Epistle of Barnabas was written between 70 and 132. This work was given some consideration to being included in the New Testament canon. Theologian Vladimir Kharlamov wrote:

> Barnabas does not specifically bring up the issue of deification. This epistle does, however, point to one aspect of Christ's Incarnation that is important to *theosis:* its connection to the divine indwelling. Precisely because of the incarnation, Christ can 'dwell in us' (6.14). Thus does he make 'a holy temple' out of 'this little house, our heart' (6.15). In this 'little house... dwells God' (16.8). In this divine indwelling is also the promise of that future goal 'when we ourselves are so perfected as to become heirs of the Lord's covenant' (6.19).[724]

722 Matt. 5:8.

723 Maloney, 19 and 43.

724 Vladimir Kharlamov, "Emergence of the Deification Theme in the Apostolic Fathers," in *Theosis Deification in Christian Doctrine*, ed. Stephen Finlan and Vladimir Kharlamov (Eugene, OR: Pickwick Publications, 2006), 56.

Within this part of the letter, there is a consistent theme: the heart as a place of dwelling ("this little house") and the reference to the indwelling divine presence. St. Paul writes, "Do you not know that your body is a temple of the Holy Spirit within you, whom you have from God, and that you are not your own?" All refer to an interior dwelling of the Divine.

St. Gregory of Nyssa rarely used the term *deification* or *divinization* in his writings, but he develops Jesus's statement: "The kingdom of God is within you."[725] He wrote in one his homilies:

> The Lord does not say it is blessed to know something about God, but to have God present within oneself. *Blessed are the clean of heart, for they shall see God.* I do not think that if the eye of one's soul has been purified, he is promised a direct vision of God; but perhaps this marvelous saying may suggest what the Word (Jesus) expresses more clearly when He says to others, *The Kingdom of God is within you.* By this, we should learn that if a man's heart has been purified from every creature and unruly affections, he will see the Image of the Divine Nature in his own beauty.[726]

St. Gregory of Nyssa also referred to the indwelling divine presence, comparable to many of the Early Greek Fathers. They understood the statement of Jesus to be "The Kingdom of God is *within* you." Thus, they described an interior reality, which is fundamental to the doctrine of *theosis*. From the Patristic perspective:

> The kingdom is a mystical reality, a divine gift to be cherished and cultivated with the inward being in the depths of the secret heart. Access to this inner reality

725 Luke 17:21, *Orthodox Study Bible*.
726 St. Gregory of Nyssa, "On the Beatitudes," 148–150. Sermon No. 6.

> is provided by prayer, particularly continual prayer that centers upon the divine Name [Jesus].[727]

We need to cultivate the soil of our hearts so that it may be fertile ground for the seed implanted there—the Word of God[728]—to grow and bear fruit.[729] These fruits are the divine virtues, of which the first is humility, St. Gregory of Nyssa and other Holy Fathers tell us.[730]

Consider the wisdom of St. Isaac the Syrian, one of the later Desert Fathers:

> The fear of God is the beginning of virtue, and it is said to be the offspring of faith. It is sown in the heart when a man withdraws his mind from the attractions of the world ....[731]

Fear in this sense and by translation means "reverential fear" and awe at the majesty of God. It is an acknowledgment of the enormous difference between Creator and created whereby we recognize and approach God with a profound sense of humility, knowing that he in all his glory desires a personal relationship with us. In many respects, this understanding underpins the Jesus Prayer. The prayer, *Lord Jesus Christ, Son of God, have mercy on me, a sinner,* acknowledges Jesus as God and us as sinners. This profound sense of awe and humility reflects a heart that begins to be conditioned to practice the virtues. It is a transformed heart, not one of a superficial or intellectualized faith. Consider again the

727 Breck, 30.

728 See Luke 8:11. "The seed is the word of God."

729 See Matt. 13:23.

730 See St. Gregory of Nyssa, "On the Beatitudes," 90. Sermon No. 1. St. Gregory believes that humility is the foundation with all other virtues flowing from it. He advises, "But let no one imagine that humility is achieved easily and without labor. On the contrary, it needs more effort than the practice of any other virtue."

731 *The Ascetical Homilies of Saint Isaac the Syrian*, 113. Homily One.

example of Zacchaeus. When he welcomes Jesus into his home, he acknowledges his past defrauding of others and his desire to make restitution. Further, he offers to give half of his wealth to the poor. This a true change of heart.

Recall Rahner's statement, "The devout Christian of the future will either be a 'mystic,' one who has 'experienced' something, or he will cease to be anything at all." Consider the axiom Stăniloae was fond of quoting: "If you are a theologian, you will pray truly. And if you pray truly, you are a theologian." Both would tell us it is about the experience, and not the intellectual knowledge. Or, as St. Isaac the Syrian put it, one cannot taste honey by reading a book.[732] It is about a genuine encounter with the Divine.

Summary

The Early Desert Fathers believed that Christianity was a divinizing process that gradually occurred within the human heart, where man and the Triune God meet. All the references and examples given are about internal conversion and a deeply rooted faith versus a faith that is intellectualized or superficial. It is not about knowledge; it is about actual experiences of the Divine. Jesus spoke of purifying the inside of the dish, criticizing the scribes and Pharisees for focusing on external observances. He was seeking interior change from his followers; Zacchaeus, the tax collector, was a prime example.

The experience of encounter is meant to warm the heart. Consider the example of the two disciples on the road to Emmaus: "Were not our hearts burning within us?" It requires constant effort and focus to cultivate the soil within our hearts, where the divine seed is planted. Thus, we need to ask ourselves, "What is the condition of the soil

---

732 Ibid., 153. Homily Four. "Therefore, O man, pay attention to what you read here. Indeed, can these things be known from [*writings of*] ink? Or can the taste of honey pass over the palate by reading books? For if you do not strive, you will not find, and if you do not knock at the door with vehemence and keep constant vigil before it, you will not be heard."

of my heart?" Is it fertile and capable of producing a rich harvest? As Jesus said, "By their fruits, you will know them."[733] We will later consider the wisdom of the Desert Fathers in how we cultivate and purify the heart through ascetical practices, which in turn increase the fruitfulness of prayer and contemplation.

Reflection Questions

1. How would I describe my faith today? What is the condition of the soil in my heart? Is it deep and fertile? Or is it rocky and shallow? Please be honest.

2. Why is my faith the way it is today? What were the key influences, positive or negative? Was my faith influenced by my parents, family, or friends? Were there circumstances in my life—crises, moments of conversion—that have influenced my faith? In some cases, did I walk away from my faith. Or am I returning to it? Please be specific.

3. What is my personal view of God? Am I afraid of God? Do I look at him with reverence? Is he at the center of my life or on the periphery? Do I dismiss him as irrelevant in my life?

4. Am I happy with my faith today? What is preventing me from deepening my faith?

Supplemental Discussion:

Understanding Luke 17:21

From the Patristic Age until about 1900,[734] Luke 17:21 was translated as "The kingdom of God is within you." However, beginning

733 Matt. 7:16.

734 See Paul M. Bretscher, "Luke 17:20–21 in Recent Investigations," *Concordia Theological Monthly* 22 (12) (1951): 900. He wrote that the shift in opinion related to translation occurred during in the past 50 years, and his article is dated 1951. Ergo, approximately 1900.

in the 20th century, certain Scripture scholars began challenging this translation, whereas NABRE 2011 now translates this passage as the kingdom as being "among you." This implies *in* one's presence but not *within*. Some translations render it as "in your midst." The *Orthodox Study Bible* and the KJV retain the original translation, "within you." At issue is how to best translate *entos hymōn*, a unique choice of words by the author of the Lucan gospel and used only one other time among the four gospels.[735] Most scholars agree this particular passage is a *logion*, or authentic statement of Jesus. Yet the translation remains problematic for several renowned modern-day Catholic scripture scholars. John P. Meier argued that Jesus, speaking to the Pharisees when he made this statement, would never have declared the kingdom of God as being "within the hearts of adversaries."[736] Luke Timothy Johnson wrote that such a statement to the Pharisees would be "unthinkable."[737] Finally, Joseph A. Fitzmyer explained, "The real problem, however, is that elsewhere in Lucan writing the kingdom is never presented as an inward reality or an inner condition of human existence."[738] This illustrates some of the challenges raised within scholarly circles.

Given the significance of this gospel passage to the doctrine of *theosis*, the author of this work conducted a detailed analysis of the disputed passage.[739] He addressed each of the challenges raised by the scholars and concluded that the translation as understood by the Early Church Fathers, "within you," is plausible. Accordingly, for purposes of our discussion, just as in the Patristic Church, the translation of *entos hymōn* is accepted as "within you."

---

735 See Matt. 23:26. "Blind Pharisee, cleanse first the *inside* of the cup, so the outside also may be clean."

736 John P. Meier, *A Marginal Jew: Rethinking the Historical Jesus*, vol. 2 (New York, NY: Doubleday, 1994), 426.

737 Luke Timothy Johnson, 263.

738 Joseph A. Fitzmyer, "The Gospel According to Luke X–XXIV" in *The Anchor Bible* (Garden City, NY: Doubleday, 1985), 1161.

739 See Edward Kleinguetl, "The Presence of Kingdom of God: An Analysis of Luke 17:20-21" (Loyola University Chicago – Institute of Pastoral Studies, IPS 416 – Christian Origins, Rev. Patrick J. Madden, PhD, Instructor, April 12, 2015). Note that Dr. Madden is also well-versed scholar of Sacred Scripture, having studied under Raymond Brown.

WHERE WE ENCOUNTER

Prayer of the Heart

"Whoever loves me will keep my word, and my Father will love him, and we will come to him and make our dwelling with him."
(John 14:23)

"Dear friend, use the spiritual prayer of the heart to beseech with fervent tears and with your whole heart and soul the architect and builder of this house, the most good Christ and most sweet Jesus, to build this spiritual house within your heart. Then invite him to come in to dwell there and to make you rich with his blessings of grace and to illumine you with the light of his divine knowledge."[740]
(St. Nikodemos the Hagiorite)

"Every prayer must come from the heart, and any other prayer is no prayer at all."
(St. Theophan the Recluse)

Opening Scripture Reading

Rom. 8:26-27 (The Spirit aids us in our prayer).

Introduction

The divinizing process to prepare for our destiny involves interior experiences of the human heart. The key to entering the heart, according to mystics such as St. Teresa of Ávila, is prayer. Others, such as Nicholas Cabasilas, would say the experiences necessary to cultivate a relationship with Christ include a sacramental life, with

740 St. Nicodemos, *A Handbook of Spiritual Counsel*, 185. Chapter Eleven: The Spiritual and Proper Delights of the Mind.

frequent reception of Eucharist, and yet is one that is rich in prayer and meditation.[741] The reality, as we noted, is that we cannot separate prayer from the sacramental life of the Church, or we would be left incomplete.

Now, after discussing the interior experience, let us revisit the Prayer of the Heart.

Seeking God in Silence

The mystical prayer tradition is at the center of Eastern Christian spirituality. Hesychasts who use this prayer technique, coupled with efforts of personal purification (such as ascetical practices), have experiences of light and other intense feelings associated with the encounter of the divine presence. It is clear from the hesychasts' descriptions that these are interior experiences, a sense of union with God in the present age. The phrase "warmth of heart" is frequently used.

A desire for God is the "impulse," or what Rahner called "dynamic movement," that leads one through ascetical struggles and personal purification to achieve *theosis*.[742] This longing becomes the initiative to pray, a desire to experience the Divine in the heart. "God reveals himself in the silence of the heart."[743] Further, as St. Isaac the Syrian wrote, "Silence is the sacrament of the world to come; words are instrument of this present age."[744] Thus, silence and solitude become a conducive environment for hesychast prayer.

The concept of silence is difficult for the modern person of the 21st century. Our culture seems to thrive on constant stimuli that divert our attention from the interior self to the external world. Prayer allows us to redirect our attention back to the heart. *Hesychia* refers

---

741 See Cabasilas. See in particular the Translator's Introduction.
742 Ibid., 25.
743 Ibid., 26.
744 Cited in Breck, 26.

to this interior stillness. It allows a person to concentrate on God, to whom the prayer is directed. Through prayer, particularly hesychast prayer, the heart learns the truth about the divine life and its purpose. This truth will help lead us to our salvation.

The Work and Gift of Prayer

As many Holy Fathers advise, prayer is both "work" and "gift." St. Seraphim of Sarov noted that "acquisition of the Holy Spirit"—the gift—is the objective of prayer and the reward for the work. In the hesychast tradition, prayer requires *synergeia,* collaboration with the Divine. Jesus tells us, "Without me you can do nothing."[745] Accordingly, we need Jesus as our guide to make progress in the spiritual life. He is "the way" and our model. We cannot achieve salvation on our own.

Prayer of the Heart begins with *praxis,* the process of learning skills, which involves active struggle through ascetical practices, living the virtues, and other spiritual disciplines such as repentance and mourning our sins (*penthos*) to achieve personal purification. *Praxis* can lead to *theoria,* which is contemplation of God or a greater sense of his presence. As hesychast prayer becomes more internalized, the ultimate degree is pure prayer or *kathara proseuche*. This last degree is where the hesychast has an experience of union with God in peace, love, and joy.

Our work alone cannot "produce" prayer. Prayer is a gift granted by God in response to our work. "The quality and intensity of prayer that leads to abiding communion with God are bestowed only by the Spirit."[746] We cannot force or manipulate prayer. For example, it is reported that St. Silouan the Athonite obtained the gift of pure prayer in a few days, whereas St. Symeon the New Theologian "implored

745 John 15:5.

746 Breck, 38. Consider Rom. 8:26: "For we do not know how to pray as we ought, but the Spirit itself intercedes with inexpressible groanings." This verse supports the concept of *synergeia,* human and divine collaboration.

God for years before receiving the gift of pure prayer."[747] As advised in the famous spiritual classic *Unseen Warfare*:

> Do not set a time for achievement in this prayer. Decide only one thing: to work, and to work. Months and years will go by before the first feeble indications of success begin to show. One of the Mount Athos fathers said of himself that two years of work passed before his heart grew warm. With another father this warmth came after eight months. With each man it comes in accordance with his powers and his diligence in the work.[748]

The Holy Fathers usually describe the Prayer in three stages: verbal, mental, and finally, Prayer of the Heart. In the first stage, the prayer is repeated verbally, out loud but quietly, which establishes a rhythm of repetition and intensity of the prayer, generally synchronized with the person's breathing. Gradually through repetition, the Prayer "seems to transcend the verbal level and root itself in the mind."[749] As a mental prayer, it begins take on a life of its own, whether awake or asleep, as the heart keeps watch. "Once the Prayer is imprinted on the mind, it appears to 'pray itself' spontaneously."[750] Finally, at the deepest level of prayer, *kathara proseuche* or pure prayer, the Prayer literally "descends from the mind into the heart."[751]

> There, as the voice of the Spirit himself, it makes its dwelling place within the inner sanctuary. The Prayer is no longer 'prayed' as a conscious deliberate act. It is

747 Ibid., 42.

748 *Unseen Warfare*: *Being the Spiritual Combat and Path to Paradise of Lorenzo Scupoli*, ed. Nicodemus of the Holy Mountain, rev. Theophan the Recluse, trans. E. Kadloubovsky and G. E. H. Palmer (London: Faber and Faber, 1963), 161.

749 Breck, 41.

750 Ibid.

751 Ibid.

> received, welcomed, and embraced as a manifestation of divine presence and life. The Prayer now associates itself with the rhythm of the heart, producing without conscious effort a ceaseless outpouring of adoration and thanksgiving. From prayer of the lips to prayer of the mind, it has become 'prayer of the heart.'[752]

All the Holy Fathers advise that those who seek to undertake hesychast prayer should have a spiritual father to help guide the process. For example, an attempt to use the Prayer as a mantra or simply exploit it as a means of relaxation "will inevitably lead to spiritual shipwreck."[753] However, given the limited number of spiritual masters available today, certain books can provide guidance to a limited extent. These would include the writings in the *Philokalia*, *The Pilgrim's Tale*, *The Art of Prayer*, and *Unseen Warfare*. These are considered classics. Any Christian can benefit from a genuine, pious practice of the Jesus Prayer[754] and is encouraged to do so.

Not all who undertake hesychast prayer can achieve these higher levels, especially that of pure prayer. Nevertheless, there is virtue in seeking the gift, whether or not it is granted, as long as it is sought out of genuine love and desire for God.[755] We can experience warmth of heart, a sense of God's presence, and experience changes within ourselves. Each of us can strive to the best of our abilities and then leave our salvation entirely in the hands of our merciful God, submitting ourselves completely to him. Alignment of will is key to the process of divinization, renouncing ourselves and taking up our crosses each day. Nicholas Cabasilas advises we need to cling to Christ, who is both our head—as in the Body of Christ—and heart, because there is no other source of life.[756] He wrote:

---

752 Ibid.
753 Ibid., 39.
754 Ibid.
755 Ibid., 42.
756 Cabasilas, 161.

> But this is impossible for those who do not will what he wills. It is necessary to train one's purpose, as far as it is humanly possible, to conform to Christ's will and prepare oneself to desire what he desires and to enjoy it, for it is impossible for contrary desires to continue in one and the same heart.[757]

This comes back to what we have discussed before, how Jesus is "the way." "If anyone wishes to come after me, he must deny himself and take up his cross daily and follow me."[758] As Cabasilas wrote, we must desire what he desires.

In concluding this topic, let us consider the words of St. Seraphim of Sarov:

> Among the works done for the love of Christ, prayer is the one that most readily obtains the grace of the Holy Spirit, because it is always at hand. It may happen that you want to go to church but there isn't one nearby; or else you want to help a poor man but you haven't anything to give or you don't come across one; or yet again you may want to remain chaste but natural weakness prevents you from resisting temptation. But prayer is within reach of all men and they can all give themselves to it, rich and poor, learned and unlearned, strong and weak, the sick and the healthy, the sinner and the righteous. Its power is immense; prayer more than anything else, brings us the grace of the Holy Spirit.[759]

The grace of the Holy Spirit leads to the presence of the indwelling Trinity within our hearts. It is a grace, freely offered by God and can

757 Ibid.
758 Luke 9:23.
759 Zander, 86.

be sought by all, most especially through prayer within the silent recesses of our hearts.

Summary

The human-divine encounter occurs within the human heart, and prayer, contemplative prayer specifically, is a key means of entering into the heart. There are three levels of prayer: *praxis, theoria,* and *kathara proseuche*. This third level is considered "pure prayer," a gift only granted by God commensurate with an individual's effort. Those who achieve this level of prayer describe it as an intense experience of union with God in the present age. Regardless of whether a person achieves the highest level of prayer, it remains beneficial to all Christians to practice contemplative prayer; such genuine effort will bear fruit. Further, having a discipline of contemplative prayer helps create an awareness of God, increasingly finding him in all things. The cultivation of prayer requires time and effort. Pope St. John Paul II would advise us to be patient in the process:

> For a stalk to grow or a flower to open there must be time that cannot be forced; nine months must go by for the birth of a child; to write a book or compose music often years must be dedicated to patient research. To find the mystery there must be patience, interior purification, silence, waiting....

Reflection Questions

1. Have I practiced the Jesus Prayer? If so, what has the experience been like?

2. Can I commit to a Rule of Prayer that I can follow each day? A starting goal with the Jesus Prayer is good, somewhere between five and 20 minutes daily. Do not increase the allotted time until you begin to enjoy the prayer.

3. What is my personal experience with spiritual direction (having a formal spiritual guide with whom to meet regularly)? Is it something I would be willing to try?

4. What is my experience with spiritual reading, gaining insights from the Holy Fathers of the Church who have gone before me?

WHERE WE ENCOUNTER

Fruits of a Transformed Heart

"If anyone hears my voice and opens the door, then I will enter his house and dine with him, and with me."
(Rev. 3:20)

"The patient and diligent practitioner of the Jesus Prayer will doubtless be content and consoled; he will find joy in the limitless bounty of such spiritual fruits ..."[760]
(St. Ignatius Brianchaninov)

Opening Scripture Reading

Rev. 3:20-21.

Encounters Lead to Conversion

Encounter occurs within the heart, which leads to conversion and transformation. The Jesus Prayer can help facilitate the result. Transformation is less dependent on the level or degree of prayer achieved, and *kathara proseuche,* or pure prayer, cannot be achieved by all. Rather, transformation is enabled by a genuine longing, desire, and love for God, which causes us to turn toward him and reach for him. It is about the journey of transcendence, reaching for the infinite horizon. In this topic, we will consider the fruits of prayer and transformation.

The first fruit is centering,[761] the ability to be centered or focused on what is essential in life. This is analogous to the story of Martha

760 Brianchaninov, 207.
761 Breck, 42.

and Mary,[762] in which Mary, according to Jesus, has chosen the better part.[763] The key point of the two sisters was that Mary listened to Jesus while Martha unilaterally decided what Jesus wanted. While service and hospitality are important, we need to listen at the feet of Jesus and first determine what he wants us to do. It is about alignment of wills, desiring, as Cabasilas wrote, what Jesus desires. Thus, we begin by becoming centered on what is important. Further, detachment from the world and material possessions, ascetical practices, and other spiritual disciplines—all efforts of self-denial—help to synthesize things down to the essentials. In time, this centering will become increasingly instinctive and consistent as we become accustomed to doing God's will.

The second fruit is considered remembrance of God.[764] Our minds and hearts are open to his presence, allowing for the "primitive experience" of God, as described by Rahner. Through these experiences, we also have certainty that Jesus remains with us; he dwells in the hearts of the faithful through the grace of the Holy Spirit. We cannot forget or be neglectful to the presence of God in our lives, nor the dynamic he plays in our personal journey of transformation.

The third fruit of a transformed heart is self-sacrificing love, or genuine expressions of *diakonia*, meaning "service" or "ministry." We place our lives at the service of others without expecting repayment, a genuine manifestation of our love for God expressed to those near us. Consider Mother Teresa's Gospel on Five Fingers: "You did it to me." This becomes an instinctive way of life in which we find order, harmony, clarity, and connectedness with our neighbors and the world. We also become less anxious by surrendering all to God, relying on Jesus to show us "the way."

---

762 See Luke 10:38-42.

763 See Luke 10:42. "There is need of only one thing. Mary has chosen the better part and it will not be taken from her."

764 See Ware, *The Philokalia: Master Reference Guide*, xxx. Remembrance of God, *Mnimi Theou*, is essentially a constant presence to God, as he is to us.

A fourth fruit brings us back to the beginning. A transformed heart desires God even more, the longing within constantly increasing. We are centered ever more on that that which is essential—"the better part." This driving force, or, in Rahner's terms, dynamic movement, enables us to pursue the spiritual journey toward *theosis*, union with God, and participate in the divine life. This journey is a constant process of longing, encounter, growth, transformation, and further longing. We struggle against our own will, the stubbornness of ego, temptations, and disordered desires while striving to cultivate the God-like virtues. Progress is incremental, sustained by our encounters with the Divine.

Returning to *diakonia*, consider the idea of being moved by compassion or pity, as in the example of Jesus. How often do we hear in the Gospel how Jesus was moved to pity?[765] The English word for pity does not adequately express the underlying Greek term, *splagchnizomai*— "to be moved as to one's bowels." It describes a deeply emotional response. One could say Jesus was sick to his stomach. As we enter more deeply into a relationship with God, as our hearts continue to be transformed, we too can be moved with pity like Jesus, and our actions of service are a response made with genuine heart-felt feeling. These are stirrings in our hearts, and as we draw closer to Jesus and increase our solidarity with the body of Christ, we find ourselves loving the presence of Christ in others. This is how we begin to love our neighbor truly, to be moved to a deeply emotional response without counting the cost, influenced by our relationship with the Divine.

Many of us are familiar with Mother Teresa's acts of love and compassion. However, what fueled this great desire to love Jesus in the poorest of the poor, in the dying, and unwanted? The underlying answer is prayer and an ever-deepening relationship with Christ. Mother Teresa often referred to her order as "contemplatives in

765 Ex. Matt. 14:14 and Matt. 20:34.

action."[766] In each house of the Missionaries of Charity, there is always a tabernacle, the presence of Jesus. Nearby is a crucifix with an inscription beside it, "I thirst." It is a constant reminder to the sisters of their call to quench the thirst of Jesus for love and for souls. The sisters attend Mass daily before starting their work; they spend one hour in Eucharistic Adoration each evening. Every seventh day is a day of prayer, every seventh week is a week of prayer. Every seventh month is a month of prayer, and every seventh year is spent at the mother house in Calcutta in a year of prayer. *That is a lot of prayer!* Remember, though, that this constant cultivation of the heart, entering more deeply into a relationship with Jesus, creates the genuine desire to serve. It enables the sisters to do their work, to be the face of the compassionate Christ to those most in distress. Such is the beginning of a transformed heart. Recall Jesus's advice to the scribes and Pharisees: "cleanse first the inside of the cup, so that the outside may also be clean."[767] It comes from within; it cannot be superficial. The underlying prayer discipline of Mother Teresa and her Missionaries of Charity provide an example of this cycle of transformation: centering, remembrance, *diakonia* (service), and centering.

Pope St. John Paul II wrote about this New Evangelization: "Those who have come into genuine contact with Christ cannot keep him for themselves; they must proclaim him."[768] The experience of encountering Christ should strengthen and encourage us into service of others.

The point of these examples is that our encounters with the Divine should increase our desire and love for God, and one of the primary ways we express love for God is by loving those whom God loves. The second (commandment) is like the first: "You shall love your

766 Langford, 186. Mother Teresa's Instructions to the MC Sisters, November 20, 1979.

767 Matt. 23:26.

768 Pope John Paul II, Apostolic Letter, *Novo Millennio Ineunte* (Rome: Libreria Editrice Vaticana, Jan. 6, 2001), no. 40.

neighbor as yourself."[769] Through our desire for God, we place our lives at the service of others. We can go back to our discussion of love of neighbor as a means of encounter and that Jesus broadened this definition of neighbor, from one who is entitled to our help to those who are in need. As St. Paul reminds us, "So, we though many, are one Body in Christ and individually members of one another."[770] Mother Teresa would tell us that the entire ocean would be impoverished if a single drop were missing. Thus, Solidarity in the Body of Christ bind us to serve those in need. Consider the concept of "The Liturgy after the Liturgy."

Finally, we should revisit the Mary-Martha dynamic described in the Gospel of Luke. Many find this interaction controversial. Was Martha not supposed to provide hospitality? Was Mary simply evading work? To answer these questions, consider the excerpt from St. John Chrysostom's homily, "Do you want to honor Christ's body?" We need to consider how Christ wants to be welcomed. Peter tried to convince Jesus not to wash his feet at the Last Supper, but this was the example Jesus wanted to give his disciples. In the Chrysostom homily, he says that if we ornately decorate our churches and neglect our brother or sister in need, whom the homilist calls "the most precious temple of all," then we are dishonoring Christ. We should not simply decide on our own what to do and assume it will honor Jesus. Remember, our spiritual journey is about collaborating with the Divine (*synergeia*), aligning our will with the divine will, desiring what Jesus desires. It is not about unilaterally deciding to do our own thing, like Adam. We need to listen to the voice of Jesus, to prayerfully discern the actions he is calling us to take. By inviting Jesus into our hearts and surrendering to him, we place him at the center and allow him to direct our actions. Thus, in the Mary-Martha example, listening first is important, and then afterwards, taking action based on that listening/discernment.

---

769 Matt. 22:39.
770 Rom. 12:5.

We do not want to underplay the importance of listening to Jesus to discern his will. It is about divine initiative and human response. This is the correct order. In the Gospel of Luke, the author uses an interesting device to illustrate this. Tax collectors and sinners were always drawing near to "listen to Jesus," while the Pharisees and scribes were complaining.[771] The former were seeking salvation, and the latter wanted to hold on to the status quo. To put this into context with the Gospel and this discussion, the Pharisaical view was that salvation could be attained by rigorously keeping the 613 *mitzvoth*, or commandments of God. Those who did not keep the *mitzvoth*, which was the vast majority of people, were simply labeled as sinners and written off. Yet to whom is Jesus drawn? Who desires to listen? Who are those complaining? We can learn much from the teachings and examples of Jesus in the context of his time. In his ministry, Jesus spoke regularly about conversion of heart, the interior versus the exterior. He spoke of whitewashed tombs[772] and seemed to find religious scrupulosity tedious. Thus, listening to Jesus is something asked of all of us, to discern how we align our will to his, to desire what he desires, and not follow our own whims. "If anyone hears my voice and opens the door, then I will enter his house and dine with him, and with me."[773] To this, Pope Benedict XVI adds, "He continues to knock gently at the doors of our hearts and slowly opens our eyes if we open the door to him."[774] Divine initiative and human response—we must listen in order to recognize God's will for us.

Throughout this section, we refer to human experience and encounter as the basis for our spiritual journey, which is different

771 Ex. Luke 15:1.

772 See Matt. 23:27-28. "Woe to you, scribes and Pharisees, you hypocrites. You are like whitewashed tombs, which appear beautiful on the outside, but inside are full of dead men's bones and every kind of filth. Even so, on the outside you appear righteous, but inside you are filled with hypocrisy and evildoing."

773 Rev. 3:20.

774 Pope Benedict XVI, *Regina Caeli* Address, May 22, 2011 (Rome: Libreria Editrice Vaticana).

from a focus on rigor and dogma. To be clear, we are not saying dogma or doctrinal theology is bad. What we have been saying is the exterior must reflect the interior. The exterior alone can be deceiving ("whitewashed tombs"). Consider the importance of balance, the dialectic of spirituality and theology.

Also, serving Jesus should never be the cause of anxiety. This is a challenge for many in ministry, whether laity or ordained. Mother Teresa always told her sisters and volunteers that they must begin with a smile, to find joy in serving Jesus. If we are anxious over many things, it is hard to be joyful, and it is hard to be the presence of Christ to others.

Summary

We continue to describe *theosis* as an incremental transformation to prepare us for union with God. This conversion occurs within the human heart and is an ever-deepening awareness of the presence of God, self-surrender, alignment of will, and response to God's love, often in service to others (*diakonia*). We also discussed the cycle of centering on what is truly important, leading to greater awareness of God's presence and love for us, which leads us to return that love through an expression of service to neighbor. Thus, we delve ever deeper into the mystery of God with the result being a continuous transformation of heart. We can never forget or become discouraged that this is an ongoing process; there will be struggles along the way, and our journey will be completed only at the resurrection of the dead.

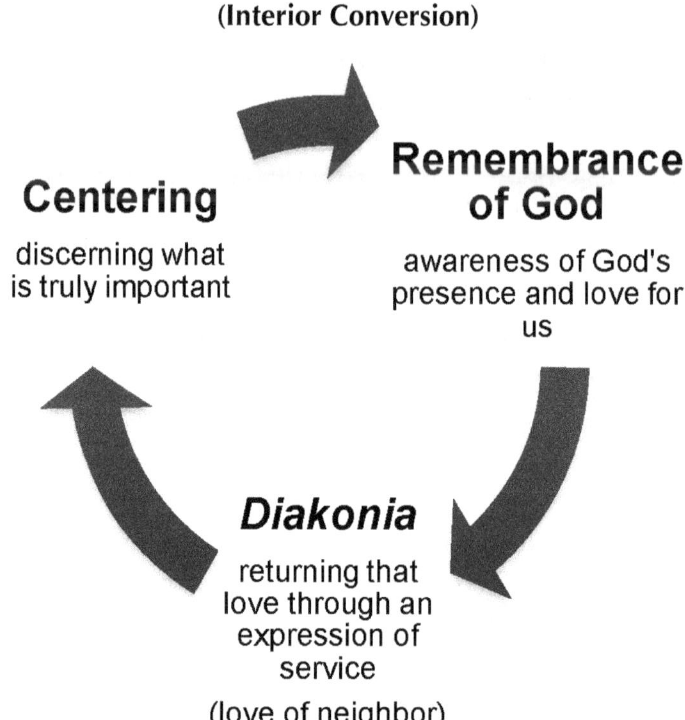

Reflection Questions

1. In my life, am I more like Martha (anxious and worried about many things) or Mary (listening at the feet of Jesus)?

2. Do I take time to listen at the feet of Jesus? Or do I usually act first? How would I describe my process of discerning God's will for my life?

3. What drives my actions in my service toward others? Am I self-directed? When does a genuine desire to serve God come into play?

Part 5

From Encounter to Destiny

FROM ENCOUNTER TO DESTINY

Introduction

It is not about the encounters, per se, but what happens to us because of these encounters. Who do we become as individuals? Are our hearts genuinely transformed? Do we increasingly live God-like virtues? Do we have better solidarity with our neighbors? Do we desire to serve others? Consider the examples from Sacred Scripture. Who did the disciples become as a result of their encounters with Jesus? How were the two disciples on the road to Emmaus changed? How were the apostles transformed at Pentecost? How was St. Paul transformed after his encounter with Jesus on the road to Damascus? They gave up everything and staked their lives on making known Jesus's message. For them to do this, Jesus could not have been an abstract concept or idea, but a real person—someone the disciples experienced and who dramatically, profoundly influenced their lives. As Jesus said to Nicodemus, "For God so loved the world that he gave his only Son, so everyone who believes in him might not perish but might have eternal life."[775] God sent his Son for an encounter with his creation, a personalized invitation to draw us into a relationship with him.

Theosis is the incremental process of divinization, slowly and persistently working to regain the likeness of God by participation in the operations of God. Fallen humanity is lifted up through Christ into the very life of God.[776] Thus, the process of divinization is to prepare us for our ultimate destiny, eternal blessedness in the life to come. Stăniloae wrote:

775 John 3:16.
776 Ware, *The Philokalia: Master Reference Guide*, xi.

> The salvation of man is assured as an eternal, happy existence only if his relation with the supreme Personal reality is so close that the powers and attributes of God will be stamped indelibly upon him through what is called deification (divinization). For this deification makes man, together with God, a bearer of the divine attributes and powers that completely overcome that tendency which the human body has toward corruption.[777]

Orthodox Theologian Andrew Louth wrote, "Deification [divinization] expresses the full extent of the consequences of the Incarnation."[778] Rahner indicated that Jesus as Savior is the gift of God who communicates himself to us, the offer of salvation, and the perfect acceptance of the gift. Because Jesus is "the way," our response is to follow his commandments and his example. This divinization finds us undergoing a personal transformation in preparation for salvation. "This reconstitution of human nature is something impossible without the grace of God."[779] Leveraging the perspective of Rahner, acceptance of God's grace is empowered by this same grace. Fulfilling our destiny to become partakers of the divine nature is enabled "by grace, progressively in this life and fully in the life to come."[780] Achieving our destiny is possible only through *synergeia*, human-divine collaboration.

Thus, our encounters with the Divine should have a transformational result, a genuine change or conversion of heart—*metanoia*—similar

777 Stăniloae, "Revelation and Knowledge of the Triune God," 65.

778 Andrew Louth, "The Place of *Theosis* in Orthodox Theology," in *Partakers of the Divine Nature: The History and Development of Deification in the Christian Traditions*, Edited by Michael J. Christiansen and Jeffery A. Wittung (Grand Rapids, MI: Baker Publishing Group, 2007), 33.

779 Ibid., 37.

780 Michael J. Christensen, "The Problem, Promise, and Process of *Theosis*," in *Partakers of the Divine Nature: The History and Development of Deification in the Christian Traditions*, 27. Reference also made to Lossky, *Vision of God* (Crestwood, NY: Saint Vladimir's Seminary Press, 1983), 134.

to the experience of Zacchaeus when he encountered Jesus.[781] Further, the spiritual life does not consist of a single conversion moment. There is no big bang. Instead, we experience an ongoing process of conversion that gradually draws us ever deeper into a relationship with God. Sometimes we have a "mountain top experience," a profound spiritual encounter with moments of intense clarity, and other times our journey will be based on the daily mundane choices to follow the way of Jesus in the ordinary, monotonous routines of our lives. Sometimes we stumble and fall. The journey of *theosis* demands struggle, resilience, persistence, and discipline. It involves taking up our crosses daily. Self-surrender is never easy, particularly given the culture of individualism that has influenced the secular world. Our experiences with the Divine give us the strength and courage to continue forward, reminding us of our longing for the infinite, the persistent "something more," always reaching for it and never giving up when we never quite reach it. These encounters also remind us that nothing finite can ever satisfy infinite longing. If we settle for something finite, the satisfaction will be temporary at best. Only God can satisfy the longing he placed in every human heart. Our journey of faith draws us ever deeper into the mystery of God, who like our own longing, is truly inexhaustible.

In the next series of topics, we will consider various elements associated with the spiritual journey leading us to our destiny. It is also important to recognize that each person is in a different place on their journey. Yet we all have the same ultimate destiny. Because human beings are related to God, we have the capacity for God (*capex Dei*), the ability to experience him. Our God is a self-communicating God who is readily available, active in his creation, and who not only is the Giver of the gift, but also *is* the gift ("Giver as gift"). Accordingly, we simply need to start from wherever we are today and move forward, drawn to the horizon of infinite possibility, toward the Infinite Being.

781 See Luke 19:1–10.

It does not matter if we are in the pigpen like the prodigal son[782] or whether our faith has grown lukewarm. Consider the Parable of the Lost Sheep.[783] It is not the sheep that went searching for the shepherd; the shepherd looked for the sheep.[784] God is always reaching for us, seeking us, inviting us, and waiting for us. He never ceases to knock at the door of our hearts. The Incarnate Christ was God's personalized message to each of us. Further, we can never forget what that message was. It is found in the prodigal son, whom the father welcomed back with immense joy. It is found in the shepherd, who does not punish the lost sheep or drive it back to the fold; he rejoices, placing it on his shoulders, and calling together his friends and neighbors to celebrate. As Jesus said, "I tell you, in just the same way there will be more joy in heaven over one sinner who repents than over ninety-nine righteous people who have no need of repentance."[785] If we accept the Giver as gift, we begin to appreciate Jesus's only explanation of mission: "For the Son of Man has come to seek and to save what was lost."[786]

At any point, we can return to our Heavenly Father, who will welcome and embrace us with open arms. We simply need to take the first step.[787]

---

782 See Luke 15:11–32. The Parable of the Prodigal Son.

783 See Luke 15:1-7.

784 See Cabasilas, 50. "It was not we ourselves who were moved towards God, nor did we ascend to him; but it was he who came and descended to us. It was not we who sought, but we who were the object of his seeking. The sheep did not seek for the shepherd, nor did the lost coin search for the master of the house; he it was who came to the earth and retrieved his own image, and he came to the place where sheep was straying and lifted it up and stopped it from straying."

785 Luke 15:7.

786 Luke 19:10.

787 See Elder Porphyrios, 192. "God is love; He is not a simple spectator in our life. He provides and cares for us as our Father, but He also respects our freedom. He does not pressure us. We should have our hope in God's providence and, since we believe that God is watching over us, we should take courage and throw ourselves into his love and then we will see him constantly beside us. We will not be afraid that we will make a false step."

Creation

"God looked at everything he had made, and found it very good."
(Gen 1:31)

"Respect all things as God's creations; preserve and use to the glory of God those which God has placed in your possession; be content with what you have, whatever its measure, and give thanks to God for it." [788]
(Unseen Warfare)

Opening Scripture Reading

Gen. 1:1-2:3 (First Creation Account).

Discussion

In Western Christianity, there is a tendency to refer to the salvation of humanity as separate from nature,[789] whereas in Eastern Christian spirituality, this separation does not exist. As Stăniloae wrote, "We are saved not *from* the world, but *with* the world."[790] In Eastern Orthodox theology, there is a greater emphasis on creation, that "God created the world for the sake of humanity."[791] The world is at the service of our movement of raising ourselves to our ultimate meaning, which is union with God.[792] "All these things impose on us a responsibility before God and before the world itself, and it is by exercising this

788 *Unseen Warfare*, 192.
789 See Stăniloae, "The World: Creation and Deification," 1.
790 Dumitru Stăniloae, "The Fulfillment of Creation," *The Experience of God: Orthodox Dogmatic Theology*, vol. 6, ed./trans. Ioan Ionita (Brookline, MA: Holy Cross Orthodox Press, 2013), xi.
791 Stăniloae, "The World: Creation and Deification," 18.
792 Ibid., 19.

responsibility that we increase our communion with God and with our fellow human beings as we 'humanize' or perfect ourselves."[793] We have a responsibility to elevate creation to its intended purpose and return it to God.[794] One key is the right use of creation and created things. Pride caused human beings to lose their way through, seduced by created things, losing sight of the Creator. As a consequence, we found ourselves outside the relationship with the Creator who gives meaning to created things.[795] We remain equally susceptible today.

Whenever we seek fulfillment in created things, we lose sight of the Creator. This could occur in anything from collecting fine art or patronizing the arts, when this becomes our primary passion or focus, to human trafficking. In all these cases, we are attempting to seek meaning in created things. As Augustine of Hippo wrote in his *Confessions*:

> Late have I loved you, beauty so old and so new: late have I loved you. And see, you were within *and I was in the external world and sought you there, and in my unlovely state I plunged into those lovely, created things which you made*. You were with me and I was not with you. The lovely things kept me far from you, though if they did not have their existence in you, they had no existence at all.[796]

St. Augustine experienced the same challenge as many: distracted by created things and directed away from the Creator. In *Gaudium et Spes*, a document from Vatican II, it says, "For creation without the Creator fades into nothingness."[797] Created things have purpose, to help us on our spiritual journey. Yet at the same time, improper use of

793 Ibid.

794 See Stăniloae, "The World: Creation and Deification," 17. "If God created all things in order that they might share in his love, their purpose is to reach full participation in this love, that is, full communion with God."

795 See Stăniloae, "The Person of Jesus Christ as God and Savior," 5–6.

796 St. Augustine, *Confessions*, 201.

797 Second Vatican Council, *Gaudium et Spes*, no. 36.

creation or substituting created things for the Creator can derail our spiritual journey.

Not surprisingly, given the Eastern Orthodox emphasis on creation in the salvation of humanity, His All-Holiness Ecumenical Patriarch Bartholomew of Constantinople has been sharing his concerns for humanity's neglect of the environment since at least 1997, earning him a reputation as the "Green Patriarch."[798] In May 2015, Pope Francis issued an encyclical on ecology and the environment entitled, *Laudato Si'*,[799] in which he references the writings of Patriarch Bartholomew. One such reference notes that "to commit a crime against the natural world is a sin against ourselves and a sin against God."[800] When we discussed "Love of Neighbor" as a means of encounter, we referenced the fact that there are seven themes in Catholic Social Teaching as identified by the United States Conference of Catholic Bishops. One of these includes "Care for God's Creation."[801]

In the creation account in Genesis, humanity was given dominion over all creation.[802] We have been entrusted as stewards of God's handiwork and are expected to use creation wisely to pursue our destiny. We are to elevate it to its intended purpose, and we are to return it to God. We are also not to become lost in created things, as St. Augustine did when he was younger, or to lose sight of the fact that creation points to the Creator, who should be our primary focus. In Eastern Christian theological teaching, we are saved *with* creation, not apart from it. St. Maximos the Confessor wrote that divine intent "is realized in the divinization of the human being *and* transfiguration of the whole cosmos."[803]

798 See Marlise Simons, "Orthodox Leader Deepens Progressive Stance on Environment," *New York Times*, December 3, 2012.

799 Pope Francis, *Laudato Si'*, no. 7-9. References to Patriarch Bartholomew.

800 See John Chryssavgis, *On Earth as in Heaven: Ecological Vision and Initiatives of Ecumenical Patriarch Bartholomew* (Bronx, NY: Fordham University Press, 2011). Ecumenical Patriarch Bartholomew, Address in Santa Barbara, California. November 8, 1997. Cited by Pope Francis in *Laudato Si'*, no. 8.

801 USCCB. "Seven Themes of Catholic Social Teaching."

802 See Gen. 1:28–30.

803 Vishnevskaya, 144.

Creation also teaches us something about God, which, as we have discussed from the beginning, is based on our lived experiences. Stăniloae wrote,

> Only by bringing [Creation] to perfection does God complete the plan of creating the world and of its deification in Christ, after everything that could have been accomplished on earth has been accomplished in its present form, through his help, so that divine reason could be made transparent in it.[804]

Today's challenge is that our interpretation of "dominion over creation" seems to have denigrated to exploitation, which ranges from a disrespect for the environment to exploitation of labor and resources in other countries. Pope Francis gives us much to consider in *Laudato Si'*, where he writes:

> The current global situation engenders a feeling of instability and uncertainty, which in turn becomes 'a seedbed for collective selfishness.' When people become self-centered and self-enclosed, their greed increases. The emptier a person's heart is, the more he or she needs things to buy, own, and consume. It becomes almost impossible to accept the limits imposed by reality. In this horizon, a genuine sense of the common good also disappears. As these attitudes become more widespread, social norms are respected only to the extent that they do not clash with personal needs. So our concern cannot be limited merely to the threat of extreme weather events, but must also extend to the catastrophic weather consequences of social unrest. Obsession with a consumerist lifestyle, above all when few

804 Stăniloae, "The Fulfillment of Creation," 119.

> people are capable of maintaining it, can only lead to violence and mutual destruction.
>
> Yet all is not lost. Human beings, while capable of the worst, are also capable of rising above themselves, choosing again what is good, and making a new start, despite their mental and social conditioning. We are able to take an honest look at ourselves, to acknowledge or deep dissatisfaction, and to embark on new paths to authentic freedom. No system can completely suppress our openness to what is good, true, and beautiful, or our God-given ability to respond to his grace at work deep in our hearts. I appeal to everyone throughout the world not to forget this dignity which is ours. No one has the right to take it from us.[805]

Patriarch Daniel of Romania asks: If humanity has lost its sense of the sacredness of life as gift of God, does this not "contribute the most to the destruction of nature, precisely because nature was no longer perceived as a gift of God, but as a domain of profitable exploitation?"[806] In other words, he would argue, the ecological crisis of today is essentially a spiritual crisis as humanity becomes increasingly separated from God and his divine plan. This, in turn, leads to poverty and suffering, solitude and despair, separation and conflicts.[807]

Summary

Creation was given to humanity to assist with our salvation. We are stewards of the gifts given to us by God, and we are expected to elevate his creation to its intended purpose and return it to him.

805 Pope Francis, *Laudato Si'*, no. 204-5.
806 Patriarch Daniel, *Confessing the Truth in Love*, 176.
807 Ibid., 177.

There are two important points to consider. First, we are entrusted with caring for our common home, as Pope Francis describes it in *Laudato Si'*. This means we are not to be wasteful, nor exploit resources, locally and globally, or take resources for granted, as may be the temptation in a throw-away culture focused on individualism. It also includes anything that could demean the value of human life, such as exploitation of low-cost labor in foreign countries and human trafficking. We are saved *with* creation and are called to be conscious of the gifts given to us by God, treating them as such.

Second, we should not become lost in created things. In his youth, St. Augustine of Hippo sought fulfillment in created things and created beauty. However, created things should point to the Creator, who should be the center of our lives. So often, consciously or unconsciously, we pursue what is created to experience fulfillment. However, only the Creator (God) can fill us. Anything finite will only temporarily satisfy our deepest longing.

Reflection Questions

1. When I read the creation account and hear that humanity is given dominion over all creation (See Gen. 1:28-30), what does that mean to me?

2. Do I feel responsibility for the environment? Why or why not?

3. If I have concerns for the environment, are they limited to my community, or home country, or do I feel a responsibility for the world?

4. Am I concerned about the exploitation of resources from other countries? Am I concerned about labor conditions in places that are considered "lower cost" but are notorious for sweatshops? Why or why not?

Freedom

"You will know the truth, and the truth will set you free."
(John 8:32)

"The highest gift that God bestowed upon man at his creation was the gift of freedom. Man was created free. It was within his will to choose one or another path in his life." [808]
(Archbishop Averky Taushev)

Opening Gospel Reading

John 8:31-36 (Freedom).

The Freedom to Choose

"The truth will set you free."[809] One difference between humanity and other creatures is that we are endowed with free will. Rahner and Stăniloae discussed the person's freedom to choose God above all else. Given our societal focus on personal freedom, it is worth investigating this concept further, in particular as it pertains to the spiritual life. While there may appear to be a contradiction relative to freedom as understood by the secular world, the reality is that the more dependent we are on God, absolute submission of our will to his, the freer we are. Yet often, we are led to believe that dependence to any degree infringes upon our personal freedom.

Rahner wrote, "When freedom is really understood, it is not

808 Archbishop Averky Taushev, *The Struggle for Virtue: Asceticism in a Modern Secular Society*, trans. David James (Jordanville, NY: Holy Trinity Publications, 2014), 71.
809 John 8:32.

the power to be able to do this or that, but the power to decide about oneself and to actualize oneself."[810] In other words, we can freely choose to become who we as human beings were created to become, fulfilling our destiny and divinely intended purpose. Consider our initial discussion about our God who communicates himself to human beings, who in turn have the capacity for a relationship with him. God's self-communication, his gift to us, is his very self, which is the transformative agent allowing us to become who we were created to be. There are two components to God's self-communication: the offer and our free-will response to this offer. In turn, we can choose how to respond, to accept the gift through the grace of God or reject it. In the Incarnation, Jesus himself is the gift, Giver as gift, and models the perfect acceptance of the gift, completely surrendering himself to the will of the Father. Jesus always said he is doing the "will of my Father,"[811] and those who do the will of the Father will enter the kingdom of heaven.[812] Jesus's consummate act of total surrender to God begins in the Garden of Gethsemane, "not as I will, but as you will,"[813] and is completed with the last words of his mortal life: "Father, into your hands I commend my spirit."[814] Jesus's "yes" to God becomes our "yes" through the Holy Spirit at Pentecost. Accordingly, Jesus is our example of true freedom, complete submission, and alignment of our will with God's, and our "way" to the Father.

We were given the ability to choose. Generally, we want the freedom to do what we like. We are free to judge, to look out for number one, to be self-centered, to be proud, to be boastful, to discriminate or belittle others, to ignore the needs of others, or to

810 Rahner, *Foundations of Christian Faith*, 38. Consider Maslow's Hierarchy of Needs and the importance of the need for self-actualization—the realization or fulfillment of one's talents and potentialities, especially considered as a drive or need present in everyone.

811 See John 6:38. "Because I came down from heaven not to do my own will but the will of the one who sent me."

812 See, for example, Matt. 7:21. "Not everyone who says to me, 'Lord, Lord,' will enter the kingdom of heaven, but only the one who does the will of my Father in heaven."

813 Matt. 26:39. See also Mark 14:35 and Luke 22:42.

814 Luke 22:46.

get our way even if it involves force or coercion. Yet, is this really freedom? Or is this enslavement to sin? True freedom, according to St. Silouan the Athonite, means constantly dwelling in God.[815] It means an alignment of our will with the Divine. Here is the paradox: We are truly free only when we deny ourselves.

Re-Forming the Modern Person

Humanity was formed in the image of God with a divinely created purpose, sharing in the abundant life of the Holy Trinity. However, attempts are underfoot to reform the modern person into an image as defined by secular society, divorced from God and his divinely intended purpose. Those who lived under Communist regimes often had experience with reeducation efforts, the objectives of which were a rejection of faith in God, giving up traditional moral values, and creating within a person a heart de-sensitized to God's grace, incapable of true and profound feelings, thus being condemned to live a superficial life.[816] Essentially, per Fr. Ciprian Grădinaru of Romania, this is the spirit of the Antichrist.[817] This well-known contemporary spiritual father states, however, that such reeducation is the same under both Communism and Capitalism. We are ceding our freedom to the spirit of the age, consciously or unconsciously.

> In the Communist prisons, torturers used all resources available to force prisoners to deny Christ. Nowadays, rejecting Christ is done voluntarily, as people are seduced from an early age to embrace a lifestyle that is opposite to the one to which Christ calls us. In prisons, torturers were trying to prevent every person

815 Cf. Archimandrite Sophrony, *St. Silouan the Athonite*, 65.

816 See Fr. Ciprian Grădinaru, "Afterword," in Monk Moise, *The Saint of the Prisons: Notes on the Life of Valeriu Gafencu*, trans. Monk Sava, Oaşa Monastery (Triada, 2019), 284.

817 Ibid., 283. Grădinaru notes that the correct translation of "Antichrist" is not "against Christ," but "in place/replacing Christ." Thus, the spirit of the age seeks to take the place of Christ, to "remove him from people's consciousness, to neutralize people's discernment and their capacity to choose freely" (284).

> from having any kind of privacy or moments of prayer. Nowadays, people voluntarily surrender their own privacy in favor of TV, the Internet or anything which might steal their serenity and opportunity to be alone with Christ.[818]

Fr. Ciprian warned that there are three means by which secular society attempts to reeducate people to form the "modern person," gradually leading him or her away from God. The first is a continuous promotion of the hedonistic message:

> The essence of life consists in enjoying oneself, feeling good, having fun, accumulating as much as possible, and being successful. Happiness in life is the generally understood as the sum of moments of pleasure. Thus, the people educated in this spirit constantly crave pleasure. Working like slaves, people chain themselves to monthly installments to the bank, or they steal and make compromises ....[819]

To be clear, this is not the abundant life God wants for us and it dilutes or dismisses our divinely created purpose. Yet, we cannot escape the truth of Fr. Ciprian's observation, and we can readily observe its impact on our society today.

The second means of molding the modern person is through "political correctness," which Fr. Ciprian describes as a "horrendous instrument of mass manipulation."[820] He wrote that this concept aims to impose a new world order, free of Christian principles, the whole concept of God being something unpleasant. The third means is the creation of new language whereby classical definitions such as marriage and family are redefined within a changing cultural norm.

818 Ibid.
819 Ibid., 285.
820 Ibid.

For example, "family" is no longer defined as "the primary social entity, established by marriage, composed by husband, wife, and their descendants." Since 2014, the Oxford Dictionary defines it as "a group consisting of two parents and their children living together as a unit."[821]

According to Fr. Ciprian, the danger is that society is attempting to re-form the modern, progressive person into one who rejects faith in Jesus Christ, does not embrace the cross, no longer places God at the center, and dismisses a divinely created purpose. Rather, secular society proposes a false god as an alternative, one who will fulfill our wishes and make our lives more comfortable on earth.[822] Yet, is this really freedom or is this a dangerous enslavement to sin? Do not be deceived! The love of God is revealed through suffering on the Cross. We can know Christ only if we follow him to Golgotha, not through a life of ease and pleasure.[823]

The Choice is Ours

We choose whether to accept our divinely created purpose. Elder Porphyrios said:

> God is love; he is not a simple spectator in our life. He provides and cares for us as our Father, but He also respects our freedom. He does not pressure us. We should have our hope in God's providence and, since we believe that God is watching over us, we should

821 Ibid., 286.

822 Ibid., 293.

823 Another illustration of this will be considered in our upcoming topic on *Synergeia*, wherein we consider Dietrich Bonhoeffer's contrast of cheap grace versus costly grace. All the Holy Fathers state that the path to salvation is the Way of the Cross, a life of self-denial. That is why spiritual fathers like Grădinaru point to the importance of cultivating our inner sense of sacrifice through ascetical practices. By resembling Christ, we hope to receive the grace of Christ, who sacrificed himself for us (Grădinaru, 292). Ascetical practices, acts of mercy, and compassion for neighbor are considered privileges, opportunities to grow closer to God, and not as obligations or constraints on one's freedom.

> take courage and throw ourselves into his love and then we will see him constantly beside us.[824]

Humanity can accept or reject the offer of our loving God, whose grace opens the door to accept his gift and the ability to achieve our divinely intended destiny. Through acceptance, we open our hearts to recognize the indwelling of the divine presence, which, in turn, will assist us in transforming our lives and continuing toward our destiny. The acceptance is through complete self-emptying (*kenosis*). This is "the way" of Jesus, which he modeled for us yet is impossible to achieve through human initiative alone. However, for God, all things are possible.[825] Thus, *kenosis* and *theosis*, self-emptying and divinization, are closely related. Russian Orthodox Theologian Sergius Bulgakov taught, "As a human being empties himself or herself of ego and sinful, fallen nature, the vessel that remains is filled with divinity."[826] This is the reason that Fr. Ciprian stressed that Christian formation, the antidote to societal reeducation, is through asceticism and the liturgical life of the Church.[827] Our only chance to fight evil is to fill ourselves with Christ. Only light can banish darkness.[828] Alfred Delp, SJ wrote, "With God the only way to complete freedom is complete surrender—there is no alternative."[829] Delp was falsely accused of plotting to kill Hitler, but executed anyway. His death was another act of true freedom: Delp remained true to himself and his personal beliefs. The same lesson is illustrated by the many witnesses, martyrs, and new confessors who refused to succumb to reeducation in Communist prisons, choosing instead to double-down on their faith in Jesus Christ. Faith tested

---

824 Elder Porphyrios, 192.

825 Cf. Matt. 19:26.

826 Boris Jakim, "Sergius Bulgakov: Russian *Theosis*," in *Partakers of the Divine Nature: The History and Development of Deification in the Christian Traditions*, ed. Michael J. Christensen and Jeffery A. Wittung (Grand Rapids, MI: Baker Publishing Group, 2008), 250

827 See Grădinaru, "Afterword," *The Saint of the Prisons*, 280.

828 Ibid., 292.

829 Alfred Delp, SJ. "Unbound," *Magnificat*. 18(8) October (2016), 341. Taken from *Prison Writings* (Maryknoll, NY: Orbis Books, 2004).

through affliction and patient endurance is akin to gold purified by fire.

In contrast, consider the example of the rich young man who asked Jesus what he must do to inherit eternal life.[830] When Jesus told him that he lacked only one thing—to sell all he had, give the money to the poor, and follow Jesus—he went away sad. He chose not to accept the offer and Jesus respected his decision. He did not pursue the young man, asking, "Are you sure?" He did not say, "If that is too difficult, perhaps we can relax the standards a bit." We are free to choose the way. But there are only two choices: with God or without God.

Summary

Society defines limitations on personal rights as an encroachment on our freedom. This reflects a culture of individualism where the individual is at the center. In the extreme, the rights and well-being of the individual supersede the well-being of society—often forced with the mantra of "political correctness." Matthew Kelly wrote, "Every type of perversion and depravity has become someone's personal preference and right."[831] However, what secular society defines as freedom is generally enslavement to sin. Patriarch Daniel of Romania encourages people to ask themselves the essential question of existence:

> What have I done with the liberty (freedom) I have found? If this liberty has helped me to love God and people more, then I have found true liberty. If the liberty I have found has removed me even farther from God, people, and myself, then I am not truly free.[832]

830 See Mark 10:17-22.

831 Kelly, *Life is Messy*, 39.

832 Patriarch Daniel, "Only Jesus Christ Gives People Complete Liberty," in *Patriarch Daniel: Rebuilding Orthodoxy in Romania*, ed. Chad Hatfield (Yonkers, NY: St. Vladimir's Seminary Press, 2021), 141.

The freedom the Creator grants us is to surrender ourselves, aligning our will with the divine will and fulfilling our true destiny. God does not superimpose his will. Jesus modeled this self-surrender and acceptance of God's will, both in the Garden of Gethsemane and in his final words as he died on the cross: "Father, into your hands I commend my spirit."[833] This is true freedom: our choice to follow God can never be taken away.

Consider the 21 Coptic Christian Martyrs beheaded on a Libyan beach.[834] They had choices. Each chose not to renounce his faith, to surrender his fate to his captors, and to have the name of Jesus on his lips as he was murdered. Same as Jesus on the cross, this was an ultimate act of self-surrender, trusting in the mercy of God over the torment inflicted by evil men. This was an act of true freedom. And in such an act, we are set free from any worries or anxieties because we have completely entrusted ourselves to God.[835]

Reflection Questions

1. How do I define freedom? What does it mean to me in my everyday life? Provide specific examples of how you feel free from limitations.

2. How do I feel when I reflect on this idea of self-surrender, of aligning my will to God's will, in other words, what God wants of me? Do I feel restricted? Do I feel like I am going against the grain? Or do I have a sense of genuine freedom? Please explain your answer.

3. How do I react to Fr. Ciprian Grădinaru's observation regarding the reeducation occurring within our secular society? Have I

---

833 Luke 23:46.

834 Decapitated by ISIS on February 15, 2015, for refusing to renounce their faith.

835 See Wis. 3:1-3. "The souls of the just are in the hand of God, and no torment will touch them. They seemed, in the view of the foolish to be dead; and their passing away thought an affliction and their going forth from us utter destruction. But they are in peace."

found my faith declining? Do I find myself wanting to be more politically correct than a Christian who is counter-cultural?

4. What are my feelings about people who gave their lives for their convictions? Consider St. Maximilian Kolbe, Dietrich Bonhoeffer, Fr. Alfred Delp, or the 21 Coptic Christian Martyrs. How do I feel about people, nameless to the world, who attend church in the Middle East, are aware of the risks, and are one day killed by a terrorist bomb?

The Fathers of the Burning Bush Movement

A gathering of bishops, priests and monks focused on the revival of the hesychast tradition (1945-1958), during Communist repression. One of the members pictured is Fr. Dumitru Stăniloae.

(Mural at Entrance of Antim Monastery, Bucharest, Romania)

FROM ENCOUNTER TO DESTINY

The Two Ways

"Enter through the narrow gate ..."
(Matt 7:13)

"There are two ways: one of life and one of death—and there is a big difference between the two." [836]
(Didache 1:1)

Opening Gospel Reading

Matt. 7:13-14 (The Narrow Gate).

The Two Ways

Today, many search for an accommodation between the Gospel of Jesus Christ and the spirit of the age. Some say Jesus's teachings need to be "modernized" as if they were outdated; some argue for re-defined or alternative meanings relative to certain scriptural teachings. However, as authentic Christian disciples, we should not be deceived between Christ and Belial.[837]

Throughout Sacred Scripture, there is a constant portrayal of two ways: one leading to life and the other to death. Never do we see

836 *The Didache: The Teaching of the Twelve Apostles*, trans. R. Joseph Owles (North Charleston, SC: CreateSpace, 2014), 1. The Didache is an important historical document of the Early Church, written in the 1st century, which includes teachings on the Christian life, virtue, Christian ethics, Church rituals (Baptism and Eucharist), and Church organization. Didache means "teaching."

837 See 2 Cor. 6:14-16. NAB. "Do not yoke yourselves in a mismatch with unbelievers. After all, what do righteousness and lawlessness have in common, or what fellowship can light have with darkness? What accord is there between Christ and Belial, what common lot between believer and unbeliever? Tell me what agreement there is between the temple of God and idols. You are the temple of the living God ..."

a middle way, or a way of compromise or accommodation. In our opening reading, St. Paul clearly delineates between these two ways, differentiating between light and darkness, or one could say, between white and black, God and idols.

In the Old Testament, Moses said to the Israelites, "I set before you life and death, the blessing and the curse. Choose life, then, that you and your descendants may live."[838] Moses places before Israel the choice to follow the Lord, and warns them what will happen if they bow down to other gods. Similarly, Joshua told the people to "choose today."

> Now, therefore, fear the Lord and serve him completely and sincerely. Cast out the gods your ancestors served beyond the River and in Egypt, and serve the Lord.
>
> If it is displeasing to you to serve the Lord, choose today whom you will serve, the gods your ancestors served beyond the River or the gods of the Amorites in whose country you are dwelling. As for me and my household, we will serve the Lord.[839]

Throughout the Old Testament, we see what happens when the Israelites go astray, abandoning the Lord, and how calamities beset them. In short, left to their own devices and initiative, nothing good happens.

Jesus differentiated between the two ways, the narrow gate that leads to salvation, the one few will find, and the wide road leading to destruction.[840] He provided the Parable of the Great Feast.[841] "Many are invited, but few are chosen."[842] When the rich young man chose

838 Deut. 30:19.
839 Josh. 24:14-15.
840 See Matt. 7:13-14.
841 See Matt. 22:1-14.
842 Matt. 22:14.

to walk away, not wanting to do what was required to obtain eternal life, Jesus did not stop him nor suggest a compromise.[843] He respected his choice. We, too, must choose who we will follow, Jesus or the Way of the World. There is no middle path.

Separating Ourselves from God

The decision confronting the "modern person" is whether he even needs a divine being. The European Enlightenment challenged this need, advocating reason over faith. Since then, the offspring of this philosophical movement has further diminished the role of God and increasingly emphasized the individual as the center of existence. We have witnessed the unfolding of a major cultural shift away from love of God to love of self. As modern people, we desire to be liberated from our Creator, rather than dependent on him, believing that he enslaves us and precludes us from happiness. Yet we know the definition of insanity: doing the same thing over and over, yet hoping for a different outcome. Straying from God led the ancient Israelites into disaster. Do not be deceived! Freedom from God is enslavement to sin.

Attempting to Lower the Bar

Some want to find an easier way, arguing that following the commandments of Jesus is too hard. There is great effort being made by the modern person to find a middle way: indulging and rationalizing our pursuit of carnal pleasures and worldly desires, while still convincing ourselves that we can attain salvation. Many want the best of both worlds, and any efforts to curb this modernism are labeled "outdated," "unwelcoming" "not being inclusive," or even "un-Christian." Yet, in reality, these labels are nothing less than striving to find accommodation with the spirit of the age with actions and behaviors contrary to the

843 See Mark 10:17-22.

Gospel of Jesus Christ. We see this in the loss of respect for the dignity of human life, great efforts to normalize immoral lifestyles and behaviors, a reliance on human initiative instead of dependence on God, and the emergence of a culture of individualism. We are in a turbulent whirlpool of apostasy that wants to create a rival to the True Faith. We are experiencing the *en masse* de-Christianization of our society. However, do not be deceived. Attempts to take our cues from the spirit of the age is a chase after wind.[844]

Abba Dorotheos of Gaza warns of this middle way, of what happens when we hold on to bad habits.

> Believe me, brothers, a man with a single passion set into a habit is destined to punishment. Maybe he will do ten good actions for every one resulting from bad habit, but the latter will prevail over the ten good actions. If an eagle gets out of a snare except for one claw which remains caught in the net, it has lost all power to escape. Though it is outside the net, is it not half-captive by it? Can the hunter not strike it down whenever he pleases? So it is with the soul: if one has one passion set into a habit, the enemy at any moment he pleases strikes it down, for he has the upper hand over the soul through that passion. This is why I am always telling you not to allow a passion to harden into a habit.[845]

Abba Dorotheos is clear: half-enslavement is still enslavement to sin. We might believe that we are mostly free, yet this is a delusion. In reality, we are still on the wide road leading to destruction. The narrow gate to salvation cannot be widened by redefining the boundaries.

---

844 See Eccl. 1:14. The author describes all futile pursuits as a "chase after wind."

845 St. Dorotheos of Gaza, *Discourses and Sayings*, trans. Eric P. Wheeler (Kalamazoo, MI: Cistercian Publications, 1977), 180-81. Discourse XI: On Cutting Off Passionate Desires.

Yes, what Jesus asks of us is not easy, but he did not establish a quota system for how many can be saved. There is no ambiguity in his teaching: "If anyone wishes to come after me, he must deny himself and take up his cross daily and follow me."[846] Having even one claw still caught in the fowler's snare prevents us from coming after Jesus, following him to eternal life.

Even in our churches, we see evidence of a dilution in the teachings of our faith. Ask yourself: when did you last hear a priest preach about the importance of repentance and confession? What about fasting, individual contemplative prayer, developing a Rule of Prayer or a spiritual program for life, greater participation in Eucharist during the week, reading Sacred Scripture, or seeking spiritual guidance from someone who has traveled the same road? How often does the priest reference the writings of the Holy Fathers? No, these are not popular topics, but these are the instructions we need on how to gain our eternal salvation. If the answer is "not recently," then the question becomes, "Can I find a parish that will help me cultivate the Art of Spiritual Life, a place where I will be nurtured and nourished, a place where the clergy will provide me the instructions needed for spiritual growth, and place where I can find like-minded people who will support me on the journey?" St. John of Kronstadt wrote, "A sleeping conscience needs a strong shaking to awaken."[847]

What is the net result of the "modern person" striving to be free of God? Are people happier? Are we experiencing the abundant life? We can observe the increases in depression, despair, burnout, nihilism, frustration from seeking and coming up empty, and an unprecedented decline in moral behavior. This is not the way to the abundant life, to salvation, or eternal happiness. Rather, separation from God results in fruitless searching, frustration, and despair—vanity, a chase after

846 Luke 9:23.
847 St. John of Kronstadt, *Ten Homilies on the Beatitudes*, trans. N. Kizenko-Frugier (Albany, NY: Corner Editions/La Pierre Angulaire, 2003), 53.

wind.[848] This is because nothing finite can ever fulfill infinite longing. Only God can do that.

Reorienting Our Perspective

Rather than deciding the commandments of Jesus are too hard and giving up without trying, let us start with the position of *how* we can we live by his commandments. What is required? As with anything in life, there is no shortcut. However, we do have the wisdom and guidance of the Holy Fathers who experienced the same struggles, temptations, search for happiness, human frailties, and other challenges. Their writings left us with instructions on achieving incremental progress to reach our true homeland, eternal blessedness with God in heaven.

St. Paul advised, "Open wide your hearts."[849] The issue is not the narrowness of the gate through which Jesus tells us to enter. As St. Paul wrote to the Corinthians, the narrowness was in their hearts.[850] They constrained themselves from the fullness of life in Christ and could not realize the abundant life. Opening our hearts means removing the constraints, to love as Christ wants us to love and live as he desires us to live. Be open to the possibility of Christ, and he will lead us along the right path. We are better with him than without. Nothing in human history suggests otherwise. So, we must choose one of the two ways, the way of life or the way of death, with God or without. We cannot straddle the issue.[851] Christ tells us we must follow him with an undivided heart.[852] This alone is the path to salvation.

---

848 Cf. Eccl. 1:14.
849 Cf. 2 Cor. 6:11.
850 Cf. 2 Cor. 6:12.
851 See 1 Kings 18:21. Elijah said to the Israelite people, "'How long will you straddle the issue? If the Lord is God, follow him; if Baal, follow him.' But the people did not answer him."
852 See Matt. 6:24.

Summary

In Jesus's teachings and throughout Sacred Scripture, there are two distinct paths: one that is faithful to God and his commandments; the other is not. Jesus says that the road to eternal life leads through the narrow gate few will find. Today, many would like to justify a middle way because the way of Jesus is too hard. However, there is no middle way, nor does Jesus have a specific quota for how many will be saved. Accordingly, we must choose between one of two paths, one leading to life and the other to death. As written in the Didache, "There is a big difference between the two."

Reflection Questions

1. What are my struggles with living by the commandments of Jesus? With what teachings of Jesus do I disagree? Why? Do I try to rationalize certain behaviors by reinterpreting what Jesus taught?

2. Do I agree with secular teachings that are in conflict to the Gospel? What are these, and why do I sometimes take the secular side?

3. What is St. Theophan telling us about outward appearances of faith and true interior disposition? How does this relate to our discussion about the two ways?

4. Do I desire to follow the path to salvation more faithfully? What am I prepared to do to gain eternal life?

Synergeia (Collaboration with the Divine)

"I do nothing on my own, but I say only what the Father taught me." (John 8:28)

"Man can be spiritually healed, enlightened, and deified only by the Living God—the Holy Trinity. However, God does not do this without man's participation, and this mystical synergy is the essence of life in the Church." [853] ***(Elder Thaddeus of Vitovnica)***

Opening Gospel Reading

John 15:1-8 ("I am the vine, you are the branches").

Freedom

Freely choosing the offer of our self-communicating God is simply the first step. The gift is the *agent* of transformation, not the transformation itself. In order to complete the journey of *theosis,* we need to collaborate with the Divine to live the God-like virtues.[854] This requires intentional human effort combined with divine collaboration, the latter of which we call *synergeia*. Striving to do our utmost best is merely preparation for the direct intervention of God, who alone can bring us to himself.[855] We cultivate the soil; God plants the seed and nurtures its growth.[856] Accordingly, the human-divine relationship

853 *Our Thoughts Determine Our* Lives, 58.

854 In Roman Catholic theology, such collaboration is called *gratia co-operans*.

855 Burrows, *To Believe in Jesus*, 22.

856 Consider the Parable of the Sower and the Seed. See Matt. 13:1-9; 18-23, Mark 4:1-9; 13-20, and Luke 8:4-8; 11-15.

requires ongoing effort to reach for the infinite horizon, striving toward our destiny. The choice is whether to opt for self-will or the divine will. In the latter, participation in uncreated grace freely given provides ongoing progress in the spiritual journey of divinization.

Scriptural Foundation: Parable of the Talents

The concept of *synergeia* can be best illustrated by the Parable of the Talents.[857] In the Gospel of Matthew, the master gives three servants talents: one received five, another received two, and the final servant received one. The first two traded and doubled their talents, whereas the third servant buried the talent in the ground and gave it back to the master on his return. The master commended the first two servants and threw the third servant out into the darkness, calling him "useless." The first two servants accepted the gifts, the talents, and did something with them. They provided the effort. The third servant did nothing and was punished. As St. Paul wrote:

> By the grace of God, I am what I am, and his grace to me has not been ineffective. Indeed, I have toiled harder than all of them; not I, however, but the grace of God that is with me.[858]

It is the same on our spiritual journey. We are expected to collaborate with the Divine, leveraging what is given us to sustain us along the way. The Parable of the Talents is also similar to our discussion of creation, wherein the servants are entrusted with something of the master's. They are expected to return it, multiplying it to its full potential.

Accordingly, this parable and the insights of St. Paul help us understand the importance of human-divine collaboration. God is

857 See Matt. 25:14–30. Luke has a similar parable, the Parable of the Ten Gold Coins (Luke 19:12–28).

858 1 Cor. 15:10.

always present and active in his creation. We cannot achieve our destiny alone or simply choose to accept the offer. Initiative and effort are required, which usually means patient endurance and perseverance. St. Paisios of Mount Athos explains this well:

> Man ... will never mature spiritually if he is constantly assisted by God without struggling himself. For this reason then, God helps man at the beginning of the spiritual life, but then gradually removes himself in order for man to realize that he must do for himself whatever he can.[859]

If we do not struggle, we will not desire God above all things. Salvation, while freely offered to all, must be properly accepted. It is not passive participation; it is a free choice to deny ourselves, take up our crosses, and follow Jesus. These are the conditions of discipleship. And St. Paisios says we will be given "spiritual examinations" along the way, to test our desire, no different than when impurities are refined from gold or silver.

Telos versus *Amartia*

Theosis is the step-by-step, transformative process that we undertake, wherein by following the commandments and example of Jesus, we begin to regain the likeness of God, preparing ourselves to live in union with him in the life to come. Consider this: every person has the potential to be another Mother Teresa of Calcutta. Despite the skepticism this statement might draw, it is true. This can be said confidently because we are all created in the divine image, patterned after the Image Absolute, and related to God. We have the blueprint of the divine attributes within us. The difference is how well we collaborate with the indwelling divine presence. However, we all possess the possibility—which we have previously described as the "likeness."

859 St. Paisios the Athonite, "Spiritual Awakening," *Spiritual Counsels*, vol. 2, trans. Fr. Peter Chamberas, ed. Anna Famellos and Andronikos Masters (Souroti, Thessaloniki, Greece: Holy Hesychasterion Evangelist John the Theologian, 2016), 325.

Jesus tells us, "Be perfect, just as your heavenly Father is perfect."[860] On the surface, this seems daunting or impossible. However, in the original New Testament Greek, the word for "perfect" is *teleios*, which is derived from *telos,* meaning "purpose" or "goal." Thus, perfect—*teleios*—means living up to the purpose we were created for and to which we have been called.[861] It is not about being perfect—nor is it simply living a good life. We are called to be much more, to be Christ-centered and God-like to fulfill our divinely intended purpose.

Contrast *telos* with the Greek word for sin, *amartia,* which does not mean "transgressing the law." It means "missing the mark."[862] The mark is our divinely intended purpose, and sin throws us off this true direction; we become self-centered, cut off from true life. We disengage ourselves from God, cutting the bond of love by which God embraces us; we lose our internal harmony and proper orientation toward God.[863] We ought to be reaching beyond the world, toward our Creator, yet we often find ourselves yielding to the pressures and temptations of the world, inescapably trapped. We have lost our purpose.

So, if we fall short of the mark, we get up again. We keep trying. In *Evangelii Gaudium,* Pope Francis describes his view of the Holy Mystery of Repentance: "An encounter with the Lord's mercy which spurs us on to do our best."[864] "What matters for Jesus is not our spiritual level but our spiritual *direction*, not our proximity to perfection but our *desire* for it."[865]

Striving for our best, striving for the infinite horizon of possibility, is what the spiritual journey is all about. Fr. Stephen Krupa, SJ, adjunct senior instructor at Loyola University Chicago, said: "If I fall short 499

860 Matt. 5:48.

861 See Coniaris, *Achieving Your Potential in Christ: Theosis*, 118.

862 Ibid., 22.

863 See Raya, *The Face of God*, 180.

864 Pope Francis, *Evangelii Gaudium*, no. 44.

865 Stephen Finlan, "Deification in Jesus's Teaching," in *Theosis: Deification in Christian Doctrine*, vol. 2, ed. Vladimir Kharlamov (Eugene, OR: Pickwick Publications, 2011), 30.

times today, I hope that tomorrow I will only fall short 498 times." St. John Climacus wrote:

> Do not be surprised if you fall every day and do not surrender. Stand your ground bravely. And you may be sure that your guardian angel will respect your endurance.... all things are possible with God.[866]

St. Paul tells us grace abounds more than sin.[867] *Theosis* is about striving to do our best, making those incremental improvements to fulfill our destiny. Realistically, we often feel somewhere between *telos* and *amartia,* striving for *telos,* yet sensing a gravitational pull toward *amartia.* It is human nature to resist the call, "the way" of Jesus. We often struggle because of personal selfishness, pursuing our own path, thinking we know better, or avoiding the cross, seeking an easier way. Yet the more we resist the passions and temptations, the more we are enabled to accept God's gift of self, to be open to his divine presence in our lives. In this daily struggle, we realize our weakness, (*limitedness,* as Rahner would say), and become increasingly aware that we cannot maintain a journey toward transcendence on our own. We can do so only by collaborating with the Divine (*synergeia*). We need deifying grace.

Closing Off Openness to God

We have the free choice of responding to God's offer, either accepting or rejecting it. To Rahner, closing our openness to the self-communicating God is sin. Stăniloae had a similar perspective of being closed off to God as the infinite source of power and also being closed off to our neighbor. Often, when we close ourselves off from God, we try to fill the inner longing with experiences involving finite things instead of that which is infinite. In doing so, we deny our created purpose by denying our dependence on God.

866 Climacus, 130. Step 5: On Penitence.
867 See Rom. 5:20.

Consider the Parable of the Fig Tree.[868] God's self-communication is always available. In the parable, the person who planted the orchard is frustrated with the fig tree, which does not bear fruit, and questions, "Why should it exhaust the soil?"[869] Similarly, the Giver has offered us the gift we need to fulfill our destiny. Do we accept, or are we simply exhausting the soil?

We must avoid three illusions. All pertain to our efforts to fill our infinite capacity with finite things, in other words, "exhausting the soil" with futile efforts that bear no fruit. The first illusion is security, which Jesus addressed in the Parable of the Rich Fool.[870] We would like to believe our lives will be better if we are secure, that the frailties of human existence can be mitigated by material possessions. However, if our planning surrounds our temporal life, we lose sight of our destiny, heaven. We depend on our initiative instead of on God. The problem with worrying about our earthly tomorrow is that too many variables are beyond our control, including our life span. Our very existence is a true blessing from God. The trappings of prosperity can be deceptive. Life is not chaotic chance; our lives are governed by the gracious gifts of God.[871] He gives us what we need when we need it, provided we open ourselves to him.

The second illusion is control, believing that we can gain control of our own lives. Yet, as the Russian proverb says, "Man proposes, God disposes." In reality, we are often tested in both prosperity and adversity, often being shown the absurdity of believing we are in control.

The final illusion is affection. Sometimes we succumb to the belief that happiness can be found in attractions to created things, be it beauty, love, addictions to pleasure and possessions, or a desire to

868 See Luke 13:6–9.
869 Luke 13:7.
870 See Luke 12:16–21.
871 Cf. Luke Timothy Johnson, 201.

reduce our pain.[872] We can delude ourselves as we saw in the Parable of the Rich Fool: "Relax! Eat heartily, drink well. Enjoy yourself!"[873] Yet the true treasure offered to us is the divine indwelling, which can be gained only by accepting the offer of our self-communicating God. Anything less, and we will always find ourselves falling short. Recall St. Gregory of Nyssa's concept of the "Experience of Our Dissatisfaction." Pursuit of finite things and pleasures will always leave us empty.

All three illusions—security, control, and affection—can cause us to lose sight of our created purpose. They are the antithesis of freedom and, in reality, they lead to enslavement to sin. Only virtue and compassion follow us after death;[874] there are no pockets in a shroud.[875] Absolute freedom solely relies on God because, if we do, we theoretically will have no worries. God is in control in all circumstances, adversity and prosperity.[876] God gives us absolute freedom to choose, to reject or not reject his offer of self, his unconditional love. As Rahner writes:

> In and through yourself, in and through what you in your innermost being are and definitely want to be, you can be a person who closes himself into the absolute, deadly and final loneliness of saying "no" to God.[877]

---

872 Consider addictions to alcohol, tobacco, drugs, pornography, sex, or even work when life becomes distorted with a constant search for "something other than God" (C. S. Lewis's term) to make us happy. Yet these are attempts to fill infinite longing with finite things, with the finite always falling short.

873 Luke 12:19.

874 St. Ambrose of Milan, "Exposition of the Gospel of Luke, Homily." 7.122. Taken from *Luke*. In "Ancient Christian Commentary on Scripture" series, New Testament, Vol. III, ed. Arthur A. Just, Jr. (Downers Grove, IL: Intervarsity Press, 2003), 208.

875 Spanish proverb. See William Barclay, *The Gospel of Luke* (Louisville, KY: Westminster John Knox Press, 2001), 197.

876 See Rom. 8:31. "If God is for us, who can be against us?"

877 Rahner, *Foundations of Christian Faith*, 103–104.

This possibility of life without God can become disquieting, especially when we strive to fill our infinite capacity or attempt to satisfy our inner longing with finite things.

Reality Check: The Spiritual Journey Involves Struggle

Being open to God's gift of self does not mean we will have a life without struggles. We do not pray for an easy life; we pray for the strength to endure a difficult one. Our faith will be tested for it to be perfected, like fire refining silver or gold. We are given struggles to increasingly place greater reliance on God, letting go of self-will and surrendering like Jesus in the Garden of Gethsemane, which will prepare us for our destiny. "The demons cleverly watch us, observe our weak points, and then attack with their fantasies."[878] A disciple of Jesus will have a cross to bear—Jesus was clear about this.[879] St. John Chrysostom wrote:

> 'Is there nobody,' someone asks, 'who enjoys comfort both here and hereafter?' This cannot be, O man, it is impossible. It is not possible, not possible at all for one who enjoys an easy life and freedom from want in this world, who continually indulges himself in every way, who lives randomly and foolishly, to enjoy honor in the other world. For if poverty does not trouble him, still desire troubles him, and he is afflicted because of this, which brings more than a little pain. If disease does not threaten him, still his temper grows hot, and it requires more than an ordinary struggle to overcome anger. If trials do not come to test him, still evil thoughts continually attack. It is no common task to bridle foolish desire, to stop vainglory, to restrain presumption, to refrain from luxury, to persevere in

878 Maloney, 105.

879 See Luke 9:23. Anyone who wishes to a disciple must take up his cross daily.

> austerity. A person who does not do these things and others like them cannot ever be saved.[880]

Each person has an individual struggle. St. Isaac the Syrian advised:

> Without actual direct experience of God's protection, the heart cannot hope in him; and if the soul does not taste Christ's sufferings consciously, she will never have communion with him.[881]

Said another way, this is how we learn self-surrender, to align our will in harmony with the will of Jesus and follow his example. We become dependent on him and no longer rely on our own initiative. This is the communion of which St. Isaac speaks, harmony with the divine will. We know this self-surrender often seems humanly impossible. However, recall what Jesus said to the rich young man who desired perfection.[882] He was told that there was one more thing to do: to sell all he had and follow Jesus. The Gospel tells us, "When he heard this statement, he went away sad, because he had many possessions."[883] He could not do what Jesus asked. The disciples asked Jesus, "Who then can be saved?"[884] Let us reflect upon Jesus's answer: *"For human beings this is impossible, but for God all things are possible."*[885] This is one of the clearest statements in Sacred Scripture showing the essential need for human-divine collaboration (*synergeia*). We simply cannot do it on our own.

As written in the Letter to the Hebrews:

> My son, do not disdain the discipline of the Lord or lose

880 Chrysostom, *On Wealth and Poverty*, 66-7.
881 *The Ascetical Homilies of Saint Isaac the* Syrian, Homily Five, 160.
882 See Matt. 19:16-26.
883 Matt. 19:22.
884 Matt. 19:25.
885 Matt. 19:26.

> heart when reproved by him; for whom the Lord loves, he disciplines; he scourges every son he acknowledges. Endure your trials as 'discipline;' God treats you as sons. For what 'son' is there whom his father does not discipline? At the time, all discipline seems a cause not for joy, but for pain, yet later it brings the peaceful fruit of righteousness to those who are trained by it.[886]

Struggles, temptations, challenges, and suffering are intended for purification of heart. As Chrysostom writes, "The more God afflicts us, the more he perfects us."[887] Thus, we accept the opportunity to encounter God in all circumstances of our lives, to assess the quality of our relationship with him.

> If God is right there, in the middle of our struggle, then our aim is to stay there. We are to remain in the cell, to stay on the road, not to forego the journey or forget the darkness. It is all too easy for us to overlook the importance of the struggle, preferring instead to secure peace and rest, or presuming to reach the stage of love prematurely."[888]
>
> When we admit our hopelessness and desperation, when recognize that we have 'hit rock bottom' in ourselves as well as in our relationships with people and with God, we also discover the compassion of God who voluntarily assumed the vulnerability of crucifixion. One would not seek divine healing unless one had to in order to survive, unless one admitted there was no other way out of the impasse.[889]

886 Heb. 12:5-7, 11.

887 Jean-Claude Larchet, *The Theology of Illness* (Crestwood, NY: St. Vladimir's Seminary Press, 2002), 66. John Chrysostom, *Homilies on Lazarus*, VI.8. Taken from

888 John Chryssavgis, *In the Heart of the Desert: The Spirituality of the Desert Fathers and Mothers* (Bloomington, IN: World Wisdom, Inc., 2003), 104.

889 Ibid., 50.

When we find ourselves in a turbulent whirlpool of despair, which we invariably will, we need our faith more than ever. Abba Dorotheos of Gaza wrote:

> In God's providence everything is absolutely right and whatever happens is for the assistance of the soul. For whatever God does with us, he does out of love and consideration for us because it is adapted to our needs.[890]

Consider the story of St. Teresa of Calcutta. Most have heard the story of her profound conversion experience, her "call within a call," on September 10, 1946. On her train ride from Calcutta to Darjeeling for her annual retreat, she encountered a dying man on a railway platform whom she heard call out, "I thirst." She saw Christ calling to her and asking her, "Will you refuse me?" On her retreat, she continued to pray about this experience, and she felt the profound sense of Christ's message of thirsting for love and for souls. She felt him calling to her, "Come be my light." and "Will you do this for me?" This motivated her to begin the monumental task of creating a new religious order, the Missionaries of Charity, to satiate the thirst of Christ for souls in service of the poorest of the poor, Christ in his "most distressing disguises." It is evident Mother Teresa had a strong interior prayer life, and her encounters with Jesus in prayer were intense. These experiences gave her the inner strength to overcome all the challenges and focus on Jesus's request to quench his thirst for love and for souls.[891]

Other saints had similar profound internal encounters, including St. Teresa of vila and St. Faustina Kowalska, a mystic who, through apparitions of Jesus, was asked to spread devotion to the Divine Mercy. Love of Christ consumed the hearts of these mystics and sustained

---

890 St. Dorotheos of Gaza, 192. Discourse XIII: On Enduring Temptation Calmly and Thankfully.

891 See Langford.

their efforts. Without their surrender, their "yes" to Christ, they could never have overcome the insurmountable obstacles they faced. And there are countless more saints with similar experiences. Addressing the collaboration occurring through prayer, Patriarch Daniel said:

> St. Gregory Palamas says that when man prays, the activity is not his alone, he is not the only one who works when he prays, but God also works in prayer, who sends the grace of his merciful love into the heart of the one who prays. So, prayer is not merely human work. It is a cooperation of the soul with God.[892]

"A cooperation of the soul with God" is a good summary of *synergeia.*

Until recently, most people did not realize that Mother Teresa had experienced over 40 years of spiritual darkness.[893] After the intensive encounters with Jesus and the start of her mission, she no longer had intense mystical experiences in prayer. They were gone, and, as exemplified in her letters, she was distressed by this darkness.[894] St. John of the Cross and other well-known mystics also experienced periods of spiritual darkness. Most, though, did not have this drought as long as Mother Teresa, which apparently lasted until her death. Yet despite no longer hearing the voice of Jesus, she still maintained her incredible pace and work, always with a smile, to care for the dying and the poorest of the poor. The inspiration she initially received sustained her for the rest of her life. She knew she was serving Jesus,

---

892 Comments of Patriarch Daniel during a conference with the clergy of the Archdiocese of Bucharest, June 6-7, 2022. See Aurelian Iftimiu, "The Year 2022 is an Opportunity to Reflect on the Romanian Hesychasts." St. Gregory Palamas is one of the three designated patron saints for the 2022 Solemn Year of Prayer.

893 See "Saint Teresa of Calcutta," *Magnificat* 19(12) (February 2018), 324. Mother Teresa's spiritual darkness and associated anguish became known through the publication of her private letters.

894 See Mother Teresa, *Come Be My Light.* A good book based on the correspondence of Mother Teresa' initial intense experiences and personal energy to undertake her work for Jesus, followed by prolonged pain and suffering from her spiritual darkness.

that she loved Jesus, even if she no longer heard his voice. All the while, she remained incredibly humble, describing herself as "a pencil in the hand of God."[895]

The story of Mother Teresa tells us that even a deeply spiritual mystic, who had an incredible desire to serve Christ through the unloved, unlovable, and unwanted, and who had an extraordinary impact on our world, was not immune from great struggles and suffering. Some say she prayed to Jesus to experience the "thirst" he felt on the cross; perhaps this spiritual dryness, this sense of abandonment, was that. It was her personal communion with the anguish of Christ, the intense feelings of rejection and abandonment he felt while hanging from the cross.[896] Recall the words of St. Isaac the Syrian: "If the soul does not taste Christ's sufferings consciously, she will never have communion with him."[897]

The reality is that God is also in the midst of our struggles, whether or not we recognize his presence. Ignatian spirituality states that "God is in the overcoming." We would like to believe God is near when we are happy or have been blessed in one way or another. This can be delusional, a superficial faith, whereby when the storms come, our faith collapses. It is also important to see God in the midst of struggle, in the "overcoming"—the actions we take to navigate through the constant difficulties of life.[898]

Jesus contrasts the house built on rock versus the one on sand and the storm's impact on each.[899] Mother Teresa was an example of someone whose house was built on rock because despite terrible personal affliction and a sense of abandonment, this storm did not diminish her passion for the work she had undertaken. Today, we need to ask ourselves this question: If we know the storm is coming, which

---

895 Ibid.
896 See "Saint Teresa of Calcutta," *Magnificat* 19(12), 324.
897 *The Ascetical Homilies of Saint Isaac the Syrian*, 160. Homily Five.
898 See Vinita Hampton Wright, "God is in the Overcoming." *Loyola Press Online*.
899 See Matt. 7:24-27.

it invariably will, which foundation do we want? Do we want rock or sand? Do we want to be grounded upon the Divine, collaborating with him through self-surrender and submission to his will, or do we want to go a different direction? Our freedom allows us to make that choice.

Accepting the Offer of Salvation

By accepting the offer of our self-communicating God, the gift of his very self ("Giver as gift"), our hearts can begin to be filled. God pours out his unconditional love to us, and if we accept his gift, his love will be poured into our hearts through the Holy Spirit.[900] The purpose of our existence, of God having created something "other than God," is for us to share in his overflowing love because self-love is not true love. True love is shared. The ongoing work of the Holy Spirit and the importance of the Spirit dwelling within is key to fulfilling our destiny. This can only be achieved by freely accepting God's offer of salvation and collaborating with his divine presence, participating in the uncreated energies of God— Eastern perspective—or uncreated grace, per Rahner, which is freely available to all.

Accepting the offer of salvation means we will accept our cross just as Jesus did: "If anyone wishes to come after me, he must deny himself and take up his cross daily and follow me."[901] For Mother Teresa, her primary cross was a protracted period of spiritual darkness. We all have crosses. Jesus's way is the Way of the Cross.[902] However, by accepting the offer as laid out by Jesus, we will be guided through the inevitable struggles on the journey to our destiny. Struggles are meant to perfect us, causing us to be increasingly reliant on God alone and his mercy. As Jesus said in our opening Gospel passage, "Without me, you can do nothing."[903] With this conviction, we should not allow

900 See Rom. 5:5.

901 Luke 9:23.

902 Burrows, *To Believe in Jesus*, 27. Sr. Ruth contrasts the Spirituality of the Cross with the Spirituality of Glory. The Way of the Cross renounces all for the sake of seeking God and not self. The Spirituality of Glory seeks itself under the guise of seeking God.

903 John 15:5.

anything to take away or even mitigate our poverty, our helplessness, our 'nothingness.'[904] Through our struggles, we will learn the absolute truth of Jesus's statement and increasingly surrender our self-will to the divine will.

Summary

Without Jesus, without collaborating with the Divine, it is impossible to achieve our destiny or fill the longing within us. Collaboration means an alignment of wills; we surrender our selfish self-will to God's will. This required surrender is a great struggle and, in fact, counter cultural. Without Jesus, without collaborating with the Divine, it is impossible.

German Pastor and Theologian Dietrich Bonhoeffer described this challenge well in his comparison of cheap grace versus costly grace:

> Cheap grace is the preaching of forgiveness without repentance, baptism without church discipline, Communion without confession, absolution without personal confession. Cheap grace is grace without discipleship, grace without the cross, grace without Jesus Christ, living and incarnate.[905]

This is the way the world tries to mold Christianity today, to accommodate the spirit of the age, trying to widen the narrow gate, and to eliminate the Cross. Thus, it tries to devalue the importance of the Gospel of Jesus Christ. To this, Bonhoeffer provides the contrast:

> Costly grace is the gospel which must be *sought* again and again, the gift which must be *asked for*, the door at which a man must *knock*. Such grace is *costly*

904 See Burrows, *Essence of Prayer*, 195.

905 Dietrich Bonhoeffer, *The Cost of Discipleship* (New York, NY: Simon & Schuster, 1995), 44-5.

> because it causes us to follow, and it is *grace* because it calls us to follow *Jesus Christ*. It is costly because it costs a man his life, and it is grace because it gives a man the only true life. It is costly because it condemns sin, and grace because it justifies the sinner. Above all, it is *costly* because it cost God the life of his Son.[906]

True faith has a price, and it must be lived authentically, staying the course and not trying to seek a non-existent easier way that is free of struggle. There is no other way except the way of the Cross, through which Jesus restored our relationship with God and invites us into eternal blessedness through union with him. This is how Christians provide witness to a broken world. Cardinal Sarah writes, "Faith is contagious. If it is not, that is because it has become insipid."[907]

To live to our divinely intended lives, to be "perfect as your heavenly Father is perfect," as Jesus taught, requires divine assistance. We make the effort, and God provides the deifying grace when we need it. By grounding our life in the Divine, having God at the center, we will have a solid foundation when the trials and storms invariably come. No one is immune from struggles on the spiritual journey, not even well-known saints such as Mother Teresa. However, the choice remains ours. We must freely choose, surrendering our self-will and choosing to collaborate with the divine will.

Reflection Questions

1. In my life today, what is the direction I find myself choosing most often? Do I try to go it alone, relying on myself? Or, do I find myself dependent upon God? Reflect upon this and provide an honest answer. It does not need to be shared.

906 Ibid., 45.
907 Sarah, *The Day is Now Far Spent*, 25.

2. What struggles do I experience? Do I recognize God's presence as I overcome them? Or, do I think he is silent and has abandoned me?

3. When I hear in the Gospel the words of Jesus that we must be perfect as our heavenly Father is perfect, what has been my response to this? Do I dismiss it as impossible? How have I reconciled this?

4. We discussed "being perfect" as *telos,* our purpose or goal, and sin as *amartia,* which is missing the mark. Does this give me a new perspective?

5. When I consider the invitation to follow Jesus, do I expect a life free from struggles and pain? If yes, why do I have this perspective?

6. How would I describe the foundation of my faith? Is it rock or sand? Please explain your choice.

The Wisdom of the Desert Fathers

"Then Jesus was led by the Spirit into the desert..."
(Matt. 4:1)

"Each time that there is a spiritual renewal in the Church, the desert fathers are present."
(Iréné̈é Hausherr, SJ)

Opening Gospel Reading

Matthew 3:16 – 4:11 (The Temptation of Jesus in the Desert).

Examples of Authentic Christian Living

We are experiencing a season of winter within our Church today, particularly in Western Europe and North America. When hearts lie fallow, it is best to return to basics. In this case, the Desert Fathers provide one of the earliest and best models of Christian living based on experience and a desire to encounter the Divine. We need to cultivate an environment in which we can experience God through prayer and the ordinariness of daily life. We need to be properly attuned to recognize his presence. Consider the example of the Prophet Elijah and his encounter with the Lord.[908] The Lord was not in the strong and violent wind, the earthquake, or the fire. He was in the "light silent sound," almost like a whisper. If our hearts are not attuned, we may not recognize or experience the Lord's presence.

---

908 See I Kings 19:9–12.

Yet God is active in his creation, ever-present to us, especially in our need.

The Desert Fathers represent a model of simple Christian living and a source of spiritual guidance. Theirs is an experienced-based journey of faith, a back-to-basics spirituality, which is crucial today. Between the third and the fifth centuries, these individuals withdrew into the Egyptian desert and later the Syrian desert for solitude in imitation of Jesus. They developed a unique form of contemplative prayer known as *hesychia*, which is how the hesychast tradition began.[909] Abba Arsenius, one of the monks, said a voice told him to "flee, keep silent, and be at rest."[910] These three injunctions are essentially the core of hesychast spirituality.[911] The Desert Fathers knew that Christianity was a divinizing process that took place gradually within the human heart, the interior focus where man and the Triune God meet. Constant vigilance, purification, and humility, silence, and solitude create a spiritual listening to God's indwelling presence.

Putting the Desert Fathers into Context (Then and Now)

Despite being part of the Ancient Church, the Desert Fathers are relevant today because, first and foremost, their spirituality was derived from simple lived experiences. They were not theologians, per se, but provided experience-based wisdom. At the same time in the history of the Early Church, the great Alexandrian and Antiochene Schools were emerging with theologians describing and debating Christian doctrines, often leveraging concepts from earlier Greek philosophers, primarily Plato or neo-platonic philosophical constructs. The period of the Desert Fathers overlapped the time of the First Seven Ecumenical Councils (325 to 787) until about 800, which

909 In descriptions of Catholic spirituality, the hesychast tradition is also referred to as Desert Spirituality.

910 *The Sayings of the Desert Fathers*, trans. Benedicta Ward, SLG (Kalamazoo, MI: Cistercian Publications, 1975), xxi.

911 See Maloney, 43.

means Desert Spirituality evolved concurrently with the development of essential Christian theological doctrines.

During this time, we see the dialectic tension in the unity of spirituality and theology. These two elements did not evolve autonomously. For example, St. Athanasius of Alexandria, one of the great theologians of the time and a participant at the First Council of Nicaea, knew St. Antony of Egypt and wrote his biography, *The Life of Antony*. Another Council Father, St. Basil the Great, visited the Desert Fathers and was a monk himself. Connections between spiritual and theological evolution were maintained.

The mystical tradition of the Eastern Churches descends directly from Desert Spirituality, and has been faithfully practiced and preserved ever since. During today's spiritual winter, it is good to return to the basics.

Lessons of Desert Spirituality

The objective of the Desert Fathers was to reside in an environment conducive to encounter. If we return to the three injunctions heard by Abba Arsenius, the latter two, "be still" (*hesychia*) and "be at rest," are reflective of prayer or contemplation in the presence of the Divine. The first injunction, "flee," is to withdraw from the attractions of the world and secular affairs—anything that might distract our hearts from God. Thus, fleeing is about creating the right environment for encounter, to be attuned to the presence of God in our lives.

If we look at Desert Spirituality even further, three general themes emerge from the "sayings" of the Desert Fathers. The first is a move toward personal purification and simplicity. Spiritual masters of the hesychast tradition did not just focus on the prayer, but also on personal purification to cultivate a relationship with the Divine Indwelling. They tilled the soil of their hearts to yield a rich harvest of prayer.

The second theme concerns interior stillness and sober vigilance. This refers to the prayer and being attuned to constant attacks from the demons who desire nothing more than to divert us from prayer. Third, the Desert Fathers believed that loving God and following the examples of Jesus were heavily predicated on love of neighbor. Notice, too, how these three themes closely align with the teachings of Jesus regarding fasting, prayer, and almsgiving.[912]

Personal Purification and Simplification

True athletes of prayer place great emphasis on preparing an interior environment conducive to encounter. The first level of participation is *praxis*, the process of learning skills. These skills involve the active struggle through ascetical practices, living the virtues, and other spiritual practices such as repentance and mourning our sins (*penthos*) to achieve personal purification. In essence, the objective is detachment from the world and abandonment of self-will, whereby we become completely dependent on God. Only in this state can the individual experience true freedom to make the free-will choice of being open to the Giver's gift.

St. Isaac the Syrian advised us:

> The beginning of a man's true life is the fear of God. But the fear of God will not be persuaded to dwell in a soul together with distraction over outward things. For by serving the senses, the heart is scattered from delight in God ...[913]

St. Isaac's "true life" is the interior life, and "fear of God" means a right-ordered relationship between Creator and created, God and the humanity. God should be held in great reverential awe because he is

912 See Matt. 6:1–8, 16–18.

913 *The Ascetical Homilies of St. Isaac the Syrian*, 114-5. Homily One.

so far beyond our understanding; he is unlimited, and we are limited. Thus, we need to approach God with a sense of humility. Further, a right-ordered relationship between God and the person has God at the center, instead of pushing him to the periphery or ignoring him.

St. Isaac says that fear of God, of proper reverence, cannot dwell in the soul distracted by outward things. This makes sense because such external attachments—pride, wealth, and sensual pleasure, to name a few—tend to push God from our center to the periphery as we make something else the priority. Accordingly, St. Isaac tells us we cannot have interior conflict within our souls. Jesus effectively told us the same thing: "No one can serve two masters. He will either hate one and love the other, or be devoted to one and despise the other. You cannot serve God and mammon."[914] Thus, to have God at our center and delight in him, we need to remove that which divides our heart.

St. Isaac tells us that "the fear of God is the beginning of virtue and, it is said to be the offspring of faith."[915] Living the God-like virtues is part of the divinizing process of *theosis*, preparing us for our destiny. The following are some spiritual practices specifically focused on purification of heart:

1. **Asceticism (*Áskēsis*)**

   Asceticism means "training" or "exercise." Ascetical practices include fasting, self-denial, and simplification to detach ourselves from worldly concerns. In the Eastern Christian tradition, there are fasting periods during the liturgical year, the most significant being the Great Fast (Lent) and the Nativity or Philip's Fast, the latter being the 40 days before Christmas. The fasts are generally more rigorous than those in the Western Church because they involve abstinence from meat, fish, dairy products, wine, and olive oil throughout

914 Matt. 6:24.

915 *The Ascetical Homilies of St. Isaac the Syrian*, 113. Homily One.

the duration. Two others are the Apostles' Fast, about two weeks from the Monday after All Saints to the Feast of SS. Peter and Paul, and the Dormition Fast, the first two weeks of August. Except for fast-free periods such as Bright Week (the week after Easter), Christians are also asked to fast on both Wednesdays, in remembrance of the betrayal of Jesus by Judas Iscariot, and Fridays, in remembrance of Christ's Crucifixion. Ascetical fasts are intended as "means of spiritual perfection, crowned in love, and aided in prayer."[916] St. Isaac tells us, "There can be no knowledge of the mysteries of God on a full stomach."[917] Without our bodies actively involved, we cannot create the proper interior disposition conducive to true prayer. As Cardinal Sarah says:

> Since the origins of the Church, prayer is often combined with fasting: our body must be completely involved in the search for God in the silence of prayer. It would be false to put God first in our lives if our bodies are not really involved.[918]

Fasting is not just from food. One should fast from anything that could steer the heart away from God. This would include slander, gossip, judgment, and excessive entertainment or Internet usage. These spiritual practices are intended to fulfill the teachings of Jesus regarding daily self-denial—these are part of the terms and conditions of authentic discipleship.[919] Ascetical practices are also intended to create a sense of spiritual poverty, increased recognition for dependence on God, and creation of an inner longing, providing a place for God to fill. Fasting can often lead to intensified experiences of

---

916 "Fasting," https://www.orthodoxwiki.org/Fasting.

917 *The Ascetical Homilies of St. Isaac the Syrian*, 146. Homily Four.

918 Sarah, *God or Nothing*, 151.

919 See Luke 9:23. "If anyone wishes to come after me, he must deny himself and take up his cross daily and follow me."

prayer because of the sense of longing derived from physical hunger. Fasting is to cultivate a hunger for God, wherein faith itself is a hunger for him.

2. Detachment (*Apatheia*)

Closely related to *áskēsis* is *apatheia,* which means "detachment from distractions," including both thoughts and material possessions. *Apatheia* is an antidote to our efforts to fill our inner longing with finite things. Our lives of "convenience" have become quite complicated. The Desert Fathers sought a life of simplicity, realizing that what people often valued in secular society has no value. As St. Paul wrote about his life before his conversion, "Whatever gains I had, these I have to consider a loss because of Christ."[920]

The approach of the Desert Fathers was to follow Jesus's commandment to the fullest: "Sell all you have, give your money to the poor … Then come, follow me."[921] Often, we believe our attachments will bring us happiness. However, only dependence upon God and allowing his plan for our lives to unfold can provide true happiness. "Therefore, I tell you, do not worry about your life, what you will eat (or drink), or about your body, what you will wear. Is not life more than food and the body more than clothing?"[922]

Rather than "building larger barns,"[923] we should ask ourselves what is necessary and avoid what is excessive. For example, attachments to designer brands, specific car models or the size of our houses, the latest technology, collections, and increasingly extravagant vacations can all creep into our lives based on secular society's measures of success. The reality is these things can impoverish us as to

920 Phil. 3:7.
921 Matt. 19:21.
922 Matt. 6:25.
923 See Luke 12:16–18. Parable of the Rich Fool.

what truly "matters to God." Attachments often come through habits or practices, and we may not even realize how many we have. Further, the culture of individualism that permeates our secular society often makes us immune to recognizing attachments, selfishness, and our gravitation toward a "throw-away" society. In some instances, these are subconscious pursuits of happiness and focus on self. Yet nothing can substitute for the presence of God in our lives, so we need to simplify and declutter. Otherwise, it is easy for us to lose our spiritual focus,[924] dividing our hearts and pushing God to the periphery.

What is truly necessary? For example, what does a concept such as "retail therapy" tell us about the condition of our secular society? Some advocate that we can identify what we think is necessary in our lives and easily cut that in half. Consider the three illusions—security, control, and affection or disordered love—described in our *Synergeia* discussion. We need to detach from material possessions and place greater dependence on God. As St. John of the Cross said, "God does not fit into an occupied heart."[925]

St. Isaac the Syrian advised:

> No one is able is able to draw near to God without leaving the world far behind. This is virtue: emptying one's mind of the world. As long as the senses are occupied with *things*, the heart cannot stop imagining them. Passions do not cease nor evil thoughts come to an end without the desert and solitude.[926]

924 See Vishnevskaya, 139. She points to St. Maximos the Confessor's analogy that loss of spiritual focus is "like a little sparrow whose foot is tied tries to fly but is pulled to earth by the cord to which it is bound."

925 "Saint John of the Cross," *Magnificat* 18(6) (August 2016), 179.

926 St. Isaac of Nineveh, *On Ascetical Life*, trans. Mary Hansbury (Crestwood, NY: St. Vladimir's Seminary Press, 1989), 26. "First Discourse," no. 4-5.

He also wrote, "Leave the things of no value that you may find the precious things."[927]

3. Mourning Our Sinfulness (*Penthos*)

Many Holy Fathers spoke of mourning our sinfulness. Consider the exchange between Abba Isaiah and Abba Macarius:[928]

Abba Isaiah:	Give me a word, father.
Abba Macarius:	Flee from men.
Abba Isaiah:	What does it mean to flee from men?
Abba Macarius:	It means to sit in your cell and weep for your sins.

Spiritual Fathers often counsel their disciples to begin their time of prayer by truly mourning their sins, realizing one's unworthiness before God. Repentance is not just the Holy Mystery of Confession, but also a state of mind with constant sorrow for sins committed. The Holy Fathers also speak of the "gift of tears," a genuine regret for the sins that distract us from God. When distracted from our prayer, some also advise recreating the atmosphere of prayer by mourning, saddened by the sins committed. This is intended to create a spirit of humility, the foundation of all virtues. Humility must be felt to achieve a proper state of prayer in which the single ask of God is for his mercy.

4. Forgiveness (*Aphesis*)

Anger and resentment are spiritual shackles that weigh us down, disturbing our inner peace. We can become embittered by remembering the wrongs committed by others or find ourselves constantly judging. One Spiritual Father

927 Ibid., 53. "Third Discourse," no. 18.

928 See *The Sayings of the Desert Fathers*, 133.

described such strife as "spiritual suicide."[929] Jesus is clear in his teaching:

> Be merciful, just as your Father is merciful. Stop judging and you will not be judged. Stop condemning and you will not be condemned. Forgive and you will be forgiven.[930]

He also describes the importance of forgiving others in the Parable of the Unforgiving Servant,[931] concluding: "So will my Heavenly Father do to you, unless each of you forgives his brother from his heart."[932] Jesus clarifies that forgiveness is not meant to be superficial or simply words, but a true movement within the heart, a letting go, which helps one to be "clean of heart"[933]—a critical concept of *theosis*. It repulses the demons that lay claim to the heart to impair our relationship with God. This can be particularly true in times of prayer. Forgiveness sets our hearts free from this emotional baggage the demons want us to carry.

Jesus modeled this from the cross when he forgave his persecutors: "Father, forgive them, for they know not what they do."[934] This is the standard of forgiveness to which each of us is called.

In the Eastern Churches, the Great Fast (Lent) begins on Cheesefare Sunday with Forgiveness Vespers, which conclude with the Ceremony of Mutual Forgiveness. Thus, the Great Fast begins in a spirit of communal forgiveness, with each

---

929 Archimandrite Seraphim Aleksiev, *The Meaning of Suffering* and *Strife & Reconciliation*, trans. Ralitsa Doynova (Wildwood, CA: St. Herman Brotherhood/St. Xenia Skete, 1994), 94.

930 Luke 6:36–37.

931 See Matt. 18:21-35.

932 Matt. 18:35.

933 See Matt. 5:8. "Bless are the clean of heart, for they will see God."

934 Luke 23:34.

person forgiving every other person. This is one of the most moving services in the Eastern Churches.

Consider the example of Vietnamese Cardinal Francis Xavier Nguyen Van Thuan, named Archbishop of Saigon shortly before the city fell to North Vietnamese forces. Because of his stature in the Church and his family's connections to the deposed South Vietnamese government, he was targeted by the Communist regime and imprisoned in a reeducation camp for 13 years, the first nine in solitary confinement. The young, zealous Communist guards tried to break him, yet they could not. He refused to be held hostage by anger, resentment, or retribution. Because of his kindness and compassion, some of his tormentors, many of whom had been lifelong atheists, joined the Christian faith. His chief jailer became Catholic. When Van Thuan was released from prison in 1988, he had no ill feelings toward his captors. In fact, like Christ on the cross, he forgave them. After all he had endured, Van Thuan had no bitterness in his heart, only a profound sense of hope in God, compassion, and forgiveness. He provides a concrete example of what it means to be "Merciful like the Father," clear evidence of how love and compassion can overcome hate and indifference. In this case, forgiveness and love even led to the conversion of one's enemies.

Shackles of hatred, anger, jealousy, or holding grudges disturb our tranquility and inner stillness, which in turn has an adverse effect on our prayer. We are called to forgive and be free, which allows us to find interior stillness in our times of silence and solitude.

5. Humility – the Foundation for the Other Virtues

The practice of the virtues also assists in creating a climate conducive to prayer. As one spiritual elder from Mount Athos advised:

> We know from the teachings of our Holy Fathers that virtues do not unite man with God perfectly, but they create the appropriate climate so that prayer comes and unites man with God the Holy Trinity.[935]

In his first sermon, "On the Beatitudes," St. Gregory of Nyssa describes the spiritual journey and how humility is the keystone from which the other virtues flow. If one virtue exists, the others are believed to exist because the virtues are indivisible.[936]

In considering the virtue of humility, we also reflect on Jesus, who is humility personified, a self-emptying love who gave himself to others. The Incarnation involved self-emptying (*kenosis*) to take on our humanity, his humble birth, his model of humility at the Last Supper by washing the feet of his disciples, and his complete surrender to his Heavenly Father in his passion and crucifixion. As Jesus said, "Whoever wishes to be first among you shall be your slave."[937] This was a clear message in his teaching, and Jesus modeled this in his life.

The Jesus Prayer is grounded in humility, acknowledging Jesus as Son of God, who we are, "a sinner," and what we desire: "mercy." This is also an example of a rightly ordered relationship predicated on "fear of God," as described by St. Isaac the Syrian. Accordingly, many of the Holy Fathers describe the importance of cultivating a spirit of humility. St. Gregory of Nyssa further writes:

> If you free a character from pride, the passion of wrath has no chance of springing up. To

935 Met. Hierotheos, 56.

936 St. Gregory of Nyssa, "On the Beatitudes," 125. Sermon No. 4. "For any one form of virtue, divorced from the others, could never by itself be a perfect virtue."

937 Matt. 20:27.

> be of this mind is precisely to be habitually profoundly humble, for if humility is well-established, wrath will find no entrance into the soul. And if wrath is absent, life will be in a settled state of peace.[938]

If humility creates a state of peace and it cannot be divorced from the other virtues, then developing a life of virtue contributes to a fitting interior environment for encounter. As St. Silouan the Athonite advised his disciple, "Therefore I tell you, humble yourself at all times, and be content with the gifts you are given, and then you will be living with God."[939]

The Holy Fathers speak of the need to overcome the passions or appetites that often drive human behavior. "But where do the passions in man come from?"[940] asks Archbishop Averky Taushev. He answers, writing:

> All of the Holy Fathers, teaching on the spiritual life, with one voice agree that the root and source of passions is egoism or self-love, that is, unreasonable, wrongful love towards oneself.[941]

Consider that the original sin of Adam was a focus on self instead of what God asked of him—a single commandment. Thus, pride is the first of these passions to be overcome, the source of all other passions. And it is rooted out through the cultivation of humility, the foundational virtue.[942] To create the right conditions for prayer and vigilance, we must overcome

938 St. Gregory of Nyssa, 104-5. Sermon No. 2.
939 Sakharov, *St. Silouan the Athonite*, 169.
940 Taushev, 128.
941 Ibid.
942 Per Isaac the Syrian, "The fear of God is the beginning of virtue." In this context, fear of God is the prerequisite and humility is the foundational virtue upon which all the other virtues are built.

our passions and channel these energies toward God. The following is a summary table for consideration.[943]

Passion to be conquered	***By being transformed into***
Pride	Humility
Lust	*Agapé* love
Anger	Righteous indignation (emotional response to injustice, mistreatment, insult, malice)
Greed	Selfless love and generosity
Unfaithfulness	Fidelity and steadfastness
Envy	Magnanimity (generous in forgiving insults or injury; free from petty resentments or vindictiveness)
Sloth	Diligence and zeal
Ingratitude/Indifference	Gratitude; a generous spirit

Passions are initially aroused by thoughts and distractions (*logismoi*). To combat these thoughts, sober vigilance and watchfulness are required.

Interior Stillness and Sober Vigilance

Stillness (*hesychia*) and sober vigilance (*nepsis*) are the "work of prayer" aimed at obtaining the gift of prayer from God commensurate with our efforts.

1. Interior Stillness (*Hesychia*)

The work of prayer and personal purification are required

943 See Ware, *The Philokalia: Master Reference Guide*, xiv. Author added "Ingratitude/Indifference" to the list.

to produce the interior stillness referred to by the Holy Fathers as *hesychia*. These cultivate the heart so that, if granted by God, the individual can experience pure prayer, whereby the individual has experiences of union with God in this life. As one spiritual elder from Mount Athos described it:

> When God comes into our heart, he gains victory over the devil and cleanses the impurities which the evil one has created. The victory, therefore, over the devil is the victory of Christ in us. Let us do the human part by inviting Christ, and he will do the divine part by defeating the devil and purifying us.[944]

The elder also explained that the Jesus Prayer consists of two basic points of dogma: acknowledgment of the divinity of Christ ("Lord Jesus Christ, Son of God") and a confession of one's inability to be saved of his or her own accord ("Have mercy on me").[945] Throughout these discussions, we have mentioned the importance of complete surrender and dependence on God, an affirmative response to his offer of salvation. The elder stated, "We are not struggling to meet an impersonal God through the Jesus Prayer. We do not seek our elevation to absolute nothingness. Our prayer focuses on the personal God, the God-man Jesus."[946]

Over time and with continued practice, there will be an insatiable thirst for the Jesus Prayer.[947] Yet, at the same time, virtually all the Holy Fathers say that attaining true prayer is a struggle, with constant attacks by the demons who wish to steal our prayer from us and derail our relationship with

944 Met. Hierotheos, 44.
945 Ibid., 45.
946 Ibid., 50.
947 Ibid. See 170–171.

God. These distractions (*logismoi*), either positive or negative thoughts or impulses, which cause one to drift away from interior stillness and prayer. Accordingly, we must remain persistent in our prayer, maintain our ardent desire, persevere in hope, retain our zeal, and exhibit immense patience, combined with faith in God's love for us.[948] As St. Silouan the Athonite advised:

> There is no comfortable armchair in the study for the monk to work out these problems. In the silence of the night, remote from the world, unheard and unseen, he falls down before God and weeps the prayer of the publican, "God be merciful to me a sinner," or cries with St. Peter, "Lord, save me!"[949]

Elder Porphyrios advises us:

> Learn to love prayer. In order not to live in darkness, turn on the switch of prayer so that divine light may flood your soul. Christ will appear in the depths of your being. There, in the deepest and most inward part, is the Kingdom of God. The Kingdom of God is within you.[950]

Prayer nurtures our personal, intimate relationship with God, who desires a personal, intimate relationship with us.

2. Sober Vigilance (*Nepsis*)

Complacency is dangerous to spiritual life. There are interior struggles, what the Holy Fathers call "unseen warfare." That is

948 Ibid., 81.
949 Sakharov, *Silouan the Athonite*, 166.
950 Elder Porphyrios, 113.

why they also speak of maintaining sober vigilance, or *nepsis*, being watchful at all times. Jesus spoke specifically about this in scripture. Consider these verses from the Gospel of Matthew:

Matt. 12:43–45

No.	Verse	Comment
43	*When an unclean spirit goes out of a person it roams through regions searching for rest but finds none.*	"The demons cleverly watch us, observe our weak points, and then attack us with their fantasies."[951] They never give up.
44	*Then it says, 'I will return to my home from which I came.' But upon returning, it finds it empty, swept clean, and put in order.*	A purified heart risks complacency. "When we have lost a sense of our sinfulness, we have also lost the sense of our constant need for the Giver of Life to come and heal us still more."[952]
45	*Then it goes and brings back with itself seven other spirits more evil than itself, and they move in and dwell there; and the last condition of that person is worse than the first.*	The complacent heart is assailed by new temptations. "When one is fighting a lion, it is fatal to glance away for even a moment. So too the man fighting against his flesh, who yields for the merest instance."[953]

951 Maloney, 105.
952 Ibid., 133.
953 Climacus, 258.

There is a reality in the spiritual life. We are not immune to struggles, trials, and temptations along the way. The lure of the secular world will always remain around us because even if we strive to renounce or flee the world, we cannot escape the reality that we still live in the world. The demons will use every means possible to disrupt our relationship with God. Temptations can be likened to a salesperson who knocks persistently at the door. If we let him in, he begins his sales pitch, and whether or not we discover that his products are undesirable, he is already inside, and it is hard to get rid of him. Worse, we consent to the "purchase," after being worn down and led astray.[954] The great irony of this unseen spiritual warfare within ourselves is the discovery that "the demons fight hardest when God is near; the darkness of the shadow is in direct proportion to the brilliance of the light."[955]

Accordingly, we must remain ever vigilant against the poisonous weeds that can creep back into our hearts, virtually undetected if we are not sufficiently vigilant. St. Antony of Egypt advised, "The proper daily labor for a man is to cast his wretchedness before God and reckon on temptation until his last breath."[956] To sustain our vigilance on the journey and make incremental progress in reclaiming the God-like virtues, we must leverage all the means for encounter we have described herein, incorporating these into our spiritual practices. These can also carry us during times of temptation or spiritual dryness. These include:

- Participate frequently in liturgy and reception of the Holy Eucharist.
- Establish a daily Rule of Prayer, including time for silence and contemplative prayer.

954 Cf. Tito Colliander, *Way of the Ascetics*, trans. Katherine Ferré (Crestwood, NY: St. Vladimir's Seminary Press, 1960), 50.

955 Chryssavgis, *In the Heart of the Desert*, xii.

956 Cited by St. Dorotheos of Gaza, 146. Discourse VII: On Self-Accusation.

- Read Sacred Scripture, gaining insight on God's plan of salvation and the mission and teachings of his Son. "Everything proceeds from Holy Scripture. You must read it continually in order to learn the secrets of spiritual struggle."[957]
- Read other spiritual writings from the Tradition, the Holy Fathers who have gone before us on the spiritual journey. They provide wisdom gained through lived experiences. St. Isaac the Syrian said: "Read often and insatiably the books of the teachers of the Church on divine providence ..."[958] Similarly, St. Teresa of Ávila suggests "reading good books" as one of the remedies left by God to his Church.[959]
- Participate regularly in the Holy Mystery of Repentance (Confession), keeping the heart cleared of weeds.
- Seek regular guidance from a Spiritual Father. In the absence of a spiritual director, regularly read from the writings of the Holy Fathers who have traveled the spiritual journey before us, gleaning their pearls of wisdom.
- Adapt other spiritual disciplines described herein: fasting, simplification, detachment from worldly or material things, mourning of our sinfulness, and forgiveness of others. Adapt to the Church's regular fasting cycles, which were established with wise purpose.
- Sustain a spirit of gratitude for all blessings, including trials, accepting all as the will of the

957 Elder Porphyrios, 110.
958 *The Ascetical Homilies of St. Isaac the Syrian*, 146. Homily Four
959 See St. Teresa of Ávila, 92.

Heavenly Father, knowing that we were created so that he could share his overflowing love with us.

- Interact with the broken Body of Christ, never losing sight of Jesus in the distressing disguise of the poor; maintain solidarity with our neighbors, especially those in need.

All these practices are means of encounter, to be leveraged like an herbicide against pesky and persistent weeds that must remain in check.[960] We can never grow weary or lose sight of our destination, union with God in the life to come. Think of the Olympic athlete who ever keeps the goal in sight, attending to every detail to achieve it.[961] So should it be with our greatest prize, eternal blessedness with God in the life to come. With the classic and practical wisdom of the Desert Fathers, Abba Poemen advised us:

> As long as a pot is on the fire, no fly nor any other animal can get near it. But as soon as it is cold, these creatures get inside. So it is for us; as long as we live lives in spiritual activities, the enemy cannot find a means of controlling us.[962]

We can never become complacent; we must remain vigilant and labor until our last breath.

Love of God Manifested in Love of Neighbor (*Agapé*)

Above, we have discussed the spiritual practices required to create a climate conducive to prayer and encounter. Next, we described interior stillness and vigilance. Finally, the fruits of a purified heart

960 Consider Matt. 13:24–29. Parable of the weeds.

961 See 1 Cor. 9:25. "Every athlete exercises discipline in every way. They do it to win a perishable crown, but we an imperishable one."

962 *The Sayings of the Desert Fathers*, 183.

should be reflected in our relationships with others. This is one gauge of our progress on the spiritual journey. Abba Moses the Black said, "If a man's deeds are not in harmony with his prayer, he labors in vain."[963] It is all about who we become from our encounters and experiences with the Divine.

We manifest our love for God in how we treat our neighbor, reflecting the indelible link Jesus made between the greatest commandment and the second, "which is like it." As we continue our spiritual journey, we must constantly reassess whether we are becoming like the Father, more God-like, more loving towards others. Are we more merciful and forgiving? Are we frequently moved to compassion like Jesus,[964] or when encountering those in need like the widow of Naim?[965] We cannot make progress in our spiritual life without the love of neighbor. Abba John the Dwarf said:

> A house is not built by beginning at the top and working down. You must begin with the foundation in order to reach the top." They asked him, "What does this saying mean?" He said, "The foundation is our neighbor, whom we must win, and that is the place to begin. For all the commandments of Christ depend on this one.[966]

Jesus speaks of almsgiving,[967] yet alms are more than money or food. Alms can include acts of kindness, especially those that restore dignity to one another. St. Teresa of Calcutta said it can begin simply with a smile that acknowledges the dignity of the other, recognizing the divine presence in all. As with everything else on the journey,

---

963 Ibid., 141.

964 See for example Matt. 9:36: "At the sight of the crowds, his heart was moved with pity for them because they were troubled and abandoned, like sheep without a shepherd." In this case, the word *pity* is from the Greek, *splanchnízomai*, "to be moved as to one's bowels." In other words, Jesus was very deeply moved.

965 See Luke 7:11–16, particularly Luke 7:13.

966 *The Sayings of the Desert Fathers*, 93.

967 See Matt. 6:1–4.

we must continue to gauge our progress and not grow slack or complacent. Abba Dorotheos of Gaza wrote:

> We really need to scrutinize our conduct every six hours and see in what way we have sinned since we sin so much and are so forgetful. And we should say to ourselves, "Have I said anything to irritate my brother? Have I seen my brother do certain things and judged him harshly or despised him or spoken evil of him? Have I asked (someone) for something and when I did not receive it murmur against him? Have I spoken ungraciously or had an argument? Have I abused someone or criticized him or when I did not like something murmured against him?" For if a man murmurs against anyone, it is a fault.[968]

Love of neighbor is indelibly linked to love of God—we cannot dispute or ignore this. Jesus was clear: we will be judged worthy of the kingdom based on how we treat the least among us.[969] St. Silouan the Athonite said, "The man who dwells in grace beholds grace in others, and he who does not know it in himself does not see it in others either."[970] He also told his disciples that one can judge the measure of grace in a man by his attitude to his neighbor.[971]

Summary

In our quest for a return to the basics of the spiritual life, the Desert Fathers provide us with much wisdom and spiritual guidance pertaining to the interior life, which ultimately manifests itself through exterior actions toward our neighbor. Significant aspects include:

968 St. Dorotheos of Gaza, 175. Discourse XI, On Cutting Off Passionate Desires.
969 Cf. Matt 25:45.
970 Archimandrite Sophrony, *Silouan the Athonite*, 101.
971 Ibid.

- St. Isaac the Syrian and "the fear of God" as the beginning of virtue.
- Personal purification and simplification, including ascetical practices, detachment, mourning of sins, forgiveness, and cultivation of humility as the foundation for the other virtues.
- Interior stillness and sober vigilance, being freed from distractions and avoiding complacency. These create the conditions necessary for prayer.
- Love of neighbor, interior love of God manifested in love for others. Our outward actions manifest our interior disposition.

These concepts are similar to the three biblical penitential practices of fasting, prayer, and almsgiving.

The wisdom of the Desert Fathers is a simple, back-to-basics spirituality developed through intense experiences of the Divine in an environment conducive to such encounters. Returning to the Holy Fathers, to their spiritual counsels, is a means for recapturing authentic Christian spirituality grounded in lived experiences. Recall the axiom: "If you are a theologian, you will pray truly. And if you pray truly, you are a theologian." This teaching, notably, originates in the writings of Evagrios the Solitary, a Desert Father.

The wisdom and spiritual practices of the Desert Fathers are timeless, as relevant today as they were in the Early Church. They struggled with similar temptations to that which we experience today. Their lives and teachings ultimately show that true transformation of heart can occur through perseverance, struggle, ascetical practices, and, most of all, prayer. Consider this example, too, in light of Pope Francis' teachings:

> The great danger in today's world, pervaded as it is by consumerism, is the desolation and anguish born of

> a complacent yet covetous heart, the feverish pursuit of frivolous pleasures, and a blunted conscience. Whenever our interior life becomes caught up in our own interests and concerns, there is no longer room for others, no place for the poor. God's voice is no longer heard, the quiet joy of his love is no longer felt, and the desire to do good fades. This is a very real danger for believers too. Many fall prey to it, and end up resentful, angry, and listless. That is no way to live a dignified and fulfilled life; it is not God's will for us, nor is it the life in the Spirit which has its source in the heart of the Risen Christ.[972]

Our hearts are filled with longing, and we seek a dignified life. The Desert Fathers provide tangible examples for those who aspire to the abundant life God wants to give each of us.

Reflection Questions

1. In my spiritual life, what are my most important practices?
2. What practices are missing from my life? What can I do about this?
3. What has the wisdom of the Desert Fathers taught me about progress in the spiritual life?

Supplemental Information

The concepts discussed in this topic are expanded in two other works:

> Edward Kleinguetl. *Into the Desert: The Wisdom of*

972 Pope Francis, *Evangelii Gaudium*, no. 2.

the Desert Fathers and Mothers. Parker, CO: Outskirts Press, 2019.

______. *The Fruit of Prayer: Spiritual Counsels of the Holy Fathers*. Parker, CO: Outskirts Press, 2021.

FROM ENCOUNTER TO DESTINY

Theosis (Transcendence)

"Through these, he has bestowed on us the precious and very great promises, so that through them you may come to share in the divine nature..."
(2 Pet. 1:4)

"Mysticism will remain the center of the Christian rebirth that is to come, for it is the means by which a Christian enters into communion with Christ through a gradual spiritual process of purification and perfection. Its starting point is when a man turns within himself in order to seek Christ and to attain to union with God through love. The inner experience transforms nature, fills the mind with knowledge, strengthens the will, purifies the heart, and makes man a bearer of Christ." [973]
(Valeriu Gafencu)

"When we turn away from the path indicated by Christ—that is, from the deification of man by the power of the Holy Spirit—the whole point of man's coming into the world disappears." [974]
(Elder Sophrony of Essex)

Opening Gospel Reading

Luke 8:40-48 (Woman with the Hemorrhage).

Encountering Jesus

An encounter with Jesus can change one's life.[975] Miracles occur

973 Monk Moise, *The Saint of the Prisons*, 228.
974 Archimandrite Sophrony, *His Life is Mine*, 70.
975 Inspired by Fr. Miron Kerul-Kmec's homily, St. Nicholas Byzantine Catholic Church, Barberton, OH, November 7, 2021. See YouTube or Podbean, "The Art of Spiritual Life."

if we approach with true faith, and our lives will be transformed. Putting the story of the woman with the hemorrhage into context, the Greek term used for "flow of blood," *rhysis haimatos*, comes from Leviticus, which tells us this condition had rendered the woman ritually unclean for twelve years[976] and unfit for contact with people. She would have been treated as an outcast—seen by the religious authorities as a sinner and only a step above the social standing of a leper. It is not surprising that she was afraid to make her presence known. Yet she had faith: "If only I can touch his cloak, I will be cured."[977] And, in fact, she was immediately healed.

In terms of this encounter, there are two key points to consider. First, God wants a personal, intimate relationship with each of us. He cares about all, so much so that every hair on our head has been counted. When Jesus asks, "Who touched me?" he knew someone made a deliberate effort to touch him and he felt the healing power go forth. The woman who had done so realized "that she had not escaped notice." She makes herself known to Jesus, explaining her situation in the presence of all. Amid a crowd that was pushing and shoving, she mattered to Jesus.

The second point is Jesus's reaction. "Daughter,"[978] he says. Her dignity is restored; she is not impure, but a child of God.[979] He adds, "Your faith has saved you." The miracle occurred because of her unconditional faith. And he tells her, "Go in peace." Encounter leads to transformation, in this case, healing, and the restoration of dignity as children of God, beings made in his image.

Miracles are possible if we touch Jesus. We can regularly contact him—prayer, liturgy, the sacraments, especially Eucharist, Sacred Scripture—and, if we do so with faith, our lives will be transformed.

---

976 See Luke Timothy Johnson, 141. See Lev. 15:25-27.

977 Matt. 9:21.

978 Luke 8:48.

979 Inspired by Fr. Miron Kerul-Kmec, Jr.'s homily, St. John Chrysostom Byzantine Catholic Church, Pittsburgh, PA, November 7, 2021. See YouTube.

Divinization

The idea of divinization is the very kernel of the religious life of the Christian East.[980] Our discussion topics have explored this concept from the perspective of encounter, a genuine experience of a God who draws us ever more deeply into a relationship and increases our desire for transcendence to fulfill our supernatural purpose. God so greatly desires this relationship that he gave us a personal invitation, becoming incarnate through his Son Jesus Christ. Archbishop Joseph Raya draws the correlation. "The Incarnation of God and deification of man mutually imply each other. What Adam ought to have attained by obedience to God, God achieved through the obedience of Christ."[981] Christ's "yes" is our "yes," giving us the example of how we are to respond to God, who communicates himself to us. Additionally, Jesus described himself as "the way" to the Father; thus, only through Christ can humanity be divinized. Through Christ, humanity achieves its divinely intended purpose—and we discover true meaning to our existence.

This striving for divinization is a lifelong effort of personal conversion (*metanoia*), possible only through human-divine collaboration (*synergeia*). When we discussed the Operations of God, we referenced Pope St. John Paul II's observations of the real possibility that man can unite himself with the Triune God in the intimacy of his heart. It is a deep union through deifying grace that Eastern theology likes to describe with the powerful term *theosis*. *Theosis* reinforces how our God is present and active in his creation, that we can tangibly experience him, and through our experiences, we can achieve a supernatural purpose intended by God. We can touch Christ every day, experience his healing power, and, if we remain faithful, experience many miracles along the way. As humans, we have the ingrained desire to transcend ourselves, strive for the horizon of infinite possibility, and, thus, move toward God. Through encounter, we can achieve genuine transcendence, filling infinite longing with an Infinite Being.

980 Popov, 42.
981 Raya, *The Face of God*, 65.

The more we grow in our relationship with God, the more attuned we will be to his presence, including the monotonous activities of everyday life. To cultivate this relationship, we leverage the various means of encounter available, preparing our hearts as a place for the indwelling divine presence. We discover that the spiritual life is not a simple upward linear progression. Rather, it is more like a series of concentric circles with an ever-increasing awareness of the divine presence through moments of conversion. We move from centering, choosing the better part, to recognizing the presence of God in daily experience, to living lives in service to others (*diakonia*), and back to centering. Thus, divinization is a continuous process of entering ever deeper into a relationship with God through participation in his divine operations. Lossky wrote:

> Desiring God more and more, the soul grows without ceasing, going beyond herself and outside herself; in the measure in which she unites herself more and more to God, her love becomes more ardent and insatiable.[982]

We become aware "that the union will never have an end, that ascent in God has no limit, that beatitude is an infinite process."[983] However, Pope St. John XXIII reassures us of the fruits of a transformed heart, writing, "It is deeply rewarding for men striving for salvation to follow Christ's footsteps and obey his commandments."[984]

Theosis requires significant effort; we have to do our part. As one Athonite spiritual elder described it, sometimes we are sailing when the wind blows, and other times the labor of rowing is needed.[985]

---

982 Lossky, *In the Image and Likeness of God*, 37.

983 Ibid.

984 Pope St. John XXIII, "Homily at the Canonization of St. Martin de Porres," in *The Liturgy of the Hours*, vol. 4 (New York, NY: Catholic Book Publishing Co, 1975), 1542. St. Martin is a great example of a person who was meek and humble, striving for holiness through simplified living and great love for others. See Giuliana Cavallini, *St. Martin de Porres: Apostle of Charity*, trans. Caroline Holland (Charlotte, NC: TAN Books, 2012).

985 See Met. Hierotheos, 86.

In other words, we can anticipate times of greater struggle, either in prayer or simply the challenges of life. We are given what we need as "our daily bread" to become less dependent on ourselves and more reliant on God. We are given crosses to bear, proving we desire God more than anything else, not growing weary. All of this is predicated on human-divine collaboration (*synergeia*), which involves spiritual practices, cultivating a life of virtue, a regular discipline of prayer, and loving our neighbor as a concrete expression of our love for God.

Jesus is both the gift of our self-communicating God and, at the same time, the perfect acceptance of the gift. Therefore, Jesus is truly our "way" when it comes to pursuing the spiritual journey. Rahner noted that "a result of the fact that God gives himself to people and dwells in them," they gradually transform, overcoming bad habits and particular sins.[986] Not only is Jesus the gift, but his spirit also dwells within the hearts of believers. By deepening our relationship with him, we multiply the talent given to us and increase its yield. Accordingly, we cultivate this relationship, recognizing that the kingdom of God is within us and that the divine presence is an interior reality. Jesus is our example of divinized humanity, who were created to be.

Regarding faith, each of us will either fulfill our supernatural purpose or bury our talent in the ground and follow a different path. Accepting anything less than our divinely intended purpose, we sell ourselves—and God—short. We make this choice with our God-given freedom; we can decide on true freedom, de-throning the ego, submitting our will to the divine will, or choosing enslavement to sin. These are the two ways, and there is no middle alternative. If we "accept the offer of salvation," we are committing ourselves to a lifetime of struggle for personal purification to prepare ourselves for our final destiny. The demons will fight us; the secular world will say we are foolish. Yet the more we strive, the more we recognize the presence of God around us and can participate in his operations. We experience God, even though he is a mystery beyond human comprehension.

986 Kilby, 22.

St. Augustine of Hippo in *Confessions* lamented how he learned to love God late in his life and how he had been lost in created things. He sought God outside when God was always within. And when he finally recognized the presence of God within himself:

> You called and cried out loud and shattered my deafness. You were radiant and resplendent, you put to flight my blindness. You were fragrant, and I drew in my breath and now pant after you. I tasted you, and I feel but hunger and thirst for you. You touched me, and I am set on fire to attain the peace which is yours.[987]

"You touched me, and I am set on fire!" Our experiences are often similar to that of St. Augustine if we remain open to God's presence. The more we experience God, the more we desire an ever-deeper relationship with him. Rahner wrote:

> There is a mysticism of everyday life, the discovery of God in all things; there is a sober intoxication of the Spirit, of which the Fathers and liturgy speak which we cannot reject or despise, because it is real. Let us look for that experience in our own lives. Let us seek the specific experiences in which something happens to us.[988]

Today, it may appear as if the anti-Christian way of life is slowly conquering the world: materialism, atheism, apatheism, immoral behaviors, decadence. Yet, people are increasingly seeking meaning in their lives—a liberation of sorts from the empty promises and enslavement of sin. God alone can satisfy our innermost longing because only he is inexhaustible. Let us embrace the advice of Rahner:

---

987 St. Augustine, *Confessions*, 201.
988 Rahner, *The Practice of Faith*, 84.

"Let us seek the specific experiences in which something happens to us." God, for his part, cannot help but share his overflowing love with us. Something happens to us if we reorient our lives back to the Creator.

Remember that choice is completely and freely ours. We can pursue the secular promises of the world or accept the gift offered by our loving God, who seeks a personal relationship with us. In the Gospel of Luke, we are presented with two outcomes:

> The Pigpen—the Prodigal Son sought the pleasures of the world through a life of dissipation and ended up with swine in the pigpen, alone and hungry.[989] He tried to fill infinite longing with finite things, resulting in "desolation and anguish born of a complacent, yet covetous heart, the feverish pursuit of frivolous pleasures, and a blunted conscience."[990]
>
> Joy-filled—the experience of the two disciples who encountered Jesus on the road to Emmaus: "Were not our hearts burning within us."[991] "The Joy of the Gospel fills the hearts and lives of all who encounter Jesus. With Christ joy is constantly born anew."[992]

The latter is the dignified life God wants for us, life in the Spirit, which has its source in the heart of the risen Christ.[993] The choice, however, is entirely ours.

Theosis is not about the encounter; it is about who we become because of our experiences with the Divine. It involves bringing God back into the center of our lives instead of leaving him at the

989 See Luke 15:15–16.
990 See Pope Francis, *Evangelii Gaudium*, no. 2.
991 Luke 24:32.
992 Pope Francis, *Evangelii Gaudium*, no. 1.
993 Ibid., no. 2.

periphery. However, for God to genuinely dwell in our hearts, we need to remove all those things that distract us from God. We cannot have a divided heart. Jesus specifically tells us in the Gospel, "No one can serve two masters."[994] Secular society makes many claims and promises; however, in the end, as many of us have experienced, we will be left empty—and sometimes find ourselves in the pigpen. Nothing finite can satisfy infinite longing.

Jesus never deluded us. The spiritual life is one of struggle; his way is the way of self-denial and the cross. We will encounter tranquility and turbulent whirlpools, mountaintop experiences and the monotony of daily life. God is present in all, not just when we experience blessings. God is in the overcoming, the times when we find ourselves able to navigate through the challenges with divine guidance. This is possible if we are firmly anchored to God, our spiritual lives built on a foundation of rock. Superficial change is not enough. Our hearts must be gradually transformed and purified. Struggles are the fire that refines gold and silver, removing impurities. Through these we prove to God our willingness to stay the course, to desire him above everything else. We can rise above the struggles if we remain dependent upon God and rely on his grace. We will discover the infinite possibility, our ability for transcendence.

Summary

In the final analysis, it is not simply about our encounters with God; it is who we become. *Theosis* or our divinization is the journey we undertake to achieve our divinely created purpose. Yet, Jesus is clear, this journey of incremental growth involves significant struggle. It is about learning to place God back in the center of our lives and allowing him to guide us, to be dependent upon and collaborate with him—even when secular culture would say this is utter foolishness. Conversion is usually not a "big bang," one-time event. It is about

994 Matt. 6:24.

the ongoing process of conversion—seeking, finding, drawing closer, serving others, and further seeking—ever purifying our hearts and simplifying our lives to fulfill our destiny. We have a supernatural destiny—union with God. Anything less and we sell ourselves—and God—short.

The empty promises of the secular world will never fill us, despite how often we give in to glitzy marketing campaigns. The definition of insanity is trying the same thing over and over and expecting a different outcome. Do not be deceived! Only the narrow gate leads to eternal life.

Reflection Questions

1. Where am I on the journey of life?
2. Where is God in my life? Is he at the center? Is he on the periphery? Do I even think of God in my life? Please be honest.
3. What brings me happiness and fulfillment? How do I seek happiness? Is it lasting? Why or why not?
4. What promises of the secular world do I find most appealing? Why? Which ones have I pursued?

Supplemental Information

More details can be found on this topic in the following two short works:

Edward Kleinguetl. *Mine Know Me: An Examination of Authentic Christian Discipleship.* Parker, CO: Outskirts Press, 2021.

______. *The Narrow Gate: Recalibration on the Spiritual Journey*. Parker, CO: Outskirts Press, 2022.

Icon of the Transfiguration of Our Lord

"Upon Mount Tabor, Jesus revealed to his disciples a heavenly mystery. While living among them he had spoken of the kingdom and of his second coming in glory, but to banish from their hearts any possible doubt concerning the kingdom and to confirm their faith in what lay in the future by its prefiguration in the present, he gave them on Mount Tabor a wonderful vision of his glory, a foreshadowing of the kingdom of heaven.

"Let us listen, then, to the sacred voice of God so compellingly calling us from on high, from the summit of the mountain, so that with the Lord's chosen disciples we may penetrate the deep meaning of these holy mysteries, so far beyond our capacity to express. Jesus goes before us to show us the way, both up the mountain and into heaven, and it is for us now to follow him with all speed, yearning for the heavenly vision that will give us a share in his radiance, renew our spiritual nature, and transform us into his own likeness, making us for ever sharers in his Godhead and raising us to heights as yet undreamed of."[995]

(Anastasios of Sinai)

995 Anastasios of Sinai, "Sermon of the Transfiguration of our Lord, in *The Liturgy of the Hours*, vol. 4 (New York, NY: Catholic Book Publishing Corp., 1975), 1285-6.

Part 6
Concluding Thoughts

CONCLUDING THOUGHTS

Relevance of Faith (Examining the Evidence)

"You will know the truth, and the truth will set you free."
(John 8:32)

"Woe to the soul that does not have Christ dwelling in it; deserted and foul with the filth of the passions, it becomes a haven for all the vices." [996]
(St. Macarius the Great)

"As we face today's phenomenon of secularization, the saints teach us that if we forget God, we will quickly forget the eternal and unique value of every human being, for the purpose of the human person's life on earth is to seek first eternal life in the kingdom of heaven." [997]
(Patriarch Daniel of Romania)

"Right belief is the foundation for everything."
(Fr. David Roşca)

Opening Gospel Reading

John 8:31-36 (You will know the truth, and the truth will set you free).

---

996 St. Macarius, "Homily 28," in *The Liturgy of the Hours*, vol. 4 (New York, NY: Catholic Book Publishing Corp., 1975), 596. See also Pseudo-Macarius, *The Fifty Spiritual Homilies and the Great Letter*, trans. George A. Maloney, SJ (New York, NY: Paulist Press, 1992), 184-5. "Woe to the soul when it does not have Christ as its Master dwelling in it, because being abandoned and filled with the foul odor of the passions, it finds itself a dwelling place of iniquity."

997 Patriarch Daniel, "The Unity of Faith and Nation is Strengthened in Prayer," in *Patriarch: Daniel: Rebuilding Orthodoxy in Romania*, ed. Chad Hatfield (Yonkers, NY: St. Vladimir's Seminary Press, 2021), 106. Reference to Matt. 6:33: "But seek first the kingdom of God and his righteousness, and all these things will be given you besides."

Summarizing the Evidence

We began this work with the question: Does faith matter? Initially, we started with our conclusion that our purpose in life as human beings is to live in union with God, that we are called to share in the very life of God. This is the reason we were created and why we exist. The same God who created the universe, the God who is "ineffable, inconceivable, invisible, incomprehensible, ever-existing, yet ever the same," a God beyond all our imagining, desires a personal, intimate relationship with each of us. In turn, our deepest longing can only be fulfilled by establishing a personal, intimate relationship with him.

That was the conclusion. Through this series of topics, we have discussed how God makes himself available to us through various means of encounter, that he invites us into a relationship, and we can experience him in tangible ways. We considered why faith remains relevant to us in our daily lives. We have set forth the value of having God at the center of our lives and allowing him to lead us to our supernatural destiny. At the outset, we asked each person to have an open mind and consider the evidence presented, contrasting this to the messages prevalent in secular society today, many of which try to dismiss the importance of faith and push God away from our center.

We are made in the divine image, capable of being filled with God's love, and capable of achieving a divine purpose. This is the abundant life Jesus came to give us.[998] We have examined the Divine that we encounter, the Triune God, and how he has acted in his creation through a twofold mission and how he remains active in his creation and in his Church. We have examined how we can encounter the Divine, how we come to know God through his Son, through his Holy Spirit, and through his operations. We considered how the location of such encounters occur in the human heart, with the objectives to transform the heart and create a deeper relationship with God. We have argued that faith requires an "all-in" response with

998 John 10:10.

an undivided heart. It cannot be God and something else. It is God alone. A superficial faith or simply going through a series of motions will never bring us to our divinely intended purpose. We must remain in God, trust him, and freely surrender ourselves completely to him. Finally, we have considered the process of divinization preparing us for union with God. After all, it is not about the encounters themselves; it is who we become because of these encounters. We are transformed from our fallen human nature to one that is renewed.

People who have engaged their faith through these topics must determine the answer for themselves: Did we prove our case for God? Did we make it clear that God wants a personal, intimate relationship with us, that we are the most prized of all his creations and we are created to be the recipients of his overflowing love? Each participant has considered the evidence and is given a free-willed choice. Do we accept God's offer of salvation?

Consider again the perspective of C.S. Lewis: "All that we call human history…[is] the long, terrible story of man trying to find something other than God which will make him happy."[999]

Closing Arguments

With that, we would like to conclude this series with a reflection that summarizes the spiritual journey itself. The following is by Sr. Ruth Burrows, a Carmelite nun from England and a well-known spiritual writer:

> If we could start from scratch, with no preconceived notions of the route, and if our hearts were firmly fixed on our journey's end, with Gospel in hand we would have no further need of route marking, no need of signposts. Jesus himself, through his Holy Spirit, would guide our hearts aright. And even now I am

999 C. S. Lewis, 53.

> convinced that anyone who truly seeks God rather than himself will find him, and this in spite of being directed in wrong paths. The Holy Spirit will lead him, secretly, probably painfully but most surely.
>
> The trouble is so very few of us really do seek God. We want something for ourselves and this is why we are anxious to be told the way. We want the path marked out for us, securely walled in, with not a chance of going astray. We are so anxious for this that we cannot afford to listen to the Lord guiding us from within. If we did listen then we would realize that we were merely going around in circles within the given confines, and that if we would find God, we must venture out into the trackless, unknown wastes. While we are busy circuiting the well-worn track described for us by others, we cannot conceive what it is like outside, or even that there is one. So to some extent signpost must replace signpost. On each signpost one word only will be written, however; the name of Jesus, for he alone is the way; there is no other.[1000]

Sr. Ruth makes a key point that we choose to seek God. We described herein the two ways and that there are only two—one leading to life and the other to death, with God or without God. There is no middle way or alternative. "All people are called to holiness, all people are called to an unceasing battle with sin, and all people are called to unseen warfare."[1001] That is the reality. We can enter eternal life only through the narrow gate that, as Jesus said, few will find. Sr. Ruth defines faith as "a sustained decision to take God with utter seriousness as the God of my life ... (and) a decision to shift the center of our lives from ourselves to him, to forgo

1000 Burrows, *To Believe in Jesus*, xii.
1001 Taushev, 115.

self-interest and to make his interest, his will, our sole concern."[1002] Without Jesus as our guide, we will be swept down the wide road to destruction. Without him, we will remain lost. With him, all things are possible.[1003]

German theologian Wolfhart Pannenberg studied the phenomenon of obsolescence in religion. He observed, "Religions die when their lights go out, that is, when their teachings no longer illuminate life as it is lived by their adherents. Where people experience God as still having something to say, the lights stay on."[1004] We hope those who have participated in these discussions discover or rediscover that the Catholic Church, enriched by its Eastern Christian patrimony, "breathing from both lungs,"[1005] does have something relevant to say about human purpose that stands in stark contrast to the empty secular messages and distortions in our society: atheism, agnosticism, relativism, secularism, religious pluralism, individualism, and, worst of all, apatheism. We retain a living faith that is ever ancient, ever new,[1006] providing us with the means to experience the Risen Jesus, Son of the Living God, who, despite being a mystery beyond human comprehension, can be encountered in our everyday lives. He is not a God of myths and legends but active in his creation, readily available and approachable by all. Thus, faith remains relevant to us in our daily lives, and faith is the foundation for hope, a desire for and belief in a greater and, in our case, a supernatural purpose. Archbishop Fulton J. Sheen said:

> It is characteristic of any decaying civilization that the great masses of people are unconscious of the tragedy. Only those who live by faith really know what is

---

1002 Burrows *Essence of Prayer*, 20.

1003 Cf. Matt. 19:26.

1004 Cited by Elizabeth A. Johnson, 22.

1005 Ex. Pope St. John Paul II, *Ut Unum Sint*, no. 54. For the Church to achieve its deepest meaning, it needs to learn to breathe again from both its lungs, one Eastern and one Western.

1006 Consider Heb. 13:8: "Jesus Christ is the same yesterday, today, and forever."

> happening in the world ... the great masses without faith are unconscious of the destructive process going on because they have lost the vision of the heights from which they fell.[1007]

Elder Sophrony of Essex wrote, "When we turn away from the path indicated by Christ, the whole point of man's coming into the world disappears."[1008] We see evidence of a secular age trying remold the modern, progress person into someone who is divorced from God and robbed of his or her divine inheritance. Yet instead of increased happiness and liberation, we readily observe the darkness, gloom, pessimism, despair, and depression that have overshadowed our society. Many have lost sight of humanity's eternal destiny, losing their way like the prodigal son mired in the mud with the swine.

Pope Francis wrote, "The Joy of the Gospel fills the hearts and lives of all who encounter Jesus. Those who accept his offer of salvation are set free from sin, sorrow, inner emptiness and loneliness. With Christ joy is constantly born anew."[1009] We have the choice to accept the offer of salvation or not—and God will respect our choice. However, consider the words of St. Paul to the fickle Galatians: "I am amazed that you are so soon deserting him who called you in accord with his gracious design in Christ, and are going over to another gospel. *But there is no other!*"[1010]

Jesus said, "I have come to set the earth on fire."[1011] Imagine the impact of people discovering or rediscovering the beauty of their faith. There would be no question: the lights would remain on as a shining witness to the world, a witness to hope, and standing in stark contrast to hate, darkness, and indifference. Imagine, indeed.

1007 Archbishop Fulton J. Sheen made this statement in 1948. Cited by Michael Cunningham, "Living the Worthy Life: Now More Than Ever We Need Jesus Christ," *Catholic365* online (February 5, 2021).

1008 Archimandrite Sophrony, *His Life is Mine*, 70.

1009 Pope Francis, *Evangelii Gaudium*, no. 1.

1010 Gal. 1:6-7. NAB. Emphasis added by the author.

1011 Luke 12:49.

Reflection Questions

1. Do I accept that God wants a personal, intimate relationship with me?

2. Do I believe that God is active in his creation today, accessible to me, and present to me in special moments and in the ordinary moments of life, in the storms and challenges? Or do I find God distant and unresponsive? Or do I simply think God pops in and out of my life as he pleases? Please explain your answer.

3. Having examined the evidence through our topics of discussion, do I believe that faith has relevance in my life today? On a zero to ten scale, how strong is my conviction?

4. Based on what I have discovered through our discussions, what do I plan to do next in my life? Am I drawn to learn more?

5. Have I gained an understanding of the Catholic Church as ever ancient, ever new? Do I appreciate that the faith is the same yesterday, today, and forever?

CONCLUDING THOUGHTS

The Call to Discipleship (Transmitting the Faith)

"Whoever follows me will not walk in darkness,
but will have the light of life."
(John 8:12)

"In a secularized and individualistic society, a young person in search of holy love and life in communion with God can become an example for his or her peers, a young confessor and missionary of great use for the life of the Church and for the good of society!" [1012]
(Patriarch Daniel of Romania)

"The only way out of the stalemate in which the world has been thrown by the failure of Christians who have failed to be true Christians is a 'reconversion' of the world to Christianity, to realize that only a renewed human being can raise the world." [1013]
(Archbishop Ioachim of Roman and Bacău)

Opening Gospel Reading

John 8:12-20 (The Light of the World).

Next Steps

Some may say, "Did we not conclude these discussions about

1012 Patriarch Daniel, "The Orthodox Youth: Confessors of Christ and Missionaries of the Church," in *Patriarch Daniel: Rebuilding Orthodoxy in Romania*, ed. Chad Hatfield (Yonkers, NY: St. Vladimir's Seminary Press, 2021), 116.

1013 Iftimiu, "Archbishop Ioachim on Episcopal Ministry in the 3rd Millennium."

faith?" The answer is yes and no. Pope Benedict XVI appealed to the faithful in one of his addresses:

> Dear friends, the commitment to proclaim Jesus Christ, 'the way and the truth and the life,' is the main task of the Church. Let us invoke the Virgin Mary that she may always assist us to proclaim the Good News of salvation, that the Word of God may spread and the number of disciples multiplied.[1014]

If we believe in the relevance of faith in our lives, then we are also called to be witnesses to the Gospel. Pope St. John Paul II wrote:

> Over the years, I have often repeated the summons to the *new evangelization*. I do so again now, especially in order to insist that we must rekindle in ourselves the impetus of the beginnings and allow ourselves to be filled with the ardor of the apostolic preaching which followed Pentecost. We must revive in ourselves the burning conviction of St. Paul, who cried out, 'Woe to me if I do not preach the Gospel' (1 Cor. 9:16). This passion will not fail to stir in the Church a new sense of mission, which cannot be left to a group of 'specialists' but must involve the responsibility of all members of the People of God. *Those who have come into genuine contact with Christ cannot keep him for themselves; they must proclaim him.*[1015]

What Pope John Paul II and the popes of the third millennium have announced is that this New Evangelization is to be undertaken by all the faithful, not just specialists. If we have come into genuine contact with Christ, we must proclaim him. The New Evangelization

---

1014 Pope Benedict XVI, *Regina Caeli* Address, May 22, 2011.
1015 Pope John Paul II, *Novo Millennio Ineunte*, no. 40. Emphasis added by the author.

is "a new mobilization of the Church to bring the good news once again to the ends of the earth—both to revitalize the lukewarm and to introduce Jesus to those who have never met him before."[1016]

What special qualifications does an ordinary person have in evangelization? Consider the axiom quoted by Stăniloae: "If you are a theologian, you will pray truly. And if you pray truly, you are a theologian." In other words, it is not about the intellectual knowledge or training, but true experiences of Christ in our lives. Patriarch Daniel of Romania stresses, "The love of Christ, the joy of Christ, and the peace of Christ that we receive through personal prayer and common Liturgy are the gifts to be shared with the world at all times, today and tomorrow."[1017]

Evangelization is generally conducted through two channels, individual witness and within the community of faith. In this final topic, let us explore these two channels.

Living as People of Encounter

Who do we become from our encounters with the divine presence? Do we as individuals live as people who believe our faith is relevant? Is it a priority in our lives? Do we bear witness to hope? Consider the wisdom of Elder Porphyrios of Kavsokalyvia:

> Living faith moves people, regenerates them and changes them, whereas words alone remain fruitless. The best form of mission is through our own example, our love and meekness.[1018]

A living faith reflects a living Church. How we live our lives is the ultimate witness to the relevance of faith. Many years ago, during

1016 Mary Healy, "Learning from Saint Mark," *Magnificat* 24(1) April (2022), 292.
1017 Patriarch Daniel, *Confessing the Truth in Love*, 107.
1018 Elder Porphyrios, 187.

a program entitled Catholics Returning Home, a young woman described the reason she came to the session. She explained the joy and happiness her husband had and said, "I want what he has." If only others might express similar sentiments when observing how we live our lives! As written in the First Letter of Peter: "Always be ready to give an explanation to anyone who asks you a reason for your hope."[1019] Or, as in the statement attributed to St. Francis of Assisi: "Preach the gospel at all times and, if necessary, use words."

Theosis is about the daily choices we make to follow the example of Christ instead of the enticing but empty offers of the secular world. Our lives should bear witness to this. Archbishop Charles Chaput wrote:

> Living in Christ requires daily conversion, discipleship, and transformation. Becoming a Christian and living in Christ imply *a lifetime of growing in Christ*. The water of Baptism gives life to the seed in our hearts that is Jesus Christ. The more the seed grows—the more we nourish and cultivate it through the sacraments, prayer, and apostolic action—the more we grow *into* Christ. We were made to do that. We were made to grow and bear the fruit of cooperating with Jesus in redeeming and sanctifying the world.[1020]

Evangelization through Community

Individual transformation should also lead to the transformation of our faith communities. The pastor of Holy Trinity Ukrainian Greek Catholic Church in Carnegie, Pennsylvania, had the following message on his parish's website:

1019 1 Pet. 3:15.
1020 Chaput, *Living the Catholic Faith*, 44.

> God made us to be eternally happy with him, beginning in this age and continuing forever in the endless age to come. Our parish exists to help you achieve that single goal: eternal happiness with God. In the history of the world, we believe there is only one way to do that and it is through knowing and loving Jesus Christ.[1021]

The first sentence reflects the overall premise of *theosis*, which has been a central theme of our discussions. It also describes the role of the parish with a single goal, to assist parishioners on the journey to fulfill their supernatural destiny. Eternal happiness or even lasting happiness is not found in finite or temporary things. We achieve our destiny by "coming to know and love Jesus Christ."

The question for us to consider in terms of evangelization is whether our parish or community helps people achieve this single goal: union with God. Look for the signs. Does our parish address our divinely intended purpose? Does the priest speak about confession and repentance, given this was the first teaching of Jesus? Is Eucharist at the center? Are we taught to pray and encouraged to nurture a relationship with Christ through prayer? Are we regularly challenged to follow in the footsteps of Christ, which means to deny ourselves, take up our cross daily, and avoid the way of the world? Are people becoming more spiritual, constantly deepening their relationship with Christ in the Holy Spirit? If not, what am I personally willing to do about it? After all, we have a collective responsibility for one another as members of the Body of Christ.[1022] Without affirmative answers to these questions, people risk having a superficial faith and being swept away by secularization. This is a dangerous path as it can lead to a falling away from faith, a lack of desire to pray, and a waning of communion with God; the soul begins to atrophy and is at risk of dying.

1021 Fr. Jason Charron, "About Us," Holy Trinity Ukrainian Catholic Church, Carnegie, PA, http://www. htucc.com/about.htm.

1022 See also Rom. 12:5.

How can I support others in my community to persevere on the journey? Recall that one of the reasons for young Catholics' disaffiliation was due to a lack of companions on the spiritual journey.[1023] How can I reach out to those who need to encounter Jesus but have no idea who he really is? We are called to care for the well-being of all our brothers and sisters. We are tasked with re-Christianization: "the strengthening of the Christian faith, the effort toward authentic Christian living, the steps toward spiritual perfection, a Christian community that is active, united, fraternal, and the determination to live the Christian life."[1024] If we are complacent in our efforts, we leave the door open to secular influences that can lead people astray. Recall what Patriarch Daniel of Romania wrote: "True theology is always born out of the life of the Church that prays, confesses, and serves."[1025] We love and serve God by loving and serving others—this is an inescapable fact from the commandments and example of Jesus.

Patriarch Daniel adds, "Youth organizations can become more relevant to the renewal of life in our communities, especially when they discover prayer as a source of changing, of inspiration, joy, and creativity ..."[1026] Are we focused on our youth? Are we teaching them how to pray?

How can we become a "community of missionary disciples,"[1027] to be in a constant state of mission to joyfully make the Risen Jesus known to others so all will have a deeper relationship with him? We can find ways to grow individually, communally, and evangelically, reaching out to others who are not practicing the Christian faith. Something happened at Pentecost, and we are entrusted with the mission to continue spreading the Good News, to pass along the spiritual treasures entrusted to us. Most importantly, we cannot overlook our youth who are the future of our Church and who are

1023 Catholic News Service, "Young Adults Want to be Heard," 2.
1024 Monk Moise, *The Saint of the Prisons*, 252.
1025 Patriarch Daniel, "The Unity Between Theology and Spirituality," 20.
1026 Patriarch Daniel, *Confessing the Truth in Love*, 162.
1027 Cf. Pope Francis, *Evangelii Gaudium*, no. 24.

hungry to know their faith and its relevance in their lives. Unfed, this demographic is leaving the Church in the greatest proportions. We must be the catalysts of conversion, not default to thinking that others will do it. Like Jesus, we must be moved to pity and do something. Inaction is not an option!

Standing in Contrast to the Prevailing Culture

In a very real way, as people transformed by our encounters with Jesus, we are to come the reality and presence of Jesus in the world.[1028] Especially during this spiritual pandemic, we cannot understate the urgency of this work. People are leaving the Church in epidemic proportions. "All the growth is on the other side of the spectrum, the so-called 'Nones,' or do not have a religious affiliation."[1029] There has been significant complacency with faith that has been handed down to us. Perhaps we took it for granted because we had a country in which freedom of religion was guaranteed and we may not have had the first-hand experiences of past generations.

In many cases, our Deposit of Faith was preserved at a great cost. Consider the Cristero Rebellion in Mexico in the 1920s, Nazism, Communism, and Socialism during the 20th century, repression during the Cultural Revolution in China, or the persecution of Christians in Africa and the Middle East today. Many of our ancestors paid a great price for what we have today. Patriarch Daniel of Romania observed, "the secularized society does not work in harmony with the ideal of the Church, but very often develops a position of hostility, owing to individualism."[1030] Further, societal attacks against the Church are often based on jealousy, since secular society prefers to be the moral authority and dismisses the Church as being a unnecessary

1028 See Burrows, *The Essence of Prayer*, 72.

1029 Dinan, "Losing our Religion."

1030 Patriarch Daniel, "Serving the Church: Sacrifice and Joy," in *Patriarch Daniel: Rebuilding Orthodoxy in Romania*, ed. Chad Hatfield (Yonkers, NY: St. Vladimir's Seminary Press, 2021), 222.

influence. This creates inherent conflict, and, to an extent, we can observe this in American culture today. Are we willing to take a stand against the influences that wish to de-Christianize our society and impose a different world order? Consider carefully what is at stake: true freedom or enslavement to sin.

Our challenge is to re-cultivate the soil for spiritual growth through genuine dialogue and engagement with our faith, specifically focused on encounter and true experiences of the Risen Jesus. We need to help people gain hearts afire with love for Jesus. In *Evangelii Gaudium,* Pope Francis referenced Mother Teresa of Calcutta: "An authentic faith—which is never comfortable or completely personal—involves a deep desire to change the world...."[1031] With Christianity under fire within secular society, we are challenged to accept our responsibilities of passing on the Deposit of Faith to the next generation. We who desire to be called Christians must be willing to act as authentic Christian disciples, living the faith we profess.

Consider the story of Cardinal Ignatius Kung Pin-Mei, Bishop of Shanghai. He was arrested in 1955 by the Communists. He spent several months in prison for intensive "re-education," after which he was brought to a stadium where several thousand people gathered. He was ordered to confess his "crimes" and renounce his ties to the Vatican. He wore Chinese pajamas, prison attire meant as a form of humiliation. With a microphone shoved in his face, he looked at the people and said, *"Long live Christ the King! Long live the Pope!"* The people responded, *"Long live Christ the King! Long live Bishop Kung!"* Immediately, he was ushered from the stage by his handlers and spent the next 30 years in solitary confinement for the embarrassment he caused.[1032] After that, he spent another two and a half years under house arrest and was expelled from the country. In 2000, shortly before his death, Cardinal Kung made a speech in Stamford, Connecticut:

1031 Pope Francis, *Evangelii Gaudium*, no. 183.
1032 See Elizabeth Scalia, "Exile: The Past is Prologue," *Patheos* (April 3, 2009).

> In America, you have freedom of expression and true freedom to worship. You honor justice and human rights. This is a nation of God. Standing with you here today, my heart is with my people in China who still do not have the freedom to worship.[1033]

Today we face a challenge in our country: that which we take for granted can be easily lost. Cardinal Kung made an ominous warning at that time:

> Liberty is not lost in a day. It is lost in increments and inches. Tomorrow the government will set your house temperature for you, while keeping their own set to their comfort levels. They will tell you how much money you may fairly earn, while "they" are not quite so limited. Next year your son will be forced to participate in mandatory volunteerism, and so will your mother. Soon you will be advised to abandon your hate-filled intolerant church for the approved and correct one. Someday, you may be asked to *bow* before someone and you will have to say "yes" and then live with yourself, or say "no" and live with those consequences. The banality of slavery…it is almost a tedious thing.[1034]

Today, almost 25 years later, we see a sharp divide between the secular messages of the world, especially in our own country, and those of the Gospel. We are drifting even further apart. We have state-mandated health care imposed on religious institutions. We see continued loss of respect for the sanctity of human life and basic human dignity. The sanctity of marriage is being challenged, e.g.,

1033 Ibid.
1034 Ibid.

the Obergefell decision.[1035] Families find it difficult to survive as households of faith. Over 65 million infants in our country have been lost through abortion. "Christmas" has become a bad word in our schools and society. Constructive dialogue among our elected officials has denigrated to personal agendas. Race relations and community outreach in recent times have experienced serious setbacks. The plight of the poor and those in need only grows greater. Crime is significantly increasing. Many say we are experiencing a profound spiritual crisis. Is there anything we can do?

Cardinal Kung did give us some words of wisdom in his speech:

> Practice prayer, which is the most subversive of liberties; it can never be taken from you, and is a source of power and strength. Train yourself in prayer. Begin now, so that you are a fit, skilled practitioner when the need arises.[1036]

The crisis of faith we are experiencing leads to significant disillusionment and a loss of hope. However, the cause of this crisis is not because structured religion or the Church has lost meaning, as some would like to argue. Rather, as Christians, we have forgotten how to be 'mystics,'[1037] to pray, to be attuned to the divine presence through genuine encounter. Cardinal Sarah said:

> Prayer is the greatest need of the contemporary world; it remains the tool with which to reform the world. In an age that no longer prays, time is, so to speak, abolished, and life turns into a rat race.[1038]

1035 *Obergefell v. Hodges* (2015). Landmark civil rights case in which the United States Supreme Court ruled that the fundamental right to marry is guaranteed to same-sex couples.

1036 See Scalia.

1037 Davies, "Lenten Mission 2018: Hope." Consider too Cole, "Saving a Dying, Shrinking Church."

1038 Sarah, *God or Nothing*, 150.

It is up to us to continue the work of Pentecost and assist others on the journey. The urgency has never been greater. What will we do? Are we stewards of the treasures passed onto us, often at a great price? As we contemplate our mission, consider the advice of Patriarch Daniel of Romania, who faced the daunting task of rebuilding faith in a country that had been devastated by decades of Communist oppression:

> Let us teach the young generations to find in prayer the fount of pure love and to live their lives on earth in the light of the blessing of our Heavenly Father and of the Church of his Son, Jesus Christ, so that they may feel the light, peace, and intense joy of the Holy Spirit.[1039]

As Christians, we have hope through our encounter with the Risen Lord.

Evangelical Renewal

During Patriarch Daniel's efforts to renew the interior life of Romanian Christians, especially amid intense secularization, he said, "Secularization means building one's personal life and life of the society without reference to God and religious values."[1040] He warns of "an attitude of indifference to the presence of God and to the need of rhythming our lives and openness to eternity."[1041] This is not unlike our "apathetics" or "Nones" in our society.

Not surprisingly, Patriarch Daniel mentions an intensive focus on the liturgical life of the Church: The Sacramental life, most notably confession and Eucharist; prayer, especially the Jesus Prayer and the mystical tradition of the Church; authentic ascetical practices from

1039 Patriarch Daniel, "The Orthodox Youth: Confessors of Christ and Missionaries," 116.
1040 Ibid., 184.
1041 Ibid.

the Tradition, including fasting; and a Patristic and Philokalic renewal, focusing on the witness of the Holy Fathers. In short, he focused on the means of encounter we described herein. In reclaiming the unity between theology and spirituality, he wrote:

> The primary premise of theology is ... to see through the eyes of Christ, to think according to Christ; to become integrated into the life of Christ—yet not with the purpose of losing oneself as a unique, unrepeatable individual, but to find in him the fullness of one's own life.[1042]

This fullness, he says, is embodied in the words of St. Paul, "We have the mind of Christ"[1043]—alignment of wills being at the heart of divinization. This, to him, is "theological knowledge"[1044] and, he adds, it "involves a transformation or sanctification of our thinking in the Holy Spirit."[1045] In a word, he focused on *theosis*. For Patriarch Daniel, it was not solely about restoring the physical infrastructure of the Church; more important was fostering inward spiritual growth of the faithful to strengthen the life of the Church. As he noted in an interview, "The faithful are the wealth of our Church. No matter how materially wealthy a church may be, if it is empty during services on Sundays or festal days, then it is spiritually poor."[1046] In another interview, he said:

> The highest priority is to call people to salvation—that is, to call them to union with God through prayer and good deeds .... I believe that the Church can have

1042 Ibid., 16.
1043 1 Cor. 2:16.
1044 Patriarch Daniel clearly subscribes to idea that theological knowledge is based on experiences with the divine presence. Recall the axiom cited by Stăniloae: "If you are a theologian you truly pray. If you truly pray you are a theologian." Patriarch Daniel was a student under Stăniloae.
1045 Patriarch Daniel, "The Unity Between Theology and Spirituality," 17.
1046 Ibid., 181.

> no priorities other than those set by the Savior Jesus Christ—namely, the tidings of the gospel of salvation; the renewal of spiritual life, of course; and third, the manifestation of faith and spirituality through concrete works for the benefit of society.[1047]

As we face a spiritual pandemic, with people turning away from God and churches emptying at an exponential rate, perhaps these lessons of Church rebuilding can be leveraged in our renewal efforts. Patriarch Daniel did not compromise with the spirit of the age—quite the contrary—nor rely on innovations or gimmickry. He focused on the basics grounded in the Sacred Tradition of the Church. We can do the same.

A Witness to the Nations

Fallen human nature is separated from God, and a soul separated from God has a 100 percent mortality rate. If one chooses to separate from God, he will respect our decision—just like Jesus's respected the decision of the rich young man who chose to walk away.[1048] God gave us free will, and we will choose whether or not to love him. However, there are consequences associated with separation from God: despair, despondency, and significant unhappiness on the way to spiritual death. This is because God is the source of all goodness, and, if we choose to separate ourselves from this source, we will be lacking in that which can lead us to true happiness and fulfillment. Unfortunately, today's secularized society provides many arguments for why we do not need God, and we can observe how darkened the world has become.

In contrast, the renewed human person lives with God, and only renewed people can raise up a fallen world. We are called to be

1047 Ibid., 231.
1048 Cf. Matt. 19:22.

Jesus's witnesses to all the nations.[1049] We begin by the witness of our lives, demonstrating what we deem important to us by the way we live. Further, we discern what we as a community can do to bring the Gospel message to those who have fallen away, the disenfranchised, and the unchurched. We are called to pass on the Deposit of Faith entrusted to us by previous generations, to become a community of missionary disciples. Missionary zeal is required more than ever to bring the good news of the Gospel to the world, offer the world a life-giving alternative, revivify those who are lukewarm in faith, and reach those who have dismissed the need for salvation. The mission fields are in our midst; reconversion and prioritization of faith are critical. "A true apostle looks for opportunities to announce Christ by words addressed either to non-believers with a view of leading them to faith, or to the faithful with a view of instructing, strengthening, and encouraging them to a more fervent life."[1050] Christians in name must live authentic Christian lives.

Reflection Questions

1. Do I live a life that bears witness to my faith being important to me? Do I live as a person with hope?

2. Do I appreciate the faith that has been handed down to me? Do I recognize it as a treasure, a pearl of great value? Do I recognize the cost at which this faith was given to me? Am I a good steward of this treasure of faith? How am I handing it down to the next generation? Do I feel a responsibility to pass on what has been given to me?

3. Does my parish or community focus on the goal of bringing its people closer to Christ to achieve their divinely intended destiny? Does it teach people how to know and love Jesus

1049 See Matt. 28:16-20. The Great Commissioning.

1050 Pope St. Paul VI, *Apostolicam Actuositatem*, Decree on the Apostolate of the Laity (Rome: Libreria Editrice Vaticana, Nov. 18, 1965), no. 6.

Christ? If so, how well are we doing as a community? If not well, what needs to be improved?

4. Is Christ authentically present in my parish church today, not just in the tabernacle, but alive in the hearts of those present?

5. What initiatives can be started in my community? What can be done to reach out to those separated from the Christian faith?

6. How do we engage our youth and help them to be solidly grounded in their Christian faith?

7. Do we experience complacency in our Church? In our parish? What are my observations regarding any changes we have made?

8. What can we do to reverse the trends that our Church is experiencing in terms of rapidly declining attendance? In particular, what can we do to engage the youth (our next generation), those who have fallen away, and those who have lost hope?

9. How do I collaborate with the Holy Spirit to continue the work that began at Pentecost (as described in the Acts of the Apostles)?

Icon of the Appearance on the Mountain
(The Great Commissioning)

"Go, therefore, and make disciples of all nations, baptizing them in the name of the Father, and of the Son, and of the holy Spirit, teaching them to observe all that I have commanded you. And behold, I am with you always, until the end of the age."
(Matt. 28:19-20)

Supplemental Information

SUPPLEMENTAL INFORMATION

Historical Perspective

Selected Christian Spiritual Traditions

The following are significant spiritual traditions within the Church that include the names of key individuals and writings from their respective periods:

East	West
Monastic Origins of Spirituality (200 – 800s)	
Desert Spirituality • St. Antony of Egypt (251-356) • Rule of St. Pachomius (292-348) • St. Macarius the Great (c.300-91) • Various monastic leaders from the Egyptian desert (330s-460s), *Sayings of the Desert Fathers (Apophthegmata Patrum)* • St. Barsanuphius the Great and St. John of Gaza, the two "Old Men," (mid-6th century), *Letters* • St. Dorotheos of Gaza (d. 565), *Discourses and Sayings* • St. John Climacus (579-606), *The Ladder of Divine Ascent* • St. Isaac the Syrian (640-700), *Ascetical Homilies* • After the Islamic conquest of Egypt in the 7th century, some monks moved from the Egyptian desert to Mount Athos.	**Desert Spirituality Moves West** • St. Augustine of Hippo (354-430), *Confessions* • St. John Cassian (360-435), *Conferences* and *Institutes* • St. Benedict of Nursia (480-543), founder of the Benedictine Order (Rule of St. Benedict), beginnings of *Lectio Divina*.

East	West
Continued Evolution of Monastic Spirituality (900 – 1200)	
Eastern Monastic Spirituality • First monasteries established on Mount Athos, which becomes the center of Eastern Orthodox spirituality • St. Symeon the New Theologian (949-1022), monk of the Monastery of St. Mammas, Constantinople, *Discourses* • St. Anthony of Kiev (983-1073), founds Pechersk Lavra, the Monastery of the Caves, bringing Athonite spirituality to Ukraine/ Russia	**Western Monastic Spirituality** • St. Bruno (1030-1101) founds Carthusian order • Robert of Molesme (1028-1111), a Benedictine abbot, founds the Cistercian order (1098) • St. Bernard of Clairvaux (1090-1153) reforms the Cistercian order
Spirituality in the Scholastic Period (1200 – 1400)	
Greek Renaissance – Jesus Prayer • Mount Athos becomes epicenter of hesychast spirituality • St. Gregory of Sinai (c.1265-1346) • St. Gregory Palamas (1296-1359), *Triads* • Hesychast Controversy (1330-54) • St. Nicholas Cabasilas (1322-92), *The Life in Christ* and *Commentary on the Divine Liturgy* **Russia** • St. Sergius of Radonezh (1314-92), a hermit and mystic, founds Holy Trinity Monastery near Moscow (Sergiev Posad). • St. Sergius and St. Herman, Athonite monks, found the Valaam Monastery at Lake Ladoga (~1389). **Serbia and Romania** • Nicodemus of Tismana (c.1320-1406), a disciple of Athonite St. Gregory of Sinai, founds one monastery in Serbia and two in Romania in the hesychast tradition	**Age of Scholasticism** *Separation of Spirituality and Theology as theological formation shifts from monasteries to universities* • St. Dominic (1170-1221), founder of the Dominican Order • St. Francis of Assisi (1182-1226), founder of the Franciscan Order • John Van Ruysbroeck (1293-1381), Flemish Mysticism • St. Catherine of Sienna (1347-80), *Dialogue of Divine Providence* • Julian of Norwich (1342-1416), *Showings* • Anonymous *Cloud of Unknowing* (late 14th century, Carthusian); first reference to a practice later known as Centering Prayer • Thomas à Kempis (1380-1471), *Imitation of Christ*

<table>
<tr><th>East</th><th>West</th></tr>
<tr><td colspan="2">Spirituality in the Age of Reformation (1400 – 1800)</td></tr>
<tr><td>
Hesychia in Russia
<ul>
<li>St. Nil Sorsky (1433-1503), disciple of St. Sergius of Radonezh, represents school of spirituality focused on the hesychast spiritual movement (Jesus Prayer, study of scripture and patristics, silence, and living simply). Contemplative mystics. Predanie (The Tradition) and Ustav (The Monastic Rule). Considered a teacher of prayer and ascetical life.</li>
<li>St. Joseph Volotsky (1440-1515), another disciple of St. Sergius, represents a different school of spirituality focused on strict obligation of obedience to God, and meticulous observance of rituals and liturgical worship. Large monasteries with estates.</li>
<li>Rivalry emerges between the two schools, with Volotsky's dominating and currying favor with the Muscovite state. Hesychast spirituality disappears from public view in Russia for almost 200 years until the Russian Spiritual Renaissance.</li>
</ul>
Under Peter the Great (1672-1725) and Catherine II (1729-96), monasticism in Russia is suppressed
<ul>
<li>St. Paisius Velichkovsky (1722-94) enters Pechersk Lavra in Kiev (1741); was told the hesychast tradition could be found in Romania, travels there (1743), becomes a disciple of Basil of Poiana Mărului (1692-1767), and later goes to Mount Athos (1746)</li>
</ul>
</td><td>
Age of Reformation
Ignatian Spirituality
<ul>
<li>St. Ignatius of Loyola (1491-1556), founder of the Jesuits, Spiritual Exercises</li>
</ul>
Carmelite Spirituality in Spain
<ul>
<li>St. Teresa of Ávila (1515-82), Interior Castle</li>
<li>St. John of the Cross (1542-91), Dark Night of the Soul and Ascent of Mount Carmel</li>
</ul>
Other Threads
<ul>
<li>St. Philip Neri (1515-95), founder of the Congregation of the Oratory</li>
<li>Lorenzo Scupoli (1530-1610), Spiritual Combat</li>
<li>St. Francis de Sales (1567-1622), founder of the Salesians, Introduction to the Devout Life</li>
<li>Pierre de Bérulle (1575-1629), founder of the French Oratory</li>
<li>St. Vincent de Paul (1580-1660) and St. Louise de Marillac (1591-1660)</li>
<li>Armand Jean le Bouthillier de Rancé (1626-1700), concerned about laxity, reforms the Cistercians in 1664 and creates the Order of Cistercians of the Strict Observance (OCSO), also known as the Trappists</li>
<li>St. Paul of the Cross (1694-1775), founder of the Passionists in 1720</li>
<li>St. Alphonsus Liguori (1696-1787), founder of the Redemptorists, The Way of the Cross</li>
</ul>
</td></tr>
</table>

East	West
Spirituality in the Age of Reason (1700 – 1925)	
Russian Spiritual Renaissance **Athonite Developments** • Kollyvades Movement – spiritual renewal emphasizing Patristic theology, liturgical life, and frequent reception of communion; reaction against the European Enlightenment • St. Paisius Velichkovsky begins translation of *Philokalia* into Slavonic (1746-64); gathers disciples • St. Nikodemos the Hagiorite (1749-1809) under influence of St. Makarios of Corinth (1731-1805), compiles original Greek *Philokalia* (1782); Nikodemos also translates *Unseen Warfare* (1796), and develops *The Handbook of Spiritual Counsel* (1801) • *Evergetinos* published (1782) **Romania / Russia** • St. Paisius Velichkovsky and his disciples return to Romania (1764), first to Dragomirna Monastery and then, as the community grows, to Neamţ (1779); continues translating *Philokalia* into Slavonic, published in 1794 (Slavonic *Philokalia*) » Created interest in and love for reading and studying spiritual books of the Holy Fathers » When St. Paisius dies, large numbers of his disciples return to Russia and significantly influence monasticism (e.g., Optina, Valaam, etc.) » Appearance of the *Starchestvo*, spiritual threads based on an elder (*staretz*) » Optina Monastery (~early 1800s), becomes a significant spirituality center through disciples of Paisius	**Age of Reason** • Jean-Baptiste Henri Lacordaire (1802-61), re-establishes the Dominican order in Post-Revolutionary France • Isaac Hecker (1819-88), co-founder of the Paulists, focuses on the evangelization of America **Oxford Movement** • Included a focus on writings of the Early Church (patristics) and mystical writers; recovery of an integrated spirituality (body, mind, and heart), interior transformation, and emphasis on the potential of union with God • Pre-cursor to *ressourcement*, leading into the Second Vatican Council • St. John Henry Newman (1801-90), key figure in the Oxford Movement; also, a founder of two Oratories in the United Kingdom, Birmingham (1848) and London (1849) **Carmelite Spirituality in France** • St. Thérèse of Lisieux, OCD (1873-97), *Story of a Soul* • St. Elizabeth of the Trinity, OCD (1880-1906)

East	West
» Optina Monastery (~early 1800s), becomes a significant spirituality center through disciples of Paisius » Optina Elders, renowned spiritual masters (*staretz*) ▪ Elder Leonid (1768-1841), established the *Starchestvo*, and was a disciple of Elder Theodore of Svir, a disciple of St. Paisius ▪ Elder Macarius (1788-1860), was a disciple of Athanasius, a disciple of St. Paisius, and, later, of Elder Leonid ▪ Elder Ambrose (1812-91), considered the pinnacle of eldership at Optina • St. Tikhon of Zadonsk (1724-83) • St. Seraphim of Sarov (1754-1833) » Sarov-Diveyevo becomes a significant spirituality center • Laity embrace Jesus Prayer and monastic spiritual practices • Anonymous classic *The Pilgrim's Tale* (~1860s); earliest redaction from Optina Monastery • St. Ignatius Brianchaninov (1807-67), *The Field*, *The Arena*, and *The Refuge* • St. Theophan the Recluse (1815-94), *Unseen Warfare* (updated) and translating the Slavonic *Philokalia* into Russian (*Dobrotolubiye*) • St. John of Kronstadt (1829-1908), *My Life in Christ* • Optina Monastery closed (1923) *Russian revolution in 1917 significantly impacts the Russian Church: Optina and other spiritual centers closed; many Russian theologians and intelligentsia emigrated to France.*	

East	West
Spirituality in the Modern Age (1925 – Today)	
Russian Diaspora • St. Sergius Orthodox Theological Institute established in Paris (1925) by Russian émigré and home to many noted Russian Orthodox theologians **Flourishing of Hesychast Tradition** **Russia and Eastern Europe** • Post-Communism (~1990s), prolific growth in monasteries in Russia, Ukraine, Romania, and Bulgaria **Russia** • Valaam Monastery returned to Orthodox Church (1989), the "Athos of the North" **Bulgaria** • Elder Seraphim Aleksiev (1912-93), *The Meaning of Suffering, Strife and Reconciliation*, and *The Forgotten Medicine: The Mystery of Repentance* **Romania** • Burning Bush movement at Antim Monastery (1945-58), a gathering of spiritual fathers focused on the revival of the hesychast tradition • Fr. Dumitru Stăniloae (1903-93) translates the original Greek *Philokalia* into Romanian (Romanian *Philokalia*) • Elder Paisius Olaru of Sihla (1897-1990) • Elder Cleopa Ilie of Sihastria (1912-98) • Elder Arsenie Papacioc (1914-2011) **Serbia (influenced by Optina/ Valaam)** • Elder Thaddeus of Vitovnica (1914-2003)	**Age of Modernity** ***Nouvelle Théologie* (1935-60)** • "New Theology," a movement of critical reaction to Neo-Scholasticism with a desire to return Catholic theology to the original sources (Sacred Scripture and Church Fathers), most notably within circles of French and German theologians • Renewed interest in biblical exegesis and mysticism • Precursor to *ressourcement* and its influence on reforms at the Second Vatican Council. **Second Vatican Council (1962-65)** • *Lumen Gentium* includes "Universal Call to Holiness" (Nov. 21, 1964) **Trappist/Contemplative Outreach (Cistercian Spirituality)** • Thomas Merton, OCSO (1915-68), coined the term "Centering Prayer" • Thomas Keating, OCSO (1923-2018) • Basil Pennington, OCSO (1931-2005) • William Meninger, OCSO (1932-2021) **World Community for Christian Meditation ("WCCM")** • Fr. John Main, OSB (1926-82) • Fr. Laurence Freeman, OSB (1951-) **Other Contemplatives** • St. Charles de Foucauld (1858-1916), hermit in North Africa • St. Teresa Benedicta of the Cross (Edith Stein) (1891-1942) • Caryll Houselander (1901-54) • Catherine Doherty (1896-1985), *Poustinia* (1975) • Mother Teresa of Calcutta (1910-97)

<table>
<tr><th>East</th><th>West</th></tr>
<tr>
<td>
Athonite Revival of Hesychast Tradition
<ul>
<li>Elder Daniel of Katounakia (1846-1929)</li>
<li>St. Silouan the Athonite (1866-1938), born in Russia
<ul>
<li>Elder Sophrony of Essex (1896-1993), a disciple of St. Silouan – a Russian who initially went to St. Sergius in Paris before going to Mount Athos where he became a disciple of Elder Silouan; later returned to St. Sergius, publishes the biography of St. Silouan, and eventually settles in Essex, UK, founding a monastery
<ul>
<li>Elder Zacharias of Essex (1946-), disciple of Elder Sophrony</li>
</ul>
</li>
</ul>
</li>
<li>Elder Joseph the Hesychast (1897-1959)
<ul>
<li>Elder Ephraim of Arizona (Philotheou) (1927-2019), a disciple of Elder Joseph</li>
</ul>
</li>
<li>Elder Porphyrios of Kavsokalyvia (1906-91)</li>
<li>Elder Paisios of Mount Athos (1924-94)</li>
<li>Elder Ephraim of Katounakia (1912-98)</li>
<li>Elder Aimilianos of Simonopetra (1934-2019)</li>
</ul>
Beginning in 2000, resurgence of monasteries on Mount Athos (Greece), many in the Hesychast tradition

Egyptian Monastic Revival
<ul>
<li>Monastic revival beginning in 1969</li>
<li>Fr. Matthew the Poor (Fr. Matta El Meskeen) (1919-2006), Orthodox Prayer Life</li>
<li>Fr. Lazarus al Anthony, video interviews (e.g., The Last Anchorite and Coptic Youth Channel's series, A Monk's Life)</li>
</ul>
</td>
<td>
Modern Spiritual Movements

Predominantly lay movements, focusing on the call to holiness and renewal, drawing together contemplation with action (evangelization, social justice); many focus on navigating the path to holiness within secular culture. Became increasingly popular after the Second Vatican Council and its teaching on the Universal Call to Holiness. Some of the more prominent examples, along with the founders, country of origin, and founding year, include:
<ul>
<li>Schoenstatt Movement (Fr. Joseph Kentenich, Germany, 1914)</li>
<li>Opus Dei (Fr. Josemaría Escrivá, Spain, 1928)</li>
<li>Catholic Worker Movement (Dorothy Day and Peter Maurin, United States, 1933)</li>
<li>Focolare Movement (Chiara Lubich, Italy, 1943)</li>
<li>Cursillo Movement (group of laymen, Spain, 1944)</li>
<li>Comunione e Liberazione (Fr. Luigi Guissani, Italy, 1954)</li>
<li>Neocatechumenal Way (Redemptoris Mater) (two laypeople, Spain, 1964)</li>
<li>Catholic Charismatic Renewal (two laymen, United States, 1967)</li>
<li>Sant'Egidio Community (group of high school students, Italy, 1968)</li>
<li>Families of Nazareth Movement (Fr. Tadeusz Dajczer, Poland, 1985)</li>
<li>Center for Contemplation and Action (Fr. Richard Rohr, OFM, United States, 1986)</li>
<li>ACTS Missions (three laymen, United States, 1986) – offshoot of the Cursillo Movement</li>
</ul>
</td>
</tr>
</table>

The roots of the Church are very deep. For more than 2,000 years, prayer has nourished the life of the saints and the disciples of Jesus. The above analysis demonstrates how the Eastern Christian spiritual tradition has revolved around the Jesus Prayer, beginning with the Desert Fathers, and continuing to modern times. Thus, this mystical tradition of the Christian East has been faithfully practiced and preserved since the time of the Early Church.

In contrast, several spiritual traditions emerged in the West. During the Scholastic Period, there was a separation between theology and spirituality as the study of theology migrated from monasteries to universities, where it became a rigorous academic discipline. The same separation did not occur in the Christian East, wherein knowledge of God was based on actual experience. The maxim of Evagrius Ponticus is often quoted by Orthodox Theologians: "If you are a theologian you truly pray. If you truly pray you are a theologian."[1051]

A significant shift occurred at the Second Vatican Council, which espoused *ressourcement*—a return to the sources. This meant a move away from Scholasticism with a renewed emphasis on Sacred Scripture and Patristic sources. The writings of Karl Rahner, SJ, for example, reflect this shift: "The devout Christian of the future will either be a 'mystic,' one who has 'experienced' something, or he [she] will cease to be anything at all."[1052]

The great beauty of the Universal Catholic Church is that it includes the spiritual patrimony of both East and West. Pope St. John Paul II believed the Church needed to learn to breathe again from both lungs, one Eastern and one Western.[1053] Recent popes have described the need to rediscover the treasures of the Eastern Catholic Churches to create a synthesis reflective of the Universal Catholic Church. Further, the reawakening of faith that followed the fall of Communism is an immense source of hope, especially for Western European

1051 Evagrius Ponticus, *The Praktikos & Chapters on Prayer*, 65.
1052 Rahner, "Christian Living Formerly and Today," 15.
1053 Ex. Pope St. John Paul II, *Ut Unum Sint* (Rome: Libreria Editrice Vaticana, 1995), no. 54.

and North America where freedom of religion was often taken for granted, leading to a more superficial faith, not tested by fire, and, in turn, people are leaving the Church in epidemic proportions. The reawakening in countries like Romania is the truly fruit of the blood of martyrs.[1054] "Communism destroyed a few hundred thousand people physically, but spiritually destroyed millions. The martyrs beneath the ground ... cry out for us to return to Christ, to the Church."[1055] In Romania, since 2007, there has been an intense focus on rebuilding the interior lives of people and, today, the Orthodox Church remains the most trusted institution in Romanian society.[1056]

One could make similar observations about the Church in Ukraine, Slovakia, and Hungary, arising from the catacombs, surviving Communist repression, and preserving the Deposit of Faith, often at a great price. These Eastern Christian experiences and perspectives provide a further richness to our Catholic faith, especially related to mysticism, the theology of encounter, and the hesychast tradition (Jesus Prayer).[1057] Encounter is essential to establishing a deep-seated relationship with Jesus Christ, the source of life, hope, and way to eternal blessedness.

With this emphasis on encounter, we begin to appreciate the spirituality of such people as Mother Teresa of Calcutta, who asks us the right question: "Do you really know the living Jesus—not from books but from being with him in your heart?"[1058] Her entire

---

1054 See Sarah, *The Day is Now Far Spent*, 239.

1055 Monk Moise, *The Saint of the Prisons*, 276-7.

1056 Ştefana Totorcea, "Poll: The Church Remains the Most Trusted Institution in Romania," *Basilica News Agency*, online, January 19, 2021. Cites a poll made by the Center for Urban and Regional Sociology conducted between January 11-15, 2021. Research showed that 62% of Romanians placed a high and very high degree of trust in the Church. In second place was local councils with 60% and these were the only two institutions trusted by more than half of the people.

1057 As an example, the hesychast tradition was core to spiritual survival in Romania. Examples include the revival of the tradition through the Burning Bush Movement at Antim Monastery in Bucharest and in prisons where many of those imprisoned adopted monastic practices in response to the brutal physical and psychological conditions. The latter is exemplified by Valeriu Gafencu. See Monk Moise's *The Saint of the Prisons*.

1058 "Jesus is My All: A Novena to Blessed Teresa of Calcutta," ed. Fr. Brian Kolodiejchuk, MC (San Diego, CA: Mother Teresa Center, 2005), 13.

apostolate to the poor and suffering was anchored in contemplative prayer. Thus, one critical aspect of the spiritual journey—to know God's plan for us—we must come to know and love his Son, Jesus Christ. One way to know him is through prayer. Recall the teaching of St. Isaac the Syrian, "You cannot taste honey by reading a book." To know Jesus is to experience him.

For further information and a concise history of Christian spirituality, including Protestant traditions, the following text is recommended:

Sheldrake, Philip, *Spirituality: A Brief History*, 2nd ed. West Sussex, UK: Wiley-Blackwell, 2013.

Glossary of Selected Terms

The following terms are related to our discussions and spirituality in general.

Acedia

From the Greek meaning "negligence." Acedia is a gloomy combination of weariness, sadness, and a lack of purposefulness. It robs a person of the capacity for joy and leaves one feeling empty, or void of meaning. In the spiritual life, this equates to a state of listlessness or despondency, making it difficult to continue spiritual practices such as prayer, fasting, or spiritual reading evidenced by falling asleep during prayer or reading, and general boredom. Some Holy Fathers have considered this the most crushing of demons because it can cause a person to give up on the struggles of the spiritual journey. In a modern context, one would equate this with a person who is demoralized, or suffering from depression or burnout. The constant bombardment of Gospel values by secular society can exacerbate this condition.

Active Prayer

See "Self-Activating Prayer."

Agapé

Greek term for the highest form of love. See "love."

Agnosticism

Rejection in belief defaulting to the view that matters of God are unknown or unknowable. God may exist but is not relevant. This is a popular perspective today.

Alexandrian School

One of two major centers for theological learning and biblical exegesis in the Ancient Church. Intellectuals of this school emphasized the allegorical interpretation of Scriptures and tended toward a Christology that emphasized the union of the human and the divine. Notable theologians associated with the school were Origen and Clement of Alexandria. Prior to Christianity, Alexandria had been a significant cultural center, strongly influenced by Greek philosophy and having the largest Jewish population outside Palestine.

Almsgiving

A penitential practice, sacrificially giving to God through charitable acts, assisting others in need. It is more than giving money or philanthropy. Rather, it is a conversion of heart, moved to compassion as Jesus was, and giving from our means, not just our surplus (see the widow's contribution, Luke 21:1-4). Almsgiving also becomes part of our prayer practice. Love of neighbor is an outflow from our love of God.

Amartia

Greek word for "sin" that is used in the New Testament, which does not mean a transgression of the law. It is better defined as "missing the mark."

Anaphora

Greek word for "sin" that is used in the New Testament, which does not mean a transgression of the law. It is better defined as "missing the mark."

Anawim

Hebrew term from the Old Testament meaning the "poor ones." These were cited as the widow, orphan, or resident alien—those who had no voice in society and were completely dependent on God. Noted in the Old Testament, God always had a special place in his heart for these and always heard their cries. In today's context, they would be considered the vulnerable, marginalized, and the socio-economically oppressed.

Antiochian School

One of two major centers for theological learning and biblical exegesis in the Ancient Church. Intellectuals of this school stressed a more literal interpretation of the Scriptures and a Christology that emphasized the distinction between the human and the divine in the person of Jesus Christ. Notable theologians included St. John Chrysostom, Theodore of Mopsuestia, and Patriarch Nestorius, who was at the center of the Nestorian heresy. See "Nestorianism."

Apatheism

An attitude of apathy toward the existence or non-existence of God. Apathetics do not see a reason to bother with religion; not engaging matters of faith, deeming them to be irrelevant. A popular perspective present in society today. Apathetics are a rapidly growing demographic, larger than atheists and agnostics combined. See also "Nones."

Apologetics

From the Greek *apologia*, meaning "speaking in defense." This is the religious discipline of defending religious doctrines through systematic argumentation and discourse. Christian apologetics is a branch of theology that aims to present historical, reasoned, and evidential bases for Christianity, defending it against objections.

Apophatic

An experience of God that cannot be defined in words. Rahner, called this "themelessness"—we cannot capture God in words, concepts, or themes. We can only say something about God through our experiences, such as inferring his love for us. This theological perspective underpins the approach in Eastern Christian theology.

Apostolic Period

The time of the Earliest Church, from the Ascension of Jesus to the death of the last apostle (ca. 100).

Apostasy

The abandonment or renunciation of a religious belief. Historically, this has been considered a serious sin because it separates one from God.

Arianism

An influential heresy denying the divinity of Christ, originating with the Alexandrian priest Arius (c. 250– c. 336). Arianism maintained that the Son of God was created by the Father and was therefore neither coeternal with the Father, nor consubstantial.

Art of Spiritual Life

Establishing a rhythm in daily living that includes key spiritual practices such as prayer, fasting, and almsgiving. See also "Interior Monasticism." Includes regular study of the ascetical teachings of the Holy Fathers of the Church. The objectives are increasing awareness of our interior longing for God, ability to recognize his presence in our daily activities, and a focus on surrender of self-will to God's will. Through these efforts, we increasingly collaborate with God's plan for our lives (see "*synergeia*") to draw closer to him, experience joy and fulfillment, and prepare ourselves for our destiny: union with God in the life to come.

Asceticism

From the Greek *áskēsis*, meaning "exercise" or "training," similar to that done by an athlete. Asceticism as a spiritual discipline has three basic goals: (1) bringing order and self-control to human passions/appetites, (2) centering a person, and (3) opening a person to God's presence. Ascetical disciplines were meant as voluntary self-denial as prescribed by Jesus in his terms and conditions of discipleship ("If anyone wishes to come after me, he must deny himself and take up his cross daily and follow me" – Luke 9:23).

Atheism

Outright rejection of a belief in God. Popular perspective present in society today.

Attentiveness

Continuous focus on God; spiritual attentiveness. See "*Nepsis.*"

Attributes of God (Divine Attributes)

A quality or characteristic of God that cannot be seen, but is inferred through our experiences. For example, we say God is love (absolute), God's love is overflowing, God's mercy is infinite (beyond measure), and God's compassion is limitless. Many of these attributes are found in Sacred Scripture, but we begin to understand them by following the example of Jesus and through our human experiences. Generally, these experiences occur when we realize our limitations and strive to move beyond them (transcendence). We discover a greater capacity than we could have imagined.

Authority of Sacred Scripture

The ability to use Sacred Scripture as a source of revelation and theological belief. This authority is supported by three attributes: Inspiration (divinely inspired), Inerrancy, and Canonicity.

Authority of Sacred Tradition

A source of Divine Revelation and theological belief by the Catholic and Eastern Christian Churches. Tradition (with a capital "T") is seen as how the faith was lived and practiced by the Apostles and their disciples, and handed down through the Early Church. This would include prayers, rites, rituals, liturgies, a sacramental system presided over by the threefold ministry of bishops, priests, and deacons, and the Church as a communion of local churches. It also includes the writings of the Holy Fathers that provide perspectives on how to live by the commandments of Jesus.

Body of Christ

An analogy of all believers united in a single body with Christ Jesus as its head. A body has many members but remains a single body (unity that retains diversity). Christ speaks of the unity of all believers in his analogy of the vine and branches (John 15:1-10). Images of the Church as the body of Christ come from Rom. 12:5, 1 Cor. 12-27, Col. 1:18, 1:24, and Eph. 5:23. As such, the Church is one with Christ. See also "*Koinonia*."

Boredom

Sad longing or emptiness; a sense of missing something to which we are attached. Previous pleasures or material things no longer satisfy the inner longing. Joy is elusive. A loss of energy, purpose, or zeal. Leads to despair, depression, despondency, and even burnout. See also "*acedia*."

Canonicity

The acceptance of a text as divinely inspired and agreed upon for inclusion into the Canon. Canonicity is one of three attributes giving authority for Sacred Scripture to be used as a source for theological belief.

Capex Dei

Capacity for God – ability of a human person to experience God and enter into relationship with him. This is predicated on humanity being created in the divine image and human fulfillment being achieved only through a relationship with God. This capacity is realized when experiencing inner longing, a desire for something more. God created this longing, so he alone can fill it. Nothing finite can fill infinite longing. Only in total communion with God do our hearts find rest and we can be who we were created to be.

Catholic Social Teaching

Expresses the Church's concerns over injustices or indignity, which includes how we as disciples should consider responding to these situations, especially by reflecting upon the mission of Jesus in the Gospel. Modern Catholic Social Teaching began with Pope Leo XIII's encyclical letter in 1891, Rerum Novarum, which discussed labor conditions and the need for just wages.

Charity

In the context of a theological virtue, we love God more than everything, and love our neighbor for the love of God. See also "Agapé." Charity is one of the three theological virtues, along with faith and hope. According to St. Paul, charity (love) is the greatest of these virtues. See 1 Cor. 13:1-13.

Christology

Study of the biblical and theological doctrine relating to the person, nature, and role of Christ.

Common Home

Term used by Pope Francis in *Laudato Si'*, describing our world and our mutual responsibility for it. This is one of the first major Catholic Social Teachings on the environment. Humanity is given dominion over Creation (see Gen. 1:28-30), but this does not mean exploitation or waste. We must never forget we are saved with Creation, that we are called to elevate it to its intended purpose and return it to God for the benefit of others.

Common Order/Path

The Holy Fathers' guidelines on the path to salvation. Includes instructions on repentance, ascetical practices, and prayer. There is a common denominator to their teachings, and they recommend when a spiritual guide cannot be found, one should follow this common order of transformation (*theosis*) to achieve eternal blessedness in heaven.

Complacency

A feeling of uncritical satisfaction with oneself or one's achievements. In the spiritual journey, a presumption that one has made enough progress toward salvation and further effort is not required. Jesus warns against this in the Parable of the Rich Fool (Luke 12:16-21). Synonyms for complacency include self-satisfaction, self-approval, self-approbation, self-admiration, and self-congratulation. When a primary objective of the spiritual journey is surrender of self-will to the Divine will, just by its definition, one can see the dangers of complacency, wherein the focus is on "self."

Compunction

Regret or remorse for sinfulness. See "*Penthos*."

Contemplation

Practices with the aim of being aware of the divine presence. Contemplative prayer follows meditation and is the highest form of prayer aiming for a close spiritual union with God.

Conversion

Transformation or change of heart, *metanoia*. For most, conversion is an ongoing, life-long process and not a "big bang" one-time event. We must choose daily to follow Jesus. ("If anyone wishes to come after me, he must deny himself and take up his cross daily and follow me" – Luke 9:23).

Creed

A system, doctrine, or formula of religious belief; the codification of belief. A creed may also be defined as an authoritative statement of basic Christian belief. During the first two Ecumenical Councils, the Church formulated its beliefs in the Nicaea-Constantinople Creed (NCC), which has remained unchanged and is still used by mainline Christian denominations.

Deification

See "Divinization." These terms are used interchangeably.

Deifying Grace

Grace of the Holy Spirit that allows union with God to take place. This grace allows the union of two distinct natures, human and divine, without mixture or loss of one within the other. St. Gregory Palamas writes: "While every virtue, including imitation of God that is within our power, prepares a capacity in the recipient for divine union, it is still grace that accomplishes the unutterable union itself. It is by means of grace that all of God co-indwells with all those who are worthy, and that the whole of the saints co-inheres wholly with the whole of God" (from *Tomos of Mount Athos in Defense of the Hesychasts*). See also "Uncreated Energies." Note that living the God-like virtues creates the capacity for receipt of grace, and God provides such grace as a gift commensurate with effort, reflective of human-divine collaboration (*synergeia*).

Delusion

See "Spiritual Delusion."

Deposit of Faith (*Depositum Fidei*)

The content of Divine Revelation (revealed truth) coming to us from the Sacred Scriptures and Sacred Tradition. Combined, these are a single Deposit of Faith that form the basis of our Catholic beliefs. It is considered sacred because it comes from God and a deposit because it has been left to us by Christ.

Desert Spirituality

Spirituality drawing from the lives of the Desert Fathers from the Early Church. This includes the hesychast tradition (Jesus Prayer) and spiritual disciplines such as ascetical practices, detachment, mourning our sinfulness, and a spirit of penance. Throughout the history of Eastern Christian Spirituality, the Ancient Church to modern times, one can observe that it is deeply rooted in Desert Spirituality. It is a "back-to-basics" spirituality—simple yet continuously relevant to the spiritual journey and personal holiness.

Desire

See "Longing."

Despair

A complete loss or absence of hope. The Good News of the Gospel is intended to give us hope, that a life of eternal blessedness awaits us. However, the demons try to exploit our weaknesses to diminish our hope.

Despondency

A state in which one's spirits are low, reflecting a loss of hope or courage. The demons try to exploit these weaknesses to disrupt our relationship with God. St. Seraphim of Sarov wrote: "Despondency is a worm gnawing the heart."[1059]

Destiny

Human destiny is union with God, sharing in the life of the Holy Trinity, eternal blessedness in the life to come (heaven). As written in 2 Pet. 1:4, we become "sharers in the divine nature." The goal of theosis is to prepare for this destiny.

Detachment

From the Greek *apatheia,* a state of mind free from passions, such as a movement of the soul toward irrational love or senseless hate. To grow in the spiritual life, especially in contemplative prayer, a person must strive for personal purification to be freed from the passions and attain the virtues. *Apatheia* is a state of total dependence on God's grace—impossible to obtain on our own. It is only possible through synergeia.

1059 Zander, 103.

Diakonia

Greek term meaning "service." In theological terms, it is a call to serve the poor and oppressed. The call of the first "deacons" in Acts 6:6, was to take care of the Greek widows, who were neglected in the daily distribution of bread. So, first and foremost, this concept is about serving the poor and marginalized. It is the type of heart and mindset to which all followers of Jesus should aspire. See also "Almsgiving."

Dialectic Tension

Concept in which two elements—often contradictions—are in play in order to create a unity. It is a tension because the two elements must be held in equal proportion without overemphasizing one or the other. An example is the two natures of Christ, wherein he is simultaneously human and divine.

Dignity of the Human Person

A Principle of Catholic Social Teaching. Every person has fundamental dignity because all are made in the divine image and, as such, all life is sacred. Nothing can strip this dignity away. Thus, the Church encourages us to address any structures or institutions that challenge the fundamental dignity of the human person: abortion, euthanasia, capital punishment, human trafficking, improper treatment of undocumented workers.

Dispassion

Free from or unaffected by the passions. This is the foundation from which to cultivate the virtues. Some Holy Fathers refer to three stages in the spiritual life. The first is to conquer the passions or eliminate them (see "Passions"). This creates the foundation to cultivate the virtues.

Distractions

From the Greek *logismoi*, invading or intrusive thoughts that disturb or sidetrack one in prayer. One must always be vigilant (*nepsis*) to maintain inner stillness (*hesychia*).

Divine

When used as a noun, Divine refers to God and is capitalized. For example, we speak about encountering "the Divine."

Divine Attributes

The attributes of God that we infer from our experience of God and the teachings of Jesus. These include goodness, love, mercy, compassion, long-suffering, patience, purity, and pure love for our neighbor. *Theosis* is the process by which the human person gradually become divinized (deified) by practicing the divine attributes (also called the God-like virtues) to fulfill our destiny: union with God.

Divine Image

How humanity is created (see "Image of God"). "God created mankind in his image; in the image of God he created them; male and female he created them" (Gen. 1:27). Early Church Fathers would say that we are patterned after the Image Absolute, which is Jesus Christ.

Divine Liturgy

See "Liturgy."

Divine Office

Official set of prayers of the Church, marking the hours of each day and sanctifying the day with prayer. With the liturgy, it constitutes the official public prayer life of the Church. Matins and Vespers are two examples of specific hours or "offices" that are prayed. There are also Little Hours in between: First, Second, Third, Sixth, and so forth. In the Eastern Churches, the book of hours is called the *Horologion*, which means "the hour-teller." The equivalent in the Roman Church is the breviary or The Liturgy of the Hours.

Divine Person

Member of the Trinity, Father, Son, or Holy Spirit, three persons, one essence.

Divine Presence

The presence of God that we experience in prayer and in our lives when we remain spiritually attuned. In Eastern Christian Spirituality, sometimes this is referred to as experiencing the "energies" or "operations" of God (see "Energies").

Divinization

Related to the concept of theosis, the process of practicing the God-like virtues, becoming more "God-like" to prepare for our destiny: union with God. Term used interchangeably with "Deification."

Divinized Humanity

Jesus is fully human and fully divine (two natures), reflecting humanity's ultimate destination, union with God. Divinization is how human beings practice God-like virtues in preparation for this destiny. This "divinized humanity" is the goal to which all should aspire.

Ecclesiology

Study of the theological doctrine as applied to the nature and structure of the Church. From the Greek *ekklēsia*.

Ecumenical Council

Council of Church authorities, generally bishops and theologians, convened to settle matters of doctrine and practice and secure approval of the whole Church. Those who are entitled to vote represent the entire Church. "Ecumenical" comes from the Greek *oikoumenikos*, meaning "from the whole world."

Elder

A Spiritual Father. See "*Staretz*."

Encounter

To come upon or meet with. In the context used herein, the premise is that God is meant to be experienced in a tangible way. "The Joy of the Gospel fills the hearts and lives of all who encounter Jesus" (Pope Francis, *Evangelii Gaudium*, no. 1).

Energies

The operations of God that can be experienced and allow us to know something about God. These are considered "uncreated energies" because they are actions of God in the world. From the Greek *energeia*.

Enlightenment (Divine Illumination)

The divine assistance or grace provided to discern whether our thoughts and actions are aligned with the divine will; to gain greater insights on the divine mysteries based on contemplation or encounters with the divine presence. Sometimes referred to as Holy Illumination. Not to be confused with the philosophical movement known as The Enlightenment (see below).

Enlightenment (Philosophical Movement)

An intellectual and philosophical movement that dominated Europe in the 18th century. It fostered a belief in the inherent goodness of humanity and confidence that humans had the capacity for greatness within themselves, dismissing the role of God (reason over faith). This spawned several movements or philosophical schools of thought, including Humanism, Rationalism, and Individualism (see below). All these schools of thought, which influence our culture today, illustrate a movement away from God and even communal responsibilities, with an increased focus on self. Accordingly, within our secular society we have developed a culture of individualism, which subconsciously influences our perspectives and actions.

Essence

The inward nature, true substance, or constitution of anything. God in his essence is a mystery and, as such, unknowable. However, we can learn something about God through our experience of his operations (energies). From the Greek *ousia*, meaning "essence" or "substance."

Human beings cannot comprehend the essence or nature of God, nor can we take on the essence. However, we can share in, partake of, or participate in the divine nature as we strive to be more like God; striving to live the virtues. This involves self-surrender of our will to the divine will, which prepares us for our destiny: union with God.

Eternal Blessedness

To live in union with God—our human purpose or destiny. Sometimes this is also referred to as "communion with God," sharing in the very life of the Holy Trinity. Theosis is the incremental process of striving to prepare ourselves for this destiny.

Faith

Confidence or trust in a person or thing. Herein, faith refers to confidence and trust in God. Faith is one of the three theological virtues, along with hope and charity (love) — gifts from God that lead us to him and allow us to live in a closer relationship with him.

Fall

Term used to describe the sin of Adam and Eve, rejecting dependence on God (preferring self over God). It represents the transition from a state of innocent obedience to God to one of disobedience. The Fall created a defect in human nature, enslaving humanity to sin and making us more susceptible to temptation. Said another way, humanity was made in the image and likeness of God (Gen. 1:27), but lost the likeness through the sin of Adam and Eve. As sung in the Troparion for the Pre-Festive Day of the Nativity: "Christ is born to raise up the likeness that had fallen."

Fallen Nature

Because of the Fall, human nature has been gravely weakened, enslaved to sin, and susceptible to temptation. Through the Incarnation, our human nature was restored to its original nobility. Through Baptism, we are granted new life and the possibility of life with God in heaven. However, we must continually strive to renew our restored nature through our daily, incremental efforts. Some spiritual writers explain that unless we understand the depth of our fallen nature, our true humanity ("sinful nature"), we will not understand our need for salvation. Further, by understanding our fallen nature, we will be more likely to mourn our sinfulness (*penthos*).

Fasting

Ascetical/penitential practice of abstaining from food, creating a physical hunger and being reminded of the spiritual void only Christ can fill. If we fast with our hearts, we express our love for God and acknowledge our sinfulness. Our sacrifice unites us to the sacrifice of Jesus Christ, who shed his blood for our salvation.

Further, self-denial disposes us to freedom from worldly distractions to create an environment conducive to prayer. Through voluntary fasting, we unite ourselves in solidarity with the poor and suffering who have no food, reminding us that we are all members of the Body of Christ and are reliant upon God for all our blessings.

Fear of God

A reverential fear or awe of God in his majesty. It is not a phobia or a negative fear, such as fear of punishment for sins (slave-like fear). Rather, it is fear of sinning, thereby offending God and being separated from him for eternity (filial fear). It implies a rightly ordered relationship between God (Creator) and the person (created). Fear of the Lord, used interchangeably herein, is considered one of the seven gifts of the Holy Spirit. St. Isaac the Syrian wrote, "The fear of God is the beginning of virtue." Sir. 1:16: "The fullness of wisdom is to fear the Lord."

Filiation

Being a child of a certain parent. Term derived from the Latin, filius, meaning "son." This is a distinct property of the Son, the Second Person of the Trinity. In the Nicaean Creed, we say: "Begotten, not made, consubstantial with the Father..." Consubstantial means "with the same substance." See "essence" above.

Forgetfulness

Loss of spiritual attentiveness or zeal; complacency. Places the soul at risk. See "*Nepsis*."

Forgiveness

From the Greek *aphesis*, meaning "dismissal" or "release" or figuratively "pardon." Forgiveness frees the mind from anger and resentment, or demons that can impair our interior stillness. In the Parable of the Unforgiving Servant (Matt. 18:21-35) Jesus concludes, "So will my Heavenly Father do to you, unless each of you forgives his brother from his heart" (Matt. 18:35). Note the emphasis on heart, which means genuine forgiveness versus superficial and is intended to assist one in remaining "clean of heart," a key concept in *theosis*.

Formation

The process of forming or the state of being formed. In this context, formation is the spiritual grounding of an individual (experiential-based encounter) opposed to catechesis, which is formal instruction, based on an academic approach to theology (intellectual knowledge). Thus, formation is coming to know and enter into a relationship with Jesus Christ, learning to live our lives with him as our guide (becoming more Christ-like) versus solely an intellectual understanding of doctrines of faith. St. Isaac the Syrian wrote, "You cannot taste honey by reading a book." See also "*Praxis*."

Freedom

The state of being without confinement or under physical restraint; exemption from external control, interference, regulation; the power to determine action without restraint. Surrender of self-will to the Divine will is an act of freedom.

Giver as gift

How God communicates (reveals) himself to us and how we enter into a relationship with him. God is the giver of the gift. The gift is Jesus Christ, his Son, who is true God and of the same essence (substance) as the Father. Rahner describes this as, "The Giver is himself the gift." In the Nicaean Creed, we describe the Son as consubstantial with the Father. Further, Jesus models the perfect acceptance of this gift through self-surrender.

God is in the Overcoming

A concept in Ignatian spirituality. Often, we see God only in the blessings and good things that happen to us, which can lead to a superficial faith. We should also recognize the presence of God in our experiences of "overcoming," which includes our struggles to navigate the difficulties of life. God is present both in the calm and in the storm.

God-like Virtues

See "Divine Attributes."

Hedonism

The ethical theory that pleasures, in the sense of satisfying desires (bodily desires, wealth, intellectual pursuits, etc.), is the highest good and proper aim of human life. Argues that human behavior is motivated by the desire to increase pleasure and decrease pain. Dismisses the true nature of humanity, spiritual, and dismisses a divinely intended purpose. Closely correlated to "Humanism" and "Individualism."

Hesychia

Stillness, watchfulness, interior silence of the heart. Hesychast prayer, commonly known as the Jesus Prayer, is a contemplative prayer practice. Hesychasm evolved from the Desert Fathers and Mothers during the third to seventh centuries and was further developed in the monasteries on Mount Athos during the Greek Spiritual Renaissance (1200-1400). It advanced further during the Russian Spiritual Renaissance (1800-1917) and is still faithfully practiced and preserved within the Eastern Christian Churches, both Catholic and Orthodox. Also called "Prayer of the Heart" or noetic prayer (see "*nous*").

Holiness

The state in which we strive to fulfill our destiny, which is union with God. It is an ongoing journey of transformation involving spiritual struggle and increasing devotion to God. See also "Universal Call to Holiness."

Holy Mysteries

Term used by the Eastern Churches for Sacraments. From the Greek *mystērion*, meaning "mystery." Emphasis is placed on the mystery of the ritual. The "holy mysteries" are considered vessels for mystical participation in divine grace.

Hope

The combination of a desire for something and an expectation of receiving it. St. Paul writes that hope is for that which is unseen (Rom. 8:24), and the ultimate hope is in our supernatural destiny of union with God. Hope brings us to desire eternal life as our ultimate happiness. "And hope does not disappoint," as St. Paul wrote (Rom. 5:5). Hope is one of the three theological virtues, along with faith and charity (love).

Human Heart

A commonly held belief, beginning with the Early Desert Fathers and Mothers, is that Christianity was a divinizing process gradually occurring within the human heart, the interior focus in which man and the Triune God meet. Humanity encounters God in the heart.

Humility

From the earth, grounded. A simple, modest opinion of oneself, avoiding honors, ranks, titles. It is the foundation for the other virtues.

Human Person

Created in the divine image, rational and with free will, with the capacity for relationship with God (*capex Dei*) and achieve a supernatural destiny (union with God). To attain this destiny, must regain the divine likeness lost through the Fall by surrendering self-will to the divine will and practicing the divine attributes.

Humanism

An outlook or system of thought attaching prime importance to human rather than divine or supernatural matters. A movement away from God spawned by the Enlightenment.

Hypostasis

One of the three real and distinct substances in the undivided essence of God; a person of Trinity. Plural is hypostases.

Image of God

The sum of our possibilities. It is imprinted upon us and can never be taken away. As human beings, we have a capacity for God (*capex Dei*) and the ability to enter into a relationship with him because we are related to him. In this context, we describe ourselves as created in the divine image.

Incarnation

The doctrine that the second person of the Trinity, the *Logos*, assumed human form in the person of Jesus Christ and is completely God and completely man without mixture or confusion. Renowned 20th century Catholic Theologian Karl Rahner, SJ, uses the term: "divinized humanity" to describe our goal as humanity: divinization (deification).

Individualism

(1) The habit or principle of being independent and self-reliant. (2) A social theory favoring freedom of action for individuals over collective or state control. A movement away from God spawned by the Enlightenment.

Indwelling Divine Presence

The presence of the Divine within the human heart. Through Baptism, we have the Indwelling Presence. We cultivate this presence by following the example of Jesus through self-surrender and aligning our will with the Divine will.

Inerrancy

Acceptance of a text as being free of error. Divinely revealed truths that cannot be overturned by historical or scientific research. Sacred Scriptures are considered inerrant in that they are written to guide us how to get to heaven, not about how the heavens go. This allows for various texts to be considered within their literary form versus a literal interpretation. Inerrancy is one of three attributes authorizing Sacred Scripture as a source for theological belief.

Infinite Horizon

An analogy of how we as finite beings can begin to understand the concept of infinity, which begins to give us preliminary understanding of God as Infinite Being. In his theological framework, Rahner discusses the infinite horizon and horizon of infinite possibility.

Inspiration

In a broad sense, varying degrees of human and divine collaboration. Inspiration refers to the texts as divinely inspired. It is one of three attributes authorizing Sacred Scripture as a source for theological belief.

Interior Monasticism

For a non-monastic, adopting certain monastic practices such as prayer and spiritual disciplines (repentance, asceticism, and detachment) to deepen one's relationship with God. See also, "Art of Spiritual Life."

Interior Stillness

See "*Hesychia*." Consider Psalm 46:11, "Be still and know that I am God!"

Interior Struggle

See "Unseen Warfare."

Jesus Prayer

A prayer tradition emerging from Desert Spirituality, focused on interior stillness to encounter the presence of God. One of the most popular forms of the prayer is "Lord Jesus Christ, Son of God, have mercy on me, a sinner." See "*Hesychia*."

Kathara Proseuche

The third and highest level of participation in prayer in the hesychast tradition, following *praxis* and *theoria*. See "Pure Prayer."

Kenosis

Renunciation of the divine nature, at least in part, by Christ in the Incarnation: "Who, though he was in the form of God, did not deem equality with God something to be grasped. Rather, he emptied himself, taking the form of a slave" (Phil. 2:6-7). This contrasts with Adam, who wanted to be "like God" (the temptation). Thus, Jesus models for us the right relationship with God (dependent through self-emptying).

Koinonia

Christian fellowship or communion or joint participation with God or, more commonly, with fellow Christians.

Knowledge from Above

Divine wisdom (grace) granted to those who seek it appropriately, namely a fervent desire for God alone, to which God responds with his grace. Appropriate spiritual guidance is required for someone to cultivate the appropriate receptivity to this divine grace. Also referred to herein as "wisdom from above." See also "*synergeia*."

Kollyvades

A movement that began in the second half of the 18th century among monastics on Mount Athos as a reaction against the secular influences of the European Enlightenment, whereby people had begun to turn away from God to secular philosophical systems for addressing issues. This was a spiritual renewal emphasizing Patristic theology, liturgical life, and frequent reception of communion. Certain Kollyvades Fathers were responsible for compiling the *Philokalia*.

Lectio Divina

Latin for "Divine Reading." A traditional Benedictine practice of scriptural reading, meditation, and prayer intended to promote communion with God and to increase the knowledge of God's Word. It does not treat Scripture as texts to be studied but as the Living Word. Traditionally, Lectio Divina has four steps: read; mediate; pray; and contemplate. First, a passage of Scripture is read, then its meaning reflected upon. This is followed by prayer and contemplation on the Word of God. The focus of this practice is not a theological analysis of biblical passages but viewing them with Christ as their key meaning. Accordingly, this illustrates how Sacred Scripture can be a means of an encounter with the Divine.

Levels of Prayer

Participation or depth of encounter, also noting the difference between beginners and experienced practitioners. In the Christian East, these levels are referred to as *praxis*, *theoria*, and *kathara proseuche*, or pure prayer. In Western spirituality, comparable levels are defined: purgative, illuminative, and unitive. In both cases, the highest level of participation (pure or unitive prayer) involves an experience of union with God and is granted only by God to practitioners based on their efforts. Those who have achieved this highest level of prayer are often called mystics.

Lex orandi, lex credendi

Latin, loosely meaning "the law of prayer is the law of believing." The thought that handed-down Tradition, such as liturgy, points to the beliefs held by the earliest disciples, showing us their beliefs and theology. It is an explanation of the importance placed on Tradition as a source of divine inspiration, drawing on how people lived their beliefs.

Likeness of God

Image of God's fulfillment, our ability to become who God wants us to be, achieving our possibilities, bringing us to our purpose: eternal blessedness, living in union with him—nothing less. We may choose not to seek to achieve our possibilities, but the Image of God can never be taken from us. The likeness, on the other hand, is achieved through struggle, purification, and divine-human collaboration (*synergeia*).

Listlessness

A lack of energy, drive, or purpose. In the absence of hope, many drift through life without a sense of purpose or meaning. The Good News of the Gospel is that humanity does have a purpose; we are created in the image of God to share eternal blessedness with him. God alone can fulfill our deepest longing.

Liturgy

"Work of the people," from the Greek *liturgeia*. Eastern Christian Eucharistic worship is called the Divine Liturgy, reflecting heaven and earth coming together in worship.

Logismoi

See "Distractions."

Logos

Greek for "Word." Jesus is referred to as the Word of God. Through Jesus, God reveals himself as the self-communicating God (see "Giver as gift"). In previous salvation history, God spoke to humanity through intermediaries such as the prophets or angels. In the present age, he spoke to us through his Son (see Heb. 1:1-2).

Longing

A desire in every human heart that aspires to something more. Every person has a desire for happiness and fulfillment, to love and be loved. Longing is a spiritual void created by God in the human person so that he alone can fill it with his love. Trying to fill that longing with finite things creates temporary fulfillment that, once it passes, often results in dissatisfaction and frustration. As part of the spiritual journey, we come to an increased realization that our longing is truly for the divine presence and that we can only be who we were created to be through him. He alone can fill our deepest longing.

Longsuffering

A long and patient endurance of injury, trouble, or provocation. More than simply perseverance, especially considering the example of Jesus, his extreme humility and self-surrender, especially during his passion.

Love (*Agapé*)

The highest form of love, charity; the love of God for man and of man for God. This is contrasted to *eros* or romantic love, *philia*, which is love as a bond of friendship, and *storgē*, which is love as a bond of empathy.

Martyr

From the Greek *mártys*, meaning "witness." The Church describes two types of martyrdom. Red martyrdom refers to those who voluntarily suffer and give their lives for their faith. White martyrdom refers to those who sacrifice through ascetical practices, such as hermits and early monks of the Egyptian desert, bearing witness to their faith by how they live.

Mass

From the Latin *missio* meaning "to be sent" or "mission." The Roman Church uses the term Mass for its Eucharistic worship.

Meditation

A form of prayer in which a structured attempt is made to become aware of and reflect upon the revelations of God.

Metanoia

True change of heart; conversion. Change in one's way of life resulting from penitence or spiritual conversion. Consider the example of Zacchaeus who, through his encounter with Jesus, said he would make four-fold restitution to all he had defrauded and give rest of his wealth to the poor (See Luke 19:1–10). See also "Conversion." Such change is brought about in the human heart by divine grace.[1060] (See "*synergeia*.")

Modernity

Also referred to as the Modern Age, which began with the Enlightenment. Central to Modernity is emancipation from religion, specifically the dominance of Roman Catholicism, and consequent secularization. Began with Descartes' methodic doubt, which transformed the concept of truth in which the guarantor is no longer God or the Church, but Man's subjective judgment. The modern person is one formed by the principles of modernity, which entails less focus on God as the center of one's life and diminished emphasis on a divinely intended purpose.

Mortification

Actions taken to subdue one's bodily or carnal desires. We seek to overcome the passions through our acts of penance, repentance, detachment, withdrawal from the world, and other means of self-denial.

Mountaintop Experience

An intense spiritual experience. These are infrequent and granted by God as gifts based on the needs of the individual.

Mount Athos

A mountain and peninsula in Greece, epicenter of Eastern Orthodox monastic spirituality. Location of 20 significant monasteries under the direct jurisdiction of the Ecumenical Patriarch of Constantinople. The term "Athonite" refers to Mount Athos (e.g., an Athonite monk).

Mourning our Sinfulness

See "*penthos*."

1060 See St. Theophan, The Path to Salvation, 87.

Mystagogia

From the Greek meaning "learning about the mysteries," to become rooted in the mysteries. In the Roman Catholic tradition, this is the final period of formation once a person has been initiated and received into the Church.

Mystic

One who has had an experience of the Divine, having an awareness of the presence of God. The adjective is "mystical." As Rahner wrote, "The devout Christian of the future will either be a 'mystic,' one who has 'experienced' something, or he [she] will cease to be anything at all."

Mysticism

Becoming one with God; mystical union or direct communion with God. This occurs when one achieves pure prayer or unitive prayer. Not all will achieve this height of prayer because it is a gift granted by God commensurate with one's efforts.

Natural Law

A body of unchanging moral principles regarded as a basis for all human conduct. A person can know the good based on these principles. Arguably, this ability reflects how the human person is made in the divine image. However, because of human weakness (fallen human nature), a person's ability to discern absolute good is distorted (human lens versus divine) and, thus, requires divine collaboration (*synergeia*) and appropriate direction from an unerring spiritual guide for proper discernment. See also "Renewed Human Nature."

Nature

The basic, real, and invariable nature of a thing or its significant individual feature or features. Humanity's union with God is a union of two distinct natures (human and divine).

Neo-Scholasticism

Revival of Scholasticism in the mid-19th century (~1840). See "Scholasticism."

Nepsis

Sober vigilance and spiritual attentiveness. Sobriety. As a person draws closer to God, it is important to remain vigilant for assaults from the Evil One, which often can be a subtle attempt to intervene in our relationship with God. Also called "sobriety" by the Holy Fathers, loss of which leads to forgetfulness, loss of zeal, and complacency. Without sobriety, temptations and evil suggestions approach the door of the heart and, finding it unguarded, enter and bring a swarm of unclean thoughts that darken the mind and heart. "To keep silence as you should and to be sober in your heart, let the Jesus Prayer cleave to your breath—and in a few days you will see it in practice."[1061]

Nestorianism

An influential heresy that undermined the unity of Christ's divine and human natures at the Incarnation. Associated with the teachings of Nestorius (386-451), Patriarch of Constantinople, advocates proposed two separate natures in Christ versus a union of natures. This was condemned by the Council of Chalcedon in 451.

New Evangelization

Term first used by Pope John Paul II in his Apostolic Letter, Novo Millennio Ineunte (2001). It is an invitation for all Catholics to renew their relationship with Jesus Christ and his Church, for each person to deepen his or her faith, have confidence in the Gospel, and possess a willingness to share the Gospel. It begins with a personal encounter with Jesus. In turn, renewed by our encounter, we are called to reach out to the baptized who have fallen away from Church. Pope Benedict XVI clarified that the New Evangelization is not new in content, but in its inner thrust and methods to confront the cultural crisis created by secularization.

Nones

Those who are religiously unaffiliated. In questionnaires when

1061 Hesychius of Jerusalem, "Texts on Sobriety and Prayer," Writings from the Philokalia on Prayer of the Heart, trans. E. Kadloubovsky and G.E.H. Palmer (London: Faber and Faber, 1992), 316.

asked regarding religious preference, they would indicate "none" versus "Catholic" or "Christian." This demographic has been significantly increasing in recent years. See also "Apatheism."

Nouvelle Théologie

French for "new theology." See "*ressourcement.*"

Nous

Equated to intellect or intelligence; the rational mind; the rational part of the soul. In hesychast prayer, practitioners place the nous into the heart to avoid distractions and achieve stillness. This is the reason the prayer practice is also called "Prayer of the Heart." Noetic is the adjective and sometimes this method of prayer is called noetic prayer.

Operations of God

God acting within his creation in which he reveals himself to us. Theologian Dumitru Stăniloae called these "new acts that guide creation" for "the needs we have at each moment."[1062] Through his operations, we experience God and infer something about God, such as his divine attributes. See also "Divine Presence" and "Energies."

Passions

Sinful habits or demons that try to prevent us from cultivating the God-like virtues that will lead us to eternal blessedness. These include pride, lust, anger, greed, unfaithfulness, envy, sloth, ingratitude, and indifference. We are inclined to the passions because of our fallen nature. In our spiritual journey, we struggle to conquer these passions (see "Unseen Warfare"). We cannot overcome these on our own, many of which are deeply ingrained in our human nature. Rather, this requires human-divine collaboration (*synergeia*).

Patriarchate

One of the five major Churches in the Early Church. There were four

1062 See Stăniloae, "Revelation and Knowledge of the Triune God," 126. "Through his attributes God makes something of his being evident to us, but this something is made specific within one vast and uninterrupted symphony of continually new acts that guide creation and each element of it separately towards the final goal of union with him."

major Churches in the East: Constantinople, Alexandria, Antioch, and Jerusalem. In each, the archbishop was titled "Patriarch." The major Church in the West is Rome; its Patriarch is the Pope of Rome. Liturgical traditions are typically based on the Patriarchate from which was received: Byzantine from traditions coming from Constantinople; Antiochene from traditions coming from Antioch, etc. Subsequently, other Eastern Orthodox patriarchates were added, such as Moscow and All Russia, Romania, Bulgaria, Serbia. However, in our discussions herein, we refer to the original five major Churches.

Patristic Period

Period of the Early Church, beginning with the end of the Apostolic Age (death of the last apostle, ca 100) and generally accepted to have ended about 800. Period during which the first seven Ecumenical Councils were held, and major doctrinal decisions were made (e.g., Christology, the Trinity, the Nicaea-Constantinople Creed).

Patristics

Reference to Early Church Fathers, both Latin and Greek, and their writings. Through a movement leading up to the Second Vatican Council, the concept of *ressourcement*, a return to the sources, means a return to the teachings of Sacred Scripture and the Church Fathers. Also refers to studies of such writings.

Pelagianism

Heresy in the Early Church, named after the British monk Pelagius (354-420), who taught that humanity could choose the good and achieve salvation through individual efforts and, most notably, without divine assistance.

Penthos

Mourning our sinfulness ("Spare your people, O Lord"). Also called compunction, and an important part of repentance as a state of mind. Some Greek Fathers also describe the gift of tears associated with such mourning, a reflection of unworthiness, and a desire for the mercy of God. This also helps to cultivate the virtue of humility.

Personal Holiness

See "Universal Call to Holiness."

Philokalic

Related to the *Philokalia*. Philokalic Fathers refer to Holy Fathers whose writings are included in the *Philokalia*. Philokalic renewal references the spiritual renewal influenced by the publication of the *Philokalia* in the 18th century.

Pigpen

Where the Prodigal Son found himself at his lowest point after pursuing the sensual way of the world. It is an analogy for the despair in which we can find ourselves after being left empty by believing in and following the broken promises made by secular society.

Pneumatology

Study of the biblical doctrine of the Holy Spirit. From the Greek *pneuma*, meaning "spirit." Related to this is being a pneumatized (spiritualized) person such as Jesus was through his Ascension, which is analogous to the divinization (deification) of the human person.

Prayer

Spending time with God, entering more deeply into a relationship with him. While there are many forms of prayer, our primary focus herein has been on contemplation and *hesychia* (hesychast prayer/Jesus Prayer). Other types of prayer include liturgical prayer and recitation of the Divine Office. Prayer is considered a penitential practice in returning to God, rending our hearts, and acknowledging our sinfulness. Through prayer, we establish a right-ordered relationship with our Creator.

Praxis

The process by which a theory, lesson, or skill is enacted, practiced, embodied, or realized. This occurs in the spiritual life as we live in conformity with Christ, adopting his teachings and the lessons he modeled and reinforced through prayer. Like any skill we desire to perfect, we must continually practice and remain steadfast in our efforts. Thus, our vocation to holiness is brought to life.

In the hesychast tradition, the first level of participation in prayer. It involves the active struggle through ascetical practices, living the virtues, and other spiritual practices such as repentance and mourning our sinfulness (*penthos*) to achieve personal purification. This is the foundation for further levels of participation in prayer. *Praxis* can lead to *theoria*.

Preferential Option for the Poor

A Principle of Catholic Social Teaching. We are asked to be concerned about the most vulnerable of our society. A basic moral test for society is to examine how well these members are faring. This reflects the compassion of God toward the anawim (see above) and Jesus's reinforcement of this in his teachings on love for neighbor, which includes strangers and all who are in need.

Prelest

See "Spiritual Delusion."

Pure Prayer

Highest level of participation in the hesychast prayer tradition, a union with God in peace, love, and joy. This is a gift from God not given to all. Those who have achieved this level of participation describe intense feelings and an experience of light. St. Gregory Palamas teaches this as an experience of Tabor Light (light experienced by the apostles at the Transfiguration of Jesus on Mount Tabor).

Purification

To purify, refine, and be set free from any impurities that could contaminate our lives. Akin to how gold is refined by fire, increasingly removing impurities, and becoming more valuable. The same is true in pursuing our vocation to holiness. This is indicative of our incremental journey of transformation, preparing ourselves for eternal blessedness (union with God, sharing in the life of the Holy Trinity). See also "Conversion," "Deification,"

"Divinization," "*Metanoia*," "Sanctification," "*Theosis*," and "Transformation."

Radiance

Related to spiritualization whereby the human person reflects the Glory of God. Jesus's Transfiguration on Mount Tabor best illustrate this. The bright light and transformation of Jesus provide a hint of the glory of heaven.

Rationalism

A belief or theory that opinions and actions should be based on reason and knowledge rather than on religious belief or emotional response. A movement away from God spawned by the Enlightenment.

Real Presence

Christian doctrine shared by Catholics and Eastern Orthodox that Jesus Christ is truly present in the Eucharist, body and blood, soul and divinity, not merely symbolically or metaphorically, but in a real, true, and substantial way.

Relativism

Belief that there is no absolute truth such as expressed by Christianity. Popular perspective present in today's society.

Recollection

Recollection means attention to the presence of God in one's soul, thus withdrawing the mind from external and earthly affairs to attend to God and divine things. It is the same as interior solitude in which the soul is alone with God. This should give one pause to stop, steering away from past sinful habits and not desiring to repeat them.

Religious Pluralism

Belief that there is more than one path to holy and ethical living. Popular perspective in today's society, which stands in opposition to the Christian faith.

Remembrance of Death

To regularly recall the inevitability of our death, wherein at some point we will stand before the fearsome judgment seat of Christ.

Through this reflection, we appreciate the need for our salvation, which increases reverential fear of God (humility) and realization that our own merits are bankrupt. We begin to appreciate better our need for divine mercy. The Jesus Prayer and remembrance of death converge. From the prayer comes a vivid remembrance of death, as if it were a foretaste of it, and from this foretaste of death, the prayer itself flares up more urgently.

One example is the Prayer of St. John of Damascus, which begins:

> O Lord, Lover of Mankind, is this bed to be my coffin or will you enlighten my wretched soul with another day? Here the coffin lies before me, and here death confronts me. I fear, O Lord, your judgment and the endless torments; yet I cease not to do evil ...[1063]

Remembrance of God

Essentially, a constant presence to God, as he is to us. We do not take God for granted or lose sight of him. In the hesychast prayer tradition, this often is accomplished through the regular invocation of the Jesus Prayer. St. Ignatius Brianchaninov wrote, "The benefit of remembrance of God is unquantifiable."[1064]

Renewed Human Nature

The condition of human beings restored to their original nature, filled with the grace of God, as intended by God before the Fall. This renewed human nature is gained by Baptism; thereafter, we strive to maintain this renewed human nature through our spiritual labors, including repentance. We strive to achieve the "likeness of God" (theosis). This renewed human nature gives us the possibility of salvation. See "Fallen Human Nature" and "Likeness of God."

Repentance

Includes the Holy Mystery of Repentance (Sacrament of Confession) and our interior disposition of mourning our sinfulness, realizing our need for God and salvation. Jesus began his ministry with the

1063 Publicans Prayer Book, 3rd ed. (Boston, MA: Sophia Press, 2017), 89-90.
1064 Brianchaninov, 161.

message: "Repent, for the kingdom of heaven is at hand" (Matt. 4:17). Accordingly, when we discuss the Jesus Prayer, part of the praxis is to develop a penitential mindset, recognizing the reality that we are sinners and in need of God's mercy.

Ressourcement

French for a "return to the sources." Leading up to the Second Vatican Council, a school of thought focused on renewed interest in biblical exegesis, mysticism, and Patristics. *Nouvelle Théologie* (New Theology) was a movement led primarily by French and German theologians. It was a return to the basics, a strong counterpoint to the dominant dogmatic theology of the day. This return to the sources had a significant influence on the Council. See "Patristics."

Rule of Prayer

The outline of our daily prayer routine—a structured rule that is practiced each day. It should specify a time, generally morning and evening, and, if possible, a place for prayer. As with any skill, prayer is something that should be practiced regularly.

Sacraments

Term used by the Western Church from the Latin *sacramentum*, meaning "sign of the sacred." The Sacraments are considered to have a visible and invisible reality—a reality open to the human senses (visible) but grasped in its God-given depths with the eyes of faith (invisible).

Salvation

The goal of Christianity and the purpose of the Church, allowing us to know and love Jesus Christ to share eternal blessedness with God in heaven. Having our likenesses restored to their original nobility, human person strives to follow the example of Jesus, to become more Christ-centric, to achieve this goal. Striving occurs through incremental efforts (see "*Theosis*"), which is how a person is divinized (see "Divinization") in preparation for his or her destiny: union with God. Salvation cannot be achieved through individual efforts but requires human-divine collaboration (*synergeia*).

Sanctification

To make holy, to purify, or to free from sin. In pursuing a vocation to holiness, we are sanctifying our lives to prepare for eternal blessedness. It is a deliberate choice, saying "yes" to Christ, and an ongoing process of purification. See also "*Theosis*."

Scholasticism

A shift from monasteries as a base for theological development to a more academic approach centered in key universities in Europe. Much of this approach was based on Aristotelian philosophy. This gave rise to dogmatic theology within the Church, influencing both Catholic theology and philosophy. Dogmatic theology was the dominant theology taught in seminaries and universities leading up to the Second Vatican Council. The primary drawback was it could create a greater focus on an intellectual knowledge of theology versus experiential knowledge (spirituality). "If you are a theologian, you will pray truly. And if you pray truly, you are a theologian." This axiom places emphasis on experiential knowledge and is reflective of the theological approach during the Patristic Period. Accordingly, ressourcement advocated a counterpoint to the predominant scholastic theology of the time. Theology and spirituality are dialectics, wherein one cannot be overemphasized over the other.

Second Vatican Council

See "Vatican II."

Secular Humanism

See "Humanism."

Secularism

Humanistic values that allow a life of ethical integrity without faith. In other words, faith is not necessary for one to live a good life. A popular perspective in society today, it opposes the Christian faith.

Secularization

Building one's personal life and the life of society without reference to God or religious values. It is not atheistic, per se, but more indifferent to the presence of God and the need to order one's life with a focus on eternity. A consequence of secularization is a move toward individualism.

Self-Activating Prayer

When the Jesus Prayer has become so internalized that the heart begins to pray the words on its own, even in one's sleep. This is a high-level of participation in the Prayer and a gift granted by God.

Self-Communication

Reference to God who is constantly seeking humanity and striving for a relationship. God reveals himself to us; he initiates the relationship and is constantly present. Related to the idea of "Giver as gift"— God gives himself to humanity through his Son Jesus. It is not about God speaking, but about God revealing himself and desiring to enter into a relationship with us.

Self-Surrender

Same as self-denial. We freely choose to surrender our own will (self-will) to the Divine will. Jesus says to be his disciple, one must deny himself, take up his cross daily, and follow him (Cf. Luke 9:23). See also "*Kenosis*."

Septuagint

Refers to the Greek translation of the Hebrew Scriptures by Jewish scholars living outside Palestine (in Alexandria) that contained a larger canon in terms of the Writings. Initially, living in a Greek-speaking world, Christians used this version of the Old Testament as their source. This translation is sometimes referred to as LXX.

Sinful Nature

Human nature's inclination toward sin because of the Fall (sin of Adam and Eve). See "Fallen Nature."

Skete

A monastic community in Eastern Christianity that allows relative isolation for the monks but also allows communal services and the safety of shared resources.

Sobor Vigilance

Spiritual attentiveness. Also referred to as "sobriety." See "*Nepsis*" and "Watchfulness."

Sobornost

Term that evolved during the Russian Spiritual Renaissance in the 1800s, it emphasizes the cooperation of people over individualism. The image used to illustrate this concept is the parish church in the middle of the village, drawing all people together and helping to provide for the needs of all, first being the spiritual needs.

Sobriety

See "*Nepsis*."

Sola Scriptura

From the Latin, "Scripture alone." This summarizes the belief of many Protestant Reformers that Scripture alone was the source of Divine Revelation. Many, however, did believe that Tradition could be confirmatory of Scripture, but did not recognize it as a source of revelation.

Solidarity

A Principle of Catholic Social Teaching. We are all members of the Body of Christ and individually responsible for one another. (See Rom. 12:5.)

Soteriology

The doctrine of salvation through Jesus Christ. From the Greek *sōtēr*, meaning "Savior."

Spiritual Accompaniment

Joining as a community of pilgrims on our journey to draw closer to God. As Pope Francis wrote that we support one another, "removing our sandals before others in humility," walking with each other "in a steady and reassuring manner, reflecting our closeness and a compassionate gaze which heals, liberates, and encourages our growth in the Christian life" (*Evangelii Gaudium*, no. 169). Spiritual accompaniment is important because as pilgrims on a journey, we are no longer orphaned, helpless, and homeless. We are not drifters, because communally we have a sense of direction with the desire to draw closer to God.

Spiritual Delusion

Disordered perceptions about personal sanctity or progress on the spiritual journey. This is the result of pride or vainglory that can encroach upon the person or belief that personal exertion can achieve progress. It can also manifest itself as complacency ("I am doing well enough compared to others"), which is also a form of pride. It is a loss of humility and a loss of the sense of dependency on God. At all points along the spiritual journey, the pilgrim must remain completely dependent on God (*synergeia*).

Spiritual Direction

The practice of accompanying people as they attempt to deepen their relationship with the Divine, or to grow in their own personal holiness. The companion (or spiritual director) accompanies the directee and is generally a Spiritual Father or Mother, often a priest, monk, or nun. See also "Elder" and "*Staretz*."

Spiritual Warfare

See "Unseen Warfare."

Spirituality

Involves the recognition of a feeling or sense or belief that there is something greater than oneself, something more to being human than sensory experience. Herein, we have considered this the experiential component of theology to be balanced with dogmatic theology. There is a well-known axiom in Eastern Christian spirituality taken from the writings of Evagrius Ponticus: "If you are a theologian you truly pray. If you truly pray you are a theologian." We also refer to this as the spiritual theology of encounter or, simply, spirituality of encounter.

Spiritualization

The transformation or divinization of the human person. See "pneumatology." Because of his spiritualization, the Risen Jesus is no longer visible to human eyes, yet can dwell in human hearts. See also "Radiance."

Stillness

See "*Hesychia*."

Starchestvo

A lineage of spiritual wisdom maintained by an elder (*staretz*). The Greek and Russian monastic traditions have a long unbroken history of elders and disciples, often centered on certain monasteries (Athonite, Optina, Pechersk Lavra, etc.). This was how the hesychast tradition was transmitted from one generation to the next. Some also include within this definition the practice of daily confession of thoughts to one's elder.

Staretz

A spiritual elder from whom people seek spiritual guidance. For example, during the Russian Spiritual Renaissance lay people would come to the monastery for spiritual counsel. An elder may also have disciples who place themselves in obedience to him. See *Starchestvo*.

Struggle

See "Unseen Warfare."

Synergeia

Greek for "synergy," the relationship between Divine grace and human freedom; collaboration with the Divine to achieve one's final destiny. God does not force his grace upon us, but guides and strengthens us when we submit to his will (self-surrender). Jesus said, "No one can come to me unless the Father who sent me draw him, and I will raise him on the last day" (John 6:44). It is about divine initiative and the human response to that initiative.

People cannot achieve salvation without divine assistance. Jesus told us, "Without me, you can do nothing" (John 15:5). Pelagianism was a heresy that taught humanity could achieve salvation through their individual efforts. Pope Francis warned against modern Pelagianism in his apostolic exhortation, *Gaudete et Exsultate*.

Telos

Greek meaning goal or purpose. We should strive for our created purpose, union with God. In the Gospel, Jesus says, "to be perfect as your heavenly Father is perfect" (Matt. 5:48).

Theologia

The study of God, or in this sense, a relationship with God that transcends knowledge. In other words, we learn something about God through our experiences with God. The human provides the desire, making the free-will choice, and God gives the grace so that through this collaboration, our destiny of union with God can be achieved. It is emphasized that this is not an intellectual endeavor, but one based on relationship and experience. A well-known axiom in Eastern Christian spirituality is taken from the writings of Evagrius Ponticus: "If you are a theologian you truly pray. If you truly pray you are a theologian."

Theological Virtues

See "Virtues."

Theoria

The second level of participation in prayer, according to the hesychast tradition. This is contemplation of God, gaining a greater sense of his presence. It is based on establishing the proper foundation through *praxis*. See "*praxis*."

Theosis

Divinization or deification. The ongoing process of transformation or conversion in which we increasingly practice the God-like virtues to prepare for our destiny: union with God. See 2 Pet. 1:4, "[Jesus] has bestowed on us the precious and very great promises, so that through them you may come to share in the divine nature ..." *Theosis* is a process that begins in our temporal life and culminates in the life to come at the Resurrection of the Dead. *Theosis* is the core of the Good News of the Gospel, namely that we are called to share in the very life of God. It is the affirmative response to God, who communicates himself to us.

Theotokos

Greek term meaning "God-bearer." Title of the Blessed Virgin Mary given to her at the Council of Ephesus (431). From this, we derive the term "Mother of God." Note that Mary was declared the *Theotokos* (God-bearer), not *Christotokos* (Christ-bearer), reinforcing the proper understanding of the Incarnation of Jesus Christ who was fully human and fully divine. The term *Theotokos* is often used in Eastern Christian prayers (e.g., "through the prayers of the *Theotokos*, O Savior save us").

Transcendence

The state of going beyond ordinary limits; surpassing; exceeding. Each human person has a desire for something greater, something that derives purpose and meaning.

Transformation

The ongoing process of conversion to achieve our destiny: union with God. See "*Theosis*," "*Metanoia*," and "Conversion."

Transubstantiation

Catholic doctrine regarding Eucharist: the substance of bread and substance of wine are transformed through consecration into the substance of Christ, even though the accidentals such as taste, color, and texture remain the same. See also "Real Presence."

Trisagion

Also known as the "Thrice Holy Hymn." It is a standard hymn or prayer for most Divine Liturgies of the Eastern Churches and included in most of the Divine Hours. The words are: "Holy God, Holy and Mighty, Holy and Immortal, have mercy on us" (said three times with reverential bows each time).

Unbegotten

Without a beginning; eternal. A property of the Father, the First Person of the Trinity.

Uncreated Energies

A term for the operations of God as described in the mystical tradition of the Christian East. Energies deemed "uncreated," contain the essence of God, because if they were created, we would not have a direct experience of the Divine. St. Gregory Palamas differentiated uncreated energies between (1) grace, which is beneficial participation in the "effects" of the uncreated energies, and (2) light, which is experienced by certain mystics who can achieve the highest levels of prayer, a temporal experience of union with God in the present life. In our spiritual journey, we encounter these energies of God, which are how he makes his presence known and provides divine assistance (*synergeia*).

Uncreated Grace

Rahner's term for God's divine assistance to those who are striving to transcend their limitations (finiteness) in order to advance in the spiritual life. It is considered "uncreated" under his concept of "Giver as gift," whereby the gift of grace is the Giver himself (God). It is through our experiences of uncreated grace that we can know something about God.

Union of Distinct Natures

See "Union with God."

Union with God

Our human destiny. See "Eternal Blessedness."

Universal Call to Holiness

The belief that all people, regardless of vocation or status, are called to personal holiness, for we all have the same destiny: union with God. It is based on Jesus's teaching, "So be perfect, just as your Heavenly Father is perfect" (Matt. 5:48). This particular term was described in Second Vatican Council document, "Dogmatic Constitution on the Church" (*Lumen Gentium*), Chapter V, November 21, 1964. "All the faithful of Christ of whatever rank or status, are called to the fullness of the Christian life and to the perfection of charity ..." (No. 40). However, this concept is not new. We see evidence of this call already playing out in everyday life throughout the history of the Church. For example, 200 years before the Vatican II in Russia, lay people, from peasants to nobility, came to such monasteries as Optina or Sarov, seeking spiritual counsel from the monks.

Universal Catholic Church

Reference to the fact that the Catholic Church is in reality a communion of Churches, the Roman Church and 23 Eastern Catholic Churches.

Unseen Warfare

The interior struggles a person has with temptations and passions, as referenced by the Church Fathers and Mothers. Sometimes also called spiritual warfare. Divinization is an ongoing struggle, striving to move from self-centered self-will to self-surrender to the Divine will. Sometimes the battle can be fierce, like the clash of tectonic plates (self-will and divine-will). Sometimes it can be more subtle, as weeds creeping into a well-managed lawn (see Parable of the Weeds among the Wheat, Matt. 13:24-30) — a reminder of the importance of constant vigilance. The Spiritual Fathers and Mothers advise us that this is a lifelong struggle; the demons will exploit any opportunity or weakness to interfere in our relationship with God.

Vainglory

Inordinate pride in oneself or one's achievements; excessive vanity.

Vatican II

The Second Vatican Council, 1962-65, an Ecumenical Council that essentially addressed the relationship between the Church and the modern world. This resulted in major reforms in the Church; however, rather than radical, many of these reforms took the Church back to its earlier roots (a return to the sources). Two major themes dominated the Council. The first was *ressourcement* (see above). The other was *aggiornamento*, a desire for renewal in response to the modern world, or in the words of Pope St. John XXIII, "to open the windows of the Church to let in some fresh air."

Vernacular

Term meaning language of the people. In the Christian East, the liturgical languages eventually transitioned from Greek to the local languages: Old Slavonic, Arabic, Coptic, Armenian, Russian. At Vatican II, the Eastern Patriarchs recommended this for the Roman Church as well. Today, the Mass is celebrated in local languages instead of Latin to increase participation. The first English liturgy in the United States occurred in 1954 by the Ruthenian Greek Catholic Church (now known as the Byzantine Catholic Church).

Vigilance

Constant watchfulness against attacks from the Evil One. See "*Nepsis*."

Virtues

Gifts from God that lead us to live in a closer relationship with him. The three theological virtues (faith, hope, and charity) come from God and lead us to God. These virtues are discussed in 1 Cor. 13:1-13. The four cardinal or moral virtues are prudence, temperance, justice, and fortitude. These are cultivated by the individual based on natural law. See "Natural Law."

Vocation to Holiness

The universal call and invitation by God to eternal blessedness (salvation). People are called to this life and invited by Jesus to follow him, preparing for a lifetime of conversion, struggles (see "Unseen Warfare"), and transformation for our ultimate destiny: eternal blessedness (union with God). See also: "Universal Call to Holiness."

Watchfulness

Term used by some spiritual writers for attentiveness or sober vigilance. See "*Nepsis*."

SUPPLEMENTAL INFORMATION

Pivotal Players

The following individuals are referenced in this work.

Amphilochios of Patmos, Elder

(1889-1970) – Greek Orthodox monk, missionary, and teacher from the island of Patmos, highly revered for his wisdom and experience as a *staretz* (elder).

Antony of Egypt, St.

(251-256) – one of the best known of the Desert Fathers, also called Antony the Great and called "The Father of Monasticism." The monastery founded beneath his cave on Mt. Golzam in Egypt is the oldest Christian monastery in the world. St. Athanasius wrote a biography of St. Antony of Egypt.

Aquinas, St. Thomas

(1225-74) – philosopher, theologian, and Dominican priest. His epic work was the *Summa Theologiae,* considered the pinnacle of scholastic, medieval, and Christian philosophy. Further, the 13th century in which he lived was considered the zenith of the Scholastic Period.

Athanasius of Alexandria, St.

(296-373) – renowned Church Father and theologian, defending the divinity of Christ against Arian teachings. Attended the First Council of Nicaea as a deacon and assistant to Patriarch Alexander of Alexandria, whom he later succeeded. Exiled five times for his uncompromising defense of the doctrine of the divinity of Christ and the Trinity. Among his famous works are *On the Incarnation* and *Life of Antony*, a biography of St. Antony of Egypt.

Augustine of Hippo, St.

(354-430) – bishop, philosopher, theologian, and prolific writer, considered one of the most important Latin Church Fathers. After a dissolute younger life, had a profound conversion experience and was brought into the Church by St. Ambrose of Milan. His *Confessions* describe his spiritual awakening.

Barlaam of Calabria

(1290-1348) – southern Italian scholar, grounded in Aristotelian Scholastic theology, and clergyman who denounced hesychast mystic assertions of being able to experience divine light during prayer. This became known as the Hesychast Controversy, wherein St. Gregory Palamas defended the experience of hesychast mystics.

Barron, Bishop Robert

(1959—). – bishop of the Diocese of Winona-Rochester (Minnesota) and founder of Word on Fire, a Catholic ministerial organization dedicated to catechesis and evangelization.

Bartholomew I, Patriarch

(1941—). – archbishop and Ecumenical Patriarch of Constantinople, since 1991. He is considered *primus inter pares,* first among equals, of the bishops of Eastern Orthodox Churches and spiritual leader of Orthodox Christians. His efforts to promote ecology and the protection of the environment have been widely noted and have earned him the title "The Green Patriarch."

Basil of Caesarea, St. (St. Basil the Great)

(330-379) – bishop and influential theologian who supported the Nicaean Creed. He is considered one of the three Cappadocian Fathers, along with his brother, St. Gregory of Nyssa, and St. Gregory the Theologian (Nazianzus), who did much to develop Trinitarian doctrine.

Bloom, Metropolitan Anthony

(1914-2003) – Russian monk and metropolitan archbishop of the Russian Orthodox Church, founder of the Diocese of Sourozh, the Patriarchate of Moscow's diocese for Great Britain and Ireland. Well known as a pastor, preacher, spiritual director, and writer on prayer and the Christian life.

Bonhoeffer, Dietrich

(1906-1945) – German pastor, theologian, spy, anti-Nazi dissident, and a key founding member of the Confessing Church, a movement within German Protestantism against efforts in Nazi Germany to combine all Protestant Churches into a single unified Pro-Reich Protestant Church. He was accused of being involved in the July 1944 plot to overthrow Adolf Hitler, sentenced, and hanged in April 1945. His writings on Christianity's role in the secular world have become widely influential, and his book, *The Cost of Discipleship*, has become a modern classic.

Brianchaninov, St. Ignatius

(1807-67) – Russian Orthodox monk, bishop, and theologian. Considered one of the greatest Patristic writers of the 19th century. His works are translated into English in three volumes: *The Field: Cultivating Salvation*, *The Refuge: Anchoring the Soul in God*, and *The Arena: Guidelines for Spiritual and Monastic Life*.

Bulgakov, Sergius

(1871-1944) – Russian Orthodox theologian, philosopher, and priest. Expelled from Russia after the 1917 revolution, he was one of the founders of St. Sergius Orthodox Theological Institute in Paris (1925), a premier center of Orthodox theology founded by Russian émigré theologians and priests, including Vladimir Lossky, Myrrha Lot-Borodine, Fr. Georges Florovsky, and Mother Maria Skobtsova. Expelled from Russia at the height of the Russian Spiritual Renaissance, they continued their work in the diaspora, heavily influencing modern Orthodox theologians including Fr.

Dumitru Stăniloae. Bulgakov is quoted in Russian writings on *theosis*, with an overview of his theology included in Andrew Louth's book, *Modern Orthodox Thinkers: From the Philokalia to the Present.*

Bunge, Gabriel

(1940—). – renowned Swiss theologian and Patristics scholar. Formerly a Benedictine monk, he was welcomed into the Russian Orthodox Church in 2010. Bunge joined the Benedictines in the Chevetogne Monastery in Belgium, unique in that it has both a Roman and Byzantine contingent of monks and was originally established by Pope Pius XI in 1924 for the reunion of the Catholic and Eastern Churches, with particular emphasis on the Russian Orthodox Church.

Burrows, Sr. Ruth, OCD

(1923—) – Carmelite nun from Quidenham Monastery in Norfolk, UK. She is the author of several bestselling books, including *Before the Living God, Essence of Prayer,* and *Guidelines for Mystical Prayer.* As a mystic, St. Teresa of Ávila's The Interior Castle highly influenced her.

Cabasilas, Nicholas

(1332-1392) – Byzantine mystic and theologian. His work, *The Life in Christ,* is considered Byzantium's last great flowering of theology. In this work, Cabasilas emphasized sacramental life, including frequent reception of Eucharist, combined with a rich life of prayer and meditation. His other great work is *Commentary on the Divine Liturgy.*

Chaput, Charles J., OFM Cap.

(1945—) – Archbishop Emeritus of Philadelphia, installed in 2011 and retired in 2020. Archbishop of Denver (1997-2011) and Bishop of Rapid City (1988-1997). He is a professed Franciscan Capuchin, and a member of the Prairie Band Potawatomi Nation, the second Native American bishop and first archbishop. A significant portion of his teaching is on evangelization. His books include *Living the Catholic Faith: Rediscovering the Basics* (2001), *Strangers in a Strange Land: Practicing the Catholic Faith in a Post-Christian World* (2017), and *Things Worth Dying For: Thoughts on a Life Worth Living* (2021).

Chesterton, G.K.

(1874-1936) – British writer, poet, philosopher, journalist, dramatist, lay theologian, and orator. Considering himself to be an "orthodox Christian," he eventually converted from High Church Anglicanism to Catholicism (1922). He wrote several works in defense of the Christian faith and is frequently quoted in modern times.

Chrysostom, St. John

(349-407) – prolific homilist and pastoral theologian. Originally from Antioch, he was first an ascetic, later a priest, and then elected as Archbishop of Constantinople in 397. Many of his homilies and writings are available to us today. He is particularly known for his teachings on wealth and poverty. In addition, he is associated with the most-used liturgical form in the Eastern Churches, the Divine Liturgy of St. John Chrysostom.

Ciszek, Fr. Walter J., SJ

(1904-1984) – Jesuit and the first American to graduate from the Russicum, a Catholic college in Rome dedicated to the study of culture and spirituality of Russia aimed at forming missionaries to be sent to that country. Ordained a priest of the Russian Byzantine Rite, he was initially assigned to an Eastern Rite parish in Poland that was overrun by Soviet forces, through which he was transferred to Siberia. Later, he was held in the KGB's infamous Lubyanka prison. He was released after spending 23 years in the Soviet Union, including five years of solitary confinement at Lubyanka and 15 years of hard labor in a Siberian gulag. His book, *He Leadeth Me,* is a spiritual autobiography. His cause for canonization is currently under investigation.

Climacus, St. John

(579-649) – a monk and later abbot of St. Catherine's Monastery on Mt. Sinai. His most notable work is *The Ladder of Divine Ascent,* which describes the ascetical and spiritual practices for raising oneself to God. He describes each practice as one of 30 steps, using the analogy of Jacob's ladder (see Gen. 28:12) for his spiritual teaching and the number of steps being the age of Jesus at his baptism. It is the most-translated book in Christianity behind the Bible and liturgical texts.

Daniel of All Romania, Patriarch (Ciobotea)

(1951—) – Patriarch of the Romanian Orthodox Church, the second-largest Orthodox Church. He became Patriarch in 2007 and tasked with significantly rebuilding the Church after a long, brutal Communist repression that ended in December 1998. He was a theology student under Fr. Dumitru Stăniloae and later, as a monk, a disciple of Elder Cleopa Ilie of Sihastria. He has placed significant emphasis on the renewal of the interior life of the faithful.

Daniélou, Jean Cardinal, SJ

(1905-74) – French Jesuit theologian, well-grounded in Patristics and a member of the *Nouvelle Théologie* movement. His doctoral thesis was on the spiritual doctrine of St. Gregory of Nyssa. He co-founded the *Sources Chrétiennes,* a collection of Patristic texts, and was appointed as a *peritus* (advisor) to the Second Vatican Council.

Day, Dorothy

(1897-1980) – American journalist and social worker. After a bohemian youth, she became a Catholic and co-founder of the Catholic Worker Movement. Establishing "houses of hospitality," she embraced the plight of the poor, unemployed, and marginalized of society. Her cause for canonization is currently under investigation.

Delp, Fr. Alfred, SJ

(1907-45) –German Jesuit priest and philosopher, member of the inner Kreisau Circle resistance group, and a significant figure in Catholic resistance to Nazism. Falsely accused of the July 1944 plot to overthrow Adolf Hitler, he was arrested, sentenced to death, and executed in 1945. Several of his writings, including those from prison, have been handed down.

Desert Fathers

Collectively, men and women who withdrew to the Egyptian and later Palestinian desert, following the example of Jesus. Theirs is an experiential faith based on simple living and from them emerged the hesychast prayer tradition. Several of them were referenced in our various topics:

- Abba Arsenius (c. 350–445)
- Abba Dorotheos of Gaza (505–65)
- Abba Isaiah the Solitary (d. 491)
- St. John Climacus (c.579-649)
- Abba John the Dwarf (c. 339–405)
- Abba Macarius the Great (c. 300-91)
- Abba Moses the Black (or Moses the Ethiopian) (330–405)
- Abba Poemen (d. 450)

Works of these Desert Fathers—except St. Dorotheos of Gaza and St. John Climacus, who were later Desert Fathers—can be found in *The Sayings of the Desert Fathers.*

Dorotheos of Gaza, St.

(c.505-65) – a later Desert Father, he joined the monastery Abba Serid near Gaza through the influence of elders Barsanuphius and John. About 540, he founded his own monastery nearby and became abbot there.

Elizabeth of the Trinity, St.

(1880-1906) – French Carmelite nun, mystic, and spiritual writer. Her writings focused on the indwelling of the Trinity. She died from Addison's disease at the age of twenty-six.

Evagrios the Solitary (Evagrius Ponticus)

(345-399) –Christian monk and ascetic. One of the most influential theologians in the late 14th century church; well-known as a thinker, speaker, and writer. His work, "On Prayer," is included in the *Philokalia*.

Francis, Pope

(1936–) – elected to the papacy on March 13, 2013. Born Jorge Maria Bergoglio in Argentina, he was previously the Cardinal Archbishop of Buenos Aires. He is the first Jesuit Pope. His Apostolic Exhortation, *Evangelii Gaudium* (November 24, 2013), provides an overview of a spiritual theology of encounter.

Frassati, Pier Giorgio

(1901-25) – a lay Dominican, dedicated to social justice issues, born to a wealthy family, but devoted himself to care of the poor. Devoted to daily Mass and the rosary. His parents were shocked when their son had died young of polio and stunned by the throngs of poor people who surrounded their mansion to pay respects. His family had no idea of his work because they disapproved of his involvement with the poor, criticizing him as lazy. Frassati's final act, as he was dying, was to write a letter ensuring someone would take medicine to a sick man who had no one to care for him. He was beatified by Pope John Paul II, who described him as someone who lived the Beatitudes.

Frassati's father was an Italian diplomat to Germany; while living in Berlin, he became acquainted with a family with a son who was so inspired by Frassati's zeal that he became a Jesuit. That young German man was Karl Rahner.

Gafencu, Valeriu

(1921-52) – modern-day Romanian confessor and new martyr of the Communist prisons. He spent his entire adult life in prison, first arrested in 1941, and later interned under the Communist regime. With other prisoners, he dedicated himself to the ascetical life, Philokalic reading, and the Jesus Prayer, contributing to the birth of Philokalic spirituality in Communist prisons (an "Ascetic of Aiud Prison"). Having encouraged fellow prisoners to spiritual purification and renewal through his sacrificial love and constant spiritual struggle, he attained significant spiritual heights. He died in Târgu Ocna, bedridden in a ward for the terminally ill with tuberculosis.

Grădinaru, Fr. Ciprian

(1971—) – popular father-confessor and spiritual father in Romania. He is a monk of Sihastria Monastery and was a disciple of Elder Cleopa Ilie. Requested by Patriarch Daniel to spend time in Bucharest as a confessor, people often spend 12-15 hours in line to confess to him and seek his spiritual counsel.

Gregory of Nyssa, St.

(c. 335–95) – one of the three Cappadocian Fathers who were bishops, including St. Basil the Great (his brother) and St. Gregory the Theologian. He was one of the Early Greek Fathers who first discussed the concept of *theosis* but rarely used the term. He also made significant contributions to the doctrine of the Trinity and Nicaean Creed. In the *ressourcement,* theologians began to consider the perspectives of these Early Church Fathers within their own theological frameworks prior to and leading up to the Second Vatican Council. Thus, one finds similarities between such theologians as St. Gregory of Nyssa of the Early Church and modern theologians such as Karl Rahner, SJ, one of the most influential Catholic theologians of the 20th century.

Hahn, Scott

(1940—) – American Catholic theologian and Christian apologist, formerly a Presbyterian who converted to Catholicism. Known for his research on Early Christianity during the Apostolic Age and various theoretical works concerning the early Church Fathers. Teaches at Franciscan University at Steubenville, Ohio, and runs the Catholic apostolate, the St. Paul Center of Biblical Theology.

Healy, Mary

(1964—) – professor of Sacred Scripture at Sacred Heart Major Seminary in Detroit and a member of the Pontifical Biblical Commission.

Hippolytus of Rome, St.

(170-235) – one of the most important 3rd century theologians in the Church of Rome. Tradition holds that he was a disciple of St. Irenaeus of Lyons, who was a disciple of St. Polycarp, who was disciple of John the Evangelist.

Irenaeus of Lyons, St.

(c. 130–200) – Greek bishop, born in Smyrna, noted for his role in guiding and expanding Christian communities in the southern regions of present-day France and, more widely, development of Christian theology that combatted heresy and defined orthodoxy. His most famous work is *Against Heresies*.

Isaac the Syrian, St.

(640–700) – a later Desert Father, originally from Qatar, he became Bishop of Nineveh (modern-day Baghdad). He is best known for his works on asceticism and is revered by monks, especially those from the Christian East. Elder Joseph, the Hesychast from Mt. Athos, advised that if one could only have a single book, it should be *The Ascetical Homilies of Saint Isaac the Syrian*. Elder Paisios of Mount Athos taught, "You can read just one sentence of Abba Isaac, and it's got enough spiritual vitamins to last for a week or a month." He also called books by Isaac the Syrian "meaty," and he is right. The writings of Abba Isaac are so rich with meaning that they need to be savored in small increments, to be reflected upon, given the depth of meaning contained therein.

Isaiah of Scetis, Abba

(5th century) – Egyptian monk who wrote a diverse anthology of essays for monks called the Asceticon; published in English as the *Ascetic Discourses.*

John of the Cross, St.

(1542-91) –well-known Spanish mystic and member of the Carmelite order. Assisted St. Teresa of Ávila in reforming the order. Two of his best-known works are *The Dark Night of the Soul* and *The Ascent of Mount Carmel.* The former narrates the journey of the soul from its bodily home to union with God. It happens during the night, representing the hardships and difficulties met in detachment from the world and reaching the light of the union with the Creator. The latter is a more systematic study of the ascetical endeavor of a soul looking for perfect union with God and the mystical events happening along the way.

John of Damaskos (Damascene), St.

(676-749) –Syrian monk and priest. In the mid-700s, a controversy arose in the Church regarding the veneration of icons, or sacred images. He wrote his treatises *On the Divine Images* that created a greater understanding of why such images do not constitute idol worship, but represent objects of devotion.

John of Kronstadt, St. (Archpriest John Iliytch Sergieff)

(1829-1908) –Russian Orthodox priest and spiritual director serving St. Andrew's Cathedral in Kronstadt, a naval base and penal colony near St. Petersburg. Living in extreme poverty, he developed a compassionate love of neighbor, evidenced by his numerous acts of social, charitable, and educational work. Yet he was most noted as a man of prayer, continuing in the tradition of the *staretz*. John was a parish priest, not a monk, yet his counsel was sought by all societal classes across Russia. He was a major influence on lay Christians. His spirituality had three important features: (1) daily Eucharist is central, (2) charity is inherent to Christian piety, and (3) the importance of personal prayer. His spiritual diary, *My Life in Christ,* is a classic of contemporary Russian Orthodox spirituality.

John Paul II, Pope St.

(1898-1963) – born Karol Józef Wojtyla in Poland, he served as Cardinal Archbishop of Kraków. Elected to the papacy in 1978, he was the second longest-serving pope in modern history. As part of his special emphasis on the Universal Call to Holiness, he beatified and canonized more than 1,800 people, more than in the preceding five centuries. As an extension of his successful work with youth as a young priest, he pioneered the International World Youth Day gatherings, beginning in Rome in 1985. Pope John Paul II wrote 14 encyclicals, several of which are particularly germane to our discussions. In *Dives et Misericordia* (1980), he stressed divine mercy being the greatest feature of God, needed especially in modern times. In *Veritatis Splendor* (1993), he discussed the dependence of humanity on God ("Without the Creator, the creature disappears"). In *Ut Unum Sint* (1995) he explained that for the Church to achieve its deepest meaning, it needed to breathe again from both lungs, one Eastern and one Western. In *Novo Millennio Ineunte* (2001), he discussed starting afresh with Christ and coined the term, "The New Evangelization."

Joseph the Hesychast, Elder

(1897-1959) – monk and spiritual elder on Mount Athos, widely acclaimed for being the spiritual father or grandfather of numerous elders credited for revitalizing six of the twenty monasteries on Mount Athos. One of his disciples, Elder Ephraim of Philotheou (later Arizona), founded 17 monasteries in North America.

Justin Martyr, St.

(c.100-65) – early Christian apologist and philosopher. Most of his works are lost, but two apologies and a dialogue did survive.

Keating, Thomas, OCSO

(1923-2018) – Trappist monk and one of the founders of Contemplative Outreach. Authored numerous books on Centering Prayer, a method of contemplative prayer popularized by the writings of Thomas Merton and originally described in *The Cloud of Unknowing,* written by an unknown Carthusian monk in Middle English during the latter half of the 14th century.

Kelly, Matthew

(1973—) – modern-day Catholic apologist, motivational speaker, author, and founder of Dynamic Catholic (See www.dynamiccatholic.com). He often discusses the value and positive inspiration of Catholicism on everyday life. Most notable among his many books are *Rediscover Catholicism: A Spiritual Guide to Living with Passion* (2010), *The Four Signs of a Dynamic Catholic* (2013), *Rediscover Jesus* (2015), *Perfectly Yourself* (2017), *Rediscover the Saints* (2019) and *Life is Messy* (2021).

Kolbe, St. Maximilian, OFM Conv.

(1894-1941) – Polish-born Franciscan friar, priest, and missionary to Japan, who promoted veneration of the Immaculate Virgin Mary. He volunteered to die in place of a stranger in the Nazi German death camp of Auschwitz, where he was a prisoner.

Kowalska, St. Faustina

(1905-38) – Polish Roman Catholic nun and mystic. Throughout her life, she reported having locutions of Jesus (Jesus speaking to her). She wrote about this in *The Diary of St. Maria Faustina Kowalska: Divine Mercy in My Soul.* She tells of how she was asked by Jesus through these apparitions to promote devotion to the Divine Mercy. Today in the Roman Catholic Church, the

Sunday after Easter, which is part of the Octave of Easter, is known as Divine Mercy Sunday. This was promulgated by Pope St. John Paul II in 2000, at the time of the canonization of St. Faustina.

Kung Pin-Mei, Cardinal Ignatius

(1901-2000) – Catholic Bishop of Shanghai, China, installed in 1950. He spent 30 years in prison for defying attempts by China's Communist government to control Catholics in the country through the government-approved Chinese Patriotic Catholic Association.

Leo XIII, Pope

(1810-1903) – Pope from 1878 to 1903. In his famous 1891 encyclical *Rerum Novarum*, he outlined workers' rights to a fair wage, safe working conditions, and the formation of trade unions, while affirming the rights of property ownership and free enterprise, opposing both socialism and laissez-faire capitalism.

Lewis, C.S.

(1898-1963) – British novelist, poet, academic, medievalist, literary critic, essayist, lay theologian, broadcaster, lecturer, and Christian apologist. He held academic positions at both Oxford University and Cambridge University. Baptized in the Church of Ireland, he fell away as an adolescent. At age 32, he returned to Anglicanism and considered himself "an ordinary layman in the Church of England." Some of his best-known works are *The Screwtape Letters*, *The Chronicles of Narnia*, and *The Space Trilogy*. *Mere Christianity* was one of his Christian apologetic writings.

Lossky, Vladimir

(1903-58) – Russian Orthodox theologian exiled in Paris and one of the founders of St. Sergius Orthodox Theological Institute. He emphasized *theosis* as the main principle of Eastern Orthodox Christianity. His work, *The Mystical Theology of the Eastern Church*, is considered a classic.

Maximos IV, Patriarch (Sayegh)

(1878-1967) – Patriarch of Antioch and All the East and Alexandria and Jerusalem of the Melkite Greek Catholic Church. He was a key father of the Second Vatican Council, championing greater receptivity to the Eastern tradition of Christianity, which won a great deal of respect from the Eastern Orthodox observers at the Council and the praise of the Ecumenical Patriarch of Constantinople Athenagoras I.

Maximos the Confessor, St.

(c.580-662) – Christian monk, theologian, and scholar from Constantinople. In his theology, he placed a great deal of emphasis on divinization/*theosis*. St. Symeon the New Theologian and St. Gregory Palamas were influenced by Maximos. Some of Maximos's works are in the *Philokalia*.

Nikodimos the Hagiorite, St. (Nicodemos of the Holy Mountain)

(1749-1809) – ascetic monk, mystic, theologian, and philosopher from Mount Athos ("Hagiorite"). Along with St. Makarios of Corinth, he compiled the Greek collection of the *Philokalia*, texts written between the fourth and fifteenth centuries by spiritual masters associated with hesychast prayer. He produced other well-known works, including *The Handbook of Spiritual Counsel* and *Unseen Warfare*, the latter originally developed by Lorenzo Scupoli and then later modified by St. Theophan the Recluse.

Paisios of Mount Athos, St.

(1924-94) – well-known ascetic from Mount Athos respected for his spiritual guidance and austere life. Many people worldwide highly venerate Elder Paisios, especially in Greece, Russia, and Romania. Five volumes of his *Spiritual Counsels* have been translated into English. Unlike many of his Athonite contemporaries, St. Paisios was not a priest, just a simple monk.

Palamas, St. Gregory

(1296-1359) – Byzantine Greek theologian and Eastern Orthodox cleric of the late Byzantine period. Originally a monk on Mount Athos and later the Archbishop of Thessaloniki. Known for defending the Hesychast tradition when controversy arose. Several of his homilies and *Triads* are published in English.

Pannenberg, Wolfhart

(1928-2014) – German theologian who made significant contributions to modern theology, including his concept of history as a form of revelation centered on the Resurrection of Christ. This concept has been widely debated in Protestant and Catholic theology. This focus on the resurrection as the key to Christ's identity stressed the experience of the risen Christ, rather than the empty tomb, in early Church history.

Papacioc, Elder Arsenie

(1914-2011) – influential monk and spiritual father in the Romanian Orthodox Church, a member of the Burning Bush movement that sought a renewal of the hesychast prayer tradition. Imprisoned and sentenced to hard labor by the Communists in 1958 and pardoned in 1964.

Paul of the Cross, St.

(1694-1775) – Catholic mystic and founder of the Passionist order, which places special emphasis on and devotion to the passion of Jesus Christ.

Pennington, Basil, OCSO

(1931-2005) – Trappist monk and one of the founders of Contemplative Outreach, along with Trappist monks Thomas Keating (1923-2018) and William Meninger (1932-2021). Through his writings, Trappist monk Thomas Merton (1915-1968) created renewed interest in Centering Prayer, a contemplative prayer method. The founders of Contemplative Outreach helped bring Merton's prayer technique out of the monastery and made it accessible to others, especially laity. Fr. Pennington also spent seven months living with the monks on Mount Athos—unusual given that most visits are limited to four days or less, particularly for those who are not Eastern Orthodox. From this experience, he compared the contemplative prayer tradition of East and West, which he discussed in a book entitled, *The Monks of Mount Athos: A Western Monk's Extraordinary Spiritual Journey on Eastern Holy Ground.*

Porphyrios of Kavsokalyvia, Elder

(1907-91) – Athonite hieromonk (priest-monk) and spiritual elder known for his gifts of spiritual discernment. He is reflective of the hesychast tradition.

Rahner, Karl, SJ

(1904-84) –German Jesuit priest and theologian considered one of the most influential Roman Catholic theologians of the 20th century. Part of the *Nouvelle Théologie* movement that significantly influenced the Second Vatican Council.

Raya, Archbishop Joseph M.

(1916-2005) – Melkite Greek Catholic archbishop, theologian, author, and civil rights advocate. Served as Metropolitan Archbishop of Akko, Haifa, Nazareth, and All Galilee. Part of the delegation of Patriarch Maximos IV to the Second Vatican Council.

Romanides, John

(1927-2001) – Greek theologian, Eastern Orthodox priest, and scholar who had a distinctive influence on post-war Greek Orthodox theology. Similar to other Greek Orthodox theologians of the 1960s, he advocated a "return to the Fathers." His theological works emphasize the experiential basis of theology, *theoria,* or vision of God, as opposed to a rational or reasoned understanding of theory. He strongly believed that the Frankish-dominated Western Church distorted this spiritual path—a strong personal indictment of spirituality from theology going separate paths with the emergence of Scholasticism.

Sakharov, Archimandrite Sophrony of Essex

(1896-1993) – Russian monk, theologian, and disciple of St. Silouan the Athonite. Born in Russia, he immigrated to Paris in 1922 and studied at the St. Sergius Orthodox Theological Institute. Finding theological studies unfulfilling, he moved to the Monastery of St. Panteleimon at Mount Athos in 1926, becoming a disciple and later biographer of St. Silouan. He stayed at the monastery until 1938, when St. Silouan reposed, and then left the monastery grounds to reside in the Athonite desert, first at Karoulia, then at a cave near St Paul's Monastery. Ordained to the priesthood in 1941, he became a spiritual father to many Athonite monks. In 1947, he left Mount Athos and returned to Paris, where he published his work on St. Silouan. He also continued his studies under Vladimir Lossky. Later, he founded the Patriarchal Stavropegic Monastery of St. John the Baptist in Tolleshunt Knights, Malden, Essex under Metropolitan Anthony (Bloom) of Sourozh. He wrote several works including *We Shall See Him as He Is* (1985) and *On Prayer*, published posthumously.

Sarah, Robert Cardinal

(1945—) – Prefect of the Congregation for Divine Worship and the Discipline of the Sacraments, part of the Roman Curia, until February 2021. Originally from Guinea, Africa, he was Archbishop of Conakry. Made a cardinal in 2010, he held several roles in the Vatican. He wrote three books in conversation with Nicolas Diat: *God or Nothing: A Conversation on Faith* (2015), *The Power of Silence: Against the Dictatorship of Noise* (2017), and *The Day is Now Far Spent* (2019).

Schneiders, Sr. Sandra M., IHM

(1945—) – professor emerita in the Jesuit School of Theology at the

Graduate Theological Union in Berkeley, California. Considered a foremost authority on the study of spirituality.

Seraphim of Sarov, St.

(1759-1833) – generally considered the greatest of the 18th century *staretz* (elders). He extended monastic teachings of contemplation and ascetical practices to lay people who sought his counsel. He taught that the purpose of the Christian life was to acquire the Holy Spirit. His most popular saying to his disciples was "acquire a peaceful spirit, and thousands around you will be saved."

Sheen, Archbishop Fulton

(1895-1979) – American archbishop well-known for his preaching and work on radio and television. Some consider him one of the first televangelists. His teachings were visionary, forewarning in 1947 an end to the American political, economic, and social life based on Christian principles. He cited symptoms such as the break-up of the family, divorce, abortion, immorality, and overall general dishonesty. Sheen urged all to pray: "The forces of evil are united; the forces of good are divided. We may not be able to meet in the same pew—would to God we did—but we can meet on our knees."

Silouan the Athonite, St.

(1866-1939) – Russian-born monk who entered the Russian monastery of St. Panteleimon on Mount Athos. An ardent ascetic, he received the grace of unceasing prayer. After long years of spiritual trial, he acquired great humility and inner stillness. He prayed and wept for the world as for himself and put great value on love for enemies. He was barely literate, yet highly sought by pilgrims for his wise counsel and revered as a spiritual elder (*staretz*). His disciple was Archimandrite Sophrony (Sakharov), who edited his writings.

Stăniloae, Fr. Dumitru

(1903-93) – a Romanian Orthodox priest, professor, and

academician, considered one of the preeminent Orthodox Theologians of the 20th century. His theological framework, *The Experience of God: Orthodox Dogmatic Theology,* is published in English in six volumes. He spent 45 years translating the *Philokalia* into Romanian with significant commentary, now published in 12 volumes. Influenced by Karl Rahner's theological framework and the Patristic Fathers of the Church.

Strickland, Bishop Joseph E.

(1945—) – Bishop of the Diocese of Tyler (Texas), outspoken proponent of the Deposit of Faith, and author of the book *Light and Leaven* (2020).

Symeon the New Theologian, St.

(949-1022) – Byzantine Christian monk and poet. He is recognized as the first Byzantine mystic to freely share his own mystical experiences. Some of his writings are included in the *Philokalia*. He wrote and spoke frequently about the importance of directly experiencing the grace of God, often talking about his own experiences of God as divine light. Outside of the *Philokalia,* his works include *The Discourses,* teachings for his monk when he was abbot of St. Mammas Monastery in Constantinople, and *Hymns of Divine Love*. Of noteworthiness in the Eastern Church, St. Symeon is only one of three saints to be given the designation "Theologian." The other two are St. John the Theologian (St. John the Evangelist) and St. Gregory the Theologian (St. Gregory of Nazianzus).

Teresa of Ávila, St.

(1515-82) –Spanish mystic and nun who reformed the Carmelite order, she was a theologian who wrote on the experiences of contemplative prayer. Her best-known works are *The Interior Castle* and *The Way of Perfection,* which guides those seeking union with God through prayer and contemplation.

Teresa of Calcutta (Kolkata), St.

(1910-97) – known also as Mother Teresa, she an Albanian-born sister who served in India, later creating an apostolate to the poorest and most abandoned through her Missionaries of Charity. She won the Nobel Peace Prize (1979), described by United Nations Secretary General Perez de Cuellar as the most powerful woman in the world, but considered herself simply "a pencil in God's hand." She described her order as "contemplatives in action" because in supporting the work with the poor and marginalized, a deep prayer life was an essential foundation.

Theophan the Recluse, St.

(1815-94) – one of the most prolific and beloved spiritual writers of 19th century Russia. Originally a monk, he was ordained the bishop of Tambov, later resigning this post and living as a recluse. He wrote an average of 30 letters per day. His best-known works in English are *The Path to Salvation, The Spiritual Life,* a series of letters of spiritual counsel, and his adaptation of *Unseen Warfare.* He translated the Slavonic collection of the *Philokalia* into Russian.

Van Thuan, Cardinal Francis Xavier Nguyen

(1928–2002) – named Coadjutor Archbishop of Saigon six days before the city fell to North Vietnamese forces. He was arrested because of his faith and also his family connections, being the nephew of the South Vietnamese President Ngo Dinh Diem. He spent 13 years in a reeducation camp, nine of these in solitary confinement. Despite the efforts of the Communist guards to break him, Van Thuan held firmly to his faith and secretly said Mass daily while in prison. During this time, he also clandestinely sent messages to his parishioners that were later collected and published as *The Road to Hope.* When released from prison in 1989, Van Thuan harbored no bitterness toward his captors, some of whom secretly converted. In 2000, Pope John Paul II asked Van Thuan to lead the Lenten Retreat that Jubilee Year and the Roman Curia. The conferences of this retreat are published in a book entitled, *Testimony of Hope* (Pauline Books & Media, 2000).

Velichkovsky, St. Paisius (St. Paisius of Neamț)

(1722–94) – Eastern Orthodox monk who was on the forefront of a spiritual revival that began on Mount Athos as a counter-response to the European Enlightenment spreading across Europe. Born in Poltava, modern-day Ukraine, he migrated to Romania where he was formed in the hesychast spiritual tradition. He subsequently went to Mount Athos, where he began compiling books of the Holy Fathers for inclusion into the *Philokalia*, having them translated from Greek into Slavonic. He later returned to Romania with his disciples through a request to renew monastic life. He brought the concept of *Starchestvo* to the Slavic lands. "By his translation of the *Philokalia* into Slavonic and through his numerous disciples, Paisius influenced the monks of Russia. All Russian mystics after Paisius may be regarded as his disciples in one way or another. The Russian mystics of Mount Athos, Valaam, Optina, Glynsky, Svensky, and Roslavl depend on Paisius."[1066] He is buried in Neamț Monastery, Romania, where, at the time of his death, he was surrounded by 700 disciples.

Vlachos, Metropolitan Hierotheos of Nafpaktos

(1945-2022) – Greek bishop and theologian. His diocese is the Metropolis of Nafpaktos and Agios Vlasios. A prolific writer, two of his best works include *A Night in the Desert of the Holy Mountain: Discussion with a Hermit on the Jesus Prayer* and *Orthodox Psychotherapy: The Science of the Fathers*.

Ware, Metropolitan Kallistos

(1934—) – English Eastern Orthodox bishop and theologian, directly under the Ecumenical Patriarch of Constantinople. Among

---

1066 Sergius Bolshakoff, *Russian Mystics* (Kalamazoo, MI: Cistercian Publications, 1980), 273.

contemporary Orthodox theologians, he is widely known for his lectures and writings. He was on the team that translated the first four volumes of the Greek *Philokalia* into English.

Zacharou, Archimandrite Zacharias of Essex

(1946—) – Eastern Orthodox monk, born in Cyprus and moved with his parents to England in 1964. Met with Elder Sophrony Sakharov in 1967, joining the Monastery of St. John the Baptist in Essex shortly thereafter. He studied theology at the Orthodox Theological Institute of Saint Sergius in Paris and, between 1996-99, worked on his doctorate at the Aristotle University of Thessaloniki. He is currently the spiritual father of the monastery and has authored several books, passing on the spiritual tradition he received from his fathers.

Bibliography

Aimilianos of Simonopetra, Archimandrite. *The Church at Prayer*. Alhambra, CA: Sebastian Press, 2012.

Al-Kalima, Dar. "The Melkite Church at the Council: Discourses and Memoranda of Patriarch Maximos IV and of the Hierarchs of His Church at the Second Vatican Ecumenical Council." Translated by Bishop Nicholas Samra. Manuscript submitted for publication. Originally published as *L'Eglise Grecque Melkite au Concile*, 1967.

Aleksiev, Archimandrite Seraphim Aleksiev. *The Meaning of Suffering* and *Strife & Reconciliation*. Translated by Ralitsa Doynova. Wildwood, CA: St. Herman Brotherhood/St. Xenia Skete, 1994.

Ambrose of Milan, St. "Exposition of the Gospel of Luke, Homily 7.122." In *Ancient Christian Commentary on Scripture*, vol. III, edited by Arthur A. Just Jr. 208. Downers Grove, IL: Intervarsity Press, 2003.

Anastasios of Sinai. "Sermon on the Transfiguration of Our Lord." In *The Liturgy of the Hours*, vol. 4. 1285-7. New York, NY: Catholic Book Publishing Corp., 1975.

Ascetical Homilies of Saint Isaac the Syrian, The. Translated by Holy Transfiguration Monastery. 2nd rev. ed. Brookline, MA: Holy Transfiguration Monastery, 2011.

Athanasius of Alexandria, St. *On the Incarnation*. Printed by Cliff Lee. Public domain text from CCEL.org. 2017.

Augustine of Hippo, St. *Confessions*. Translated by Henry Chadwick. New York, NY: Oxford University Press, 1998.

Baktis, Peter Anthony. "Orthodox Ecclesiology for the New Millennium," *Pro Ecclesia* 10, no. 3 (Summer 2001): 321–28.

Barclay, William. *The Gospel of Luke*. Louisville, KY: Westminster John Knox Press, 2001.

Barron, Bishop Robert with John L. Allen, Jr. *To Light a Fire on the Earth: Proclaiming the Gospel in a Secular Age*. New York, NY: Image Books, 2017.

Barry, William A., SJ. *Finding God in All Things*. Notre Dame, IN: Ave Maria Press, 1991.

Basil the Great, St. *On Social Justice*. Translated by C. Paul Schroeder. Crestwood, NY: St. Vladimir's Seminary Press, 2009.

Benedict XVI, Pope. *Regina Caeli* Address. May 22, 2011. Rome: Libreria Editrice Vaticana.

Bialas, Martin. *The Mysticism of the Passion in St. Paul of the Cross*. San Francisco, CA: Ignatius Press, 1990.

Bloom, Metropolitan Anthony, and Georges LeFebvre. *Courage to Pray*. Crestwood, NY: St. Vladimir's Seminary Press, 1973.

Bolshakoff, Sergius. *Russian Mystics*. Kalamazoo, MI: Cistercian Publications, 1980.

Bonhoeffer, Dietrich *The Cost of Discipleship*. New York, NY: Simon & Schuster, 1995.

Breck, John. "Prayer of the Heart: Sacrament of the Presence of God," *St. Vladimir's Theological Quarterly* 29, no. 1 (1995): 25–45.

Bretscher, Paul M. "Luke 17:20–21 in Recent Investigations," *Concordia Theological Monthly* 22, no. 12 (1951): 895–907.

Brianchaninov, St. Ignatius. *The Refuge: Anchoring the Soul in God*. Translated by Nicholas Kotar. Jordanville, NY: Holy Trinity Publications, 2019.

Brown, Raymond E. *An Introduction to the New Testament*. New York, NY: Doubleday, 1997.

Bucur, Bogdan G. "Exegesis of Biblical Theophanies in Byzantine Hymnology: Rewritten Bible?" *Theological Studies* 68, no. 1 (Mar. 2007): 92-112.

Bunge, Gabriel, OSB. *Earthen Vessels: The Practice of Personal Prayer According to the Patristic Tradition*. San Francisco, CA: Ignatius Press, 2002.

Burrows, Sr. Ruth, OCD. *Essence of Prayer.* Mahwah, NJ: Paulist Press, 2006.

———. *To Believe in Jesus*. Mahwah, NJ: Paulist Press, 2010.

Cabasilas, Nicholas. *The Life in Christ*. Translated by Carmino J. DeCatanzaro. Crestwood, NY: St. Vladimir's Seminary Press, 1974.

Catechism of the Catholic Church, 2nd ed. Rome: Libreria Editrice Vaticana, 1997.

Catholic News Service. "Young Adults Want to be Heard by the Church, Study Finds." *Texas Catholic Herald*, January 23, 2018.

Chaput, Charles J., OFM Cap. *Living the Catholic Faith: Rediscovering the Basics*. Cincinnati, OH: St. Anthony Messenger Press, 2001.

———. *Strangers in a Strange Land: Practicing the Catholic Faith in a Post-Christian World*. New York, NY: Henry Holt, 2017.

______. *Things Worth Dying For: Thoughts on a Life Worth Living*. New York, NY: Henry Holt, 2021.

Charron, Fr. Jason. Carnegie, PA: Holy Trinity Ukrainian Catholic Church website. http://www. http://htucc.com.

Christensen, Michael J. "The Problem, Promise, and Process of *Theosis*." In *Partakers of the Divine Nature: The History and Development of Deification in the Christian Traditions*. Edited by Michael J. Christensen and Jeffery A. Wittung. 23-31. Grand Rapids, MI: Baker Publishing Group, 2008.

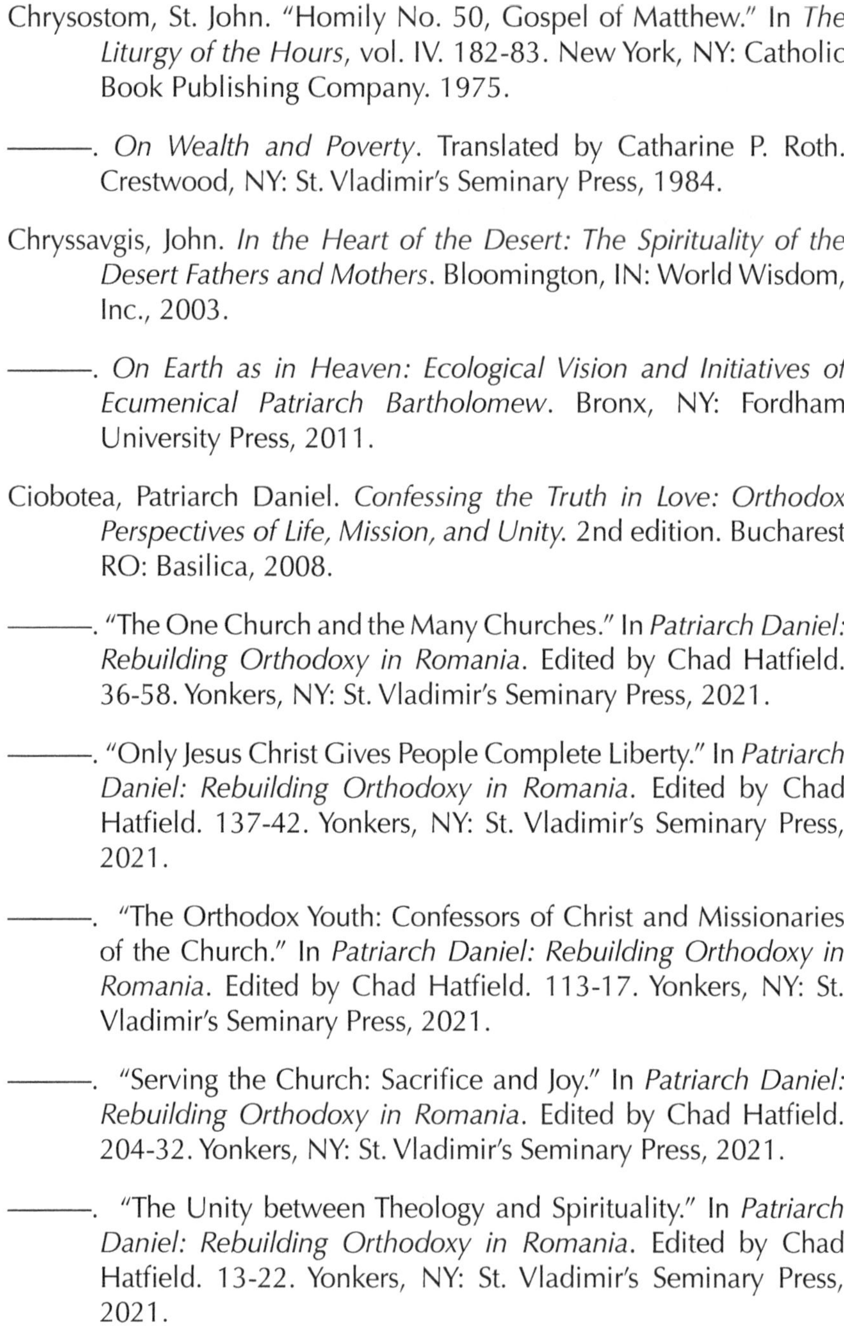

Chrysostom, St. John. "Homily No. 50, Gospel of Matthew." In *The Liturgy of the Hours*, vol. IV. 182-83. New York, NY: Catholic Book Publishing Company. 1975.

———. *On Wealth and Poverty*. Translated by Catharine P. Roth. Crestwood, NY: St. Vladimir's Seminary Press, 1984.

Chryssavgis, John. *In the Heart of the Desert: The Spirituality of the Desert Fathers and Mothers*. Bloomington, IN: World Wisdom, Inc., 2003.

———. *On Earth as in Heaven: Ecological Vision and Initiatives of Ecumenical Patriarch Bartholomew*. Bronx, NY: Fordham University Press, 2011.

Ciobotea, Patriarch Daniel. *Confessing the Truth in Love: Orthodox Perspectives of Life, Mission, and Unity.* 2nd edition. Bucharest RO: Basilica, 2008.

———. "The One Church and the Many Churches." In *Patriarch Daniel: Rebuilding Orthodoxy in Romania*. Edited by Chad Hatfield. 36-58. Yonkers, NY: St. Vladimir's Seminary Press, 2021.

———. "Only Jesus Christ Gives People Complete Liberty." In *Patriarch Daniel: Rebuilding Orthodoxy in Romania*. Edited by Chad Hatfield. 137-42. Yonkers, NY: St. Vladimir's Seminary Press, 2021.

———. "The Orthodox Youth: Confessors of Christ and Missionaries of the Church." In *Patriarch Daniel: Rebuilding Orthodoxy in Romania*. Edited by Chad Hatfield. 113-17. Yonkers, NY: St. Vladimir's Seminary Press, 2021.

———. "Serving the Church: Sacrifice and Joy." In *Patriarch Daniel: Rebuilding Orthodoxy in Romania*. Edited by Chad Hatfield. 204-32. Yonkers, NY: St. Vladimir's Seminary Press, 2021.

———. "The Unity between Theology and Spirituality." In *Patriarch Daniel: Rebuilding Orthodoxy in Romania*. Edited by Chad Hatfield. 13-22. Yonkers, NY: St. Vladimir's Seminary Press, 2021.

———. "Spiritual Life and Theology in Contemporary Orthodoxy: A Short Presentation." In *Patriarch Daniel: Rebuilding Orthodoxy in Romania*. Edited by Chad Hatfield. 23-35. Yonkers, NY: St. Vladimir's Seminary Press, 2021.

———. "The Unity between Theology and Spirituality." In *Patriarch Daniel: Rebuilding Orthodoxy in Romania*. Edited by Chad Hatfield. 13-22. Yonkers, NY: St. Vladimir's Seminary Press, 2021.

———. "The Unity of Faith and Nation is Strengthened in Prayer." In *Patriarch Daniel: Rebuilding Orthodoxy in Romania*. Edited by Chad Hatfield. 103-8. Yonkers, NY: St. Vladimir's Seminary Press, 2021.

Ciszek, Fr. Walter J., SJ, with Daniel Flaherty, SJ, *He Leadeth Me*. San Francisco, CA: Ignatius Press, 1973.

Climacus, St. John. *The Ladder of Divine Ascent*. Translated by Colm Luibheid and Norman Russell. New York, NY: Paulist Press, 1982.

Cole, Casey, OFM. "Saving a Dying, Shrinking Church," *Breaking in the Habit*. YouTube. April 15, 2020.

Colliander, Tito. *Way of the Ascetics*. Translated by Katherine Ferré. Crestwood, NY: St. Vladimir's Seminary Press, 1960.

Coniaris, Anthony M. *Achieving Your Potential in Christ: Theosis*. Minneapolis: Light & Life Publishing Company, 2004.

———. *A Beginner's Introduction to the Philokalia*. Minneapolis, MN: Light & Life Publishing Company, 2016.

———. *Tools for Theosis: Becoming God-like in Christ*. Minneapolis, MN: Light & Life Publishing Company, 2014.

Consiglio, Cyprian. *Prayer in the Cave of the Heart: The Universal Call to Contemplation*. Collegeville, MN: The Liturgical Press, 2010.

Costache, Doru. "Experiencing the Divine Life: Levels of Participation in St. Gregory Palamas's 'On the Divine and Deifying Participation.'" *Phronema* 26, no. 1 (2011): 9–25.

Cunningham, Michael. "Living the Worthy Life: Now More Than Ever We Need Jesus Christ." *Catholic365* (February 5, 2021).

Daniélou, Jean. "The Joy of Angels." *Magnificat* 18, no. 7 (September 2016): 407. Taken from *The Angels and Their Missions*. Translated by David Hermann. Baltimore: The Newman Press, 1957.

Davies, Hieromonk Maximos. "Lenten Mission 2018: Hope." Delivered at St. Sophia Ukrainian Greek Catholic Church, The Colony, Texas, February 23-25, 2018.

Day, Dorothy. *Selected Writings*. Edited by Robert Ellsberg. Maryknoll, NY: Orbis Books, 2005.

Delp, Alfred, SJ. "Unbound." *Magnificat* 18, no. 8 (October 2016): 340–41. Taken from *Prison Writings*. Maryknoll, NY: Orbis Books, 2004.

Diadochos of Photike, St. "On Spiritual Knowledge and Discrimination." In *The Philokalia: The Complete Text*, vol. 1. 253-96. Compiled by St. Nikodimos of the Holy Mountain and St. Makarios of Corinth. Translated by G.E.H. Palmer, P. Sherrard, and K. Ware. London: Faber & Faber, 1979.

Didache: The Teaching of the Twelve Apostles. Translated by R. Joseph Owles. North Charleston, SC: CreateSpace, 2014.

Dinan, Stephen. "Losing Our Religion: America Becoming 'Pagan' as Christianity Cedes to Culture." *Washington Times*, online, December 30, 2019.

Ditewig, William T. "A Spiritual Theology of Encounter." *Deacon Digest* 33, no. 6 (2016): 8–11.

Divine Liturgies of Our Holy Fathers John Chrysostom and Basil the Great, The. Pittsburgh: Byzantine Seminary Press, 2006.

Donahue, John R., and Daniel J. Harrington. *The Gospel of Mark*. In the "Sacra Pagina" series, vol. 2. Collegeville, MN: Liturgical Press, 2002.

Dorotheos of Gaza, St. *Discourses and Sayings*. Translated by Eric P. Wheeler. Kalamazoo, MI: Cistercian Publications, 1977.

Dumitraşcu, Deacon Iulian. "Repentance Must Be a Permanent State for All Christians, Says the Patriarch of Romania." *Basilica News Agency*. Online Edition. February 20, 2022.

Elizabeth of the Trinity. *I Have Found God: Complete Works*, vol. 1. Translated by Sr. Aletheia Kane, OCD. Washington, DC: ICS Publications, 1984.

Enzler, Clarence. *Everyone's Way of the Cross*. Notre Dame, IN: Ave Maria Press, 1986.

Ephraim, Elder. *My Elder Joseph the Hesychast*. Florence, AZ: Saint Anthony's Greek Orthodox Monastery, 2013.

Evagrius Ponticus. *The Praktikos & Chapters on Prayer*. Translated by John Eudes Bamberger, OCSO. Trappist, KY: Cistercian Publications, 1972.

Finch, Jeffrey D. "Neo-Palamism: Divinizing Grace, and the Breach between East and West." In *Partakers of the Divine Nature: The History and Development of Deification in the Christian Traditions*. Edited by Michael J. Christensen and Jeffery A. Wittung. 233-249. Grand Rapids, MI: Baker Publishing Group, 2008.

Finlan, Stephen. "Deification in Jesus' Teaching." In *Theosis: Deification in Christian Doctrine*, vol. 2. Edited by Vladimir Kharlamov. 21-41. Eugene, OR: Pickwick Publications, 2011.

Fischer, Mark F. *The Foundations of Karl Rahner*. New York, NY: The Crossroad Publishing Company, 2016.

Fitzmyer, Joseph A. "The Gospel According to Luke X–XXIV." *The Anchor Bible*, vol. 28a, 1157–63. Garden City, NY: Doubleday & Company, Inc., 1985.

Fowler, James W. *Becoming Adult, Becoming Christian: Adult Development and Christian Faith*. San Francisco, CA: Jossey-Bass Publishers, 2000.

Fowler, Richard J. *Celebration of Discipline: The Path to Spiritual Growth*. New York, NY: Harper One, 1998.

Francis, Pope. *Evangelii Gaudium*. Rome: Libreria Editrice Vaticana, 2013.

———. *Laudato Si'*. Rome: Libreria Editrice Vaticana, 2015.

———. *Misericordiae Vultus*. Rome: Libreria Editrice Vaticana, 2015.

Freeman, Stephen "The Beautiful God," *Glory to God for All Things*. Ancient Faith Ministries, May 25, 2010.

George, Archimandrite. *Theosis: The True Purpose of Human Life*. Mount Athos: Holy Monastery of St. Gregorios, 2006.

Grădinaru, Fr. Ciprian. "Afterword," to Monk Moise's *The Saint of the Prisons: Notes on the Life of Valeriu Gafencu*. Translated by Monk Sava, Oaşa Monastery. 278-94. Triada, 2019.

Gregory of Nyssa, St. "On the Beatitudes." *Ancient Christian Writers: The Works of the Fathers in Translation*, vol. 18, 143–53. Edited by Johannes Quasten and Joseph C. Plumpe. Translated by Hilda C. Graef. New York, NY: Paulist Press, 1954.

Gregory of Sinai, St. "Instruction to Hesychasts," In *Writings from the Philokalia in Prayer of the Heart*, 74-94. Translated by E. Kadloubovsky and G.E.H. Palmer. London: Faber and Faber, 1992.

Hahn, Scott. *First Comes Love*. New York, NY: Doubleday, 2002.

Hahn, Scott, and Brandon McGinley. *It is Right and Just: Why The Future of Civilization Depends on True Religion*. Steubenville, OH: Emmaus Road Publishing, 2020.

Healy, Mary. "Apostolic Intimacy, Apostolic Charity," *Magnificat* 23, no. 8 (2021): 400-01.

———. "Learning from Saint Mark," *Magnificat* 24, no. 1 (2022): 290-2.

Hesychius of Jerusalem, St. "Texts on Sobriety and Prayer for the Saving of the Soul." In *Writings from the Philokalia on Prayer of the Heart*. 279-321. Translated by E. Kadloubovsky and G.E.H. Palmer. London: Faber and Faber, 1992.

Hierotheos of Nafpaktos, Metropolitan. *A Night in the Desert of the Holy Mountain: Discussion with a Hermit on the Jesus Prayer*. Translated by Effie Mavromichali. Levadia, Greece: Birth of the Theotokos Monastery, 2009.

History of Vatican II. vol. 1. Edited by Giuseppe Alberigo. Translated by Joseph A. Komonchak. Maryknoll, NY: Orbis Books, 1996.

Iftimiu, Aurelian. "Archbishop Ioachim on Episcopal Ministry in the 3rd Millennium: Christianity is Just Beginning!" *Basilica News Agency*. Online Edition. February 21, 2022.

———. "Patriarch Daniel Proclaims 2022 Solemn Year of Prayer, Commemorative Year of Hesychast Saints." *Basilica News Agency*. Online Edition. January 1, 2022.

———. "The Year 2022 is an Opportunity to Reflect on the Romanian Hesychasts, Patriarch Daniel Says at Bucharest Clergy Conference." *Basilica News Agency*. Online Edition. June 8, 2022.

Irenaeus of Lyons, St. *Against Heresies*. Public Domain.

———. *Against Heresies*. In *The Liturgy of the Hours*, vol. 1. 337-38. New York, NY: Catholic Book Publishing Co., 1975.

Isaac of Nineveh, St. *On Ascetical Life*. Translated by Mary Hansbury. Crestwood, NY: St. Vladimir's Seminary Press, 1989.

Isaiah of Scetis, Abba. *Ascetic Discourses*. Translated by John Chryssavgis and Pachomios Penkett. Kalamazoo, MI: Cistercian Publications, 2002.

Jakim, Boris. "Sergius Bulgakov: Russian *Theosis*." In *Partakers of the Divine Nature: The History and Development of Deification in the Christian Traditions*. Edited by Michael J. Christensen and Jeffery A. Wittung. 250-58. Grand Rapids, MI: Baker Publishing Group, 2008.

"Jesus is My All: A Novena to Blessed Teresa of Calcutta." Edited by Fr. Brian Kolodiejchuk, MC. San Diego, CA: Mother Teresa Center, 2005.

John XXIII, Pope St. "Homily at the Canonization of St. Martin de Porres." In *The Liturgy of the Hours*, vol. 4. New York, NY: Catholic Book Publishing Co, 1975. 1541-2.

John of Damascus, St. *Three Treatises on the Divine Images*. 1st edition. Translated by Andrew Louth. Crestwood, NY: St. Vladimir's Seminary Press, 2003.

John of Kronstadt, St. *Ten Homilies on the Beatitudes*. Translated by Nadieszda Kizenko-Frugier. Albany, NY: Corner Editions/La Pierre Angulaire, 2003.

John Paul II, Pope St. *Crossing the Threshold of Hope*. New York, NY: Alfred A. Knopf Publishing Company, 1995.

———. "Eastern Theology has enriched the Whole Church." Angelus address. Aug. 11, 1996. Rome: *L'Osservatore Romano*, 1996.

———. Homily. Puebla de Los Angeles. Jan. 28, 1979. Rome: Libreria Editrice Vaticana.

———. *Novo Millennio Ineunte*. Rome: Libreria Editrice Vaticana, 2001.

———. *Ut Unum Sint*. Rome: Libreria Editrice Vaticana, 1995.

Johnson, Elizabeth A. *Quest for the Living God: Mapping Frontiers in the Theology of God*. New York, NY: The Continuum International Publishing Group, Inc., 2007.

Johnson, Luke Timothy. *The Gospel of Luke*. "Sacra Pagina" series, vol. 3. Collegeville, MN: Liturgical Press, 1991.

Justin Martyr, St. *First Apology*. Chap. 65. Public domain.

Kaisch, Ken. *Finding God: A Handbook of Christian Meditation*. New York, NY: Paulist Press, 1994.

Kariatlis, Philip. "Affirming Koinonia Ecclesiology: An Orthodox Perspective." *Phronema* 27, no. 1 (2012): 51–65.

Kärkkäinen, Veli-Matti. *An Introduction to Ecclesiology: Ecumenical, Historical and Global Perspectives*. Downers Grove, IL: InterVarsity Press, 2002.

Keating, Thomas, OCSO. *Intimacy with God*. New York, NY: The Crossroad Publishing Company, 2002.

Kelly, Matthew. *Life is Messy*. North Palm Beach, FL: Blue Sparrow Publishing, 2021.

———. *Perfectly Yourself*, 3rd ed. North Palm Beach, FL: Beacon Publishing, 2017.

———. *Rediscover Jesus*. Ellicott City, MD: Beacon Publishing, 2015.

———. *Rediscover the Saints*. Assam, India: Blue Sparrow Books, 2019.

Kerul-Kmec, Fr. Miron. Homily. St. Nicholas Byzantine Catholic Church, Barberton, OH, November 7, 2021.

Kerul-Kmec, Jr., Fr. Miron. Homily. St. John Chrysostom Byzantine Catholic Church, Pittsburgh, PA, November 7, 2021.

Kharlamov, Vladimir. "Emergence of the Deification Theme in the Apostolic Fathers." In *Theosis Deification in Christian Doctrine*. Edited by Stephen Finlan and Vladimir. 51-66. Eugene, OR: Pickwick Publications, 2006.

Kilby, Karen. *Karl Rahner: A Brief Introduction*. New York, NY: The Crossroad Publishing Company, 2007.

Klauser, Theodor. *A Short History of the Western Liturgy*. Translated by John Halliburton. London: Oxford University Press, 1969.

Kleinguetl, Edward. "The Presence of Kingdom of God: An Analysis of Luke 17:20-21." Loyola University Chicago – Institute of Pastoral Studies, IPS 416 – Christian Origins. Rev. Patrick J. Madden, PhD, Instructor. April 12, 2015.

Knoebel, Thomas Louis. "Grace in the Theology of Karl Rahner: A Systematic Presentation." PhD diss., Fordham University, 1980.

Krupa, Steve, SJ. "The World of Jesus: Parties and Sects within Judaism." Lecture notes, Foundations of Christian Spirituality, Loyola University Chicago, Fall 2014.

Laird, Martin, OSA. *Into the Silent Land: A Guide to the Christian Practice of Contemplation*. Oxford University Press, 2006.

Langford, Joseph, MC. *Mother Teresa's Secret Fire: The Encounter that Changed Her Life and How It Can Transform Your Own.* Huntington, IN: Our Sunday Visitor Publishing Division, 2008.

Larchet, Jean-Claude. *The Theology of Illness*. Crestwood, NY: St. Vladimir's Seminary Press, 2002.

Leo the Great, St., Letter 31. In *The Liturgy of the Hours,* vol. 1. 320-21. New York, NY: Catholic Book Publishing Co., 1975.

———. Sermon No. 2, On the Ascension. In *The Liturgy of the Hours,* vol. 2. 937-38. New York, NY: Catholic Book Publishing Co., 1976.

Lewis, C. S. *Mere Christianity*. New York, NY: Harper-Collins, 1952.

Lossky, Vladimir. *In the Image and Likeness of God*. Edited by John H. Erickson and Thomas E. Bird. Crestwood, NY: St. Vladimir's Seminary Press, 1974.

———. *The Mystical Theology of the Eastern Church*. Crestwood, NY: St. Vladimir's Seminary Press, 1998.

———. *Vision of God*. Crestwood, NY: Saint Vladimir's Seminary Press, 1983.

Louth, Andrew. "The Place of *Theosis* in Orthodox Theology." In *Partakers of the Divine Nature: The History and Development of Deification in the Christian Traditions*. Edited by Michael J. Christiansen and Jeffery A. Wittung. 32-44. Grand Rapids, MI: Baker Publishing Group, 2007.

Meier, John P. *A Marginal Jew: Rethinking the Historical Jesus*, vol. 2. New York, NY: Doubleday, 1994.

Maloney, George, SJ. *Prayer of the Heart: The Contemplative Tradition of the Christian East*. Notre Dame, IN: Ave Maria Press, 2008.

Maasburg, Leo. *Mother Teresa of Calcutta: A Personal Portrait*. Translated by Michael J. Miller. San Francisco, CA: Ignatius Press, 2010.

Macarius, St. "Homily 28." In *The Liturgy of the Hours*, vol. 4, 595-6. New York, NY: Catholic Book Publishing Corp., 1975.

McFarland, Alex. *The 10 Most Common Objections to Christianity*. Ventura, CA: Regal Books, 2007.

Meyendorff, John. "Doctrine of Grace in St. Gregory Palamas." *St. Vladimir's Seminary Quarterly* 2, no. 2 (Winter 1954): 17–26.

Moise, Monk. *The Saint of the Prisons: Notes on the Life of Valeriu Gafencu*. Translated by Monk Sava, Oaşa Monastery. Triada, 2019.

Monk of Mount Athos, A. *The Watchful Mind: Teachings on the Prayer of the Heart*. Translated by George Dokos. Yonkers, NY: St. Vladimir's Seminary Press, 2014.

Murray, Gerald E. "Cardinal Sarah and Our Silent Apostasy." *The Catholic Thing*. Online Edition. January 16, 2016.

Nichols, Aidan. *The Shape of Catholic Theology*. Collegeville, MN: The Liturgical Press, 1991.

Nicodemos of the Holy Mountain, St. *A Handbook of Spiritual Counsel*. Translated by Fr. Peter A. Chamberas. New York, NY: Paulist Press, 1989.

Nikodimos the Hagiorite, St. *Concerning Frequent Communion of the Immaculate Mysteries of Christ*. Translated by George Dokos. Thessaloniki, Greece: Uncut Mountain Press, 2006.

Nolan, Albert. *Jesus Before Christianity*. Maryknoll, NY: Orbis Books, 2013.

O'Brien, David J., and Thomas A. Shannon. *Catholic Social Thought: The Documentary Heritage*. Maryknoll, NY: Orbis Books, 2004.

O'Connor, John Cardinal. "The One We Have Looked For," *Magnificat*, 23, no. 10 (2021): 204-5.

Our Thoughts Determine Our Lives: The Life and Teachings of Elder Thaddeus of Vitovnica. Compiled by St Herman of Alaska Brotherhood. Translated by Ana Smiljanic. Platina, CA: St. Herman of Alaska Brotherhood, 2017.

Paisios the Athonite, St. "With Pain and Love for Contemporary Man," *Spiritual Counsels*, vol. 1. Translated by Cornelia A. Tsakiridou and Maria Spanou. Edited by Fr. Peter Chamberas and Eleftheria Kaimakliotis. Souroti, Thessaloniki, Greece: Holy Hesychasterion Evangelist John the Theologian, 2019.

________. "Spiritual Awakening," *Spiritual Counsels*, vol. 2. Translated by Fr. Peter Chamberas. Edited by Anna Famellos and Andronikos Masters. Souroti, Thessaloniki, Greece: Holy Hesychasterion Evangelist John the Theologian, 2016.

________. "Spiritual Struggle," *Spiritual Counsels*, vol. 3. Translated by Peter Chamberas. Edited by Anna Famellos and Andronikos Masters. Souroti, Thessaloniki, Greece: Holy Monastery of Evangelist John the Theologian, 2014.

Palamas, St. Gregory. "Three Texts on Prayer and Purity of Heart." In *The Philokalia: The Complete Text*. vol. IV. Compiled by St. Nikodemos of the Holy Mountain and St. Makarios of Corinth. Translated and edited by G. E. H. Palmer, Philip Sherrard, and Kallistos Ware. 343-45. London: Faber and Faber. 1995.

———. *The Triads*. Translated by Nicholas Gendle. Mahwah, NJ: Paulist Press, 1983.

Paul VI, Pope St. *Apostolicam Actuositatem*. Rome: Libreria Editrice Vaticana, 1965.

Pentin, Edward. "Pope: 'How I Wish for a Church That is Poor and for the Poor!" *National Catholic Register*. Online Edition. March 16, 2013.

Peter of Damaskos, St. "Twenty-Four Discourses." In *The Philokalia: The Complete Text*, vol. 3. 211-81. Compiled by St. Nikodimos of the Holy Mountain and St. Makarios of Corinth. Translated by G.E.H. Palmer, P. Sherrard, and K. Ware. London: Faber & Faber, 1984.

Pilgrim's Tale, The. Translated by T. Allan Smith. New York, NY/ Mahwah, NJ: Paulist Press, 1999.

Pius XII, Pope. *Mediator Dei*. Rome: Libreria Editrice Vaticana, 1947.

Popov, Ivan V. "The Idea of Deification in the Early Eastern Church." In *Theosis: Deification in Christian Doctrine*, vol. 2. Edited by Vladimir Kharlamov. 42-82. Eugene, OR: Pickwick Publications, 2011.

Porphyrios, Elder. *Wound by Love: The Life and Wisdom of Elder Porphyrios*. Edited by Sisters of the Holy Convent of Chrysopigi. Translated by John Raffan. Limni, Evia, Greece: Denise Harvey, 2013.

Pronechen, Joseph. "Archbishop Sheen's Warning of a Crisis in Christendom." *National Catholic Register*. Online Edition. July 29, 2018.

Pseudo-Macarius. *The Fifty Spiritual Homilies and the Great Letter*. Translated and edited by George A. Maloney, SJ. New York, NY: Paulist Press, 1992.

Publicans Prayer Book. 3rd edition. Boston, MA: Sophia Press, 2017.

Rahner, Karl. "Christian Living Formerly and Today." In *Theological Investigations*, vol. 7. 3-24. Translated by David Bourke. New York, NY: Herder and Herder, 1971.

———. *Foundations of Christian Faith: An Introduction to the Idea of Christianity*. Translated by William V. Dych. New York, NY: Crossroad Publishing Company, 1990.

———. *The Practice of Faith: A Handbook of Contemporary Spirituality*. Edited by Karl Lehmann and Albert Raffelt. New York, NY: Crossroad Publishing, 1986.

———. *Theological Investigations*, vol. 1. Baltimore: Helicon Press, 1963.

Raya, Archbishop Joseph M. *The Face of God: Essays on Byzantine Spirituality*. Woodland Park, NJ: God With Us Publications, 2012.

———. "Where His Body Is, There We Gather," *Magnificat*, 23, no. 4 (2021): 160.

Russell, Heidi. "Efficacious and Sufficient Grace: God's One Offer of Self-Communication as Accepted or Rejected." *Philosophy & Theology* 22, no. 1-2 (2010): 353–72.

———. "Karl Rahner: Christology and Trinity," Lecture notes, Christian Doctrine and Its History, Loyola University Chicago, Spring 2016.

———. "Karl Rahner: Philosophical Foundations." Lecture notes, Christian Doctrine and Its History, Loyola University Chicago, Spring 2016.

———. "Karl Rahner: Sin, Grace, Salvation, Revelation." Lecture notes, Christian Doctrine and Its History, Loyola University Chicago, Spring 2016.

———. *The Source of All Love*. Maryknoll, NY: Orbis Books, 2016.

Russell, Norman. *Fellow Workers with God: Orthodox Thinking on Theosis*. Crestwood, NY: St. Vladimir's Seminary Press, 2009.

Russo, Gerry. "Rahner and Palamas: A Unity of Grace." *St. Vladimir's Theological Quarterly* 32, no. 2 (1988): 157–80.

St. George Greek Orthodox Cathedral. "God's Uncreated Energies." http://www.stgeorgegreenville.org/OrthodoxLife/Chapter2/Chap2-5.html.

Saint Gregory Palamas: The Homilies. Edited and translated by Christopher Veniamin. Dalton, PA: Mount Thabor Publishing, 2016.

"Saint John of the Cross," *Magnificat* 18, no. 6 (August 2016): 179.

"Saint Teresa of Calcutta." *Magnificat* 19, no. 12 (February 2018): 324.

Sakharov, Archimandrite Sophrony. *His Life is Mine*. Translated by Rosemary Edmonds. Crestwood, NY: St. Vladimir's Seminary Press, 1977.

———. *St. Silouan the Athonite*. Translated by Rosemary Edmonds. Crestwood, NY: St. Vladimir's Seminary Press, 1991.

Samra, Bishop Nicholas. Homily, Friday Evening Vespers. Sacred Heart Co-Cathedral, Houston, TX (Sept. 11, 2009).

Sarah, Robert Cardinal. "You follow me," *Magnificat,* 19, no. 4 (2017): 54.

Sarah, Robert Cardinal, in conversation with Nicolas Diat. *The Day is Now Far Spent.* Translated by Michael J. Miller. San Francisco, CA: Ignatius Press, 2019.

———. *God or Nothing*. Translated by Michael J. Miller. San Francisco, CA: Ignatius Press, 2015.

———. *The Power of Silence: Against the Dictatorship of Noise.* Translated by Michael J. Miller. San Francisco, CA: Ignatius Press, 2017.

Sayings of the Desert Fathers, The. Translated by Benedicta Ward, SLG. Kalamazoo, MI: Cistercian Publications, 1975.

Scalia, Elizabeth. "Exile: The Past is Prologue." *Patheos*. Online Edition. April 3, 2009.

Schneiders, Sandra M. "Religion vs. Spirituality: A Contemporary Conundrum." *Spiritus: A Journal of Christian Spirituality* 3, no. 2 (2003): 163–85.

Second Vatican Council. *Constitution on the Sacred Liturgy: Sacrosanctum Concilium, solemnly promulgated by His Holiness, Pope Paul VI on December 4, 1963*. In *Vatican Council II: The Basic Sixteen Documents*. General Editor, Austin Flannery, OP. 117-61. Northport, NY: Costello Publishing Company, 1996.

———. *Decree on the Catholic Eastern Churches: Orientalium Ecclesiarum, solemnly promulgated by His Holiness, Pope Paul VI on November 21, 1964*. In *Vatican Council II: The Basic Sixteen Documents*. General Editor, Austin Flannery, OP. 525-38. Northport, NY: Costello Publishing Company, 1996.

———. *Dogmatic Constitution on the Church: Lumen Gentium, solemnly promulgated by His Holiness, Pope Paul VI on November 21, 1964*. In *Vatican Council II: The Basic Sixteen Documents*. General Editor, Austin Flannery, OP. 1-95. Northport, NY: Costello Publishing Company, 1996.

———. *Pastoral Constitution on the Church in the Modern World: Gaudium et Spes, solemnly promulgated by His Holiness, Pope Paul VI on December 7, 1965*. In *Vatican Council II: The Basic Sixteen Documents*. General Editor, Austin Flannery, OP. 163-282. Northport, NY: Costello Publishing Company, 1996.

Simons, Marlise. "Orthodox Leader Deepens Progressive Stance on Environment." *New York Times*. Online Edition. December 3, 2012.

Smith, Gregory A. "Just One-Third of U.S. Catholics Agree with Their Church that Eucharist is Body, Blood of Christ." Pew Research Center. Online. August 5, 2019.

Smith, Peter. "Catholic Panel Recommends Parish Mergers." *Pittsburgh Post-Gazette*. Online Edition. September 16, 2017.

Stăniloae, Dumitru. "The Church: Communion in the Holy Spirit," *The Experience of God: Orthodox Dogmatic Theology*, vol. 4. Translated and edited by Ioan Ionita. Brookline, MA: Holy Cross Orthodox Press, 2012.

———. "The Fulfillment of Creation," *The Experience of God: Orthodox Dogmatic Theology*, vol. 6. Translated and edited by Ioan Ionita. Brookline, MA: Holy Cross Orthodox Press, 2013.

———. "The Person of Jesus Christ as God and Savior," *The Experience of God: Orthodox Dogmatic Theology*, vol. 3. Translated and edited by Ioan Ionita. Brookline, MA: Holy Cross Orthodox Press, 2011.

———. "Revelation and Knowledge of the Triune God," *The Experience of God: Orthodox Dogmatic Theology*, vol. 1. Translated and edited by Ioan Ionita and Robert Barringer. Brookline, MA: Holy Cross Orthodox Press, 1998.

———. "The World: Creation and Deification," *The Experience of God: Orthodox Dogmatic Theology*, vol. 2. Translated and edited by Ioan Ionita and Robert Barringer. Brookline, MA: Holy Cross Orthodox Press, 2000.

Stavropoulos, Archimandrite Christoforos. *Partakers of Divine Nature*. Translated by Rev. Dr. Stanley Harakas. Minneapolis, MN: Light & Life Publishing Company, 1976.

Strickland, Bishop Joseph E. *Light and Leaven: The Challenge of the Laity in the Twenty-First Century.* El Cajon, CA: Catholic Answers Press, 2020.

Taft, Robert F. "The Authenticity of the Chrysostom Anaphora Revisited. Determining the Authorship of the Liturgical Texts by Computer," *Orientalia Christiana Periodica*. 56(1) (1990): 28–29.

Taushev, Archbishop Averky. The *Struggle for Virtue: Asceticism in a Modern Secular Society*. Translated by David James. Jordanville, NY: Holy Trinity Publications, 2014.

Teresa of Ávila, St. *The Interior Castle*. Translated by Kieran Kavanaugh, OCD and Otilio Rodriguez, OCD. Mahwah, NJ, Paulist Press, 1979.

Teresa of Calcutta, Mother. *Come Be My Light: The Private Writings of the Saint of Calcutta*. Edited by Brian Kolodiejchuk, MC. New York, NY: Doubleday, 2007.

———. *In the Heart of the World: Thoughts, Stories & Prayers*. Novato, CA: New World Library, 1997.

Theodoros the Great Ascetic, St. "A Century of Spiritual Texts." In *The Philokalia: The Complete Text*, vol. 2. 14-37. Compiled by St. Nikodimos of the Holy Mountain and St. *Makarios* of Corinth. Translated by G.E.H. Palmer, P. Sherrard, and K. Ware. London: Faber & Faber, 1981.

Theophan the Recluse, St. *The Path to Salvation: A Concise Outline of Christian Ascesis*. Translated by Seraphim Rose. Stafford, AZ: The Holy Monastery of St. Paisius.

________. *The Spiritual Life: And How to be Attuned to It*. Translated by Alexandra Dockham. Safford, AZ: The Holy Monastery of St. Paisius, 2017.

Totorcea, Ştefana. "Poll: The Church Remains the Most Trusted Institution in Romania." *Basilica News Agency* (January 19, 2021).

________. "Prayer and Communion are Fundamental Pillars of the Living Church: Bishop Ioan Casian." *Basilica News Agency* (April 21, 2022).

United States Conference of Catholic Bishops. "Seven Themes of Catholic Social Teaching." www.usccb.org.

Unseen Warfare. Being the "Spiritual Combat" and "Path to Paradise" of Lorenzo Scupoli. Edited by Nicodemus of the Holy Mountain. Revised by Theophan the Recluse. Translated by E. Kadloubovsky and G.E.H. Palmer. London: Faber and Faber, 1963.

Velichkovsky, St. Paisius. "Field Flowers," *Little Russian Philokalia*, vol. 4. 57-128. Platina, CA: St. Herman of Alaska Brotherhood, 1994.

Vishnevskaya, Elena. "Divinization and Spiritual Progress in Maximus the Confessor." In *Theosis: Deification in Christian Doctrine*. Edited by Stephen Finlan and Vladimir Kharlamov. 134-145. Eugene, OR: Pickwick Publications. 2006.

Ware, Kallistos. "Foreword" to Dumitru Stăniloae's "Revelation and Knowledge of the Triune God," *The Experience of God: Orthodox Theology*, vol. 1. Translated and edited by Ioan Ionita and Robert Barringer. Brookline, MA: Holy Cross Orthodox Press, 1998.

———. "Introduction," *John Climacus: The Ladder of Divine Ascent*. 1-70.

———. *The Philokalia: Master Reference Guide*. Compiled Basileios S. Stapkis. Edited by Gerald Eustace Howell Palmer and Philip Sherrard. Minneapolis: Light & Life Publishing Company, 2004.

Weigel, George. "Liquid Catholicism and the German Synodal Path." *First Things* (February 16, 2022).

Wikipedia, The Free Encyclopedia, s.v. "Fasting."

______. "Filioque."

______. "Hesychast Controversy.

———. "Marriage in the Eastern Orthodox Church."

———. "Tabor Light."

Wright, Vinita Hampton. "God is in the Overcoming." *Loyola Press Online: A Jesuit Ministry*.

Yáñez, Humberto Miguel. "Opting for the Poor in the Face of Growing Poverty." In *Applied Ethics in a World Church: The Padua Conference*. Edited by Linda Hogan. 13-20. Maryknoll, NY: Orbis Books, 2008.

Zacharou, Archimandrite Zacharias of Essex. "Introduction," *Sermons on the Spiritual Life: Saint Philaret of Moscow*, ix-xiv. Riverside, CA: Patristic Nectar Publications, 2020.

Zander, Valentine. *St. Seraphim of Sarov.* Translated by Sister Gabriel Anne, SSC. Crestwood, NY: St. Vladimir's Seminary Press, 1975.

Acknowledgments

An undertaking such as this requires a great deal of inspiration. We are undeniably amid a spiritual pandemic with increasing numbers who are spiritually lukewarm or do not recognize the need for salvation in a country that has rapidly divorced itself from its Christian roots, in what seems like a single generation. Yet the divine truths do not change. We were created for a divinely intended purpose that can only be realized through a personal relationship with God, whereas a soul separated from him has a 100 percent mortality rate. Despite the spiritual winter that has settled into our land, there are a few signs of a spring thaw, indicators of new life and hope. Some bishops and priests are returning to Patristic teachings, the spiritual roots of our Church, and courageously proclaiming the good news. Young people are turning to the Church, seeking answers outside of secular society. Many hungry, weary people want to rediscover their faith.

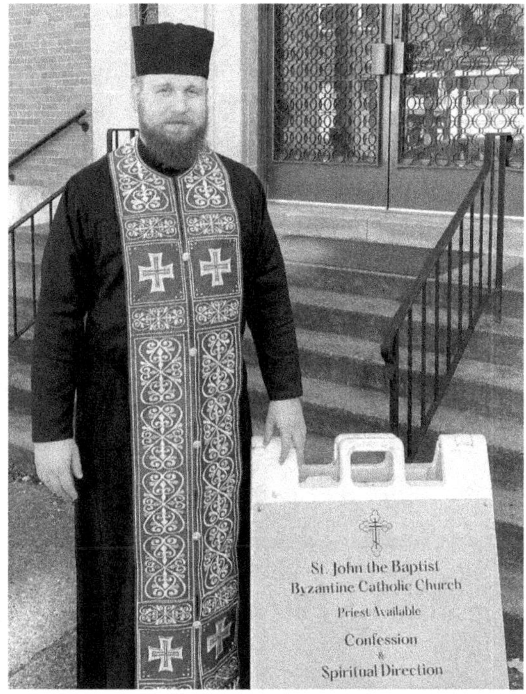

This book is dedicated to Fr. Miron Kerul-Kmec, Jr. and the priests ordained in the past five years—new missionaries with apostolic zeal to bring the good news of the Gospel to a world in need of re-Christianization. We see evidence of the basics—confession, prayer, a renewed focus on Eucharist, spiritual direction, a return to Scripture, and the writings of the Holy Fathers—bringing people to the Church. Our faith does not need to be watered down, sugar-coated, or repackaged to be more appealing to a secular culture. New programs are not required. People simply want a source of truth, the truth that will set them free. This requires a spiritual renewal in the Patristic tradition and fidelity to the Deposit of Faith already entrusted to us. Fr. Miron has started his priestly ministry working to grow two parishes, engaging college students, and bringing back spiritual guidance and confession. May Christ continue to form you after his own heart, may the Holy Spirit direct your steps, and may the wisdom of the Holy Fathers provide the example of perseverance in imitation of Christ. I wish you much success and many blessings in your vocational calling and your wife, *Pani* Sarah Marie. Thank you for your friendship and always making me feel like part of your family.

Fr. Miron Kerul-Kmec, Sr. has been a constant source of inspiration as someone who encourages me on the spiritual journey, recommends spiritual reading, and has a passion for evangelization, specifically helping people rediscover the importance of the interior life. He models for me perseverance and patience. His focus on the teachings of the Holy Fathers has manifested itself in impactful homilies and his formation class exploring the writings of St. Ignatius Brianchaninov.[1067] Thank you for your friendship, support, and encouragement. Thank you to *Pani* Marcelka for her generous hospitality, and all the parishioners of St. Nicholas Byzantine Catholic Church in Barberton, Ohio—example of a vibrant parish with fertile soil to cultivate the Art of Spiritual Life.

Speaking of a vibrant Church, significant inspiration for this second edition came from a two-week visit to Romania in summer 2021. While previously having read the writings of certain contemporary Romanian Holy Fathers—Elder Cleopa of Sihastria, Elder Paisius Olaru of Sihla, and Elder Arsenie Papacioc, and of course, the theological

1067 These are accessible to the public as podcasts. See Podbean, *The Art of Spiritual Life*.

framework of Fr. Dumitru Stăniloae—none of this did justice to a first-hand experience: Churches throughout the week were full for the divine services that lasted up to four hours! The reverence and awe of the liturgical experience truly gave the impression of heaven united with the earth. Further, Monasteries are thriving with vocations. They are filled with pilgrims. People were waiting to meet with the *staretz* of the monastery, and there were lines for father-confessors. It was gratifying to see the number of young families, especially their reverence for the icons and the veneration of relics of the saints. Many monks and nuns were also quite young. To be honest, when I read about laypeople in the 19th century waiting for a full day at a monastery to meet with the spiritual father, I had a hard time imagining this, wondering if this was just pious sentiment—until I had to wait over more than five hours to meet with a well-known spiritual father, Fr. David Roşca, at Schitul Maicii Domnului Grabnic-Ascultătoare in Vicovu de Jos, Suceava. Virtually all those waiting were young families with children. Maica (Abbess) Sotiria Ciobanu, my translator, encouraged me to afterward write down the conversation to remember the spiritual guidance. Her generous hospitality during that day was appreciated, as was the hospitality of so many throughout this journey! It was a truly a grace-filled experience, which led to my reading of the writings of His Beatitude Patriarch Daniel of Romania, explaining the immense spiritual renewal in a country where the Church had been brutally repressed under a Communist regime. Today, the Church is vibrant and alive! Further, there is an explicit focus on young people being integrated into the life of the Church. And there is no dilution of the faith to accommodate the spirit of the age. Further, a section of Patriarch Daniel's doctoral thesis, written under Fr. Stăniloae, is entitled, "The Unity of Theology and Spirituality."[1068] The essential theme of this book is to reclaim that dynamic. Thus, in exploring the writings and efforts of Patriarch Daniel, it suddenly felt as if we were two streams of a river coming from a common source. Further

1068 See Patriarch Daniel, "The Unity of Theology and Spirituality," in *Rebuilding Orthodoxy in Romania*, ed. Chad Hatfield (Crestwood, NY: St. Vladimir's Seminary Press, 2021), 13-22.

supporting this interior renewal is Aurelian Iftimiu and the team at Basilica News Agency, promoting through articles and social media, the Solemn Year of Prayer and providing other spiritual inspiration.

I am eternally grateful to His Grace Bishop John M. Kudrick, Bishop Emeritus of the Eparchy of Parma, who had a great desire for his flock to be well-grounded in the beauty of the Eastern Christian traditions so that they could be shared with others. He had a vision to develop an "Americanized" *theosis* program, which has influenced many of our works to date. He had the foresight to prepare us for today's environment.

I commend the courageous shepherds who consistently speak out, unwilling to compromise the Deposit of Faith. People today need spiritual truth, especially when it involves a hard stand against beliefs supported by the spirit of the age (*Zeitgeist*) and which conflict with Church teachings. People want men of clarity, conviction, and courage. In the American Church, we acknowledge His Excellency Bishop Joseph E. Strickland of Tyler, who tirelessly promotes the Good News of the Gospel and refuses to water down Church teaching, evidenced by his book, *Light and Leaven*. Also, we are grateful to His Eminence Robert Cardinal Sarah who in *The Day is Now Far Spent* was clear about priorities: personal sanctification must supersede all other activity, and clergy must primarily prioritize evangelization. Thank you to all the courageous shepherds who uphold the truth, especially when it runs contrary to public sentiment.

I am grateful to Donna Rueby, who envisioned the importance of planting and nurturing the seeds of faith in our high school youth. She understood years ago the importance of silence and contemplation. Thank you to Fr. Mark Goring, CC, for his passionate and enthusiastic evangelization, especially his YouTube videos, his courage to uphold the truth of the Gospel, love of Sacred Scripture, love of the Jesus Prayer, and appreciation for the teachings of the Holy Fathers in the *Philokalia*. Leveraging your sentiment, yes, the world has indeed gone bonkers; however, we can continue to challenge the status quo, plant seeds for spiritual renewal, and never waiver from a message of hope. May you continue to be filled with the necessary missionary zeal for your work: *¡Viva Cristo Rey!*

In terms of Philokalic renewal, I am inspired by Fr. David Abernethy and his Philokalia Ministries, which include directed book studies covering selected writings of the Holy Fathers. Thank you for your passion, zeal, enthusiasm, and willingness to break open these soul-profiting and life-giving texts for people and making them available via podcast.

Others also encouraged me on my spiritual journey: My priest-mentor, Fr. Edward Zavell, adopted me as a young man in high school seminary and inflamed my passion for Byzantine Catholicism. When we first met, he welcomed me with open arms and was the catalyst for my desire to know more about the Christian East. He is also a reminder of why a visitor's first contact at a parish can make a significant difference in someone's life.

Where would one be in the Eastern Christian spiritual tradition without an outstanding Spiritual Father? For me, that person is Fr. Damon Geiger, my spiritual guide during my first three years of ordained ministry. He helped me delve much more deeply into the beauty of the Eastern Christian mystical tradition and was the first to introduce me to the doctrine of *theosis*. What Fr. Ed planted, Fr. Damon cultivated by opening my eyes to the true beauty that lay beneath the ornate liturgies and traditions.

Sometimes we do not realize how much one individual has influenced us until much later. I am incredibly grateful to Fr. Nicholas Weibl, rector of Holy Spirit Seminary in Toledo, Ohio. In his class during my third year, 1976-1977, he introduced me to the Jesus Prayer, Mount Athos, and the concept of the *staretz*. It was also in his class when I heard of Mother Teresa of Calcutta and Dorothy Day for the first time. These people, places, and concepts have significantly influenced my life and have emerged in many of our works. Fr. Weibl set a foundation I did not fully appreciate at the time. Today, I am in awe of what I learned and say with heartfelt gratitude, "Thank you."

Our youth are the future of our Church, and we are entrusted to pass along our spiritual treasures to them. They truly desire to know how to pray and to understand the Catholic faith they profess. Persevere, and you will discover the pearl of great price.

I thank Gene Kirsch for his passion and enthusiasm in presenting his own witness about developing a personal relationship with Jesus and perspectives on prayer. I also am grateful to Fr. Rafa Becerra for his friendship and encouraging me to keep writing, especially during this time of pandemic. Thank you to Deacon Phillip Jackson, a classmate and the Director of the Permanent Diaconate for the Archdiocese of Galveston-Houston. He supported me and believed in me through extremely difficult trials. And finally, I acknowledge my father-confessor, Fr. T.J. Dolce, who has been of great inspiration, strength, and guidance for the past two years—both for his pastoral witness and zeal outside the confessional and his spiritual counsel inside. May God continue to grant you the energy and fortitude as a true shepherd within the Church.

To all the servants of God who influenced this work—His Beatitude Patriarch Daniel of Romania, His Eminence Robert Cardinal Sarah, His Grace Bishop John, His Excellency Bishop Joseph, Fr. Miron and *Pani* Marcelka, the parishioners of St. Nicholas Byzantine Catholic Church in Barberton, Ohio, Fr. Miron, Jr., *Pani* Sarah Marie, their son Miron Theophan and their daughter Emilia Kathryn-Jean, Fr. David Roşca, Fr. Mark, Fr. David Abernethy, Fr. Damon, Fr. Nicholas, Fr. Rafa, Fr. T.J., Deacon Phillip, Maica Sotiria, Donna, Gene and his daughters Kathrine, Nicole, and Kimberly, Aurelian and the team at Basilica News Agency, the young people of our parishes who are our future, and all others too numerous to mention—may God grant you many blessed years in peace, health, and happiness. *Mnohaja I blahaja lita*.

To my priest-mentor, Fr. Ed, may God grant him eternal memory and blessed repose. *Vičnaja jemu pamjat'*.

Fr. Deacon Edward Kleinguetl

Fr. Deacon Edward Kleinguetl, MASp
June 12, 2022
Sunday of All Saints

St. Paisius Velichkovsky
Catalyst of the Philokalic Renewal in the 18th Century and Patron Saint of this Project

(Icon written by the hand of Fr. Miron Kerul-Kmec, Jr.)

Other Resources Available

Podcasts – Directed Book Studies/Formation Sessions

Fr. Miron Kerul-Kmec, St. Nicholas Byzantine Catholic Church, Barberton, Ohio, The Art of Spiritual Life

https://artofspirituallife.podbean.com/

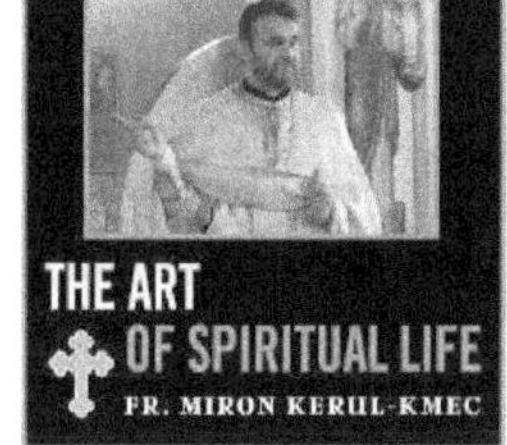

- St. Ignatius Brianchaninov, *The Field*.
- St. Theodoros the Great Ascetic
- Homilies

Fr. David Abernethy, Philokalia Ministries

https://philokalia.podbean.com/

- St. John Cassian, *The Conferences*.
- St. John Climacus, *The Ladder*.
- St. Isaac the Syrian, *The Ascetical Homilies*.
- St. Theophan the Recluse, *The Spiritual Life*.
- *The Evergetinos*.
- City a Desert, reflections from the *Philokalia*.

Books by This Author

Encounter series

Encounter: Experiencing the Divine Presence. Second Edition.

Into the Desert: The Wisdom of the Desert Fathers and Mothers.

The Art of Spiritual Life series

Choosing Life in Christ: A Vocation to Holiness.

The Fruit of Silence: The Jesus Prayer as a Foundation to the Art of Spiritual Life.

The Fruit of Prayer: Spiritual Counsels of the Holy Fathers.

Retreats

Mine Know Me: An Examination of Authentic Christian Discipleship.

The Narrow Gate: Recalibration on the Spiritual Journey.

CPSIA information can be obtained
at www.ICGtesting.com
Printed in the USA
JSHW061923160922
30644JS00004B/19